GLOBAL POLITICAL ECONOMY

Global Political Economy

Evolution and Dynamics

Robert O'Brien and Marc Williams

First published 2004 by
PALGRAVE MACMILLAN
Houndmills, Basingstoke, Hampshire RG21 6XS and
175 Fifth Avenue, New York, N.Y. 10010
Companies and representatives throughout the world

PALGRAVE MACMILLAN is the global academic imprint of the Palgrave Macmillan
division of St. Martin's Press, LLC and of Palgrave Macmillan Ltd. Macmillan® is a
registered trademark in the United States, United Kingdom and other countries.
Palgrave is a registered trademark in the European Union and other countries.

ISBN 0–333–68962–3 hardback
ISBN 0–333–68963–1 paperback

This book is printed on paper suitable for recycling and made from fully
managed and sustained forest sources.

A catalogue record for this book is available from the British Library.

Library of Congress Cataloging-in-Publication Data
O'Brien, Robert, 1963–
   Global political economy : evolution and dynamics / Robert O'Brien,
Marc Williams.
      p. cm.
   Includes bibliographical references and index.
   ISBN 0–333–68962–3 (cloth) — ISBN 0–333–68963–1 (pbk.)
      1. International economic relations—History. 2. International trade—History.
3. International finance—History. 4. International division of labor—History.
5. International business enterprises—History. 6. Corporate governance—History.
7. Globalization—Economic aspects—History. 8. Globalization—Environmental
aspects—History. 9. Economic development—History. 10. Economic history.
I. Williams, Marc. II. Title.

HF1359.O26 2004
337—dc22   2003060891

10   9   8   7   6   5   4   3   2   1
13 12 11 10 09 08 07 06 05 04

Printed and bound in Great Britain by
Creative Print & Design (Wales), Ebbw Vale

To our daughters

Isabella and Louisa

The world is yours to explore and improve

Contents

List of Boxes, Tables, Figures and Maps

Boxes

Figures

Tables

Maps

Acknowledgements

This project began while both authors were teaching in the International Relations group at the University of Sussex in the United Kingdom. Our colleagues at Sussex were instrumental in causing us to think more deeply about IPE. In particular we would like to acknowledge the influence of Anne Marie Goetz, John MacLean, Ronen Palan, Fiona Robinson, Julian Saurin and Jan Aart Scholte. Just as significant an influence were the many Sussex undergraduate and graduate students who shared a desire to learn more about how the world works and how it might be changed. In Britain the thriving academic community surrounding the International Political Economy Group (IPEG) of the British International Studies Association provided an excellent environment to learn and debate IPE topics. A debt is owed to past IPEG coordinators Susan Strange, Geoffrey Underhill and Randall Germain for nurturing a constructive academic environment. The framework of the book was the basis for a course taught to several years of a 4th year seminar at McMaster University. Students in those classes gave valuable feedback. Also at McMaster, Tony Porter assisted with advice on the new financial architecture debates and graduate student Austina Reed helped with manuscript preparation and conducted the research and presentation for several of the figures. At UNSW, students in a pre-Honours seminar provided a stimulating environment for discussion of some of the themes in the book; and Natalie Elkaim read and commented on parts of the manuscript and provided assistance with tables and statistics.

Several anonymous reviewers provided useful, but contradictory advice on early drafts of this book. We are grateful to them for their time and effort. Finally, we thank our very patient publisher Steven Kennedy for shepherding this project through the many delays caused by competing demands upon our time.

ROBERT O'BRIEN
MARC WILLIAMS

List of Abbreviations

AEZ	Agri-Export Zone
AFL–CIO	American Federation of Labor and Congress of Industrial Organizations
APEC	Asia–Pacific Economic Cooperation
ASEAN	Association of South-east Asian Nations
BIS	Bank for International Settlements
BST	Bovine Somatropin
COMECON	Council for Mutual Economic Assistance
CP	Commercial Paper
CTM	Confederation of Mexican Workers
DSU	Dispute Settlement Understanding
ECB	European Central Bank
ECPAT	End Child Prostitution in Asian Tourism
ECSC	European Coal and Steel Community
EEC	European Economic Community
EFTA	European Free Trade Association
EOI	Export-Oriented Industrialization
EPZ	Export Processing Zone
ERM	Exchange Rate Mechanism
EU	European Union
FDI	Foreign Direct Investment
FSF	Financial Stability Forum
FZLN	Zapatista Front of National Liberation
G8	Group of 8
G20	Group of 20
G77	Group of 77
GATS	General Agreement on Trade in Services
GATT	General Agreement on Tariffs and Trade
GDP	Gross Domestic Product
GNP	Gross National Product
GPE	Global Political Economy
HDI	Human Development Index
HIPC	Heavily Indebted Poor Countries
IBRD	International Bank for Reconstruction and Development
ICFTU	International Confederation of Free Trade Unions
ICSID	International Centre for the Settlement of Investment Disputes
IDA	International Development Association

IEOs	International Economic Organizations
IFC	International Finance Corporation
ILO	International Labour Organization
IMF	International Monetary Fund
IMS	International Monetary System
IPE	International Political Economy
IPRs	Intellectual Property Rights
IR	International Relations
ISI	Import Substitution Industrialization
ITO	International Trade Organization
JIT	Just-In-Time
KMP	Peasant Movement of the Philippines
KRRS	Karnataka State Farmers' Association
MAD	Mutual Assured Destruction
MAI	Multilateral Agreement on Investment
MEA	Multilateral Environmental Agreement
MERCOSUR	Common Market of the South
MFA	Multi-Fiber Agreement
MFN	Most Favoured Nation
MIC	Methyl Isocyanate
MIGA	Multilateral Investment Guarantee Agency
MNC	Multinational Corporation
MNE	Multinational Enterprise
MST	Landless Workers' Movement
MTN	Multilateral Trade Negotiations
NAFTA	North American Free Trade Agreement
NAM	Non Aligned Movement
NATO	North Atlantic Treaty Organization
NGOs	Non Governmental Organizations
NICs	Newly Industrializing Countries
NIEO	New International Economic Order
NTBs	Non Tariff Barriers
ODA	Official Development Assistance
OECD	Organisation for Economic Co-operation and Development
OLI	Ownership, Location, and Internalization
OPEC	Organization of Petroleum Exporting Countries
PGA	Peoples' Global Action
PPMs	Process and Production Methods
R & D	Research and Development
S & D	Special and Differential Treatment
SAPs	Structural Adjustment Programmes
SPS	Sanitary and Phytosanitary Measures
TBT	Technical Barriers to Trade

TNC	Transnational Corporation
TNE	Transnational Enterprise
TPRM	Trade Policy Review Mechanism
TRIMs	Trade-Related Investment Measures
TRIPs	Trade-Related Intellectual Property Rights
UN	United Nations
UNCED	United Nations Conference on Environment and Development
UNCHE	United Nations Conference on the Human Environment
UNCTAD	United Nations Conference on Trade and Development
UNDP	United Nations Development Programme
UNHCR	United Nations High Commissioner for Refugees
UNEP	United Nations Environment Programme
UNICEF	United Nations Children's Fund
VERs	Voluntary Export Restraints
WHO	World Health Organization
WTO	World Trade Organization

Introduction

International political economy (IPE) emerged as a subject of study in Western universities in the mid-1970s. From its tentative beginnings as one course within a degree program, IPE has developed into a distinct sub-field of International Relations. In some universities IPE has even grown large enough to overshadow both political science and international relations departments. Similar to its 'parent' disciplines IPE remains a field in which different theoretical traditions present the student with competing descriptions of 'reality' and conflicting explanatory frameworks. A review of the teaching and study of IPE in the past 25 years would identify both continuities and change in the issues considered important by scholars (Denemark and O'Brien, 1997). Some issues such as the impact of transnational corporations, international finance and international trade have remained central to the core issues covered in IPE courses. The centrality given to issues such as Third World development and the North–South conflict have varied over the past quarter of a century. Meanwhile, issues such as the East–West relations, energy and the impact of producer cartels have vanished to be replaced by a focus on environmental concerns and gender. In terms of a broad overview of the international political economy analysis has shifted from a concern with interdependence to an obsession with globalization.

The aim of this textbook is to provide an accessible introduction to the study of IPE. In pursuit of this aim, it follows two strategies that distinguish it from many other IPE textbooks. First, it adopts an historical approach to the study of IPE, and offers students, the interested public and scholars a broad overview of how the modern global political economy has come into being. Instead of beginning with an analysis of contemporary global political and economic structures, the book seeks to provide an easily accessible but brief history that draws out important factors in the creation of our present situation. For example, every major IPE text discusses post-war monetary relations, but few take the time to explain the origins of monetary systems and the various forms of money. In our teaching we have found that the best way for students to appreciate the nuances of the present international monetary system is to consider the development of money and credit in its historical context. Secondly, the book seeks to move beyond the repetition of the three dominant theoretical perspectives (mercantilism, liberalism, Marxism) on IPE as a framework of analysis. It seeks to reflect both the developments in IPE scholarship in the past 25 years and the main debates between orthodox and radical scholars through attention to a broad range of themes, issues and perspectives in IPE. Radical and unorthodox or heterodox approaches to IPE have become much more developed since the first wave of IPE texts in the 1980s by Joan Spero (1981), Robert Gilpin (1987) Susan Strange (1988), Stephen Gill and David Law (1988). Ecological, feminist and neo-Gramscian perspectives now compete with traditional perspectives and shed new light on old problems. Central to our strategy is a framework that integrates material and ideational aspects of IPE.

This book also differs from historical overviews of the global political economy which attempt to explain why particular states have accumulated or lost power. For example, Paul Kennedy's (1987) historical work explained the rise and fall of great powers in terms of states exploiting economic advantages and then overextending themselves in the military realm. Another group of analysts have suggested that the emergence of powerful states is linked to waves of economic innovation and dominance in particular technologies (Thompson, 2000). This study is less concerned with why a particular state accumulated more power or wealth than another state, than it is with how the system operates and the effects it has on people from many different states.

In attempting to trace the evolution of a global political economy and provide an introduction to key dynamics in the contemporary world economy, this book focuses on a number of activities and institutions. The primary activities are production, trade, finance, and war. Production is the process of creating goods and services. It is the process of making things for survival, consumption and pleasure. The organization of production leads to a division of labour which has a great influence on how people live. Trade is the exchange of these products and services across state borders. Finance is a broad term that includes the creation and distribution of money and credit. War is organized international violence that is usually thought of as the military of one state engaged in conflict with the military of another. The key institutions are the state and world order. The state is the political unit that has its origins in Europe during the 1600s and is the primary political community for human organization. World order is a term that is meant to signify the principles and rules upon which interaction on a world level is based.

We also attribute salience to the effects of technology and ideas, as well as the interaction between humans and their natural environment. Technology is an aspect of production. It is the knowledge applied to create tools to perform particular tasks. Ideas are views that we have about how society and the world should be organized. All of these elements exist in a dynamic and sometimes destructive relationship with the natural environment. Our approach is concerned with how these factors have evolved and changed over the previous 600 years and, more importantly, their relationship to each other. Thus we raise questions such as: How have trade and finance been linked? How have changes in warfare affected the state and production? In what ways has the role of the state changed with the global economy? How has human activity been shaped by environmental factors and how are humans changing or degrading the natural environment?

Croce's argument that 'however remote in time events thus recounted may seem to be, the history in reality refers to present needs and present situation wherein those events vibrate' (Croce, 1941 p. 19) implies that history is constantly rewritten in light of existing debates and sensibilities. New histories often tell us as much about the times in which they were written as they do about the historical events themselves. An interesting example of this can be seen in the last decade of the twentieth century when several prominent scholars engaged in a debate about the 'Rise of the West'. They tried to explain why political and economic power was concentrated in the hands of several Western states (Western Europe and the United States). On one side of the debate were those who congratulated today's winners in the global economy by arguing that the rich were wealthy because they had the most virtuous social, economic and political institutions. We can call this the cultural approach. The rich are rich because they have a culture that supports success. The most prominent exponent of this view is Harvard historian David Landes in his book *The Wealth and Poverty of Nations* (1998). The other side of the debate argued that Western success was accidental and temporary and was built upon force and expropriation as much as any positive cultural attributes. We can call this the global historical approach because it stresses the role of other civilizations and refutes the historical claims of the culturalists. Such an approach challenges the notion that history has ended because Western states have discovered the ultimate model for structuring economic, social and political relations. A prominent illustration of this approach can be found in Andre Gunder Frank's (1998) *ReOrient: Global Economy in the Asian Age.*

The debate between cultural and global historical explanations about the 'Rise of the West' became heated because it concerned the present and the future as much as it did the past. Participants claimed that they had discovered the secrets to why some are rich and others are poor. Such knowledge can be used by others to restructure their societies in hopes of similar success. The practical implications are immense. The culturalists see the cause of poverty as the behaviour of the poor while the global historicists side sees it as a result of the relationship between the poor and the rich. The policy implications of the first view are that the poor are themselves primarily responsible for improving their position while the implications of the second view is that the system of political and economic relations must be changed to create greater equity. The first message offers comfort to those already enjoying economic success while the second urges mobilization and change. This book joins the debate about the history and structure of the emerging global economy.

Plan of the book

Following the first theoretical chapter the text is divided into two parts. Part I (Chapters 2–4) considers the evolution and eventual domination of a European-based world economy. Part II (Chapters 5–11) focuses on the recent dynamics of the global political economy through an examination of a number of key frameworks and structures.

The concerns of IPE span a broad range of contemporary human activity. Policy makers and citizens are concerned with a myriad of issues including the role of transnational corporations, the rise of economic nationalism, economic justice, environmental degradation and the merits of free trade. The complexities of these issues cannot be properly under-stood through a study of the 'facts' without any recourse to theories of IPE. Because the meaning and impact of economic and political change are controversial and contested, Chapter 1 provides an introduction to the main competing perspectives in IPE. The first part of the chapter intro-duces the traditional IPE debate between economic nationalism, liberalism, and Marxism. We provide an overview of these schools of thought by focusing on the key actors, dynamics and views on conflict and coopera-tion. The second part of the chapter outlines how the field has developed since the 1970s by considering the careers and work of three prominent IPE scholars (Susan Strange, Robert Keohane, Robert Cox) and the issues around which existing scholarship clusters. The chapter concludes by out-lining the book's own theoretical approach.

Chapters 2–4 consider the historical evolution of the global political economy. Chapter 2 provides an overview of key historical processes that led to the transformation of regional economies and the beginnings of the creation of the contemporary global economic system. It is organized into two main sections. The first part contrasts various regional political economies – the Middle East, China, India, Africa, the Americas and Europe. This overview of centres of world civilization prior to European expansion compares and contrasts political economies with specific atten-tion to the form of political units, trade, money, finance, technology and social structure. This brief comparative analysis has two aims. The first is to highlight the differences between Europe and other world economies that might explain the relative success of the Western system. The second is to demonstrate the advanced state of political economy in areas outside

Europe which helps to explain the various patterns of European and non-European interaction. In this section we also introduce key concepts and features of the international political economy such as the role of money and finance, patterns of trade and the resulting pressures of supply and demand, the role of political and state structures, and the impact of warfare or security arrangements.

The second part of Chapter 2 charts the expansion of a European-centred international political economy into other areas of the world, namely Africa, the Americas and Asia. It stresses the variety of patterns of interaction including slavery, genocide, war and trade. The mercantilist system is explained and the fortunes of rival colonial empires charted. The chapter assesses the varied pattern of European – non-European interaction. It introduces mercantilist thought and practice and the early prominence of Portuguese and Dutch commerce. The forces pushing and pulling Europeans to leave their continent are examined. Examples include the need for precious metals and secure routes to the spices of Asia. The significance of the slave trade in European expansion and development is outlined. The various forms of European – non-European interaction is surveyed. For example, the pattern of conquest in the Americas is contrasted to the trade for slaves in Africa and the limiting of Europeans to trading outposts in Asia. The long process of opening up Asian economies to Western commerce, including the conquest of India and the forced sale of opium to China will be examined.

Chapter 3 examines the domestic and international basis of British power in the mid-nineteenth century, the development of the Pax Britannica as a structure of international governance and the rise of imperialism in the nineteenth century. The first section focuses on the industrial revolution, growth of the liberal state and the influence of liberal ideology as represented in the works of Adam Smith and David Ricardo. The origins of the industrial revolution are explained and its effects upon British society and economy are examined. The transformation in British politics and society, including the rise of the liberal state and ideology is grounded in this historical context. The second section of the chapter examines the Pax Britannica and explores three key features of this system – the gold standard, free trade, and the balance of power. It demonstrates how these international structures were based on domestic developments within Britain. This discussion shows the importance of domestic structures for international orders and the relationship between these levels of analysis. In addition, the British case allows for study of particular arrangements in the areas of trade and finance which are fundamental to understanding the liberal system and ideology. The third part of the chapter charts the relative decline of British power, and the rise of rival imperialisms. It provides a brief introduction to rival theories of imperialism.

Chapter 4 begins with an assessment of the impact of the two world wars on the international political economy. It thus continues exploration of the relationship between security, violence, state structures and economic outcomes. The second part of the chapter focuses on the inter-war years (1919–1939) and the attempt to rebuild the international economy during what E.H. Carr (1939) termed the 'Twenty Years' Crisis'. Important subjects include the fragile financial structure, weak security arrangements and social discontent. Such a study is important because the inter-war years were foremost in the minds of British and US planners of the post-1945 world order. The final section of this chapter continues the historical overview by examining the key post-war developments of the global political economy. Its purpose is to bring readers up to date with the major post-war trends before they move on to examine some of the frameworks in more detail in the second section of the book. Attention will be drawn to the five following trends: the role of the United States as a major power and the creation of a Western system; the process of decolonization and the pursuit of development; the changes in the structure of the state; the growth in international organizations in both the inter- and non-governmental sectors; the rapid pace of technological innovation and how this is both changing the form of economic activity and serving as a source of power. Finally, the chapter concludes by raising the issue of globalization.

In one sense the global political economy can be treated as a single whole, as we do in Part I of this book, but in another sense it is also composed of various structures or frameworks each with its own set of actors, processes, institutions, and rules. Of course many actors participate in more than one framework and there are linkages between them. Nevertheless, in common with standard texts in economics and political economy we have classified the diverse practices in the world economy into certain key frameworks. We do not claim that any single framework is dominant, but we do suggest that the seven frameworks (production, trade, division of labour, finance and credit, development, environment, governance) analysed in this book constitute critical spheres of activity in the world economy.

The argument in each chapter is divided into four sections – definitions, theoretical perspectives, major developments, and key issues. The section on definitions provides an introduction to some of the key terms and concepts used in analysis of the particular framework. The aim here is not to proffer definitive definitions but rather to discuss some of the key issues pertinent to an understanding of the framework. The theoretical perspectives section is important in raising key issues related to the normative elements of the global political economy framework. First, it shows the importance of knowledge in the construction of frameworks or structures in the global political economy. In our analysis, knowledge and knowledge claims are co-constitutive parts of the framework. That is, knowledge is internal and integral to the structure rather than an external set of considerations. What counts as knowledge is not secondary but rather a central feature of the political economy framework. The beliefs that actors hold about cause–effect relations will influence the actions they will take. Within the world economy, states, firms, international organizations and social movement actors have conflicting views about the issues under scrutiny. In keeping with the historical focus of this book, the section on major developments provides an overview of key changes within the particular framework in the period since 1945. Finally, in each chapter we focus on three current issues. In choosing these issues we have tried to combine topicality with relevance to the evolution of the global political economy and contrasting IPE perspectives.

Chapter 5 focuses on our first key framework in the global economy – the growth of international trade. The first section introduces readers to some of the key terms used in discussions of international trade. This is followed by an introduction to liberal trade theory which familiarizes readers with some of the main criticisms of the liberal approach. The concept of comparative advantage is reviewed and more recent theories such as strategic trade theory are outlined. The third section of the chapter describes the developments in international trade in the post-1945 international trading system, including the growth of trade, the resurgence of economic nationalism, protectionism and the role of the GATT/WTO in managing the international trading regime. The final section of the chapter examines three current issues in the world trading system. It looks at the problems faced by developing countries, the challenge of regionalism and the conflict over the legitimacy of trade rules.

Chapter 6 analyses the growth and spread of transnational production. It explores the rise to prominence of transnational corporations and the evolving relationship between firms and states. A preliminary definitional section discusses the phenomenon of TNC investment. The theoretical section of the chapter considers explanations for this spread such as Vernon's product cycle theory, and the debate concerning the impact of TNCs on host societies. The major developments section of the chapter analyses the globalization of production. The key issues section of the chapter examines the relationship between states and firms. Implications for host and home states of increased transnational investment are explored. The increasing cooperation between states and firms in the 1980s and 1990s is considered. The advent of what Stopford and Strange (1991) labelled triangular diplomacy is explored.

Chapter 7 begins by outlining some of the variations in terms surrounding the division of labour such as the international, global and gendered division of labour. In the theoretical perspectives section we consider the liberal theory of division of labour and objections to these from nationalist and critical perspectives. Under major developments we consider changes in the production process (how things are made) and the move from an international to a global division of labour. The key issues considered in the chapter are: the gendered division of labour; the global struggle for worker's rights; and the relationship between workers' rights and global stability.

Chapter 8 analyses the global financial framework by focusing on the international monetary system and the global credit system. It begins by reviewing the initial creation of a post-war financial system which was characterized by fixed exchange rates, limited capital mobility and public provision of international liquidity. The theoretical perspectives section outlines a key theory about the relationship between capital flows, exchange rates and domestic policy. The third section outlines three major developments in the global financial system since the Second World War. These are the move from fixed to floating exchange rates, financial innovation and the 1980s' debt crisis. The final section provides readers with an overview of three key issues facing the global financial system. These issues are the rise of regional currencies, dealing with global financial crisis and the debate over autonomy, convergence and democracy.

Chapter 9 considers the issue of development and dependency in the global economy. It begins with a survey of the concept of development before examining the way in which the development project has unfolded in the period since the Second World War. It looks at the implications of the shift from a Keynesian based development model to one oriented toward neo-liberal principles. The final section of the chapter considers the way in which international organizations have contributed to development, the impact of foreign aid, and the power of developing countries acting collectively to influence international development diplomacy.

Chapter 10 begins by looking at some of the different ways in which IPE studies have approached the study of global environmental degradation. It then traces the evolution of the environment as an international issue and the form it has taken in recent years. In addition to outlining the challenges of environmental problems it also considers whether those issues may change the way in which international political economy is conducted and studied. It then focuses on the debate on sustainable development; the relationship between international trade and environmental degradation; and attempts to conclude international environmental agreements.

The concluding chapter (11) examines governance in the global political economy. Specific attention is given to current understandings of governance, contemporary issues facing the global political economy, and the attendant challenges ahead for global managers and citizens. We paint a picture of increasingly global political economic relations with states, firms and citizens struggling to create, manage and distribute wealth and power. The first section examines the issue of how rules are created and maintained. It argues that an understanding of global governance requires an exploration of the complex relationship between state, corporate and civil society actors. Or to put this another way we focus on three different types of agents whose activities help provide answers to the paradox of global governance. The second section identifies key challenges facing the evolution of the global political economy. These challenges are: development and economic growth; equality and justice; democracy and regulation.

Globalization

Writing at the beginning of the twenty-first century it is impossible to ignore the phenomenon of globalization. An intense debate currently exists between proponents and opponents of what may be termed globalization studies. For the former, globalization represents a decisive configuration of social, economic, political, and cultural changes which consequently has transformed key institutions and practices of the modern world (Scholte, 2000a). Although there is immense variation among these scholars with some emphasising economic variables while others stress cultural ones, and no agreement exists on either the date at which this transformation occurred or its impact on state policies, these writers have reached the conclusion that the term globalization captures the key features of the contemporary age. On the other hand, a disparate group of analysts insist that the political, cultural, social and economic changes described by globalization theorists either do not amount to new developments in the international system, or are merely aspects of quantitative rather than qualitative change (Hirst and Thompson, 1996).

This book is not about globalization although it is possible to interpret the historical developments portrayed here in that light. The book enters the globalization debate through a number of its concerns. One of the central issues of contention in the controversy over globalization is that of historical evidence. In delineating the scope, nature, depth and breadth of change in the global economy this book contributes to this debate. Moreover, in so far as globalization is a process of historical change rather than a specific condition, the evidence here contributes to an assessment of this process. Secondly, in charting the evolution of the modern state the book confronts a central issue in the globalization debate. We reveal the historical development of the modern state, and consequently challenge arguments that present essentialized portraits of the state.

In this book we reserve the term 'global political economy' to describe the environment from the last quarter of the twentieth century until today.

Prior to this we speak of the world economy or international political economy. We use the short form 'IPE' to indicate the field of study surrounding the interaction of economic and political phenomena across state borders.

Chapter 1

Understanding the Global Political Economy

During 1996 and into 1997 a small number of investors and currency traders began to have doubts about whether Thailand's economy would be able to continue its record of remarkable growth. Fearing a reduction in economic prosperity and profit, some of these investors began to withdraw their money and investments. The outflow of money forced the Thai central bank to devalue it currency, the Bhat. This began a process which was later called the 1997 Asian financial crisis. By the time the crisis had run its course several Asian countries experienced economic depression, the government of Indonesia was overthrown, countries previously labelled economic miracles (e.g. South Korea) were forced to seek loans from the International Monetary Fund (IMF) and the viability of the international financial system was called into question.

Although the 1997 Asian financial crisis was clearly a significant development in the global political economy it was not immediately apparent what caused the events, what were its most significant aspects or what lessons might be drawn from the crisis to prevent a similar event from occurring. Indeed, a number of different stories can be told about the crisis (see Table 1.1). One story, which we'll call the liberal story, would locate the causes of the crisis primarily in the financial policies followed by Asian states (McLeod and Garnaut, 1998). This view suggests that resources were directed to inefficient uses because of corrupt business practices and political influence over financial institutions. The term 'crony capitalism' was developed to capture this inappropriate model of political economy. The lesson to be drawn from the crisis is that financial markets will eventually punish economic activity which violates or ignores liberal economic principles. The solution is for developing countries to have more transparent financial practices and follow a more liberal economic model.

A second story would stress the significance of state power in creating and exploiting the crisis (Weiss, 1999). In this view the problem arose because developing countries liberalized their economy prematurely and allowed large amounts of money to flow into and out of their countries too quickly. This undermined the East Asian model of political economy and caused a crisis. This approach would stress how the US used the Asian crisis as an opportunity to force some states to restructure along lines that benefited American business. During the crisis Asian states attempted to counter American initiatives at the IMF and continue to resist the undermining of their particular form of capitalism (Higgott, 1998). The lessons from the crisis are that states need to be careful about liberalizing their economic activity and must pay attention to guarding their national interest.

A third story (critical) would focus on the role of US private business interests and the US government in creating the conditions for a financial collapse. It would suggest that the US government pressured developing states into liberalizing their economies because this suited the interests of the US Treasury and leading financial firms on Wall Street (Wade and Veneroso, 1998). Once the crisis took place, the same interests pressed the IMF to demand that Asian economies restructure in a way that would open markets for US firms. This story would probably also stress the high degree of suffering caused by the financial collapse and the fact that its costs were very unevenly distributed. For example, the collapse of the Indonesian economy pushed millions further into poverty, but left wealthy financial interests in developed countries relatively untouched. In this view the international financial system facilitates the rapid movement of money between countries and contributes to the reoccurrence of financial crisis in many parts of the world (Walton, 2002). Action needs to be taken to curb financial speculation, such as a tax on large short-term foreign exchange transactions. States should also consider restricting the ability of investors rapidly to move their funds abroad.

Table 1.1   *Interpretations of the Asian financial crisis*

	Liberal	*State power*	*Critical*
Causes	Crony capitalism, lack of transparency	Over-rapid liberalization, reduced state capacity to regulate	Predatory liberalism, power of financial interests, Systemic flaws
Key Issue(s)	Corruption, lack of liberal economic practices	Clash of Anglo-American vs. Asian models	Human suffering caused by financial collapse
Lessons	Increase transparency and good practice in developing countries	Limit financial speculation through state policies	Reform international financial system, defend national financial system

This brief example of the Asian financial crisis demonstrates that the same event can be analysed in several different ways. Indeed, most major developments are interpreted through competing explanations. This chapter provides the reader with an overview of the key approaches to IPE that will be encountered in the book. In the first part of the chapter we introduce the debate that has shaped and moulded thinking about international political economy. IPE is often characterized as the site of a dispute between three contending paradigms or perspectives – economic nationalism or mercantilism, liberalism, and Marxism. We provide an overview of these schools of thought by focusing on their respective assessments of the key actors, dynamics and prospects for conflict and cooperation in international political economy. The second part of the chapter outlines how the field has developed since the 1970s by considering the careers and work of three prominent major IPE scholars (Susan Strange, Robert Keohane, Robert Cox) and the issues around which existing scholarship clusters. The final brief section outlines the approach of the book.

Contending perspectives on international political economy

Facts do not exist independently of explanatory frameworks. Facts are pieces of information that are thought to correspond to reality and be true, but the way in which they are perceived and judged is influenced by theory. In order to make sense of the world and to enable us to take constructive action, humans develop theories to help determine which facts are most important and what significant relationships there are between different events. Theories are used for a variety of purposes: they can prioritize information and allow individuals to turn their attention to the most important issues; they can be used to make predictions about the future so that action can be taken to prepare for upcoming events; they can be used to plan action or mobilize support for particular action. Every person utilizes theory to run their lives even if they do not engage in explicit theorizing.

Actors in the global political economy and those studying it use a variety of theories and use them for a variety of purposes. Some people are interested in prediction. For example, they would like to be able to predict what type of monetary system would lead to stable economic growth, or to predict the likelihood of war between democratic states. Others believe that prediction is nearly impossible because so many factors come together to influence events. These people are more likely to use theory in an attempt to understand the world rather than to predict what will happen next.

In this book we will use and describe a number of theories in order to better understand the world around us. The development of IPE is often constructed around a debate between three contending schools of thought, paradigms or approaches. Some commentators refer to contending paradigms, others to different schools of thought and yet others to competing approaches but it does not really matter for our purposes whether they are seen as paradigms, schools of thought or approaches. The central point is that three main contending perspectives exist on how we are best to explain developments in the global political economy. It will be evident that although analysts distinguish between these three approaches there is a wide variety of thought within each approach and indeed that much work in IPE draws on more than one of them. Before addressing the current state of theory, however, we will next introduce the key propositions of the three perspectives and highlight the major differences between them.

The economic nationalist perspective

One school of thought brings together analysts who focus on the role of the state and the importance of power in shaping outcomes in the international political economy. These theories stress the importance of the interest of the nation or the state in understanding activity in international relations. This grouping is variously termed mercantilist, neo-mercantilist, statist, state-based theory, power politics or economic nationalist. We will use the term economic nationalism to refer to this perspective because at the centre of such analyses is the protection of the national unit. The underlying economic argumentation may alter, for example, but the objective of economic intercourse remains the same. The origin of this school of thought can be traced back to the emergence and expansion of the nation-state in Europe in the fifteenth century. Mercantilism was a doctrine of political economy that governed the actions of many states until the liberal revolution in Britain in the mid-nineteenth century. Mercantilists believed that there was only a limited amount of wealth in the world and that each state must secure its interests by blocking the economic interests of other states. This is known as a zero-sum game. One state's gain is another state's loss. From the fifteenth until the nineteenth centuries European states strove to establish overseas empires that would be as self-sufficient as possible. Trade between neighbouring colonies of rival empires was discouraged.

Two famous advocates of mercantilist theory were Alexander Hamilton (1791/1991) and Fredrick List (1885/1991). Alexander Hamilton was a founding father of the United States. Writing in the 1790s he urged

Americans to protect their manufacturers from foreign competition so that they could industrialize and increase their power. Almost a hundred years later, Fredrick List argued that Germany should industrialize behind trade barriers so that it could catch up to the economic might of Great Britain. He believed that only the economically strong advocated free-trade policies because others would lose out in the ensuing competition.

One central question for students of the contemporary global economy relates to the persistence of mercantilist thought. It could be assumed that an economic perspective based upon unrivalled state power is of limited relevance in a world characterized by globalization. While this may be correct, contemporary economic nationalist thought should not be dismissed as some atavistic throwback to an earlier era. It reflects, on the one hand, an acknowledgement that states remain at the centre of power within the global political economy, and on the other, that there is an intimate connection between power and wealth. Thus economic nationalist thinking whether it is termed neo-mercantilism or statism remains important in both analysis and practice in the contemporary global economy. For example, states may protect strategic industries against foreign rivals or attempt to export more than they import for long periods of time. Japan has been accused of being a mercantilist state because in comparison to other advanced industrialized countries, its economy is relatively closed.

Key actors. Economic nationalist or mercantilist theories view the state as the main actor in the global political economy. A major assumption of economic nationalists is the primacy of the political over other aspects of social life. Statist writers begin from a focus on the group (the state or nation) rather than the individual. Economic nationalist thought begins from two major assumptions. The first is that the inter-state system is anarchical and that it is therefore the duty of each state to protect its own interests. At the core of the various historical versions of economic nationalism is the belief that an economic community persists and acts for the good of all its members. The second assumption concerns the primacy of the state in political life. As the state is the central instrument through which people can fulfil their goals it follows that the state remains the preeminent actor in the domestic and international domains. Economic policy should be used to build a more powerful state.

From this perspective the state is prior to the market, and market relations are shaped by political power. Economic nationalist thought is both descriptive and predictive. Descriptively economic nationalists maintain that production, consumption, exchange, and investment are all governed by political power. Markets are not 'natural', they can only exist within a social context. For mercantilists political needs and purposes are seen largely as being achieved through the form of the state. It remains at the core of social life. But economic nationalists move beyond description and also provide policy advice. Given their analysis of the dynamics of political economy such advice is geared towards supporting and maintaining state power.

Economic nationalists recognize the importance of market-based actors such as firms but subordinate their importance to that of the state. Within this perspective the economic power of transnational corporations is acknowledged, but the overall power of such firms remains limited. In the end firms are subject to the dictates of states. Insofar as firms have become important economic actors this is only because states have abandoned regulation or lessened controls on the movement of capital.

Key dynamics. From an economic nationalist perspective international political economy (IPE) is constituted through the actions of rational states. If international relations are conceived as a struggle for power, international political economy is a struggle for power *and* wealth. The determination of a state's fate resides in its ability to ensure that its citizens reap advantages from international production and exchange. Market relations are important indicators of power and wealth but the market is governed by the activities of states. Economic activity is subordinate to political goals and objectives. Furthermore, economic actors are subject to political authority. The consequence of the salience of the state is that international economic relations are international political relations. The global economy in this view is subordinate to the international political system.

IPE scholars working in this perspective argue that the nature of the global economy reflects the interests of the most powerful states. For example, Krasner (1976) has suggested that systems of free trade are most likely when a single power dominates the international system. This dominant, or hegemonic power, is needed to provide leadership and absorb the short-term costs of maintaining a free-trade regime. Analysts such as Robert Gilpin (1981) have argued that changes in the distribution of power between states increase the chances of conflict in the international system. Because of this view considerable time can be devoted to contemplating the rise and fall of great powers (Gilpin, 1987; Kennedy, 1987).

In the heated debate over globalization both defensive and sceptical economic nationalist perspectives can be heard. The defensive posture arises from a fear that globalization may prevent state actors from fulfilling their goals. This, of course, is merely the continuation of the long-held suspicion of economic exchange held by economic nationalist thinkers. Unlike proponents of free trade, economic nationalists believe that the gains from trade are unequally distributed and favour those with greater economic and political power. Thus defensive economic nationalists can recognize globalization as a threat and seek to counter its impacts. On the other hand, sceptical economic nationalists reject many of the current liberal arguments about globalization. They contend that globalization is largely a myth and that the power of the state remains undiminished. Since economic actors are subordinate to political power these analysts argue that the policy environment conducive to globalization has been created by states. It therefore follows that states can alter this environment by changing their policies. Moreover, it can be claimed that since states remain powerful actors and the only legitimate centres of authority in the modern world, nothing significant has occurred in the global political economy.

Conflict and cooperation. Within international relations theory, realism, with its focus on the primacy of the state, the anarchical nature of international relations, and the inevitability of conflict, provides the foundation for economic nationalist thought. If realism is the perspective in international politics, economic nationalism is its equivalent doctrine in political economy. Both share a commitment to the state and to the role of power in social life. Power-based theories such as economic nationalism and realism view the world as anarchic, lacking any central authority. Relations between states are thus characterized by unending conflict and the pursuit of power.

International economic relations are therefore perceived in zero-sum terms, that is, the gain of one party necessitates a loss for another party. The system structure is perceived in conflictual terms. While economic nationalists believe that market relations can be positive they also think that such activity can also be negative. Since participating in markets is potentially negative, economic nationalists argue in favour of state control of key economic activities or for state assistance to central economic sectors. The continued salience of economic nationalist perspectives is easily visible today in production, consumption, trade and investment. In terms of production, economic nationalist sentiment is visible in arguments concerning the continued production of some good or service within particular national borders. This can be seen in terms of security concerns, that is, a state should not be reliant on the import of a specific good otherwise in times of conflict this good may be unavailable. Some countries such as France protect their agricultural sector while the US defends defence technology. It can also be seen in terms of the preservation of the cultural values of the nation. For example, many economic nationalists believe that it is vital to maintain the production of certain cultural products, for example, film and music within national borders. In relation to consumption, economic nationalist arguments have been made against cultural imperialism, that is, the view that the import of some products pollutes the nation through the introduction of foreign values. Whereas a liberal would argue that the sovereignty of the consumer is paramount, economic nationalists maintain that the values of the nation are more important. From the foregoing it is easy to see how in the sphere of exchange, economic nationalists support protection of domestic industries. Furthermore, economic nationalist thought is behind arguments that seek to restrict foreign investment, and supports the 'rights' of local investors over foreigners.

The liberal perspective

In contrast to the economic nationalist theories, liberals focus either upon the individual or a wide range of actors from the state to the corporation to interest groups. They do not see the state as a unitary actor, but as influenced by numerous factors. Rather than stress the inevitability of conflict, liberals search out the conditions for cooperation. They tend to underplay the role of force and coercion in human affairs and emphasize the ability of individuals to choose between attractive courses of action. Liberals see the world system as one of interdependence rather than anarchy. States and peoples can cooperate for mutual benefit in the liberal view. Rather than a zero-sum game where one's gains are the other's losses, liberals see a positive-sum game where the pie grows bigger and everyone gains. Liberal theories of political economy emerged in eighteenth- and nineteenth-century Britain in the wake of the industrial revolution. Political economists such as Adam Smith (1776/1983) and David Ricardo (1817/ 1992) preached the virtues of government non-interference in the economy and free trade.

Today's global economy is governed largely according to liberal principles. For example, the trade regime is based upon the goal of free trade: money flows into and out of most countries without great difficulty and all forms of economic activity are increasingly liberalized. There is a wide variety of liberal thought. It ranges from those who see the state fading away in an emerging borderless world (Ohmae 1990) that will be dominated by private business to liberal institutionalists (Keohane and Nye, 1977) who stress the continuing importance of the state, but see it enmeshed in webs of interdependence and international organization. The book by Landes (1998), mentioned in the Introduction, takes a particular type of liberal approach. It argues that those with liberal values have been most successful in the global economy and implies that these values were freely chosen by people in Europe and the West. However, he parts ways with those liberals who argue that individual choice is more significant than cultural institutions.

Key actors. Within the liberal perspective there are a number of key actors. For liberals the starting point of analysis is the individual. Liberal economic theory, of which neoclassical economic theory is a variant, begins from the analysis of individual wants and preferences and has constructed a powerful explanatory framework on this basis. In the context of analysis of the global economy, liberal theorists focus on the behaviour of individuals, firms and states. Unlike economic nationalists the key economic actor is the individual rather than the state. Individuals in pursuit of self-interest will maximize the benefits of economic exchange for society. Within liberal theory the firm plays an important role. Unlike mercantilists who view the firm with a degree of suspicion liberals see the firm as a source of economic wealth. The state is viewed with hostility by many liberals since it brings politics into the realm of economics. Liberals believe that if individuals are left freely to engage in production, exchange and consumption all would benefit and that the insertion of state control distorts benefits and adds costs to participants in the market. From a liberal perspective the transnational corporation is a positive force. Transnational corporations (TNCs) bring advantages to both home and host countries. From the perspective of the home country the TNC represents an optimal mix of technology, managerial skill and capital. For host countries TNCs boost their economies through the transfer of capital, technology, and access to markets.

Key dynamics. For liberal theorists the market lies at the centre of economic life. Economic progress results from the interaction of diverse individuals pursuing their own ends. While liberals acknowledge that market relations are not always optimal they tend to argue that intervention in the market is most likely to produce suboptimal outcomes. There is, of course a broad spectrum of liberal thought. For example, both John Maynard Keynes (1936), whose economic theories laid the foundation for interventionist, welfare governments in the immediate post-World War II period, and Friedrich Hayek, whose free-market philosophy guided the neo-liberal revolution of the 1980s are both economic liberals. They both subscribe to a belief in the positive role of markets and the ability of the market to lead to prosperity. Liberals differ over the importance of market imperfections and the policies that ought to be implemented to deal with market failure.

For liberal theorists IPE is constituted by a search for wealth. On the whole open markets will enhance growth and wealth, and firms will disseminate material wealth across the globe. Economic failure in this perspective is often the result of government intervention. Many liberal theorists have been at the forefront of the debate on globalization. For what can be termed hyper-liberals, globalization is not only a reality (indeed an inevitability!), it is a positive force for good. Globalization breaks down artificial (for which read political) barriers and by unleashing the force of production it can contribute to enhanced happiness for humankind. Thus, hyper-liberals welcome globalization. Keynesian influenced liberals or those of a reformist stance perceive certain problems with the unfettered operation of the free market and, therefore, are sensitive to some unwanted consequences of globalization. They therefore support globalization but emphasize the need for attention to market reform.

Conflict and cooperation. Liberal theorists view international relations and the international political economy as essentially cooperative. Indeed, they believe that market relations will lead to positive outcomes for all. In other words, economic relations are positive-sum. A standard liberal theory that exemplifies this belief is the theory of comparative advantage which shows that even in a situation where one country enjoys a superiority in the production of all goods and services over a second country, trade between the two countries will benefit both countries.

One persistent liberal belief has been that economic nationalist policies lead to conflict. Unlike Marxist writers who denounce the growth of global capitalism as a cause of war, liberal theorists view increased international interaction as a source of prosperity and peace. The liberal belief in the connection between protectionist polices and conflict and the reverse argument, namely that capitalism favours peace, is central to liberal critiques of the international economic order. The German philosopher Immanuel Kant (1795/1991) foresaw an era of perpetual peace when systems of free trade, a coalition of Republican states and the fear of destructive warfare would bring about an era of calm and prosperity. Near the end of the First World War, US president Woodrow Wilson (1918/1986) advocated liberal principles of free trade, self-determination and the use of international organizations to settle disputes between states.

The framers of international economic institutions after the Second World War were supporters of this view. It was argued that the war had its origins in the economic nationalist policies of the 1930s. As a consequence of the Great Depression, governments resorted to a series of protectionist measures that eroded confidence in international cooperation. As a result of economic nationalist policies the basis of collective security was shattered and an atmosphere conducive to dictators was created. The shift from economic competition to military conflict was in this view inevitable. Hence, there was the need to design institutions after the war to foster international economic cooperation and to include within those institutions mechanisms to prevent states from resorting to competitively nationalist policies.

Within the study of international relations, liberal theories of world politics and liberal theories of political economy share assumptions concerning the pluralist nature of the international system, and the feasibility of cooperation. Theories of interdependence developed in the 1960s to explain the connection between increased economic exchange and interconnectedness and the long peace among Western nations after 1945 represent classical liberal political economy. These theories emphasized the economic and political benefits of economic interchange. Interdependence was proffered as both a description of events and a prescription for the solution of conflict.

In the 1980s and 1990s liberals continued to argue that international cooperation was both possible and desirable. In contrast to economic nationalists or realists, liberals illustrated that international agreements or regimes would maintain international economic order even if hegemonic states declined (Keohane, 1984). With the end of the Cold War and the rapid spread of liberal economic models to many states in the 1990s, it appeared that the liberal faith in cooperation and progress was justified. Some even went as far as to claim that history had ended because the liberal democratic model had triumphed over other forms of social organization (Fukuyama, 1992)

The critical perspective

Another set of theories emerged in the nineteenth century in reaction to liberal thought. These theories move away from the individual and states to consider other units of analysis. They are sometimes called critical theories because they question the way the world is organized and sometimes they are labelled as radical because they challenge established forms of organization. These theories have also been termed collectivist since they focus on collectivities of people. The three most common variants of critical thought in IPE are Marxist, feminist and environmentalist theories. We will concentrate on Marxist theories here, although environmental and feminist theories will be considered in following chapters, especially those on environmental degradation and division of labour.

Marxist theories focus upon class and the interest of workers rather than state interests. Writing during the English industrial revolution, Karl Marx took issue with the idea of a harmony of interests that the liberals advocated. Marx and his co-author, Engels, discerned an ongoing conflict between workers and capitalists that would only be resolved when the workers seized power (Marx and Engels, 1848/1977). Another example is feminist theories which look at gender relations between women and men. They seek to uncover how our ideas about what men and women are supposed to be shape the ways in which society is organized. An eighteenth-century early feminist writer, Mary Wollstonecraft (1792/1992), criticized male liberal theorists for ignoring the role and interests of women in their political theories. Green theories have taken the environment and the planet as the object to be highlighted. They examine how people shape and are shaped by the environment. Neo-Gramscian theories which evolve out of Marxism stress the role of transnational classes and ideology in their efforts to understand the global economy. We will, however, use the term 'critical' to apply to these theories partly because state-based theories also focus on a collective unit, and partly because these theories are united by a critical attitude to prevailing social arrangements. In what follows we will focus on Marxism since it is the most influential of the group of theories grouped together under the heading of critical perspectives.

These critical theories stress the nature of oppression within and across societies and the struggle for justice waged by and on behalf of workers, women and the environment. Frank's (1998) study, *ReOrient*, is close to this form of analysis because he stresses European exploitation of other's resources in the 'Rise of the West'. However, he differs from traditional Marxists who have seen Western civilization as being at the forefront of human development because it was the birthplace of capitalism. He disputes both the claim that capitalism originated in Europe and that European developments are more significant to world history than development in Asia. For radical analysts, the world appears as a layer cake with one group sitting on top of another, across state boundaries.

Key actors. Marxist writers begin with a focus on class as the main 'actor' in the global political economy. They reject the individualism of liberal theory and embrace the collectivist approach of economic nationalist perspectives. However, Marxist theory rejects statism and focuses instead on the significance of class. This focus arises from the Marxist account of capitalist relations which are predicated on exploitation. The Marxist concept of class has been open to various interpretations and critiques. We will define class simply as arising from one's position in the structure of production. Marx defined class in relation to the structure of production which creates owners of the means of production (the bourgeoisie) and the labourers who sell their labour power to the bourgeoisie (the workers).

Within Marxist writing the firm is an instrument of exploitation. In this sense TNCs contribute to the exploitation and oppression of the working class. The centralization and concentration of capital visible in the form of TNCs are a key feature of imperialism whereby dominance is expressed in the global political economy. In this perspective the state is the representative of class interests rather than the expression of the harmony of communal interests posited by mercantilists.

Key dynamics. Dominance and exploitation among and within societies provide the main dynamic for Marxist theories of international political economy. Unlike liberals Marxists view market relations as inherently exploitative. Under capitalism workers are denied a fair remuneration because capitalists pay workers less than their labour is worth. Marxists view international economic relations as inherently unstable and conflictual. First, the tendency for the rate of profit to fall sees capitalists engaged in fierce competition with each other and, also according to Marxists, will tend to drive down the wages of workers. Secondly, capitalism leads to uneven development as some centres increase their wealth and growth at the expense of others. Uneven development sets the seeds of conflict between countries. Thirdly, Marxists argue that capitalism leads to overproduction or underconsumption giving rise to fluctuations in the business cycle and undermining social stability.

A revision of Marxist thought called 'dependency' theory has been used to explain the persisting poverty of many states. Dependency theory suggests that poor countries faced immense obstacles to development because they were vulnerable to economic exploitation from developed states (Dos Santos, 1970). The links between the rich and the poor were thought to make the poor poorer and the rich richer. Underdevelopment of some parts of the world was caused by development in other parts of the world. This school of thought informed developing countries' attempts to create a new international economic order in the 1970s (Cox, 1979). This approach was undermined in the 1980s as many developing states adopted liberal economic policies in the wake of the debt crisis.

Radical theorists, have tended, for a variety of reasons, to oppose globalization. It has been argued, for example, that globalization is a myth or merely imperialism in modern clothes. According to this argument, globalization represents an ideological intervention into political economy. It ostensibly describes changes in the world but in reality it is a set of prescriptions in support of free markets and an instrument to increase the power of capital over labour, the West over other states, and an instrument designed to further the interests of the leading capitalist power, the United States. In this sense globalization has to be resisted since it too maintains and increases exploitative relations. At the heart of the radical argument is the view that globalization is not distinctive. That is, discussion of globalization is merely the contemporary version of imperialism. To discuss political economy in terms of globalization may mask real power relations.

In the 1980s and 1990s, Marxist IPE was reinvigorated by the work of scholars drawing inspiration from Antonio Gramsci. Writers such as Robert Cox (1996a) and Stephen Gill (1993) focused on the role of social forces and ideology in liberalizing and globalizing economic relations. They argued that globalization based on neoclassical liberal economic principles was a political project which transformed national states into instruments of global liberalization and economic management. Part of this project involves convincing people that neo-liberal policies were actually in their best interest. In this view, the hegemony of a particular world order requires an ideological dominance which secures the broad consent of those ruled in an unequal and unjust manner.

Conflict and cooperation. Critical writers tend to perceive international economic relations as a zero-sum game. The structure of global capitalism is fundamentally conflictual. Two forms of conflict are prevalent in the global economy. Within states capitalists and workers have competing interests and the state is the scene of a class struggle as the workers and bourgeoisie clash. According to Marxists this conflict is objective and arises from the law of motion of capital. In the international arena the clash between workers and capitalists is often obscured by nationalism and the intervention of the state. Through the mechanism of imperialism dominant states oppress weaker ones and this sets up an international struggle between imperialists and their victims.

International conflict is inevitable because of the drive for profit. Different capitalists seek the protection of their state and this leads to war. Marxist theories of imperialism have in different ways accounted for the tendency of capitalist states to go to war. The most well-known of these theories, Lenin's theory of imperialism, combined two different explanations of capitalist development. One part of his theory focused on underconsumption in domestic markets. Because of underconsumption capitalists were compelled into overseas adventures since they could not maintain their rates of profit on the basis of domestic demand. Another part of his theory focused on the growth of finance capital and the merger between finance and industrial capital to form monopoly capital that sought to gain profit through overseas lending. He argued that conflict and war are a necessary end result of this competition.

At the turn of the twenty-first century conflict between social forces was also seen to take place on a global scale. Elites attempting to constitutionalize neo-liberal principles in institutions such as the World Trade Organization and the International Monetary Fund met with opposition from social movements trying to safeguard environmental regulation, raise labour standards, improve gender equity and lobby for economic justice (O'Brien *et al.*, 2000) Critical analysts depict a global conflict which takes place within, above and across states (Gill, 2003).

Contending perspectives: a summary. The question arises as to why there are so many theories and what the relationship is between various theories. There are several reasons for the existence of multiple theories. Two of the reasons are described by Robert Cox (1986, p. 207) 'Theory is always *for* someone and *for* some purpose.' Each theory has a different goal in mind, for example, economic nationalist theories are concerned with the security of the state, liberal theories with building wealth or cooperation and critical theories in pursuing economic, gender or environmental equity. While they are all trying to understand the world, they are looking at different aspects of human existence. A second and related reason is that a particular theory usually advances the causes or interests of a particular group. Richer, more satisfied people and states tend to favour liberal theories which do not threaten their interests while those disadvantaged by the system are more likely to espouse critical theories. A third explanation is that it is impossible to prove a theory right or wrong. Evidence is often disputed and interpreted in different ways. Moreover, unlike the laws of nature, people are able to reflect upon their behaviour and change their form of organization and interaction. People may act according to mercantilist theories in some eras or situations and along liberal principles in others.

Table 1.2 presents a summary of the theories. In the discussion so far our intention has been to highlight the existence of various interpretations. But what is the relationship between various theories? Are they in conflict or can they be made compatible? At their core, theories about international political economy are incompatible because they have different basic assumptions about the units of analysis, nature of the system and the motivation of actors. Yet, each theory can point to some evidence to support its existence and each seems to be useful in explaining some aspect of the global political economy. Some theorists (Strange, 1988) have suggested that people take an eclectic approach to theory – picking and choosing as they wish. This can have some advantages, but risks incoherence as one jumps from perspective to perspective. Readers should consider some systemized form of integration where various theories may be used under particular circumstances or in a hierarchy. For example, one could have a general power politics approach while conceding that the system is also characterized by class and gender exploitation and that there are times when cooperation can be more beneficial than conflict. Alternatively, some theories may be more applicable in selected time periods.

Three major figures and today's debates

This section provides an overview of the body of work of three major figures in IPE in the last quarter of the twentieth century. The review is undertaken for three reasons. First, it illustrates how the field has evolved over recent years. Secondly, attention to each scholar's work will demonstrate how they combine or mix insights from different intellectual traditions and that the student of IPE need not be imprisoned in any particular approach. Finally, it will become apparent how misleading labels can be

Table 1.2 *Comparing the perspectives*

Perspective	Economic nationalist	Liberal	Critical
Historical origins	15th century	19th century	19th century
Major figures	Hamilton, List, Krasner, Gilpin, Strange	Smith, Ricardo, Kant, Wilson, Keynes, Hayeck, Keohane and Nye	Marx, Lenin, Frank, Cox
Variants	Mercantilism, realism	Free trade, inter-dependence,	Marxism feminism, environmentalism
Level	State-centric; atomistic	Pluralist atomistic	Global structure
Human Nature	Aggressive	Cooperative	Malleable
Units	States	Firms, states, NGOs, IGOs	Class, gender, planet, global capitalism
View of the state	Unitary actor	Pluralist state: diverse interest groups	Representative of class interests
View of TNCs	Beneficial/ harmful	Beneficial	Exploitative
Behavioural dynamic	State as rational actor	Individual as rational actor but outcomes not always optimal	Dominance and exploitation within and between societies
Market relations	Potentially negative	Positive	Exploitative
System structure	Anarchy / conflictual	Cooperative / interdependence	Hierarchy / conflictual
Game Metaphor	Zero-sum	Positive-sum	Zero-sum
Hegemony	Importance of a dominant state	Post-hegemonic cooperation	Hegemony in state and society
International institutions	Not very significant	Important	Serve interests of wealthy (states, firms and classes)

when applied to particular pieces of work or collections of work which are more nuanced than a label might suggest. For each scholar we will discuss their career path, theoretical orientation, major works and issues and contributions to the field.

Susan Strange – an unorthodox realist

Susan Strange (2002) admitted that she never meant to become a professor, but ended up in the role after stints in journalism (with the *Observer* and *The Economist*) and working at a British foreign affairs research institute (Chatham House). She eventually established herself teaching in the International Relations Department of the London School of Economics. In later years she moved to Warwick University and contributed to the growth of its IPE program.

Strange's theoretical approach is difficult to characterize neatly (Tooze and May, 2002). It contains a strong element of power politics or economic nationalism in that she focuses upon the exercise of power and pays considerable attention to key state policies in structuring the global economy. She takes a realist approach in advising students to focus upon the role of interests and to constantly ask the question 'Who benefits?'. Yet, her work is also unorthodox because Strange urged observers to take account of the growing role of markets, corporations and technological innovations in changing the environment in which state operates. In a series of exchanges with American IPE scholars Susan Strange continuously went against the mainstream by variously arguing that the study of regimes was faddish and mistaken (1982), that US hegemony was not declining in the 1980s (1987), and that globalization was transforming the nature of state authority (1996).

Strange's early work concentrated on international monetary affairs such as Britain's policy for the pound sterling. In writing about the field of IPE she constantly argued that it should be an interdisciplinary area that brought together international relations and international economics. She argued against international relations specialists who she saw as fixated on the state and questions of war and peace, as well as international economists who ignored questions of power.

Strange viewed IPE as a method of understanding the world that focused upon the relationship between markets and authority. Her broad approach is set out in a 1988 textbook called *States and Markets*. The text argues that in addition to relational power (A forces B to do A's will) power resides in structures. Structural power is the ability to shape the rules of the game in a particular area. Those who create the operating framework for everyone's activities exercise power by eliminating some possibilities and making some outcomes more likely than others. Strange maintained that there were four key structures of power (security, production, finance, knowledge) and numerous secondary structures (transport, trade, energy, welfare). Strange reasoned that since the US exercised considerable structural power in the key structures, talk of US decline was mistaken.

In the 1990s Strange increasingly turned her attention to non-state actors. In a major collaboration with a business school professor (Stopford and Strange, 1991) she argued that traditional notions of diplomacy being an interstate practice had to be expanded to include state–firm and firm–firm interactions. In a following book Strange identified other actors such as business associations, bureaucrats and even mafias that were operating transnationally and undermining the authority of states.

Strange conducted most of her empirical research in the area of finance and credit. She argued that the creation and control of credit was a significant source of power in the global economy. True to her realist roots she traced the liberalization and globalization of finance to particular decisions or non-decisions of the most powerful states. Finance was globalized because it suited the interests of the most powerful states (principally the US and the UK). However, Strange also worried that the failure of states to exercise proper regulatory control over financial flows was turning the system into a form of 'casino capitalism' (1986). She questioned the stability of a liberal global financial system that outgrew government control. Her fear was that a widespread financial collapse would lead to a closing of the global economy (1998).

Susan Strange played a prominent role in founding and supporting the study of IPE as an interdisciplinary field in Britain. Her pioneering studies in the field of finance inspired a new generation to examine the power relations flowing around credit issues. Strange's insistence that IPE be an open field of intellectual inquiry influenced the development of the field in Britain by bringing in work from a number of different disciplines. Her stinging criticism of US intellectual trends provided room for British scholars and students to ask different types of questions and use different methodologies from their US counterparts. She left a rich legacy of scholarship, inquiry and institutions in her wake.

Robert Keohane – liberal institutionalist

Robert Keohane was born into an academic family and began a US teaching career after graduating from Harvard in 1965 (Keohane 1989a). His academic career took him to Stanford, Brandeis, Harvard and Duke universities. His research has had a major role in influencing the study of IPE and IR in the US and beyond.

Keohane is a central figure in what has become known as the liberal institutionalist approach to IPE and world politics (1989b). This approach suggests that institutions or sets of rules and norms can have a significant effect upon state behaviour if they have mutual interests. Institutions include formal international organizations, international regimes or conventions and custom. Liberal institutionalism was developed as a critique of realist / power politics / economic nationalist approaches to international relations and IPE. The emphasis is on how institutions can help states overcome barriers to cooperation. Although Keohane himself now prefers to be known simply as an institutionalist (2002, p. 3), the adjective 'liberal' is still useful because it refers to some of the liberal attributes than underlie his approach. These include a focus on the individual and a belief that properly designed international institutions can go some way to creating a more humane global system.

Keohane's first major work was written with Joseph Nye and tried to integrate realist (power politics) and liberal thought by focusing on bargaining in situations of interdependence. In *Power and Interdependence* Keohane and Nye (1977) argued that there were certain times and issue areas when the assumptions of realist or power politics approaches did not hold sway. They labelled these situations as 'complex interdependence' and argued that under certain circumstances states could use international institutions to bolster cooperation. They also argued that in such situations cross-border links between officials could lead to outcomes different from those that power politics approaches would have predicted.

In 1984 Keohane published a book called *After Hegemony*. It sought to explain why, contrary to realist assumptions, states continued to cooperate and participate in international agreements even after the major power which sponsored the agreements entered a period of relative decline. This was a significant issue because many analysts were worried about the decline of US power relative to other states and feared that this would make the international political economy increasingly unstable. Keohane focused on post-1945 arrangements in the issue areas of money, trade and oil. He argued that the benefits of arrangements in these issue areas, or regimes, continued independent of the rise or decline of the power of particular states. Regimes exist because they facilitate negotiations between states and allow states to overcome barriers to collective action such as uncertainty. Keohane's work helped to spark increasing attention to the issue of regime creation and maintenance. Indeed regime theory became a mainstay of US IPE scholarship.

Another important aspect of *After Hegemony* was Keohane's use of economic theory to explain the activity of states. Drawing inspiration from economic theories that claimed to explain the activity of corporations, Keohane analysed state behaviour in terms of market failure, transactions costs and uncertainty. Market failure refers to a situation where transactions do not take place because the market is arranged in such a way as to make otherwise rational activity irrational. In the case of IPE states might not agree to cooperate because they are unsure of the motives of other states. Regimes help to resolve this market failure by providing information about other states' behaviour and an element of predictability in interstate interactions. States cooperated in international regimes because these regimes solved particular problems such as lack of information and uncertainty about other states' intentions and behaviour. Keohane's use of economic models and theories of rational choice coincided and blended well with the importation of economic models in other areas of US political science. The success of his book and persuasiveness of his argument helped to bolster rational choice methodology in US IPE.

In the 1990s Keohane (2002) turned his attention to two issues raised in his earlier work – domestic politics and problem of state compliance with international regimes. The issue of domestic politics concerned how state based theories of international interaction might be integrated with understandings of nationally based politics. How do domestic politics affect international relations? The issue of compliance moves on from considering the origins and maintenance of regimes to thinking about why and how states obey international rules. This path leads towards more study of the role of international law in influencing state behaviour.

Robert Keohane has been one of the most influential US writers in the field of IPE and IR. His work has advanced understanding of the conditions under which states are able to cooperate through international regimes.

Robert Cox – historical materialist

For Canadian-born Robert Cox academic life was a second career after spending twenty-five years in the international civil service at the International Labour Organization. At the ILO Cox served as a staff officer to the Director General, Chief of the Program and Planning division and as Director of the International Institute for Labor Studies. After leaving the ILO, Cox took a teaching position at Columbia University in New York before settling at Toronto's York University in 1977.

Robert Cox describes his approach to IPE and IR as historical materialist (2002, pp. 27–9). The historical part involves recognizing that each historical era has a particular sensibility and set of institutions and understandings. This contrasts with approaches which claim there are universal laws of human behaviour which apply across time. The materialist part places the organization of production and the social relations around production at the centre of analysis. In other words, class and class conflict play an import part in understanding political economy. Cox takes a particular approach to historical materialism which mixes theoretical insights from Marx with scholars such as Vico, Sorel, Weber, Gramsci and Polanyi. The result is that many liberals and economic nationalists label Cox a Marxist while many Marxists argue that he has deviated from the Marxist path (Schecter, 2002). Thus, the labels one picks up depend heavily upon who is doing the labelling.

As the title of a collection of Cox's essays indicates, his primary interest has been *Approaches to World Order* (1996a). However, the specific focus moved from international organizations to social forces to civilizations. Cox's early work focused upon international organizations, especially the ILO. In the 1970s he and Harold Jacobson (1974) worked on decision-making in international organizations. They tried to understand what factors were most influential in shaping the programs of international organizations.

Cox' s experience at the ILO and his study of international organizations prompted him to think about the nature of power and dominance in the global economy. He (1983) theorized that powerful states exercise a form of hegemony that goes far beyond military strength. Hegemonic states such as Britain in the nineteenth century or the US in the twentieth century drew their power from a particular form of production and social relations. Hegemony require dominance in the economic, political, social and ideological realm. A hegemonic power was able to convince others that their interests were the same as those of the dominant power. As a result, hegemonic states tried to express their interests as universal norms and used international organizations to influence other states.

Central to Cox's work has been the idea that 'production generates the capacity to exercise power, but power determines the manner in which production takes place' (1987, p. 1). The ability to produce things generates resources and objects that can be used to influence events, but the production of things takes place under the shadow of coercion. For example, the industrial revolution boosted British productivity and allowed it to exercise an international role in the nineteenth century. However, the organization of production was accomplished by the use of force whether it was in the case of slavery in the cotton industry or forcing people out of the countryside into factories in Britain.

Cox also argued that it was a mistake to focus on the state and ignore the role of social forces (1986). Social forces are groups of people who occupy a particular place in the global economy by virtue of their role in the organization of production. Some social forces such as the people who own or work in internationally competitive industry advocate free trade while other social forces will oppose free trade as a threat to their interests.

In the theoretical realm Cox (1986) was significant for highlighting the differences between critical theory and problem solving theory. Problem solving theory looks at the world as it is and concentrates on how issues can be addressed in the existing system. Critical theory stands back from the existing order and asks how that order came about and under what conditions it could be changed to a different form of order. Critical theorists seek to contribute to a better social order. They thus embrace emancipatory strategies. Problem solving theory is about managing the system and critical theory is about changing the system. Most radical analysis which call for major changes in the global political economy fit into this critical category.

Cox's latest work shifted to new areas of investigation. He acknowledged two weaknesses in his earlier work – the neglect of gender and environmental issues (2002). Attempts to theorize world order need to take account of how men and women are differentially incorporated into the global economy and of people's relationship to the environment. The key question that drew his attention in later years was 'How can a global system function in a non-hegemonic or pluralist manner? How can people who have different understandings of how the world operates and how it should operate create a system for humane global governance?'. The two areas he chose to explore were civil society and civilizational interchange (2002).

Cox's most significant impact in the study of IPE has been to raise critical questions about the system of international order and to contemplate how one might get to a more egalitarian and sustainable system. This has led him to disagree with the normative and practical implications of economic liberalism and the fatality of economic nationalism.

Where are we now? Globalization and IPE

In trying to capture the field of IPE today it is helpful to think about two key features. One is an ongoing debate about methodology which is summarised in Box 1.1. The second, to which we will devote more attention given the focus of this text is the way in which debates about globalization have impacted on research priorities.

In this respect there are clear echoes of the problems addressed by Strange, Keohane and Cox. As we have argued above (and will in the remainder of this book) international political economy as an approach to explaining developments in the global political economy has to be understood in relation to a changing historical context. It is possible to conceive IPE as marked by three major debates – interdependence, declining American hegemony, and globalization. Recent and current research in IPE is informed by the contemporary debate on globalization, and within this debate four issues have informed scholarship. These themes are the changing role of the state, regionalism, inequality and governance.

Research on the state arises from the central question of the contemporary relevance of the state in an age of globalization. Two distinct but interrelated clusters of scholarship have emerged. The first focuses on the ways in which the authority of the state has been disrupted or enhanced by the processes of globalization. The empirical focus is on the impact of changes in the production and finance structures on state authority, legitimacy and autonomy. However, no consensus exists in the literature and a vigorous debate continues with three identifiable research streams. Some authors argue that globalization is forcing the state into retreat (Strange, 1996); others contend that the state is changing but in ways that signal complex transformation rather than a decline in its role (Cerny, 2000); and another group of scholars provide evidence to support their claim that state structures remain resilient in the face of a changing global economy (Garrett, 2000).

The second cluster emerges from the earlier studies of Keohane on the determinants of the conditions under which states cooperate. Recently two issues have come to the fore in this scholarship. First, the question of how domestic politics might be integrated into our understanding of international affairs (Milner, 1997) and secondly, the legalization of international relations (Goldstein *et al.*, 2000).

Research on regionalism was stimulated by the emergence in the late 1980s of the so-called new regionalism. Expansion and transformation of existing regional organizations such as the Association of South-east Asian Nations (ASEAN) and the European Union (EU) and the emergence of new regional groupings, for example, the Asia–Pacific Economic Cooperation (APEC) and the North American Free Trade Agreement (NAFTA) led to a reawakening of interest in regionalism and a the construction of new agenda in the study of regionalism (Hurrell, 1995). Research on regional integration was transformed in two significant ways. First, one of the main normative goals has been discarded. Studies of both old and new regionalism are concerned with the transformation of political community but whereas in the 1960s and early 1970s scholars' interest was particularly concerned with the role of regional organizations in fostering cooperative and peaceful relations among states, current research is less concerned with the peace dividend. Instead contemporary research is concerned with the shift of authority from national to regional levels, the distributional impact of regional groupings and the relationship between regionalism and globalization (Coleman and Underhill, 1998, Gamble and Payne, 1996). Secondly, the scope of research has broadened to focus on the role of non-state actors such as transnational corporations and social movements rather than the previous concentration on interstate activity (O'Brien, 1995).

Box 1.1 The methodological debate

Alongside discussion of the three main perspectives a debate about method emerged in the 1990s. Three prominent methodologies were rational choice theory, neo-institutionalism, and constructivism. Adherents of the different perspectives could in principle use any methodology, but it has tended to be the case that economic nationalists and liberals favour rational choice or institutionalism while critical theorists favour variants of constructivism.

Rational Choice. Rational choice theory or rational choice analysis focuses on individual choice under conditions of uncertainty. It is dominant in contemporary neo-classical economic scholarship, and extremely influential in US political science. It explains outcomes in the global political economy on the basis of the preferences of individual actors (either an individual person or a group considered to be acting as an individual). Within this framework actors are assumed to be utility maximizers (they attempt to maximize their gains and minimize their losses). Individuals try to make themselves better off by calculating costs and benefits before choosing the best path of action. This simple framework provides a powerful starting point for analysis. Rational choice theory has been used extensively to analyse trade and cooperation problems in IPE (Carlson, 2000).

Institutionalism. As a methodology institutionalism focuses on the importance of formal and informal institutions in producing political outcomes. At the core of what has been termed the new institutionalism is an emphasis on the importance of rules. If the main tenet of rational choice theory is that individuals pursue self-interest, for insti-

→

The problem of national and global inequality while central to critical perspectives in IPE was until recently of limited concern to other more orthodox approaches. Globalization has brought to the fore concerns with the politics of change and global restructuring thus highlighting the issue of inequality (Hurrell and Woods, 1995). Scholars from the economic nationalist (Banuri *et al.*, 1997; Hines, 2000) and critical perspectives (Amin, 1997; Hoogvelt, 1997) have developed research agendas to document the ways in which processes of global restructuring lead to increased marginalization and social exclusion. This in turn has stimulated research by liberal IPE scholars (Bourgignon and Morrison, 1992; Burtless *et al.*, 1998; Krugman and Venables, 1995; Stewart and Berry, 1999). Two issues have been at the forefront of this scholarship. The first issue concerns the

→

tutionalists it is that rules matter. The global economy is conceived not as the result of the actions of diverse individuals but as the outcome of the interaction of simple and complex institutions which shape individual decisions (Spruyt, 2000). In IPE institutionalism is most familiar in the writings of liberal scholars who emphasize the powerfully constraining and beneficial impact of institutions. A more radical version of new institutionalism concentrates on the institutional forms and the institutional dynamics of capitalism.

Constructivism. Constructivism begins from the premise that there is an intimate and reciprocal connection between human subjects and the social world (Palan, 2000). Whereas rational choice analysis takes values and beliefs for granted, constructivists see beliefs and values as something that have to be explained and as crucial in shaping and determining 'reality'. Whereas institutionalists focus on rules as the driving forces in constraining and shaping behaviour in a context where identity is essentially fixed, constructivism posits that norms and values go beyond shaping actors' interests – they in themselves constitute identities and hence interests. From this perspective the global political economy is a set of material conditions and practices, a set of normative statements about the world and an academic discipline. It is not reducible to one of these but is always constructed as the interaction of these three 'structures'. This is also true for any 'issue' in IPE. For example, to understand development we have to look at development in relation to material privation, the values attached to economic growth and prosperity (as well as negative values attributed to poverty), and the ways in which development is studied and analysed.

implications of transformations in the global political economy for public and private actors in the developing world. The central question concerns the benefits and costs of globalization for developing countries and for the poor in developing countries. Feminist scholars with a focus on gender issues provide an important contribution to this stream of analysis (Ashfar and Berrientos 1999; Dickenson and Shaeffer 2001; Marchand and Runyan 2000). The second major issue is that of the role of global economic institutions in the management of globalization. Here attention has focused on the adjustment policies, liberalization strategies and the normative function of major global economic organizations (Mihevc, 1995; Stewart, 1995; Stiglitz, 2002; Williams, 1994).

The fourth major theme in contemporary empirical research focuses on the problems of (global) governance (Nye and Donahue, 2000; Hewson and Sinclair, 1999). At issue are the various ways in which states, firms, social movements and individuals are coping with transformations in the global economy. One strand of research is concerned with the politics of resistance and investigates the diverse ways in which labour unions, NGOs, and civil society groups articulate resistance against practices of change and (global) restructuring (Khagram, Riker and Sikkink, 2002). A second strand of research concentrates on assessing the extent to which non-state actors including firms and non-governmental organizations (NGOs) intersect with national, regional and global governance structures. In response to recent civic action and protest against international organizations and globalization, work on civic associations, NGOs and social movements is increasing (O'Brien *et al.*, 2000). This work expands upon the neo-Gramscian IPE approaches by shifting the focus from elite groups to non-elites. It has been greatly strengthened by the empirical studies and theoretical challenges of feminist and environmentalist scholars incorporating gender and the environment. Another research trajectory focuses on the role of the corporation in the international political economy. This can take the form of studies investigating the role that corporations have played in influencing state and international organization policies. For example, leading US and European pharmaceutical, information technology, and entertainment companies have been very successful in protecting their patent rights through changes to international trade law (Sell, 1999). Other studies have looked at the activity of corporations which are trying to set up their own forms of authority through market mechanisms (Cutler *et al.*, 1999). For example, bond rating agencies evaluate the credit worthiness of states and firms, giving an authoritative verdict on how much they should pay in order to borrow money (Sinclair, 1994). These two strands of research are linked but the literature on the firm gives more attention to the nature of rule-making by private actors while the NGO literature is often concerned with how citizen groups try to shape economic relations in a more equitable manner.

Approach of the book

As argued above, all IPE analyses are written from a particular theoretical perspective. Theoretical assumptions guide choices about which theories and events should be highlighted and which will not make it into the study. This book returns to the three main approaches when they are helpful for understanding particular developments. For example, liberal theories help us understand some of the elements of British policy in the nineteenth century and the thinking behind multilateral trade institutions in the twentieth century. However, in assembling the material for the book we have been guided by an approach that reflects our view about how international or global political economy should be understood. It reflects our synthesis of elements of the three contending paradigms. There are six main components of this approach which we develop below.

First, our approach is historicist in that it is sensitive to historical change. The nature of political economy, its major institutions and ideas about it how it operates change over time (Cox, 1996a, pp. 49–59). This book places historical development at the centre of its explanatory framework, and recognizes history as both the context or framework within which meaning is located, and an ideological concept which is evident in various perspectives on political economy. Theories about how the world work arise in particular historical contexts and need to be linked to those contexts. A historical sensitivity is also important to understand the path dependent nature of the evolution of the global political economy. Some states and groups of people have become locked into particular development patterns because of events that took place many years ago. For example, many developing countries export low-value commodities because their economies were orientated to this task during the age of imperialism.

The role of historical practices in development raises a second point which is the relationship between structure and agency. Put simply this is the question of whether overreaching structures such as the organization of production or the institution of patriarchy determine the action of agents (states, firms, people) or whether agents engage in free choice and construct their own environments (Wendt, 1987). We view the relationship as dynamic and do not to privilege either systemic or unit level variables. There are dangers in reifying structures on one hand, and reducing complex events to individual action on the other. In rejecting structural determinism and methodological individualism we seek to understand the ways in which structures constrain action, and agency impacts on structural constraints. The existence of a structure of patriarchy does not, for example, determine that all males will exploit women.

Thirdly, we recognize the salience of ideas or cognitive structures as significant elements in the GPE and examine the role of ideas in structuring outcomes (Finnemore and Sikkink, 1998). Norms, values, ideologies, and ideas are constitutive elements of the global political economy. This means that they help to make the world the way it is rather than only reflecting how we think about the world. They are not secondary to material developments, and are not derived solely from the material structures of the global economy. On the contrary ideas shape, mould, facilitate, and constrain the activities of economic agents. For example, if it is believed that inflation is the economic problem most destructive of stability, harmony and progress this becomes an economic 'fact' and redistributivist policies are subsumed to the dictates of the fight against inflation. Fighting inflation ceases to be perceived as a policy choice and instead is taken to be a central and natural feature of economic governance. Another example would be the ideas supporting patriarchy. It might be assumed that women are naturally docile and dextrous, thus making them the ideal choice for particular types of employment. The importance of ideas, intellectual schemes and ideologies will therefore be investigated rather than taken as given. Certain claims to the contrary notwithstanding political economy is not value free and arguments over economic theories cannot be dismissed as rhetoric.

Fourthly, we stress the inseparability of economics and politics, and therefore reject the separation of the economic from the political at the core of liberal and mercantilist approaches. Whereas liberalism separates the economic from the political and mercantilism subsumes the economic to the political we insist that the economic constitutes the political and the political constitutes the economic. One of the ways that this becomes apparent in the text is that we link events in the field of economic development with the deployment of organized violence and the ramifications of warfare.

Fifthly, we view institutions as constantly undergoing change. Perspectives that take the institutional context as a given are deficient. Recently economics and political science have recognized the importance of social institutions in structuring market behaviour. We begin from the recognition that formal and informal institutions play significant roles in structuring outcomes in the international system. We therefore investigate the impact of institutions and emphasize the contribution of formal organizations to the evolution of the global economy. Two of the significant institutions we examine in the text are the changing nature of the state and the organization of international or world order. For example, the states discussed in the second chapter have mercantilist and imperialist characteristics while the industrial revolution sees the emergence of a liberal British state. Following the Second World War, many Third World countries were characterized by developmental states and Western countries adopted some form of the Keynesian state.

Finally, our view of the global political economy is sensitive to the relationship between changes in domestic social orders and structures of international order and global political economy (Skidmore, 1997; Cox, 1986). Social and class conflict in key states can bolster or undermine the principles and institutions upon which a particular world order rests. A leading explanation for the success of European expansionist activity in the sixteenth and seventeenth centuries was the greater relative autonomy that merchants enjoyed in Europe compared to empires in other parts of the world. Another example is the role that mobilized populations played in thwarting the attempts to build a stable liberal international system between 1918–1939. Changes in citizen expectations about government behaviour made it impossible to impose the economic medicine that liberal theory demanded.

Keeping the three main approaches and our own blend of important characteristics in mind we now turn our attention to the evolution and dynamics of the global political economy.

Part I

Evolution

Part 1

Evolution

Chapter 2

Forging a World Economy 1400–1800

Why do we inhabit a world where there are such great inequalities of wealth and life chances between regions? Why do some countries seem to be caught in a trap of producing products whose value decline over time, such as sugar or coffee? What accounts for the racial hierarchies in countries such as the United States and South Africa? Why do some societies and countries seem suspicious of the foreign and economic policies of Western states, corporations and civic associations? The answers to these questions are partially rooted in the origins of the global economy. Indeed, a full understanding of today's global economy requires a familiarity of patterns that were initiated hundreds of years ago.

Today's global political economy has its roots in the late 1400s when Spanish adventurers forcefully integrated sections of the Americas into an intercontinental economy that already linked parts of Europe, Africa and Asia. This chapter focuses on the period when the major regional economies in Asia, Africa, Europe and the Americas were brought into increased contact through the persistence of European expansionism. This will be accomplished in two sections. First, we will provide a brief overview of the major economic areas before the Spanish conquest of the 1500s. This will give us an understanding of the diversity of political economy arrangements around the world and will lay the groundwork for understanding the varying pattern of European – non-European interaction in subsequent centuries. Secondly, we will look at the pattern of European engagement with other parts of the world from the 1490s until the early 1800s. The conclusion analyses the historical record in terms of the key frameworks used in Part II of the book (trade, production, labour, finance, development, environment, and governance).

The chapter has two major arguments. First, the regional political economies that were connecting during this period varied greatly in terms of social, political and economic organization. Secondly, this heterogeneity created a variety of interactions from free exchange to open warfare and slavery. A third point, explored in following chapters, is that these interactions would have long lasting effects.

Regions of the world economy

This section provides a snapshot of several areas of the world prior to European contact with the Americas which created the first truly world-wide political economy. In the year 1400 there was little hint that the residents of Europe would have such an influence upon the majority of people who lived in other regions. As the Portuguese, Spanish, Dutch, English and French steadily moved outward from their own continents they encountered a variety of people and social organizations. Rather than expanding into a vacuum, the Europeans interacted with established civilizations, economic systems and military forces.

There are several points to keep in mind. First, with few exceptions economic activity was on a local level. Agricultural production was the norm and this was usually centred upon a market town with an agricultural hinterland of about 30 kilometres (Swartz, 1994, p. 13). Secondly, despite the predominance of this local activity, intercontinental trade routes moving luxury goods had existed for thousands of years. Thirdly, at the heart of these trade routes lay very different civilizations with distinct political economies. Indeed, some approaches to international relations and global history take different civilizations as their starting point (Cox, 1996b; Braudel, 1994).

Janet Abu-Lughod (1989) has provided an interesting account of the world system before Europeans began their transatlantic voyages. Her research reveals a system of trade and economic exchange reaching from China to Europe. The system was composed of seven overlapping regions. Economic activity was concentrated within these regions, but they were linked to neighbouring regions allowing products to move from east Asia to western Europe. Map 2.1 reproduces Lughod's diagram showing the regions, but it also adds four additional regions that will be discussed below under 'Africa' and 'Americas'. Moving from west to east on the Eurasian continent, the first area is the region which brought together northern and southern Europe. The second region sits above the Mediterranean, crossing the divide between Christian southern Europe and the Islamic centres of Egypt. This Mediterranean region overlapped with three central regions. Region 3 covered the overland trade routes which stretched across central Asia to China which was maintained by the Mongols. Region 4 included the territory around the Tigris and Euphrates rivers down to the Persian Gulf. Region 5 also joined the Mediterranean and the Indian Ocean, but through Egypt and the Red Sea. Products making their way into the Indian Ocean were then transported across Region 6 which covered the Arabian Sea, linking Arabia with the west coast of India. Region 7 linked India with South-east Asia while Region 8 finished the route by taking in China and South-east Asia. This meant that there were three routes for products to move from China to Europe. The northern route moved goods overland from China via central Asia through the Mediterranean into the European region. Alternatively, products could move by sea through South-east Asia, the Indian ocean and then into the Mediterranean either through the Persian Gulf or the Red Sea.

Abu Lughod's work omits African trading regions, so we have added two regions which cover certain areas of sub-Saharan Africa. One region brought goods from sub-Saharan Africa into North Africa and the Mediterranean / European world (Region 9). The other brought African goods into the Middle East and Asia via the Indian ocean (Region 10) Our map also includes two regions in the Americas which were not joined to the African–European–Asian system. These are Region 11 which belonged to the Aztec empire and Region 12 ruled by the Incas.

Although it would take years to travel around this circuit of trade in the 1400s and the volumes of trade were minuscule by today's standards, economic activity was increasing across the system. Let's turn our attention to each of these regions to get a brief idea of their nature. We are particularly interested in the types of economic activity and political relations that characterized each region.

The Middle East

In Abu-Lughod's diagram of fourteenth century regions, the Middle East acts as the key gateway between the Mediterranean / European and the Eastern worlds. Indeed, the desire to get around this gateway was one of the key motivations driving European merchants into the Atlantic Ocean, around Africa and across to the Americas. By the time of Christopher Columbus' voyage across the Atlantic, there had already been a seven hundred year history of bloody and lucrative interchange between European Christendom and Middle Eastern Islam. Islamic and Christian clashes took place from the south of France through modern day Egypt, Israel and Turkey to the gates of Vienna. Yet, this rivalry was balanced by many instances of cooperation with alliances and economic interchange between Europeans and Middle Easterners. For example, the Genovese sold Christian and pagan slaves to the Mamlukes in Egypt who then trained them as soldiers to be used against the Crusaders while the Venetians financed an Ottoman fleet to battle the Portuguese in the Red Sea.

For almost a thousand years Islamic warriors waged successful military campaigns against European forces. Behind those Middle Eastern armies stood a dynamic economy, extensive trade networks, bustling cities and great centres of learning. In retrospect we can see that the fifteenth century

Map 2.1   Regions of the 15th century world economy

Adapted from Abu-Lughod (1989) p. 34.

was a period of transition in the Middle East. While the religion of Islam was dominant, forms of political authority were the object of intense rivalry. Although ultimate political authority eventually came to rest in the hands of the Sultan of the Ottoman empire, this occurred only after a period of conflict with and between Turkish tribes, Mongols, Persians and Mamlukes. The competition between rival sources of political power characteristic of Europe was not absent in the Middle East. However, by the early 1500s one Empire, the Ottomans, held the upper hand. They proceeded to extend their rule eastwards and westwards toward Europe. On land and at sea the Europeans had great difficulty matching the might of Islamic forces in the fifteenth century. It would not be until the second siege of Vienna in 1683 that European militaries would start to win consistent victories.

The Mamlukes, followed by the Ottomans, presided over a thriving trading economy. In the fourteenth century, Cairo had a population of approximately half a million and was only exceeded by one or two cities in China (Abu-Lughod, 1989, p. 212). The Mamlukes developed a structured and prosperous trading relationship with the Venetians. Through force of arms they prevented Europeans from seizing Egyptian territory that would have granted direct access to the wealth of India and China via the Red Sea. Venetians docked in Alexandria to wait for access to spices, dyes, pepper, silk, cotton and porcelains from Malaysia, India and China.

Outside of the Mediterranean, Arab traders pursued economic activity along the coast of East Africa, the western coast of India and into Southeast Asia. Zanzibar, off the coast of East Africa, was occupied by Arab traders as early as the eighth century. The cultural remnants of this early commercial activity can be seen in the Muslim populations of countries such as Malaysia and Indonesia (the largest Muslim country in the world).

China

Of all the great civilizations of the fifteenth century, China was the largest and most powerful. It produced products that were greatly desired by the elite in other regions of the world. Chief among these products were ceramics and silk. China contained the world's largest cities, advanced technology and impressive military forces. Indeed, the wonders of China were so great that when the Italian Marco Polo returned from his travels to that land, his observations were often dismissed as being fanciful.

During the fourteenth and fifteenth centuries China was also undergoing dramatic changes. In 1370 the Chinese had finally succeeded in driving out Mongol rulers and reestablished a Chinese emperor. This line of rulers was called the Ming dynasty (1368–1644). Initially, the Mings launched several long range trading voyages as far as the eastern coast of Africa. Their ships were five times as large as later Portuguese ships and they contained far more cargo space and cannons. They would have been capable of crossing the Pacific Ocean if they had attempted the task (McNeill, 1982, pp. 44–5). Indeed, had the voyages continued it is possible that the Chinese might have sailed around Africa and reached Portugal, as well as 'discovered' the Americas. However, expeditions to the West (1405–1433) were eventually halted by the Ming emperors and the sea going fleet decommissioned. For the next several hundred years, the Chinese were less engaged with the outside world and fell behind relative to the expanding Europeans.

There are several possible explanations for why the naval excursions were ended. One has to do with court politics. The leader of the expeditions (Chen Ho) was both a Muslim and a eunuch and eventually lost the support of the emperors. Another explanation is that although the voyages brought back interesting goods, there was little that the Chinese found that they actually needed. Unlike the Europeans who were desperate for spices and silks, the Chinese did not find anything so attractive that it would justify the expense of further exploration. Finally, the centre of gravity in China shifted toward the north and internal development. The Mings moved the capital from Nanjing northwards to Beijing and became more concerned with land rather than sea threats. In addition, new locks on the Grand Canal joined the Yangtze and Yellow river valleys securing year round rice transport in internal waters. This greatly reduced the importance of any maritime threats to Chinese stability and hence the need for a powerful navy (McNeill, 1982, p. 47).

In terms of political structures, the Ming Chinese emperor was the sole source of law. His views might be restrained by appeal to precedent and scholarly discussions or debates, but power was absolute (Mote, 1999, p. 637). China was governed by a single political authority unlike the rival states that fought continuously in Europe. The court sat in Beijing and governors of provinces reported to the bureaucracy and the court in the capital city. The emperor was supported by a well trained bureaucracy that was selected through a process of examination. Confucian scholar–officials played the major role in running the bureaucracy and advising the emperor. Increasingly during the Ming Dynasty, eunuchs played a key role in running the court and providing services to the emperor. In some cases, such as the admiral Cheng Ho, they accomplished great feats. In other cases they advanced their interests over that of the empire and cut the emperor off from developments in his realm.

India

Like China, India also possessed an ancient civilization, considerable economic wealth and military might. However, India was a more diverse and decentralized political economy than China. The northern section of India had experienced a series of invasions from Iranian, Mongol, Turkish and Afghan tribes. In the fifteenth century, the northern region, known as the Delhi Sultanate, was ruled by descendants of invading Islamic forces, but they were constantly under attack from new waves of invaders. The Sultanate was ravaged by the Mongol descendant Timur (Tarmalane) in 1388 and Delhi was sacked in 1398. Internal cohesion was difficult to maintain. A hundred and twenty-five years later a descendant of Timur (Barbur) invaded India and set up the Mughul (Mongol) dynasty. Many of India's architectural wonders such as the Taj Mahal date from the Mughul era.

Other parts of India were ruled by independent kingdoms. The southern region was dominated by the Hindu kingdom of Vijayanagar from 1336–1565. It was often engaged in conflict with its neighbour, the Bahmani empire. The eastern province of Bengal was usually controlled by independent rulers and the western coastal area of Gujarat also enjoyed independence. There were numerous other smaller kingdoms during this period.

Ports in coastal areas of India enjoyed a great deal of autonomy from the inland empires and economic activity was conducted by a wide range of social and economic groups. In Kerala external trade was conducted by Jews and Christians who had been resident since the sixth century. In other parts of India, Jains, Buddhists, Muslims and Hindus were involved in trade (Bouchon and Lombard, 1987). On the west coast of India, the state of Gujarat dominated trade moving from the Middle East to the east coast of India. On the east coast, Bengal play a major part in moving goods on to South-east Asia. However, these coastal areas were relatively peripheral to the land based empire. For example, it is reported that when the Mughal emperor Akbar visited the recently conquered Indian ports of Cambay and Surat in the late 1500s, it was the first time that he had ever seen the ocean (Risso, 1995).

Reflecting on the experiences of the Middle East, China and India it is noteworthy that while these civilizations engaged in maritime activity, it was difficult for maritime interests to influence political power. The large land-based empires engaged in seaborne trade and established wide ranging activity crossing the Mediterranean, Red Sea, Persian Gulf, Indian Ocean and around the seas to China. However, the Ottomans, Chinese and Mughals were primarily concerned with events within their existing empires and concentrated most of their effort in land-based expansion and defence. This was a very different pattern from the maritime dependent Portuguese, Spanish, Dutch and British empires.

Africa

To Abu-Lughod's diagram of trading networks outside of the Americas we added two ellipses to cover interaction with sub-Saharan Africa. One ellipse covers land on either side of the Sahara desert and the difficult trade across that arid sea. In West Africa gold mines supplied European demand for currency while pepper was shipped north for consumption in food seasoning. This trade eventually encouraged the Portuguese to sail around the desert to establish direct trading contacts. The second ellipse integrates the trade of East Africa with that of the Indian Ocean. In East Africa trading posts exported slaves, ivory, iron, rhinoceros horn, turtle shell, amber and leopard skins to India and beyond. Both of these networks had existed for thousands of years.

Africa contained a large variety of political groups (Shillington 1995). North African states were integrated into the Islamic empire. In Ethiopia, a Christian Kingdom was founded in the fourth century which maintained its independence until the late 1930s. In the Shona state of Great Zimbabwe ten-metre high stone enclosures surrounded the King's residence. Around the great lakes area of Central Africa, the Luba and Lunda empires concentrated on fishing and hunting. They purchased iron and salt from the north and copper from the south which was made into rings, bracelets and necklaces. In summary, the large continent contained a number of different political economies linked together through trade.

Americas

Although the existence of the Americas came as a surprise to Europeans, many areas were marked by advanced civilizations. Advanced civilization, in terms of intensive agricultural activity and large cities with complicated architecture, took place in two regions of the Americas. One region was the Incan empire in the Andes in Peru and Bolivia which stretched from Equador to Chile. The other was in Mesoamerica – Mexico and Guatemala. This was the home of the Maya who were starting to decline and the Aztecs who were in the process of creating a large empire.

The Spanish encountered a well developed empire when they began contact with the population of Mexico. The Aztecs ruled Mexico and were the successor to a series of civilizations which included the Olmec, Teotihuacan, and Toltecs. Although there were differences between these civilizations some continuities are noticeable (Davies, 1982). Similar to old world civilizations, the Americans demonstrated an ability to build and maintain cities, erect large monuments and support sophisticated forms of art. The Aztec capital, Tenochtitlan, dazzled the Spanish invaders because of its large population and elaborate beauty. Its population was over ten times that of leading Spanish cities of the same era. Unlike the Europeans and Asians, the Americans faced greater transportation difficulties. Lacking beasts of burden most goods were carried by foot. Water transport was also limited due to the presence of mountain ranges (Andes) or inland empires. This meant that more energy had to be expended for transportation than in other parts of the world.

Exchange of goods was primarily in the form of tribute rather than trade. Goods were traded, but the empires tended to accumulate things by demanding them as tribute from weaker states. Dominated cities provided goods for the elite of the empire. Under the Aztecs, political relations were characterized by the use of force. There was severe punishment for disobeying the king and the Aztecs engaged in the practice of human sacrifice to appease the gods. The Aztec civilization exploited conquered peoples to amass wealth. Thus, when the Spaniard Cortes began his conquest of Mexico he found willing local allies eager to throw off Aztec oppression.

Europe

The political economy of the area now known as Western Europe underwent significant changes during the thirteenth to fifteenth centuries which placed a series of European states in a much stronger position in relation to outside powers. The two most significant changes were: increased economic activity and integration across Europe, and the consolidation of European political authority into rival states. We'll examine the increased economic activity by considering new trading patterns and the role of money and finance. Under consolidation of rival states, we'll review both the emergence of nation-states and the consequences of changing forms of European warfare. The combination of these changes set the stage for European expansion.

New patterns of trade. The fourteenth and fifteenth centuries saw the Western European economy build bridges between its southern and northern centres. In the south a handful of small Italian cities (Venice, Amalfi, Pisa and Genoa) began to develop their commercial roles while in northern Europe economic activity developed in the low countries of present day Belgium and Holland and in the North and Baltic seas. Gradually, economic activity began to link together these two poles of European commerce.

The Italian cities amassed wealth by tapping into the lucrative trade in the Mediterranean. They gathered silk from China, ivory from Africa, and spices from India, Africa and South-east Asia. Spices were in high demand

Map 2.2   *European political economy 1400–1500*

amongst the European elites because they masked the taste of rotten food in an era before refrigeration. Key spices included ginger, saffron, mace, cinnamon, rhubarb, sugar, cloves, nutmeg, nuts. The favourite spice, however was pepper. Some years, a million pounds of pepper would pass through Venice. In return for such goods the Italians were required to either pay in gold and silver, or ship goods to other regions in the Mediterranean. These products included timber, grain, linen, cloth, salt and slaves from the European interior (Braudel, 1984, p. 107).

Although the Italians were developing their commercial and financial skills, the rise of the Italian cities depended upon war just as much as upon trading skills. It was the Crusades which launched the trading fortunes of Christendom and Venice. The men of northern Europe spent large sums of money in Italy as they paid for their passage to the Holy Land. Christian states in the Middle East opened an additional gateway to secure pepper, spices, silk and drugs. For the struggling Italian city states the main battle was not between Christian and Muslims, but with their fellow Italians. Venice and Genoa engaged in a long and difficult commercial rivalry across the Mediterranean.

Simultaneously, a commercial network was developing in northern Europe with the Belgian city of Bruges emerging as a second Venice. Bruges participated in a series of Flemish fairs by 1200, exploited its English contacts and welcomed Genovese ships in 1277. Its population grew from 35 000 in 1340 to 100 000 by 1500 (Braudel, 1984, p. 99). Its textile industry thrived and by 1309, Bruges had set up its own stock market, the Bourse. Outside of Belgium, northern economic activity was facilitated by the seaborne commercial triumph of the 'Hansa' (a group of merchants) which operated in the Baltic, North Sea, English Channel and Irish Sea. In 1356 the Hanseatic League, an alliance of trading ports, was created. The products of the north and east (wood, wax, fur, rye and wheat) were sent west for salt, cloth and wine. In contrast to the Italian luxury trade, most northern products were bulky items such as Polish grain, herring, salt, wine, wood, or Swedish iron. Raw wool was the most valued product, much of it finding its way into the manufacturing of textiles in Flemish industry or into Italy. There were some northern luxury products however. These included fine Flemish cloth, northern furs, amber for jewellery, beeswax for candles, and honey.

Although this economic activity increased wealth in many parts of Europe, there was an imbalance in trade. Money drained from the north of Europe to the south and eventually to the east of the Mediterranean and beyond. High priced and desirable goods came into Europe from China, India, the Middle East and Africa. In return the Europeans had some large bulk goods to offer, but this was often not sufficient. Luxury goods that could not be offset with trade had to be purchased with silver or gold. However, there was a limit as to how much silver or gold Europeans were able to mine. Eventually this would leave Europeans with three choices: they could find new sources of silver and gold; they could try and seize the goods they wanted by force; or they could develop more desirable goods for trade purposes. As we shall see in later chapters, all of these strategies were pursued with varying degrees of success. Their biggest breakthrough was seizing American silver to buy Asian products.

Money and Finance. Now that we have raised the issue of finance and money, it is appropriate to take a detour to consider the growth of financial innovation in Europe. New forms of money, credit and the control of money developed in this period and were crucial to the growing wealth and military power in Europe and beyond. For people today, living in the age of electronic banking and credit cards it is easy to take the presence of money and credit for granted. Yet, these institutions have not always existed as they do today. Moreover, the existence of an accepted form of money which is easily interchangeable and the instrument of credit is essential for anything more than a primitive economy.

Box 2.1 The utility of money

Consider a fanciful, but useful example from an era before money existed. In this context, money can be defined simply as an object that is commonly offered or received for the purchase or sale of goods or services. When there is no money, economic activity must take place on the basis of barter. One product is exchanged for another product rather than for money. For example, your neighbours might give you some firewood if you baked some bread for them. Now, imagine a gathering of four people seeking to exchange products in a society that does not have money. One is a farmer who has brought several bushels of wheat, another is a shepherd bringing some wool from his sheep, a third has brought a horse for exchange and the fourth is a blacksmith with some simple tools such as knives. One problem arises when people try to exchange products of unequal value. Suppose that the person with the horse would like to barter for a single knife. The trade may not take place because the tool maker can't make change for a horse. Another problem could arise if one person does not want the product of another. For example, the shepherd may want the farmer's wheat, but the farmer may not want the shepherd's wool. The shepherd might have to trade his wool for a knife and then trade the knife for the wheat. Alternatively, he may not be able to barter for a product that the farmer wants and the economic exchange is frustrated. The problem is only solved if all of these people value a single commodity. They could sell their own products for that commodity and use it to purchase other people's goods. That valued commodity is called money.

Although various forms of money have been in existence for approximately 4000 years (iron, tobacco, cattle, shells, beads, whiskey, stones), it is only in the last century or so that the value of money has been readily accepted by the public without intense scrutiny (Galbraith, 1996). There has often been doubt about how much value was stored in the commodities used as money. In the case of metal coins there has always been the risk that the issuing authority would debase the currency. Debasement occurred when the person minting the coins diluted the content with other metals and passed it off as a pure product. For example, rather than issuing a gold coin which contained a 100 per cent gold, a ruler might be tempted to claim that it was 100 per cent gold but put in 15 per cent copper. The hope was that the coin would still purchase the same amount of goods as the original gold coin, but cost less to make because there was a smaller gold content. Eventually, users of the coin would discover the change and would demand more of it to pay for the same amount of goods. The amount of goods the coin could buy would decrease over time as it became debased. A modern form of debasement is inflation where money loses its value as prices for goods rise.

Another difficulty in the age of multiple coins was the problem of exchanging money from various jurisdictions. How could one be sure of the value of a foreign coin? Even more serious was the possibility of counterfeit coins. When people from diverse jurisdictions met at trading centres they would often prefer to be paid in coins that had a better reputation for keeping their value than others. The result was that traders would take the valued ones and keep them for private use while the debased ones were passed on. This habit of hoarding good currency led to Thomas Gresham's famous observation in 1558 that bad money always drives out good. The problem of creating a stable international monetary system which facilitates the exchange of foreign currencies and trade continues to this day. We will explore some of its dimensions in Chapter 8.

A key advance in financial history was the development of banking and provision of credit. Today we tend to encounter three types of banks. Most people will be aware of deposit banks, also sometimes called commercial or clearing banks. They take deposits and give loans to individuals and corporations. Examples include Citibank, Barclays or Deutsche Bank. These banks project a serious image and rely upon their reputation for sound finance to attract and keep customers. Investment or merchant banks are a second type of bank. They make deals between rich individuals or companies to finance business investments and corporate takeovers. They tend to be more aggressive than deposit banks. Finally, countries also have a third type of bank – the central bank. This is the bank of the country. It is run by the government and is tasked with printing and distributing money and controlling the supply of money within a country.

The creation of credit greatly facilitated the growth of European economic activity. Credit notes allowed a person to buy now and pay later. This facilitated economic growth as some people and enterprises were able to conduct business that otherwise would not have taken place. A modern example of such activity is the house mortgage. Very few people would be able to buy a house if they were required to pay for it in cash. However, by taking a loan and paying it off over a long time period, many people can own houses. A similar mechanism was needed to finance long distance trade.

Another significant development in this area was the beginning of companies with partners or shareholders rather than a single owner. For example, in Italy there was an arrangement called the commenda. When launching a trading voyage one merchant would supply two-thirds of the

Box 2.2 Banks and financial instability

Although banks and credit allow people to undertake more economic activity, they also pose a financial risk. People, companies or states can take on too much debt and have difficulty repaying the loan. In the case of the banking industry there is always risk that customers panic and cause the collapse of a bank. Banks lend money out of their deposits via currency or notes of credit. However, there is a problem if all depositors come to the bank at once to ask for their money back. The bank will be unable to pay because the money has been distributed to other customers in the form of loans which cannot be instantly recalled. If there is a hint that a bank may be in financial trouble, depositors will rush to withdraw their money, thereby guaranteeing the bank's collapse. A bank must be able to retain the confidence of its depositors if it is to survive. In national banking systems the central bank often acts as a lender of last resort. The lender of last resort guarantees a proportion of depositors' money in the hope that this will prevent a run on the bank. There is no lender of last resort in the international system.

capital while another would supply one-third and manage the enterprise abroad. Both would share the profits. This allowed young adventurous merchants to trade with other merchants' capital. As trade was conducted over greater distances and time periods there was more demand for pooling investment in the form of the corporation. Large infrastructure projects such as canal building and, later, railroads contributed to the rise of shareholding companies and eventually the creation of stock exchanges (Kindleberger, 1993, pp. 190–8).

The development of accepted forms of money, credit and banks was a precondition for financing European economic, political and military expansion from the 1400s until today.

Rise of sovereign territorial states. A key development in Europe during the fifteenth to seventeenth centuries was the transition from feudal forms of organization to new political structures to the eventual emergence of sovereign territorial states. The push for political formations such as city states, leagues and sovereign states came from merchants in cities seeking greater economic freedom to capitalize on growing long distance trade (Spruyt, 1994). In Italy, the wealth of the luxury trade with the East allowed particular cities to develop resources great enough to guarantee their economic and military independence. In France, merchants allied with the king to undercut the power of the nobility and free up commerce.

This led to the creation of the centralized state. In Germany the king sided with the nobles, forcing cities such as Lubeck and Bremen to band together in the Hanseatic League.

Over time, the state form of organization proved to be more successful than the league or city state. The state differed from other forms of medieval political organization because it was both sovereign and territorial. Sovereignty meant that there was no higher form of political authority than the states. The king or the parliament was the ultimate legal authority, concentrating law making and use of violence in its hands. This contrasts with the feudal system where sovereignty was diffuse and authority was shared or contested amongst various actors such as the church, the empire, cities and lords. It also contrasted with leagues of cities where decision-making was difficult to achieve and more difficult to enforce.

The state was also territorial which means that its authority was confined to a particular geographic area. Unlike universalistic organizations such as the church which claimed authority over all Christians, states limited their jurisdiction to confined borders. The French king claimed authority over people living in France, but recognized the authority of the English king over people living in England. France and England might dispute the specific borders of each country or even try to conquer each other, but there was no question that they recognized each sovereign's right to govern his or her own people as they wished.

The emergence of the sovereign territorial state had several important consequences. First, it proved to be more efficient at mobilizing economic resources than other forms of organizations. A single power with a given territory was gradually able to create national markets for commerce. This involved the destruction of the numerous barriers to economic activity that had grown up in the feudal era. Prominent among these barriers were varying customary laws, dangerous travel conditions, tolls on roads or waterways, a multitude of currencies and diverse weights and measures. By standardizing coinage, weights and measures, developing common laws protecting private property and ensuring safe and easier transit, states were able to increase economic activity and resources into their own treasures.

A second important consequence was the competition created by a system of sovereign states. European states engaged in deadly economic and military competition with each other for hundreds of years. At times this weakened their position with the rest of the world, as in the aftermath of the First and Second World Wars. However, this state rivalry and the inability of any single European state to create a lasting empire over Europe (with the brief exception of Napoleon) injected a certain dynamic in European relations. Innovation in one European state would often be copied in others seeking to keep up in the competitive battle. City states and states turned to the external world to gain an advantage over their European rivals. For example, as Venice grew stronger, Genoa supported Portuguese and Spanish attempts to break Venetian power by sailing around Africa or across the Atlantic. Although Columbus sailed for Spain he was originally from Genoa and had approached the Portuguese for support.

As Charles Tilly (1999) points out, wars drove European state formation. Conflict between European political authorities and their need for capital to finance ever more destructive wars contributed to the rise of nation-states. Nation-states proved to be more efficient at raising revenue and mobilizing military forces than either the city states of Italy or leagues of cities such as the Baltic based Hanseatic League. The centralization of violence within a state's control was so significant that the sociologist Max Weber concentrated on this feature when he defined a state as 'a human community that (successfully) claims the monopoly of the legitimate use of physical force within a given territory' (Gerth and Mills, 1958, p. 78).

This competitive European state system often had negative implications for people outside of Europe. Where they were strong enough, Europeans used other parts of the world either as a battleground for their struggles or as venues to mobilize resources that they could use to further their rivalry. European strength depended upon their ability to reap the benefits from increased trade, financial innovation and military developments.

European expansion

In the middle of the 1400s Portugal, and then Spain, began a process of European exploration, expansion and conquest that would continue in various forms and guises for over five hundred years. In time, the Portuguese and Spanish were surpassed by the Dutch, French and English states. Europeans launched a three-pronged attack on the political, economic and cultural foundations of the societies they encountered (Abernethy, 2000). Where they had power over other groups, Europeans established new political structures ruling over local peoples in the form of colonies. They restructured local economies, transferring new forms of production oriented to satisfying European demands and tastes. They also transformed local cultures by introducing Christianity, notions of European racial superiority, and eventually western political ideologies such as nationalism, liberalism and Marxism. This section sketches out the reasons for this expansion and the varying patterns of interaction established between Europeans and Americans, Africans and Asians, from the Italian Renaissance until the industrial revolution.

The causes of European expansion have generated considerable academic and political debate. This chapter highlights several important factors: greed, fear, knowledge and biological good fortune. The greed was for valued products from outside Europe. Fear was created by the competition from other European powers and the Islamic forces of Egypt blocking trade routes to the Far East. Knowledge was contained in the crucial technologies enabling the development of the sea going cannon-carrying sailing ship. The biological good fortune of the Europeans lay in their possession of a stock of threatening diseases and productive domesticated animals.

The waves of European expansion are summarized in Table 2.1. It lists the major expansionist powers, their period of greatest activity, the regions they operated in, the types of local activity they conducted and the major economic sectors that they dominated. The first four countries are prominent in this chapter while the next countries are featured in following chapters.

Into the Americas

We begin our survey of European contact with the Americas because this is the area of the world where Europeans had an early and dramatic success in subjugating the peoples and environment of another continent. In the fifteenth century the sailors of Portugal and Spain sailed west into the Atlantic Ocean in an effort to secure the luxuries of the East. As will be discussed below, the Portuguese sailed down the African coast and eventually into Asia. The Spanish headed west across the Atlantic hoping to reach China. Rather than reaching China the Spanish encountered the Americas and quickly went about plundering its wealth. The resulting collision of European and American civilizations can be compared to an avalanche. A combination of European disease, livestock and force of arms swept American civilization before it, creating waves of destruction.

A key factor in explaining this swift collapse of American civilization is the role played by the introduction of European diseases. Diseases such as smallpox, measles and to a lesser extent malaria ravaged aboriginal populations causing up to a hundred million deaths in less than one hundred years. It has been estimated that the pre-Spanish conquest population of Central America and Mexico of 25 million declined to 1.5 million by 1650. Similarly, the population of Peru may have declined from 5 million to 300 000 in 1780s (Wolf, 1982, p. 134).

Prior to the Spanish arrival, Americans were a very healthy group of people. Their migration to the American continent via the frozen Bering Strait and subsequent isolation from other parts of the world meant that the humans living there developed free of the numerous deadly pathogens breeding on the Euro-Afro-Asian land mass. The peoples of the Old World

Table 2.1 *Summary of European expansionist activity*

European power	Most active years	Countries/regions	Local interaction	Economic activity
Portugal	Mid 1400s to late 1600s	Brazil, West and Southern Africa, coastal ports in India and China	Conquest, trade, coastal ports	Fish, spices, sugar, slaving, intra Asian trade
Spain	Late 1400s to late 1700s	North Africa, Americas, Philippines	Conquest	Silver and gold extraction
Holland	Early 1600s to late 1700s	Indonesia, North America	Trade, port seizure, conquest	Spices, intra Asian trade, slaving
Great Britain	Early 1700s to mid 1900s	North America and Caribbean, Africa, Middle East, South and South-east Asia, Australia, New Zealand	Conquest, settler colonies, trade	Fish, furs, raw materials, sugar, cotton, slaving, drugs
France	1600s to mid 1900s	North America, Caribbean, North and West Africa, India, South-east Asia, Oceania	Conquest, trade	Spices, furs, sugar, slaving
Belgium	Late 1800s to 1960s	Congo	Conquest	Rubber extraction
Germany	Late 1800s to 1940s	South-west and East Africa	Conquest	Minor economic interests
Italy	Late 1800s to 1940s	Libya, Ethiopia	Conquest	Minor economic interests
United States	Early 1800s to ?	North and Central America, Caribbean, Hawaii, Philippines, Vietnam, Middle East	Conquest, occupation, trade	Natural resources

had created crowded civilizations, engaged in extensive agriculture and domesticated large numbers of animals. Each of these steps resulted in the creation and spread of new forms of disease. For example, living in dirty cities close to human garbage bred cholera and dysentery; close human contact with cows, sheep and chickens led to the spread of animal diseases into the human population in the form of tuberculosis and smallpox (Nikiforuk, 1996).

When the Spanish arrived in the Americas they unknowingly unleashed their pathogens upon a vulnerable American population. Smallpox was the most devastating disease, exterminating villages and tribes. The spread of disease was facilitated by bringing large numbers of native inhabitants together as slaves for the mines. Living in unhealthy conditions they were made even more vulnerable to illness. Smallpox spread across the continent, preceding the arrival of Europeans into the American interior. The continent seemed empty to many European settlers as they spread across the Americas partly because so much of the population had already been killed.

Europe's ecological imperialism was not confined to disease. Another element in the success of the European invaders was the livestock they introduced into the Americas. Horses provided power for agricultural development and military advantage over the native population; pigs, rabbits and cattle provided for food and changed the environment to pasture land; bees provided settlers with honey. All of these animals were strangers to the Americas and provided their owners with a significant advantage in surviving in a new environment. Europeans came to the Americas not only as individual warriors, settlers or traders, but as 'part of a grunting, lowing, neighing, crowing, chirping, snarling, buzzing, self-replicating avalanche' (Crosby, 1996, p. 194). That avalanche buried the majority of the native population and set the groundwork for the creation of a 'new' world.

The Euro-American political economy. European political–economic strategy in what they termed the 'new world' was both mercantilist and imperialist. Europe's relations with the Americas were imperialist in that they subjugated local economies to the power of the European states and reoriented economic activity to serve only the interests of those states. Leading European states used the Americas as the basis of their empires. Many local economies and polities were destroyed and refashioned to serve the Spanish, Portuguese, French and English crowns. With regards to relations between European states, commercial activity was mercantilist. Economic activity was designed to increase the wealth and power of particular states and economic barriers were created to keep out contact with other states. For example, efforts were made to prevent Spanish and

Portuguese or English and French colonies from trading with each other. Economic activity was viewed as a zero-sum game. Each country tried to be as self-sufficient as possible and to deny their rivals the opportunity of creating wealth. The British and French crowns licensed private individuals to raid the fleets of opposing nations. The Spanish viewed such activity as piracy.

The Spanish initially came to the Americas seeking a route to China and India. In their first encounters with native Americans, it was gold which caught their eye. Although gold continued to be a source of fascination for the Spanish and other Europeans, it was silver which accounted for the majority of the wealth confiscated from the Americas. Spanish silver did not flow only to Europe: large quantities were shipped across the Pacific Ocean. Silver was shipped from Acapulco in Mexico to the Spanish controlled Philippines where it was exchanged for Chinese goods, especially textiles (silk). In 1797 more Spanish bullion went from Acapulco to Manila than was transferred across the Atlantic Ocean. Between 1570–1780 it is estimated that four to five thousand tons of silver went to the Far East to pay for goods. (Wolf, 1982, p. 154). The Americas had been forcibly entered into the world economy and Europeans were consuming the benefits of the integration.

The effort to mine silver led to a transformation of the American economy. The Spanish needed labour for their mines, and supplies to maintain the mining industry. Labour was provided by native American and African slaves. Silver processing was exceedingly dangerous as it involved the use of mercury and resulted in mercury poising. The mines were at high altitude, and work was conducted under physically draining conditions. Desperate for relief, the native working population increasingly turned to a substance previously confined to Inca religious ceremonies – coca leaf. Chewing the leaves dulled the workers' pain and the Spanish were happy to democratize coca consumption to keep the silver flowing (Pomeranz and Topik, 1999, pp. 156–8).

Mining also shifted the local economy away from pre-Hispanic agriculture to the silver veins of the Sierra Madre and Volibian mountains. It created a demand for food and supplies. Drawing upon their feudal heritage the Spanish introduced a system of large land holdings called 'haciendas'. These were landed estates worked by labourers settled upon them and directly dependent upon the estate owners. The highly unequal pattern of land ownership and resulting political influence of a land holding elite frustrated economic and political transition for hundreds of years.

After the Spanish conquest, the surviving native American communities played a vital, but unequal role in what is now Latin America. Spain and Portugal focused upon resource extraction and never engaged in large-scale emigration to the Americas. In contrast to what became the United States and Canada, the Spanish relied upon local labour and integrated native Americans into their society in a hierarchical manner. The former native nobility often supervised local communities but were deprived of power. Locals were converted to Christianity, although Christianity itself was forced to accommodate local forms of worship and myths. In general, native Americans were integrated into the Spanish system as reservoirs of labour, and sources of cheap agricultural and craft products. They were often subject to Spanish tribute or taxes and were forced to hire themselves out to pay their forced debts.

Spanish settlement in the Americas, similar to European settlement in other territories, created a racial division of labour that would last for centuries. In the Spanish case, relatively few Europeans emigrated to the Americas. Europeans and their descendants dominated the elite levels of society with the children of Spanish / native American unions taking a secondary role. At the bottom of the society were native Americans, excluded from the political system, and providing labour. In North America the pattern was different as native Americans were excluded from society and Africans were imported for the intensive labour role.

Spain was not the only European state to carry out economic activity in the Americas before the industrial revolution. Two years after the Spanish contact with the Americas Portugal and Spain signed a Treaty which granted Spain all the lands 370 leagues west of the Cape Verde Islands and Portugal all lands east. Portugal took Brazil and the South Atlantic which lead to Asia while Spain took the rest of the Americas. In Brazil, the Portuguese concentrated on the production of sugar on large plantations as an export crop. This activity spread to the Caribbean where it was copied by the Dutch, French and English who became rivals. This will be dealt with in greater detail in the following section on relations with Africa.

In North America, a number of states were engaged in economic activity. The Portuguese were attracted by the fish off the banks of Newfoundland and New England. They were followed by French and English fleets. As Portuguese and Spanish maritime power decreased around 1600 the French, British and Dutch were able to establish permanent settlements along the eastern seaboard and pursue a four legged form of gold – the beaver. The demand for beaver to make expensive and fashionable hats for the European upper classes drove Europeans further into the American continent. As a result of the beaver trade, native American groups within the interior became involved in hunting the increasingly scarce mammal. Over time, native Americans moved from being partners in the fur trade to subordinate producers (Wolf, 1982, p. 194). As Canada and the United States became settler colonies for an overflow of Europeans in the eighteenth and nineteenth centuries an even worse fate awaited aboriginal inhabitants. Some groups were eliminated through genocidal warfare, others were made economically dependent and herded onto reserves.

Along Africa: the slave trade and the triangular trade

In contrast to the Americas, Europeans did not enjoy a pathogen advantage in their relations with Africa. In fact, the presence of malaria on the African continent dictated a very different relationship. Europeans were confined to the coasts of sub-Saharan Africa, depending upon Africans being willing to engage in trade. Attempts to proceed further into the continent (with the exception of South Africa which had a more moderate climate) met with disease and death for most Europeans. Large scale colonization of Africa would not occur for another four hundred years until the development of improved rifle technology and the anti-malarial drug quinine.

Europe's maritime engagement with sub-Saharan Africa began with the Portuguese. The initial desire to sail along Africa came from the hope that they could secure gold without having to rely on the trans-Saharan trade which brought the commodity up from Senegal. In addition to gold, the Portuguese sought pepper, ivory, dyewoods, beeswax, leather and timber as well as some slaves from Africa. In return they exchanged textiles, wheat, brass utensils and glass beads. In later years they brought Brazilian tobacco. Slaves purchased from African traders were originally sent back to Portugal. Since slavery marked the prime economic interaction between Europe and Africa in the period under discussion it is useful to focus upon this activity.

Slavery was not a new institution either to the Europeans or the Africans. In African tradition, slaves were usually acquired as a result of unpaid debts, the judicial process or war. They were not used as the basis for economic activity. In Europe, the Roman and Greek Empires rested upon slave power. During the Crusades, Europeans and Muslims enslaved each other. In the thirteenth century Venetians and Genovese imported Turkish and Mongol slaves. Slaves were used to grow sugar cane in Cyprus and Sicily and to work in mines. In the fourteenth century Europe imported Slavs and Greeks. In Scotland miners and saltpan workers were still enslaved in the seventeenth and eighteenth centuries.

The beginning of the slave trade was thus not unusual for either of the parties. The transatlantic slave trade took the form of a joint European – African operation. Europeans financed, organized and drew the primary benefits from the trade. The capture, delivery, control and maintenance before the voyage was primarily an African affair. Europeans took over for ocean transport and beyond. Although some Europeans seized Africans directly as slaves, they usually exchanged metal, firearms, textiles, rum and tobacco for their human cargo.

As Europeans began to mine for silver and gold and introduce new crops into the Americas, the nature and size of the slave trade changed dramatically. Slaves were required for mining silver and gold. Portugal introduced sugar from the Mediterranean into Brazil and it later spread to the Caribbean. American tobacco was exported to Europe while cotton plantations were introduced from Asia. All of these products required a large workforce for their harvesting.

A number of forms of labour were harnessed to this activity. To state the obvious, this was back-breaking work that few people would freely choose. The Europeans first enslaved the local native American population. Their numbers were limited however. Many died from disease while others escaped to form rebel communities. The Europeans also tried indentured labour from their home countries. Impoverished Europeans would agree to work for a number of years as labourers in return for their eventual freedom and an opportunity for a new life in the Americas. However, many European labourers died before their term was up and it became an increasingly unattractive option.

The solution for plantation and mine owners was to move labour in large numbers from Africa to the Americas in the form of slaves. Many Africans would die in the plantations, but they were replaced by more slaves. Why did Africa become the source of slave labour? As mentioned earlier, there was already trade in slaves preceding the introduction of plantation economies into the Americas which provided a precedent. Furthermore, Africans transported across the Atlantic were at a greater disadvantage than native American slaves. It was virtually impossible for Africans to return home while many Americans were able to flee to neighbouring areas. Those Africans that survived transport to the Americas faced years of hard labour before dying in poverty. Their descendants could expect much the same fate. When slavery was finally abolished Africans would remain on the bottom of the socio-economic scale stigmatized by poverty and racism for generations.

Similar to many historical events, there is some dispute about the number of Africans that were forcefully moved from their homes to slavery in the Americas. It is estimated that between 1450 and 1900 somewhere between 9 and 13 million Africans were transported to the Americas (Iliffe, 1995, p. 131). The trade began relatively slowly with some 275 000 – 370 000 being sent from 1451–1600. Almost 2 million were sent in the following hundred years and about 6 million between 1700 and 1800 as the plantation economies grew. An additional 3 million were transported in the nineteenth century. Mortality rates from the brutal methods of transportation were high – as much as 14 per cent on Dutch ships. Exact figures are difficult to establish, but one estimate is that of 100 Angolans taken as slaves in the eighteenth century, 10 died during initial capture, 22 died on the way to the coast, 10 in coastal holding areas, 6 died on the voyage and 3 in the Americas before starting work (Iliffe, 1995, p. 135).

This horrendous economic activity was one side in what was called the triangular trade. Europeans manufactured various goods such as textiles, guns, beads and semi-precious stones and exchanged them for slaves in Africa. The slaves were transported across the Atlantic where they worked on plantations and in mines. The products of their labour – silver, cotton, sugar – were then exported at great profit to Europe and beyond. English cities such as Bristol and Liverpool became major slaving ports until Britain ended its participation in 1807. Large fortunes were created on the backs of slave labour.

Map 2.3   *Transatlantic triangular trade*

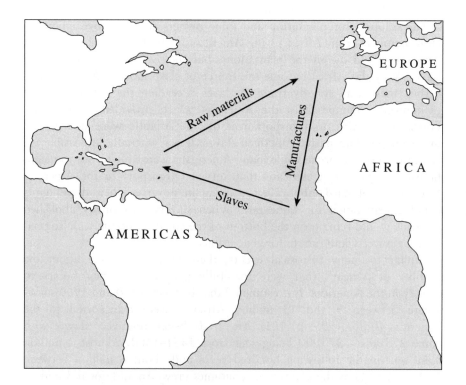

The triangular trade allowed Europeans to export more products to Africa and use cheap labour to produce commodities in the Americas. The growing slave plantations and American colonies also served as a market for European manufactured goods. In a controversial book Eric Williams (1944) suggested that the profits from the slave trade fuelled the industrial revolution in Britain. While Williams may have underestimated the importance of the European market to the industrial revolution, the triangular trade certainly did contribute to the European economic take-off in the 1800s (Wolf, 1982, pp. 199–200).

On a personal level and in terms of specific communities the consequences of the transatlantic slave trade were horrific. Individuals suffered immense deprivation, families and communities were shattered and millions died. The effects upon African civilization were more mixed. In West Africa groups along the coast were able to use trade with the Europeans to strengthen their hands against interior rivals. For example, the Asante were able to build an empire in the eighteenth and nineteenth centuries by using Dutch weapons to enlarge their territory and acquire more slaves. In the Niger Delta it transformed society into slave accumulating organizations and subjugated people further inland. In the Congo it had the opposite effect, devastating the polity and creating rival groups engaged in slavery and war. In general, Africa suffered from the slave trade as its political economy was rearranged and millions were transported to another continent. However, it continued to resist European encroachment and would do so for many years.

On the peripheries of Asia

Voyages to America and Africa grew out of the European search for new trade routes to Asia. In the 1490s Vasco da Gama sailed around Africa and reached India, with the assistance of an Arab navigator. A new route to the wealth of Asia was opened. However, the pattern of interaction with Asian political economies was far different from European experience in the Americas and Africa. The Asian empires were often larger, more densely populated and more productive than the Europeans. For several hundred years Europeans were confined to seaports and trading posts. In some cases they faced military defeat and in others they were frustrated by the lack of goods of sufficient quality to trade with Asians.

The Portuguese were the first Europeans to sail around Africa. They immediately came into contact with an expanding Muslim trade network. The Portuguese could not hope to compete with Asians in a head-to-head struggle so they attempted to control strategic pressure points, such as Goa, Hormuz and Malacca. Their attempt to expand into China was defeated in battle in 1521. The pattern of seizing coastal ports to gain a foothold in lucrative Asian trade was repeated by the Dutch and the British.

The Europeans were confined to working the sea lanes between trading outposts in Asia. The Portuguese, then Dutch and the English moved cargo between Asian ports and back to Europe, amassing wealth for their own countries, but making limited progress into the Asian heartland. Although mercantilist economic theory posited a world where European states would trade with their colonies on a North – South basis, the economic realities dictated a much more profitable trade for Europeans in facilitating economic relations between different parts of the non-European world.

The success that the Europeans did enjoy was due to the gun-bearing sailing ship. Around 1400 AD the Europeans combined the square rig of their designs with the lateen rig of the Arabs. They then equipped this with cannon. After 1500, cannons were installed below decks and the galleon made its appearance – half warship, half merchantship. It overwhelmed Arab and Asian naval opposition in direct confrontations, but could do little to subdue large land empires or stop the local trade conducted by smaller vessels.

Early Portuguese and Dutch economic activity in South-east Asia relied heavily upon a relatively egalitarian gendered division of labour between European traders and native business women (Pomeranz and Topik, 1999, pp. 28–31). The European merchants encountered existing commercial networks that were often run by local women. Local women had well established business connections and a familiarity with the economy that proved invaluable to the Europeans. The business opportunities provided by these women, combined with the extreme difficulty of attracting European women to the colonies, led to widespread intermarriage between Portuguese / Dutch merchants and Asian businesswomen. In many cases local women were able to continue amassing wealth as their sickly European partners succumbed to tropical diseases. This state of affairs lasted for about two hundred years until the nineteenth century. As technical inventions took hold such as the Suez Canal, telegraph, and vaccinations it became more possible to pursue a 'European' lifestyle in Asia. This resulted in European men bringing European wives to the colonies, causing the marginalization of native women and increasing differentiation between European and non-Europeans. As Europeans became more entrenched and powerful, their need and tolerance for local cultures decreased.

The British followed the Portuguese and Dutch into the Indian Ocean and eventually gained direct control over a large Asian land-based power – India. Colonization of India proved to be a financial windfall for the British which then enabled them to build a much larger empire. As British school children were taught, the Empire spanned the globe so that the sun never set over it.

The British began very modestly in India. The British East India Company initially accepted the sovereignty of local Indian rulers. However, in 1757 the company intervened in a local power struggle in Bengal and ended up taking power in the territory. At about this time the Muslim-dominated Mughal Empire entered a stage of crisis. This allowed the English to defeat local Indian forces in battle at Hyderabad in 1789 and Mysore in 1799.

British participation in Indian trade created large private fortunes which were brought back to England. With each new success the Indian economy was reorganized to pay for English warfare and conquest. Indian agriculture was switched to export crops that would benefit Britain such as cotton, sugar, tobacco, jute, indigo and opium. The English also imposed new patterns of tax and introduced English law. English machine-produced cottons were introduced after 1814, destroying the high quality Indian textile industry. A new army was created with English officers and Indian troops. The British forces succeeded in suppressing an 1875 revolt against the Company's role in India, but the British government was so concerned that it relieved the East India Company from ruling India and took direct control.

Although the British had succeeded in subjugating India, it was unable to make much progress with China. The Chinese were not very interested in trade with red-haired barbarians. The English were confined to the trading port of Canton and sought silks, porcelain and medicines. In exchange for these products the English had to pay in silver, since they possessed no goods that the Chinese wanted. The situation became more serious as the English developed a taste for tea. Tea drinking had begun in England in 1664, introduced by the Dutch. By 1783 consumption was 6 million pounds a year, later rising to 15 million pounds (Wolf, 1982, p. 255). All of this consumption had to be paid for in silver, which originated in the Americas. China became the tomb of American silver.

England desperately needed to find a commodity that they could exchange in return for desired Chinese goods. They could not export silver to China indefinitely. British harvesting of sandalwood devastated the forests of Fiji between 1804–1810 and Hawaii 1811–1830s, but this was not sufficient to pay for Chinese products (Pomeranz and Topik, 1999, p. 161). The answer to British problems was to export drugs grown in India. The drug of choice was opium which is highly addictive and is known in other forms as heroin. In 1773 the East India Company established a monopoly over the opium trade and smuggled it into China. US traders also became involved, shipping opium from Turkey to New York to China. The Chinese declared the trade illegal, but this did not stop British and

American entrepreneurs. By 1828 the British had been able to reverse the flow of silver so that more left China than entered it. Not content with smuggling drugs, British and US merchants pushed for the right to sell them openly to China. The Chinese market was finally opened as a result of British victory over the Chinese in the Opium Wars (1839–1842). British gunboats were the crucial ingredient in persuading the Chinese to open their border to drugs. The European drug strategy was a success for their trade balances, but a disaster for China. It shifted the economic balance in favour of Europe and created millions of opium addicts in China. The present-day export of cocaine from Colombia to the United States which has sparked a 'drug war' in the United States and Latin America pales in comparison to this historical episode.

It was in this era that we see the beginnings of the modern corporation in the form of the Dutch and British East India Companies (Pomeranz and Topik, 1999, pp. 163–6). These companies were different from other forms of business such as family firms or temporary companies in several ways. First, they were impersonal in the sense that partners in the company did not have to all know each other. Secondly, the owners of the companies did not directly control the companies. Directors were elected to run the companies and owners or investors either accepted their decisions or sold their share of ownership. Thirdly, the companies were designed to be permanent. They would survive change in owners and were founded for an unlimited time period. Earlier ventures were usually created for a limited time such as the completion of a single voyage or for a series of voyages. The expectation of the East Indian Companies was that they would engage in commercial activity for as long as it was financially viable.

This new type of economic organization was needed because the commercial activity undertaken demanded large amounts of capital over a long time-period. Return voyages from Europe to Asia could take up to three years. Capital invested would often need to be spread over several voyages due to the possibility that any single trip would not be successful. Another significant reason for huge capital expenditures is that much of the commercial activity was combined with expensive military action. In this mercantilist era, European intercontinental trade was typified by the seizure of territory, building of forts and provision of armed vessels. This greatly increased the cost of commercial activity, but was essential if merchants were to ward off their European rivals and cling to their footholds on the Asian mainland.

Conclusion

The early era of forging a world economy from the 1400s until the mid-1800s was not a savoury process. Coercion was often more in evidence than cooperation. European expansion decimated civilizations with disease, enslaved millions of Americans and Africans, worked millions of others to death, reoriented local economies to serve European elite interests and trafficked in drugs to undermine other civilizations. The period saw great transformation in key frameworks of political economy as Europeans increasingly collided with other centres of wealth and power. In this section we will review these changes using the frameworks that serve as separate chapters in the second part of the book (trade, production, labour, finance, development, environment, and governance).

It has been said that *trade* is an activity as old as human civilization and this chapter has outlined various trading systems in existence between 1400–1800. Apart from forms of local exchange, international trade (that is, cross-border trade) is a significant feature of this period. We showed the importance of long-distance trade and intercontinental trade routes to a number of societies. No simple or single imperative accounts for this trade although trade was mainly stimulated by the desire to attain goods not produced domestically. This differs from the current international trading system where developed states import goods that are also produced locally. The trade discussed above varied from the exotic to the tragic; from the sale of spices and metals to the sale of human beings. This chapter shows both some of the continuities in the history of international trade and some of the contingent features of trade. Among the continuities are the search for exotica (today this is apt to be found through tourism or the purchase of a bird or reptile). On the other hand, the chapter alerts us to the fact that goods considered moral in one epoch may not be perceived as such at another period in history. For example, while slavery and the trade in slaves still exists it is universally condemned as a practice.

The push and pull of markets played a key role in driving European expansion. European lust for luxury goods from the East motivated states and merchants to find new sources of supply. It was European inability to produce particular products such as silk and spices which drove them out of their regional shell. When they could not take what they wanted by force (which was most of the time), Europeans engaged in trade. However, in several locations trade which originally was conducted upon the basis of relative equality eventually had disastrous effects upon local economies. The fur trade in North America eventually undermined the independence of native Americans while the slave trade devastated large parts of Africa as it evolved from a minor activity to a large-scale operation.

During the four centuries covered in this chapter *production* remained primarily agricultural and was largely designed for local use. Although there were not great advances in the technology of production, there were significant changes in who produced what and for whom. European conquest of the Americas radically altered the production structure of two continents. Native economies were either destroyed or reorganized to supply raw materials (metals, crops, furs) to European states. In the southern US, Latin America and the Caribbean the patterns of production relations consisted of a small wealthy land-holding class and a large disempowered and sometimes enslaved labouring class working in agriculture or mining. In the northern US and parts of Canada settler colonies were set up with a more equal distribution of land and an industrial base was slowly nurtured. In Africa, the capture and export of slaves grew from a relatively minor practice to a large economic activity which destabilized some societies and brought resources to others.

The reorientation of production in various continents led to the emergence of a division of *labour* which increasingly grouped the export sector of countries into particular tasks. Europeans took on the roles of producing manufactured goods, shipping goods between continents and running plantations and mines on several continents. Africans were incorporated into the division of labour as providers of slaves. Native Americans were either exterminated, marginalized on reserves or poor land, or integrated into subordinated labour relations. In Asia, large land empires ensured more balanced relations with the European adventurers and traders. Indian, south-east Asian and Chinese producers continued to make highly desirable products and insisted upon fair compensation for their goods.

Long distance trade led to *financial* innovation and the appearance of the predecessor to the transnational corporation. An important element in European expansion was the development of financial instruments to fund exploration, trade and war. The development of banking and provision of credit was a key advance. Money had to be lent over long periods of time so that risky but highly profitable trade could take place. Economic activity over great distances and long time-periods also encouraged the development of impersonal and long-standing corporations. Giant economic actors such as the British and Dutch East India companies were required to engage in intercontinental trade. They were also needed because economic activity often required military security from foreign rivals and local populations. As a result, these companies employed military forces to protect and extend their interests.

In this era we can see the origins of some of today's *development* dilemmas. The economies of what is now Latin America and the Caribbean were forcefully integrated into the world economy in the role of natural resource producers. European and Asian crops (e.g., cotton, sugar cane) were introduced and the economy was organized to benefit Western capitalists. This resulted in two developments: certain areas were locked into producing products whose value would decrease over time, and wealth was transferred from the producers of the products (often native Americans or slaves) to the owners of the mines and plantations (European landholders, capitalists and settlers). In Africa the slave trade allowed some tribes to increase their power relative to African rivals, but it destroyed other societies and weakened the continent as a whole. In Asia, European impact was far less significant until the nineteenth century. Indeed, it is likely that the transfer of European silver (taken from the Americas) to pay for goods stimulated Asian industry.

During this period the natural *environment* in the Americas went through massive change. European introduction of crops and animals shifted the existing balance between people and nature to a new dynamic which saw the increasing subjugation of nature to human economic activity.

The growth of the international economy cannot be separated from developments in domestic and international *governance* arrangements, including the use of organized violence. In terms of domestic arrangements, the most significant political development was the rise of the modern state in Europe. As the reigning monarchs of Europe fought each other they needed to finance their wars. The discovery that the centralized state was more efficient at raising revenue for the purposes of conducting military campaigns contributed to the demise of city states and the various leagues of states. Competition spurred innovation within states and resulted in other areas feeling the impact of European struggles.

The emergence of a new form of political organization was intimately linked with developments in the market. First, the territorial state was effective in the removal of barriers to economic activity across space and place. A multiplicity of political authorities had resulted in an often insurmountable range of barriers to commerce, for example, customs duties, and tolls. The creation of a single political authority (similar to the creation of a common market or free-trade area today) breaks down barriers within the same territorial space. Secondly, the emergence of the state not only abolished various barriers to commerce but also encouraged trade through legislation. The development of law, common currencies, and various methods of standardization, for example, weights and measures, facilitated economic exchange and the development of the market.

Although organized state violence played an important role in European expansion, it was only one of several factors. Some historians (Parker, 1996) have argued that European military superiority was the key variable in explaining the success of European endeavours, but this is unlikely. Spanish military technology was not much more advanced than that of the native Americans. In Asia, the Indian and Chinese military were for centuries more than capable of resisting European arms. It is true that Western naval technology proved crucial for securing coastal ports, but Western land forces would have to await the invention of better rifle, artillery and machine gun technology in the nineteenth century before gaining a decisive edge over non-Europeans.

The relative equality in arms suggests that European military success was often dependent upon the cooperation of local collaborators (Thompson, 2000, p. 79). Americans, Africans and Asians were in competition with other Americans, Africans and Asians just as European states were struggling against each other. Alliances between locals and Europeans against other locals or other Europeans were common. For example, Cortes relied upon local tribes to help defeat the Aztecs. Europeans needed Africans to supply slaves to their coastal stations. The British allied with Indians who opposed Mughal rule to gradually take over the whole country. European success depended upon local cooperation.

The pattern of European interaction and the rules that governed interaction across civilizations varied greatly according to the ability of other groups to resist European dominance. In the case of the Americas, Europeans imposed their own form of political economy as they overwhelmed local groups. In Africa, Europeans were prevented from moving in much beyond the coastal regions, but their thirst for slaves reshaped African societies. In most parts of Asia, Europeans were confined to coastal trading cities by larger and more powerful Asian empires. Some European advance was made in India after two hundred years, but China resisted European power well into the nineteenth century. European expansionism also resulted in widely diverse patterns of cultural transformation in the societies they encountered (Curtain, 2000). In some cases, such as South Africa, new racial hierarchies were introduced through migration while in others cases, such as Mexico, European and native cultures fused into a new entity.

Interactions brought about by European expansion had great implications for Europe, as well as those it encountered. 'Discovery' of the Americas caused Europeans to re-evaluate their place in the cosmos and reconsider their relationship to other peoples. Did these other peoples have similar rights to Europeans? Were they equal in the eyes of God? While European actions often seemed to answer these questions in the negative, a more egalitarian view of non-Europeans would eventually emerge in the late twentieth century. In commercial terms new products flooded into Europe changing social and political organizations. One example was the introduction of the potato which allowed millions of poorer Europeans to have a richer diet. More significantly, the flow of American silver allowed Europe to engage in greater trade with Asian centres.

Finally, the role of *ideas* played an important part in the period between 1400–1800 as a world economy was in the process of formation. At the simplest level the knowledge structure provides the technology and know-how of societies and civilizations. We have shown how different societies, empires and civilizations had developed various levels of technological sophistication at the beginning of this period and how the technological bases of these societies changed over the course of these four centuries. There is no need to recap this history here except to reinforce the point that during this period Europe rose from a subordinate position to a potentially dominant one.

The knowledge structure also provides what can be termed worldviews, that is that meta-structure determining the reception of knowledge and structuring perception of human–environment relations. Once again this period provides an example of the wide diversity in human thought and behaviour. It also shows how some world-views proved more adaptable to changing environmental conditions while others failed to cope with advances in technology.

The third aspect relating to the role of knowledge pertains to ideas about the relationship between humans. The organization of society, of economics and politics rests on ideas about social relations. From the Incas, to the Chinese, to Africans, to Europeans, different systems were developed during this period. And yet at the end of this period we stand on the verge of the global dominance of just one of these systems of thought. The analysis above has attempted to provide some answers to the rise of Europe while acknowledging that no definitive answer can be given. It has shown that in all three areas of the knowledge structure identified – technical, rational and social, that the world in 1400 exhibited greater diversity than our world at the beginning of the twentieth century. It also has demonstrated that working on very different principles peoples were able to develop functioning polities and economies. By the end of this period the ideational structure of one group of people was becoming dominant. This chapter has argued that this is not because these ideas were, in themselves, superior but that in combination with other themes examined they contributed to the transformation of Europe in a manner that resulted in European dominance and expansion as other societies experienced conquest, decay and decline.

Entering the nineteenth century, Europe had increased its wealth and power relative to other parts of the world. It had wrought destruction upon the Americas, weakened Africa, but was held at a distance in much of Asia. It would await the industrial revolution before European expansion could progress further. We begin with this development in the following chapter.

Chapter 3

The Industrial Revolution, Pax Britannica and Imperialism

In the long and painful process of forging a global political economy there are three events that stand out above all others. The first is the European conquest of the Americas and the integration of that hemisphere into a worldwide economy. The second is the industrial revolution which transformed economic, political and social relations in Europe and echoed around the world. The third is the information revolution whose effects are only now starting to become more clear. This chapter concentrates on the second key event, the industrial revolution and its consequences. We begin by recounting the origins of the industrial revolution in Britain and the factors which facilitated it. The second section focuses upon the international system that was created as a result of the advantages the revolution gave to Great Britain and other Western powers (Pax Britannica). The third section examines one of the consequences of the increased power flowing from the industrial revolution – the era of renewed imperialism.

There are several points we can take from this historical overview of the nineteenth century. First, both wealth and power flowed to the elites of states which were able to harness innovation in production technologies. The industrial revolution increased British power and wealth to such an extent that some scholars describe the mid-1800s as a period of British hegemony or Pax Britannica. The German and US lead in the second industrial revolution at the end of the nineteenth century propelled them into prominent roles in the early twentieth century. Technological innovation and the ability to adapt to new methods of production are important.

Secondly, the liberal market of the nineteenth century was created at some human cost. Within Britain people were herded into cities and factories. Vulnerable women and children were the initial factory labour forces until a 'free' labour market eventually dragged in male workers. In international terms, the wealth generated by the British textile industry relied upon US slave labour to produce the input of raw cotton. Progress had its costs and they were distributed very unevenly.

Thirdly, although the benefits of free trade were loudly proclaimed, the practice was much more limited. Bolstered by the productivity increases of the industrial revolution, Britain led the way in pursuing free trade unilaterally. Some countries followed the example in order to secure key technologies. However, once other countries felt themselves in direct competition with Britain, they often erected protectionist barriers. Britain was eventually surpassed in the second industrial revolution by two highly protectionist countries – the United States and Germany.

A fourth point is that the international order required particular domestic arrangements to function smoothly. Two of the important mechanisms of the nineteenth century system relied upon the exclusion of public opinion from policy-making. The gold standard required automatic social and economic adjustment to trade flows. The balance of power necessitated strategic decisions based upon calculation of interest to the exclusion of ideology or affinity. These practices were possible because the mass of the people were excluded from political participation. However, as democratization continued in the nineteenth century and a rising tide of nationalism spread across all European states, it was much more difficult to control policy options.

A final point is that the developments in European industrial innovation shifted the balance of power between Europeans and non-Europeans, sparking a renewed bout of expansionism and competition. Large parts of Africa and Asia which had previously resisted European expansion succumbed to the force of European arms and industrial might. Once again, economies were reoriented to serve foreign interests, often with disastrous consequences for local populations.

The industrial revolution

What was the industrial revolution?

To simplify a complex phenomenon, the industrial revolution involved the application of machinery to production, the introduction of new energy sources to power the machines, and the reorganization of the labour force into factories. The first industrial revolution began in Britain and lasted about one hundred years from the mid-1700s until the 1870s. Changes began in the textile industry with cotton and were followed by the steel industry, especially in the form of railroads. In the 1870s a second industrial revolution focusing upon new products and technologies swept the Western world, led by Germany and the United States. Elsewhere, the results were much more varied. A few states such as Japan, Russia and Canada successfully mimicked the British example while many other states are still attempting to industrialize their societies at the beginning of the twenty-first century.

Let us begin by looking at the British textile industry in the 1700s. At this time the British were engaged in serious competition with Dutch and

Indian textile producers. While they were able to combat Dutch production because of cheaper products and labour costs, they were unable to compete with Indian products. Indian textiles were both cheaper and of a better quality than those produced in England. The solution to this competitive problem was the protection of the domestic market by forbidding the British East India Company to import Indian textiles into the UK.

The British wanted to improve their productivity, but ran into a serious technical barrier. The key problem was the lack of synchronization between spinning and weaving. It took a long time to use a spinning wheel to spin the cotton into thread and a relatively short time to weave it into a garment. The pace of weaving was dependent upon the speed at which cotton could be spun. A series of inventions in the late 1700s remedied these problems. The invention of the spinning jenny allowed a spinner to spin several threads of yarn simultaneously. The waterframe drew out fibres on rollers and wound them on upright spindles. The 'mule' combined the features of the waterframe and jenny. By 1790 steam power was applied to the mule, massively increasing the amount of cotton that could be processed in a specific time.

The application of steam-powered machinery to the production of textiles increased productivity and led to the creation of the factory system. The dramatic improvement can be illustrated if we compare how British production increased in relationship to their Indian rivals. An Indian hand spinner in the 1700s took about 50 000 hours to process 100 pounds of cotton suitable for weaving. In England, Crompton's mule cut the time to 2000 hours, power-assisted mules of 1795 cut it to 300 hours, and by 1825 it was down to 135 hours (Wolf, 1982, p. 273). Being able to produce the same product in 1/370th of the time it took competitors had devastating consequences for those not experiencing the industrial revolution. The British could make far more products in the same time period and sell them for much lower prices than their rivals.

The introduction of mechanized production meant that the labour force had to gather in a single place to work with the machines. This resulted in the development of the factory system. The factory system concentrated a large number of workers engaged in different technical operations on one site. It took over from the putting-out system in which small household establishments processed raw materials. Under the putting-out system, producers would have to distribute material to be assembled or processed to individual households and await the finished product. This was not an ideal system from the owner's perspective because they had little control over work intensity, the duration of labour, embezzlement, pilfering, or quality which all resulted in delays in processing and delivery. It was more advantageous for workers who would sometimes spend most of the week engaged in other activities and then work very hard for a couple of days to fulfil their quota.

The cotton factories of the industrial revolution were essentially spin-ning mills. Weaving kept pace by a multiplication of hand looms and manual weavers. From 1805 the working day was lengthened by intro-ducing artificial light with gas lighting. Factory work was extremely unpopular with the British population. They exhibited a general unwilling-ness to work in factories. Although factory wages were sometimes higher than other unskilled industries, male workers were originally reluctant to enter the workforce because they lost independence. As a result, the bulk of the factory workforce came from the more exploitable sector of the population – women and children. It is estimated that in 1838 only 23 per cent of textile workers were adult men (Hobsbawm, 1987, p. 68). As the factory system progressed, more men entered the workforce and women were gradually confined to the domestic sphere. Early unions were often male dominated and saw women workers as competition. Many men who lost control over their work by being reduced to factory automatons reasserted control through domestic violence at home or against women in the workplace. (Stearns, 1993, p. 62). The difficult working conditions in factories sparked waves of resistance from the activity of Luddites destroying machines to the formation of trade unions and the growth of Democratic and Chartist movements.

The growth of cotton and other types of factories had a number of effects on British society. In some locations it led to the creation of great metropolitan areas. For example, the population of Manchester expanded from 24 000 people in 1773 to over 250 000 people by 1851 (Wolf, 1982, p. 276). According to Hobsbawm (1987, p. 65) the industrial revolution ushered in a new economic relationship between people, a new system of production, a new rhythm of life, a new society and a new historical era. This new system had three primary elements. First, the industrial popula-tion was divided into capitalist employers who owned the factories and materials, and workers who owned nothing but their labour which they sold for wages. Secondly, production was organized in the factory with specialized machines and specialized labour. Thirdly, the entire economy became dominated by capitalists pursuing profit.

There was a crucial international dimension to the industrial revolution both in terms of demand and supply. In terms of supply, the cotton came from outside of Europe. In the late 1700s most came from the Caribbean, but by 1807 more than 60 per cent came from the US. Between 1815 and 1860 cotton proved vital to US economic health as it accounted for more than half of the total value of US exports (Wolf, 1982, p. 279). The pro-duction of this vital input to the industrial revolution was undertaken through the use of slave labour and the removal of native Americans from their land as the plantations moved further west in the United States. On the demand side, Western states created foreign markets for their products.

For example, once British manufacturers held the competitive advantage they were able to destroy the Indian textile industry by exporting machine-made cloth and yarn at prices far lower than their handicraft rivals. By 1840 the Indian industry was destroyed and India was reduced to providing raw cotton as a British export to China.

The second phase of the industrial revolution was characterized by developments in iron and coal power. Its most visible aspect was the tremendous growth in railroad building. The first railroad connected the coalfields of Durham, England with the coast. After Britain, the United States became the centre of railroad growth. (Wolf, 1982, p. 292). Railroading sponsored the second phase of the industrial revolution shifting production away from cotton to iron and steel. England turned to coal as the energy source for this economic activity. Railroad construction rose from 45 000 miles in 1840 to 228 000 miles in 1880. British iron production reached 2.5 million tons in 1850s. Exports of railroad iron and steel tripled between 1845–1875 while exports of machinery increased 10 times (Wolf, 1982, pp. 291–3). Railroads became the shock troops of industrialization from Argentina to the Punjab. They opened up vast new areas to further economic activity and tied parts of the world closer together.

A revolution in transport was also part of the industrial revolution. In the last quarter of the nineteenth century overland freight rates declined 90 per cent due to the railroads. Shipping also made dramatic strides. In 1853 iron-hulled ships were introduced while steel hulls made an appearance in 1864. Sailing ships were eclipsed by steamships which had greater tonnage and speed. A clipper ship with 1000 tons cargo capacity took 120–130 days to go from London to the south coast of China. In 1865 a steamship with 3000 tons could undertake the journey in 77 days (Wolf, 1982, p. 293). Steamship conquered the Atlantic in the 1840s and 1850s, and Asian seas by the 1890s. Alongside the triumph of steamships came the building of canals across Egypt and Panama. The Suez Canal in Egypt was completed in 1869 and cut the sailing time to Asia from England in half. Unfortunately for Egypt, it also resulted in their bankruptcy and virtual rule from Britain. Approximately 50 years later US companies would overcome even greater obstacles (primarily malaria) to finish the Panama Canal in 1915 through the use of Jamaican and Chinese labour. From this time on, the US actively intervened in the operation of Central American states to ensure the safety of 'its' canal.

The advent of the railroad also saw the rediscovery of a particular form of business enterprize – the corporation. As outlined in the previous chapter today's transnational corporations were foreshadowed by the British and the Dutch East Indian Companies. Although the early phase of the industrial revolution was conducted by family businesses, a more permanent and long-term organization such as the corporation was needed for the railway expansion. This was because the sums of money needed for investment were very large and the time-frame for realizing profits was long term. (Pomeranz and Topik, 1999, p. 164).

Why Britain, why then?

The industrial revolution catapulted Britain into a world power and decisively tilted the balance between Asia and Europe. The question arises as to why it occurred in Britain and why it happened at this time. Although there is a great debate on the subject, most analysts highlight three factors: the growth in European knowledge and technology, the rise of the liberal state, and Britain's unique role in the international economy. We will deal with these in turn.

David Landes (1998, pp. 200–9) puts a great deal of emphasis on the development of a culture of knowledge in Europe and Britain. He stresses the European scientific revolution and the Enlightenment which sought to move understanding beyond religious interpretation. Europe developed three key characteristics. First, there was a growing autonomy of intellectual inquiry. Scientists were gradually able to break free of the church and state to pursue their discoveries according to scientific rather than theocratic dogma. Secondly, a language of proof was developed in the scientific method. This required that knowledge be backed up by verifiable experiments. Finally, there was a routinization of research which turned the pursuit of invention into a regular practice.

Technical expertise was not the preserve of Europeans or the British, it was shared by other civilizations. In order to prosper, technological changes had to be supported by a political and economic structure. The industrial revolution required tremendous changes in many aspects of people's lives. What type of environment facilitated such changes? In Britain it was the advent of the liberal state.

The liberal state facilitated the industrial revolution by giving more power to markets and rewarding or punishing behaviour which assisted or retarded the efforts of the emerging industrial capitalists. The liberal state and economy had to be forcefully created (Polanyi, 1957). People had to be forced out of home production and into factories if the cotton mills were to operate. This was called creating a free labour market. The political power of agricultural labour and landholders had to be curbed so that the rising merchant class would be free to import and export products and hire and fire labour.

An example of the type of changes that was required was the 1834 Reform of the Poor Law Act. This law repealed the previous system of poor relief which had stipulated that individual parishes were responsible for their own poor people. Under the new system the poor were encouraged to move to cities to work in the new industrial system rather than face even more horrendous conditions in poorhouses. A national police force was also assembled to deal with the violence caused by forcing people into new forms of labour. A liberal state is not necessarily a less active state.

The creation of the liberal state while supported by a particular class alliance was informed and inspired by liberal ideology. An ideology is a world-view which advocates a particular way of organising social, political and economic life. Nineteenth-century Britain saw the blossoming of liberal ideology. On the economic side, liberalism promoted the ability of economic agents to engage in activity with limited interference from state authorities. Adam Smith (1776/1983), the Scottish philosopher, is even today well-known for expounding the doctrine of laissez-faire – laissez-passer. The English translation (from French) is 'let it be, let it pass'. This refers to letting goods pass between points without hindrance such as tolls, taxes or other state interference. On the political side, liberalism was known for advancing the civil rights of individuals against the powers of the state. Theorists such as John Stuart Mill (1859/1980) pushed for responsible and representative government which respected individual's civil and political rights. Although such rights were articulated in universal terms, in practice they excluded the majority of Britain's population by limiting them to property-owning men. As Mary Wollstonecraft (1792/1992) had pointed out in the previous century, the emerging liberal system was flawed because of its treatment of women.

The horrors of the industrial revolution caused a reaction on the part of those forced to bear the cost. This period saw the formation of trade unions and democratic movements. In the ideological realm, Karl Marx emerged as the dominant theorist of class relations. His writings urged the working class to unite and overthrow the capitalist class. The publication of the *Communist Manifesto* served to inspire millions of people around the world struggling for a more equal society. Marx and Engels (1848/ 1977, p. 224) described 'The need of a constantly expanding market for its products chases the bourgeoisie over the whole surface of the globe. It must nestle everywhere, settle everywhere, establish connections everywhere'. This captured the dynamic of the industrial revolution, but also resonates with global activity in the early twenty-first century. Marx envisioned a new form of society (communism) that would be based upon the common ownership of production which would distribute the fruits of people's labour evenly throughout society.

In addition to benefiting from a scientific base and a liberal state, Britain was located in a favourable international position. Due to its naval supremacy it was able to import cotton easily from the American hemisphere and to transport slaves across the Atlantic. Once textile production picked up, it was able to access foreign markets. This was important because many people in Britain were too poor to afford the volume of products being produced. The navy also acted as a source of demand for the emerging iron industry because of its need for weapons.

Following upon the heels of the industrial revolution and the transformation of transportation technology the world economy experienced tremendous growth. For example, whereas international trade increased in value by 30 per cent from £300 million to £400 million between 1800–1830 it jumped five times to £2000 million between 1840–1870. Whereas in the early 1840s Britain accumulated £160 million credits abroad, this rose to £250 million in the 1850s and exploded to £1000 million by 1873 (Hobsbawm, 1987, p. 139). People joined the increasing international flow of goods and capital. Whereas over one million Europeans emigrated to the USA between 1800–1840, over seven million emigrated between 1840–1870.

While we can identify various factors that contributed to the industrial revolution taking place in Britain in the nineteenth century it is more difficult determining if this is the only mix that would have led to such a dramatic increase in productivity. Certainly scientific knowledge was necessary for the application of machinery to production. It is harder to say whether a particular place in the international economy was a prerequisite. Increasing demand and supply in a national market may have been sufficient. A liberal state facilitated the required social transformation, but less market-oriented states could also transfer resources. Indeed, the spread of industrialization to several different types of societies at different times suggests that the British were the first to hit upon one of potentially several different mix of factors which catapulted humanity into a new era.

What did the others do?

The surge of industrial activity in Great Britain caused considerable concern in other states. British industry was becoming more productive and competitive while the British state was becoming more powerful. European rivals and the newly emergent United States struggled to catch up. The race to catch up created a wide series of policy mixes from industrial sabotage, to brief periods of free trade to protectionist polices to defend industry.

In the early part of the industrial revolution France was Britain's most serious rival. The French monarch tried to modernize his own economy by importing British technicians to update industrial techniques. The commercial rivalry was overshadowed as France plunged into revolution and confrontations generated by the Napoleanic wars. The two countries which surpassed British accomplishments and led the way into the second industrial revolution of chemicals and electricity were Germany and the United States. Both followed protectionist paths toward industrialization. German theorist Fredrick List (1885/1991) was critical of the British notion that free trade was the best method to advance economic growth. He argued that if Germany were to catch up with Britain it must protect its fledging industries or risk being confined to primary products. List's writings echoed the mercantilist views of an earlier era and foreshadowed protective policies such as strategic trade theory in the 1990s.

The United States used British capital to finance its industrialization. The US civil war gave a boost to northern arms manufactures that contributed to further industrialization in the 1870s and 1880s. Increasing immigration and westward expansion fed continued economic growth behind high tariff barriers. By the early 1900s the US was leading in many industries and introducing new forms of production such as mass production of the automobile.

Japan was the only Asian state able to respond rapidly to the challenge of Western industrialization. Following the abolition of feudalism and political reform known as the Meiji Restoration (1868), the Japanese government began a process of state led industrialization (Stearns, 1993, pp. 113–29). Government-led companies began the initial investment in railroads, mines, shipping and textiles. Private enterprise followed government action. For example, Mitsubishi, which was run by former samurai warriors, launched itself into the shipping industry. Japanese industrialization relied even more heavily on female labour than European industrialization and the working conditions for most Japanese workers were worse for a longer period of time than their European counterparts. The success of its efforts were proved when, much to the shock of Europe, Japan defeated Russia in the Russo-Japanese war of 1905. Japan's industrial prowess was felt by much of the rest of Asia in the Second World War.

The Pax Britannica

The rise of British industrial and military power led to a particular form of international system that is sometimes called the Pax Britannica. This translates into the British peace and is an allusion to the famous Pax Romanica which was the relative peace and order characteristic of the Roman Empire at its height. The term is clearly an exaggeration because there were many areas where British power was limited and there were many violent wars. However, it does focus attention on an emerging international system which reached further than previous attempts at international order. The period is significant because it was generally based upon liberal principles that are similar to the guiding principles of today's dominant powers and institutions. Three of the international arrangements that Britain tried to make the basis of the international system were: the gold standard, free trade, and the balance of power.

The gold standard and capital flows

Activity in the international economy such as the exchange of goods and services is facilitated by a recognized form of money. Just as sound money helps move a local or national economy past the shortcomings of barter, a sound international monetary system will assist the exchange of goods and services across borders. In the international sphere there is no international money and no international central bank. The international monetary system (IMS) is the mechanism for exchanging one currency for another. This is necessary because in order to import a product you need to pay the exporter in a currency that they can use. If they are not intending to buy one of your products, they will probably want to be paid in their own currency. The international monetary system helps to determine on what terms and by what methods others will accept your currency.

It is useful to outline some of the key elements of the IMS before explaining the nineteenth century arrangement. A monetary system must address three issues (Cooper, 1987, p. 4). The first is the role of exchange rates. Will they be fixed in relation to other currencies or will they float, with their value changing in response to the market? A second issue is the nature of reserve assets. This refers to the commodity or form of money that the central bank will hold on hand to meet demands for payment of currency. A bank's reserves could be composed of gold or foreign currencies. The final issue is the control of capital movement. Does a state allow money to flow freely in and out of its borders or are there restrictions as to how much can be moved over a particular period? In Chapter 8 we will see systems that vary from the gold standard in each of these areas.

A major problem for countries participating in an international monetary system is the balance of payments. The balance of payments is the total of the value of goods and capital flowing in and out of their states. Crudely, do you sell enough to pay for what you buy abroad? If you are buying more than you are selling you have a balance of payments deficit: you run the risk of running out of money. There are several steps that can be taken in this situation. You can reduce imports or increase exports. In economies that are heavily influenced by state policy, it is possible to increase or decrease the amount of imports by command. In more open economies one can either deflate the economy, devalue the currency or

Box 3.1   The Gold Standard

Imagine two countries who are members of the gold standard and their trade is in balance. Let us choose England and France. Remember that their currencies are fixed to gold, but can freely move in relationship to each other. The values are not historically accurate, but serve to illustrate the principle. Their situation is illustrated in Stage 1 below.

Now consider a change in their trading relationship. The British begin to import more from France than they export to it. This might be because the drinking of French wine becomes more fashionable in Britain. This change in trade increases the British demand for French Francs (FFs) because they are required to pay for more French imports. However, the French don't have as strong a demand for British pound sterling (£s) because they have not increased their consumption of British goods. The French must be encouraged to sell their FFs for £s by offering a greater rate of exchange. It thus costs more £s to buy FFs on the market. The hypothetical result is that the British must now give £15 for FF10. This is illustrated in Stage 2.

If this state of affairs were to last for too long, the eventual result would be a gold drain from Britain. An entrepreneurial French citizen could use their FF10 to buy £15. This could then be exchanged in Britain for 1.5 ozs of gold. The gold could then be brought back to France and exchanged for FF15. The money changer would make a profit of FF5 minus the cost of exchanging money and transporting the gold. If this was done on a large enough level, the profits could be great. This is an early version of a common practice in today's global financial markets – making a profit from the changing value of a currency's foreign exchange rate.

→

increase the competitiveness of local products. Increasing the competitiveness of domestic products is the most attractive strategy: Better products will sell more easily, increasing revenues. However, this may take time or may be difficult to achieve. A second possibility is that the economy may be deliberately deflated or slowed down. If the economy slows, imports will decrease and the balance of payments should improve. The third option is to devalue or lower the value of your currency in relationship to your trading partners. This should make the cost of your products cheaper to foreigners and lead to an increase in sales. Both of these policies have costs. Deflating puts people out of work. Devaluation lowers real wages by making imports more expensive. It also risks inflation or price rises as foreign products become more expensive.

The era of British economic prominence in the nineteenth century is

---

→

The next part of the process contained the element that would bring the system back into balance. In each country the supply of money was determined by central banks based upon the ratio of gold they held. When gold started to flow out, the bank would have to call money in or reduce the amount it loaned out by raising interest rates. This in turn, slowed growth and reduced imports. In our example, as the British had less money to spend, they would reduce their import of French wine, reduce the need for French Francs, restore the exchange rate and stop the outflow of gold. In France the inflow of gold would have the opposite effect – expanding their money supply, increasing imports, and depreciating the currency.

The result would be stage 4 which is the same as stage 1. This equilibrium would hold only for a brief moment in time as tastes and competition quickly moved the flows of trade and gold again. The model becomes more complicated as other countries are added. The two key points are that it tended toward re-establishing balance and it provided the security for people to exchange currencies, knowing that they were backed by gold.

	French currency			*British currency*	
Stage 1:	1 oz gold =	10FF	trades for	10£	=1 oz gold
Stage 2:	1 oz gold =	10FF	trades for	15£	=1.5 oz gold
Stage 3:	10FF exchanged for 15£s exchanged for 1.5 ozs exchanged for 15FFs				
Stage 4:	1 oz gold =	10FF	trades for	10£	=1 oz gold

---

noted for its particular solution to the problem of exchanging currencies. It was called the Gold Standard. Although the British were on a gold standard from the end of the Napoleonic Wars to 1914, the heyday of the international gold standard was 1875–1914. The gold standard was never completely respected, but many states adhered to its principles in a consistent manner. In order for the gold standard to work three factors had to hold true. First, countries were required to fix their currencies in relation to gold. This meant that they had to declare that their currency was worth a particular amount of gold and then be willing to exchange it for gold. The second requirement was to allow the relatively free movement of gold across state boundaries. The third requirement was that currencies would be able to change value in relationship to each other while staying fixed to gold. An example of the operation of the gold standard is provided in Box 3.1.

This system required two prerequisites if it was to function smoothly. The first was an outflow of capital to assist countries in temporary difficulty with balance of payments problems. Countries might require some time to adjust to the flow of money and need to borrow to manage the transition. This role was played by the financial services sector of the City of London. After 1815 London became the financial centre of the world as its banks were able to draw in British money and invest it where the profit was greatest in Britain or abroad. In 1873 deposits in London banks were £120 million compared to £40 million in New York, £13 million in Paris and £8 million in Germany (Hobsbawm, 1987, p. 152).

A second important element was that the national state and society must be willing to accept automatic deflation. This required a politically inert population where the lower classes were shut out of decision making. In Britain this was accomplished by only allowing a minority of the population to vote. This kind of a system often exposed class divisions. In general political and economic elites favoured the gold standard because it came close to automatically maintaining balance of payments equilibrium. However, the working class resisted the mechanisms because they bore the cost of deflation and unemployment.

The presence of London as a financial anchor and the creation of the gold standard facilitated the movement of money from one country to another (Germain, 1997, pp. 44–58). Indeed, the nineteenth century saw the beginning of very large capital flows through the international system. In the 1800s, French money poured into Russia, German capital into the Americas and Africa. As previously mentioned British money helped the United States industrialize. Japan also benefited from British loans and modernized, quickly becoming a world power.

There were differing views as to the political impact of such capital flows. Lenin (1916/1969), the Communist theorist and revolutionary, saw these flows as leading to imperialism and eventually war. Karl Polanyi (1957) saw the interest of capitalist investors or *haute finance* as contributing to peace amongst the major powers. The wealthiest investors who had a stake in the prosperity of many different countries would lobby their national governments for the cause of peace. Although bankers appeared to have limitless power, when the clouds of war gathered in the early 1900s they had a minor political role compared to mass nationalism.

Free trade

The nineteenth century international system was notable for the appearance of the doctrine and practice of free trade. This doctrine is even more prominent today. The key date in the nineteenth century was 1846, the year Britain repealed the Corn Laws. The Corn Laws had protected British aristocrats and farmers from the import of corn. At the time, corn was used to make bread. The dispute pitted industrialists and many workers against landowners and farmers. The industrialists wanted cheap corn so that the cost of bread would be lowered and they could reduce or limit their workers' wages. This would give their products a competitive advantage in international markets over products from countries where food, and therefore wages, were more expensive. British workers also supported the repeal of the Corn Laws because they wanted to pay less for bread. The farmers and landowners feared that foreign competition would lower or eliminate their profits.

David Ricardo, a stock trader and Member of Parliament, articulated the liberal theory of comparative advantage which made the intellectual case for free trade. It remains in force today and is the bedrock of those arguing for economic integration and free trade. Prior to Ricardo, many liberals believed that you should engage in trade if you had an absolute advantage in a product. If you made the best cloth or wine, you would gain from a system that allowed for the freer trade of goods. Ricardo's (1817/1992) theory was more revolutionary. He suggested that by specializing in the product that you make best and engaging in free trade you can benefit even if other people make the products better than you do. Under this theory even countries that are economically weak will benefit from a free trade system because their resources will be used more efficiently. Free trade was a universal good.

For many people at the time, and even today, the notion of comparative advantage is counter intuitive. How is it possible that one can benefit from trade with a country that is more efficient? Box 3.2 illustrates how Ricardo's theory operates.

Although the British state signed on to the free trade economic policy, the wider international acceptance of the doctrine was mixed. The golden era lasted for about 35 years from 1846–1870s. Some European states initially participated, but the United States did not. Once lagging states had acquired some basic ingredients of the industrial revolution, protectionist policies were seen by most countries as the key to catching and surpassing Britain's economic power. Renewed moves to free trade would have to await the post-1945 US-led trading system which is examined in Chapter 5.

The last third of the nineteenth century combines a number of apparently contradictory trends. As the world fragments into rival imperialisms, capital and human mobility are at record levels. Britain loses its productive advantage, but maintains its commitment to economic liberalism because of the strength of its financial industry. Germany and the United States which are becoming more advanced in production remain protectionist

Box 3.2 Comparative advantage example

Stage 1: No trade

In the first stage, two countries (the United States and the United Kingdom) produce two products, but do not engage in trade. Each country employs 100 workers in the steel industry and 100 workers in the textile industry. The Americans have newer plants, so they are more productive. Thus, 100 US workers make 900 units of steel while 100 British workers only make 400 units of steel. One hundred US weavers make 300 units of cloth while 100 British weavers make only 200 units of cloth.

Country	Resources	Products
US	100 steel workers	900 units steel (1:9)
UK	100 steel workers	400 units steel (1:4)
Total		1300 units steel
US	100 weavers	300 units cloth (1:3)
UK	100 weavers	200 units cloth (1:2)
Total		500 units cloth

US makes Steel and Cloth more efficiently.

Stage 2: Specialization

In preparation for trade relations each country shifts resources to specialize in products in which they are comparatively stronger. While the US makes both products more efficiently it has a greater advantage in steel (9 units per worker vs. 4 units per worker) than cloth (3 units per worker vs. 2 units per worker. The US will shift workers into its strongest product while the UK will shift workers into the product that it is most competitive in, compared to the US. The UK will move more resources than the US because it needs to make a greater adjustment due to its relative inefficiency. The US shifts 10 workers out of cloth to steel, UK shifts 20 workers out of steel to cloth.

→

rather than embracing free trade as the British did when at the height of the industrial revolution.

In the recent debate about globalization some scholars have pointed to this era as evidence that today's openness is not unique. For example, Hirst and Thomspon (1996) argue that the high rates of migration, trade and investment just before World War I indicates a very open system. While there was indeed a great deal of activity it often took place in the context of empire and at much slower speeds than in the twenty-first century.

→

Country	Resources	Products
US	110 steel workers	990 units steel (1:9)
UK	80 steel workers	320 units steel (1:4)
Total		1310 units steel
US	90 weavers	270 units cloth (1:3)
UK	120 weavers	240 units cloth (1:2)
Total		510 Units cloth

Stage 3: Trade
However, the US still needs 30 units of cloth and UK needs 80 units of steel. So:
The US can trade 80 units of steel for 30 cloth from the UK.

Stage 4: Results after trade
US   990 units of steel produced – 80 units traded
         = 910 units of steel, **an increase of 10 units of steel.**

      270 units of cloth produced + 30 units imported
         = 300 units of cloth. Same as pre-trade number.

UK   320 units of steel produced + 80 units traded
         = 400 units of steel. Same as pre-trade number.

      240 units of cloth produced – 30 units exported
         = 210 units of cloth, **an increase of 10 units of cloth.**

Even though the US had an absolute advantage (it could produce both products more efficiently) both countries were still able to gain from trade after specializing in their areas of comparative advantage. Both countries are wealthier after specializing in the products in which they have a comparative advantage.

The balance of power

The hundred years from the end of the Napoleonic Wars in 1815 until the outbreak of the First World War in 1914 passed without a major war involving all the European powers. There were localized wars such as the Crimean War which pitted Britain, France and Turkey against Russia and the Franco-Prussian war, but not the kind of systemic conflict such as raged in the early nineteenth and twentieth centuries. Under the balance of power system, violence was not ruled out. Force could be used to contain rivals or in the case of the popular revolutions of 1848 to support particular regimes against democratic movements. The key was to prevent conflict from degenerating into a system-wide war. This relatively peaceful era contributed to an international system that favoured a growth in international trade and finance.

We are interested in why the leading European military states were able to prevent a general war. The security arrangements or structure at this time is known as the balance of power. It had three characteristics. The first characteristic was that there was a general agreement on what was called the Concert of Europe. This was an arrangement between the major European powers following the turmoil of the Napoleonic Wars. It provided for communication and consultation between the powers to ensure that no single state grew too strong. A second characteristic was that states would shift alliances and allegiances to balance the growing power of any particular state. If any state seemed to be getting too powerful, a coalition would emerge to contain that state. This led a British statesman, (Castlereagh) to famously declare that there are 'No permanent alliances just permanent interests.'

The third characteristic of this system was that consideration of other states' ideology and domestic public opinion had to be excluded from the decision-making process. If alliances and military action were designed for keeping a balance of power, cooperation with any form or nature of state would be pursued if it kept the balance. Maintenance of the balance might require constitutional democracies to cooperate with absolute monarchies against other constitutional democracies. Public opinion would also be excluded because it might be necessary to ally with a state that had recently been an enemy. The general public might not support sudden shifts in diplomacy so their views would have to be ignored. This was not a difficult task since none of the states in question would qualify as democracies by today's standards.

The primary balancing role in this environment went to Britain. It had two considerable weapons that it could launch against the growing power of rival states. The first was the British navy which enjoyed supremacy over the waters of the world. During the mid-nineteenth century the Royal Navy was as powerful as the next three or four navies combined. (Kennedy, 1987, p. 154). The navy could be used to interfere with opponents' supplies, support allies or to raid coastal waters. The second advantage was Britain's wealth which could be funnelled to allies on the continent. The British government was able to provide financing to other states to keep armies in the field against Britain's rivals.

While this system appeared stable and lasted for a hundred years, it went through a series of changes, becoming rigid in the first decade of the twentieth century (Craig and George, 1983, pp. 28–48) As the century progressed, states continued to build their overseas empires, and engaged in imperialist rivalry. The industrialization of Germany threatened British dominance as the two countries engaged in naval and imperial competition. The system of flexible and shifting alliances gradually hardened as Europe became divided into two camps. The Triple Entente of France, Britain and Russia confronted the Triple Alliance of Germany, Austria and Italy. Formal treaties were bolstered with secret treaties pledging one state to come to the aid of another. States committed themselves to disastrous policies without understanding the severe consequences. The assassination in August 1914 of the Archduke of Serbia sparked a series of events that gradually drew European states, the United States and the British commonwealth into a long and bloody war. Ignoring the example of the US civil war which previewed industrial warfare, leaders foolishly predicted speedy victory.

Peace and wealth for whom? The notion of a Pax Britannica helps us understand some aspects of an evolving global political economy but obscures others. One problem is that it tends to focus on inter-European affairs and fails to consider a crucial aspect of the industrial revolution which was a new wave of European imperialism sweeping over the African continent and parts of Asia. Secondly, it overstated the degree to which liberal principles governed the system and downplayed the flaws that led to its demise. These shortcomings are so serious that the next section is devoted to considering the new imperialism and the breakdown of the liberal system.

An additional problem with the Pax Britannica approach is that it ignores the very large-scale violence taking place in several parts of the world that was linked to the growth of the international market. In the United States, tensions between the export oriented, commodity producing south and the protectionist north erupted in the US civil war. This was the most violent and costly war in American history. In China the social dislocation from the opium war provided the background for a Christian influenced rebellion against the Emperor (Waley-Cohen, 1999, p. 159). It is estimated that 10–20 million Chinese died during the Taiping Rebellion and the ensuing conflicts (Pomeranz and Topik, 1999, p. 169). In the Congo, the King of Belgium carved out his own private empire. Approximately 10 million Africans died in the effort to harvest rubber for export (Hochschild, 1999). These are forgotten lives in a Western centred view emerging with the Pax Britannica. One needs to ask, peace and wealth for whom?

Renewed imperialism

Is it a coincidence that the era of unprecedented economic growth known as the industrial revolution was quickly followed by an era of unprecedented imperial expansion? Was this 'new imperialism' an inevitable consequence of capitalism or the result of political rivalry between European states? We'll first review the events surrounding the new imperialism and then consider some alternative explanations.

As described in Chapter 2, European expansionism began in the 1400s and proceeded with varying speeds and intensities in different parts of the world. In the first half of the 1800s European powers relinquished formal control in the Americas, but created new colonies in South Africa, Algeria, India and southern Vietnam. In the Americas, Spanish colonies were able to assert their independence, but remained economically vulnerable to Europe and later the United States. European expansion accelerated in the last quarter of the century. Between 1878 and 1913 Europeans extended their control over an additional one-sixth of the earth's surface. (Abernethy, 2000, p. 81). Moving from coastal settlements, Europeans expanded into the interior of the African and Asian continents. No longer satisfied with economic exchange, European traders and states insisted upon formal political control in the form of new colonies. China was not colonized, but Western powers carved out spheres of influence in the country.

This era of expanding Western powers had four significant developments (Abernethy, 2000, pp. 84–7). First, traditional European powers enlarged their empires. Holland expanded its reach in what is today known as Indonesia. Portugal pushed out from its coastal areas in Southern Africa to take over Angola and Mozambique. France established colonies in north and west Africa, as well as in Madagascar, Indochina and islands of the Pacific. Britain expanded its hold over India and attempted to dominate a portion of African territory stretching from Egypt to South Africa. Spain was an exception to this trend as a series of wars of independence deprived it of its Latin American colonies.

Secondly, three new European states entered the colonial movement. Following their own unification as nation-states Italy, Belgium and Germany rushed to seize colonies in Africa. The Italians were the least successful, suffering defeat at the hands of the Ethiopians in 1896, but managing to conquer Libya. Belgium carved out an immense territory in the Congo. Germany, riding the power derived from the second industrial revolution seized territory in southern, western and eastern Africa.

Thirdly, two Western states outside the European core completed continental expansions subduing native populations and creating large states. In the Americas, the United States rolled over native Americans and

Mexicans as it completed its drive to the Pacific Ocean. It then engaged upon a policy of expanding overseas by seizing the Spanish colonies of Puerto Rico and the Philippines and invading Cuba. Control of the Hawaiian Islands were also taken from their native inhabitants. This expansion had its counterpart in Asia as Russia extended eastward dominating large stretches of land in its drive to the Pacific Ocean.

Finally, an Asian state was able to adapt to the industrial revolution, and began its process of empire building. In the 1890s Japan seized Taiwan and it took control of Korea in 1905. Japanese interests in Manchuria continued to grow and its imperial ambitions were later pursued in the 1930s, leading to war with the United States.

The most dramatic bout of this expansionism was called the 'Scramble for Africa'. This was literally a race between European powers to divide the African content among themselves. Over a period of approximately 35 years the African continent was transformed from being relatively independent with Europeans confined along its edges to being completely under foreign control with the sole exception of Ethiopia (See Map 3.1). When the scramble was over, 10 million square miles, 110 million people and 30 colonies were added to European possession (Pakenham, 1991, p. xxiii).

The subjugation of Africa was marked by what Pakenham (1991) calls the four Cs: Commerce, Christianity, Civilization and Conquest. Europeans first engaged with Africa because of commerce. During the scramble immense fortunes were made. Consider the case of Cecil Rhodes the diamond and gold magnate. His actions resulted in the accumulation of vast wealth, the subjugation of an African nation (the Ndebele), and the creation of a country by him and named after him (Rhodesia). In addition, his name lives on through the establishment of the Rhodes Scholarship at Oxford University. Christianity also played a role as missionaries flocked to Africa. They moved deeper into the interior, converting natives in the hope that this might save their souls and spare them from the Arab slave trade. European troops soon followed as one group or another of missionaries had to be saved from the local inhabitants. European explorers, settlers and traders justified their activity in terms of civilizing Africans. It was claimed that they were bringing the virtues of advanced civilization to Africa.

As Africans resisted, it increasingly became necessary to use military force or conquest to establish European goals. There were some African successes in resisting European imperialism. For example, the Zulus defeated a British force at Isandlwana in 1879. For almost twenty years (1880s and 1890s) Samori Tourè led African resistance to French colonialism in West Africa. In 1896, 100 000 Ethiopian soldiers maintained the independence of their state by defeating an Italian force of 15 000 at the battle of Adowa. However, the overall trend was one of European imperial

Map 3.1 Pre- and post-scramble Africa

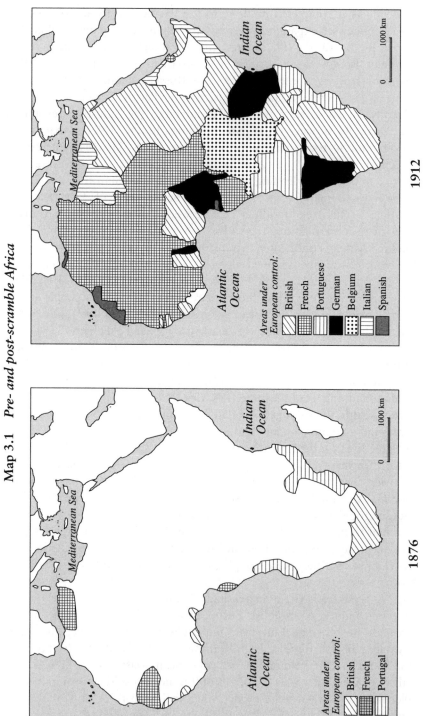

1912

1876

Adapted from Pakenham (1991) pp. 19, 670.

armies and their African conscripts inflicting large-scale defeats and harsh reprisals on African forces. Examples include the Battle of Omdurman (1898) where a British-led force killed 10 000 Sudanese warriors to the cost of 26 British soldiers. The Germans dealt with rebellion by the Hereros in South West Africa by exiling a tribe of 20 000 to die in the desert in 1904. With the exception of Ethiopia, all of Africa fell to European arms.

Many different explanations have been advanced to help us understand the imperialism of the late nineteenth century. Some of the theories stress developments in European countries while others focus on developments outside Europe; some see the imperial drives as motivated by economic factors while others stress the role of military competition.

The two most prominent explanations centre on Europe and financial factors. A liberal, John Hobson (1902) argued that imperialism was caused by underconsumption in Western states. The mass of the population were kept poor and could not buy the goods being produced. Economic interests such as the finance industry, arms exporters and shipping pushed government into expanding overseas so that they could continue to make a profit. Hobson's solution to this situation was a redistribution of income within Western states. This would allow people to buy the goods being produced and would end the need for imperialism in other parts of the world. For Hobson, the design of the Western economic system promoted imperialism, but this could be reversed by changing public policy.

Lenin's (1917/1969)) famous analysis of imperialism was informed by Marxism. Similarly to Hobson, he thought that imperialism was caused by the economic system in Western states. Industrialists and bankers combined their interests in pursuing overseas markets. Lenin saw this as the highest and last from of capitalism. Unlike Hobson, he argued that this imperialist impulse was an inevitable feature of capitalism and could only be ended by revolution in the colonized world and in the imperial metropole. He contributed his part to this development by leading the Russian revolution and creating the Soviet Union in 1917.

Another European-focused explanation argues that the imperialist upsurge was the result of military and strategic competition between European states. The scramble for colonies was the result of European competition between Britain, France, Germany, Italy, Portugal, Belgium, and Spain. Colonies were seized not because they were economically profitable, but because they blocked the ambitions of rival states or served as a symbol of power and prestige. Africa was carved up as the great power game extended to new regions of the world.

Other analysts have tried to locate relevant explanation in the colonized societies instead of Europe. For example, Ronald Robinson (1972) suggests that the fate of imperial adventures was determined, to a large extent,

Box 3.3 Imperialism in the Congo

One of the most horrific events in the new wave of imperialism was Belgian King Leopold II's exploitation of the Congo. Belgium activity in the Congo was somewhat unique because a vast area of land became the personal property of a king rather than the state. It was horrific because millions of Africans died, and brutal methods such as severing people's hands were used to force local people into labour.

Through clever diplomacy during the Berlin Conference of 1884–5 King Leopold II of Belgium was able to establish a personal protectorate over large areas of central Africa (Pakenham, 1991, pp. 239–55). This area became known as the Congo Free State. It was more than seventy times the size of Belgium itself and about one thirteenth of Africa. The King was tasked with developing the Congo for the benefit of its people, but used the territory to amass a large personal fortune and to finance monuments and buildings in Brussels.

The King of the Belgians became very rich and millions of Africans died because of the international desire for a new, modern commodity – rubber (Hochschild, 1999, pp. 158–66). The demand for rubber increased dramatically in the 1890s as the technology to refine rubber into a host of products was perfected. Rubber was needed for tires, hoses, tubes and electrical wiring covers. Demand for rubber could be met most efficiently by planting and cultivating rubber trees in Latin America and Asia. However, this required considerable care and years before a harvest would be ready. The Congo contained wild rubber trees which could be harvested immediately to meet the spiralling demand. This was the source of Leopold's wealth.

→

by the nature of local collaborators rather than European power or abilities. He argues that European powers relied upon local elites (collaborators or mediators) to manage relations with the local population. When these elites were weakened or in danger from local forces, Europeans had to expand their participation into outright rule. When the Europeans ran out of local collaborators, a process of decolonization began.

The upsurge in imperialism in the late nineteenth century was such a widespread phenomenon that a combination of factors and theories is necessary to gain a full understanding. We can begin by agreeing with Geoffrey Barraclough (1967, pp. 43–64) that the process of industrialization enabled Western states (and Japan) to dominate areas of the world that had previously been beyond their reach. Scientific advance gave some states, societies and businesses the means to dominate other states, societies and businesses. However, to explain why a certain imperial power

→

In order to harvest wild rubber, workers had to venture into the forest and engage in the difficult and dangerous practice of draining sap from rubber vines. African males were pressed into this labour by rubber agents who took their families hostage until a certain amount of rubber was harvested. Another common practice in this 'rubber terror' was to chop off the hands of Africans who failed to meet their quotas or who resisted European demands for more rubber. Although it is difficult to establish the numbers of lives lost because of the rubber trade, one credible estimate is that up to 10 million people died through a combination of murder, starvation exhaustion, disease and a plummeting birth rate (Hochschild, 1999, pp. 225–33).

The horror of this Western atrocity comes down to us in English literature through Joseph Conrad's (1902/1999) novel *The Heart of Darkness*. Conrad worked for four months on a steamship travelling the Congo river. The terrible events he saw in the Congo caused him to write a novel about the voyage of a man up a river to find a European who crossed the line into brutal insanity. The same story was later adapted as the movie *Apocalypse Now*.

A final interesting note about the sad history of Belgian intervention in the Congo was that it gave rise to the first international human rights campaign of the twentieth century (Hochschild, 1999). In 1903 the Congo Reform Association was formed to lobby against the human rights abuses in that country. It campaigned in Europe and the United States until 1913 when it was determined that the Belgian government which had taken over running the Congo from the King had instituted sufficient reforms.

expanded in a particular area, one needs to assess the factors in Europe, in the target states and ties that bound the two areas together (Doyle, 1996).

Conclusion

Looking back at the nineteenth century international system from today, we can see elements that are strikingly familiar. Some parts of the international economy were characterized by large-scale flows of capital, goods and people across state boundaries. Several advanced countries were experiencing a revolution in production which increased inequality within and between countries. Liberal economic principles dominated in some states while others sought to develop through more mercantilist policies. Several

Western states possessed the military capability of using force to intervene or dominate affairs in other continents.

The differences are also notable. In our present era, formal political control which characterized the imperial activities of Western states has largely disappeared. Information technologies have accelerated the speed of economic activities and created new channels of communication within firms and between peoples. Rules for international activity have been formalized into international law and a host of international organizations facilitate coordination between states, firms and citizens. Finally, a series of global issues such as human rights, economic justice and environmental sustainability have created new transnational coalitions.

The nineteenth century is known as the century of free *trade,* although our analysis shows that this is an overstatement since the practice was often not observed by many states. Nevertheless, from the mid-nineteenth century the dominant power, Great Britain, led the way in promoting and supporting free trade. The British did so not seeking reciprocity but on a unilateral basis. But many countries feeling unable to compete with British economic dominance erected protectionist barriers. However, the practice of free trade only tells part of the story. Equally crucial in the emergence of a global economy was the ideology of free trade. It was during the nineteenth century that this pervasive modern economic ideology was born.

There were important changes in the *production* structure in this period. The most important was the industrial revolution and the attendant developments in its wake. These included the development of industrial capitalism and the export of capital from Europe to North America, South America and Asia. Capitalism emerged as a dominant economic, political and social system in the mid-nineteenth century in the aftermath of the industrial revolution. The new power of industrial production, with its division of labour and emphasis on new technological improvements, initiated fundamental changes in the relations between individuals and communities. The developments in production were harnessed by national elites to supplement their power domestically in intra-state struggles and to enhance the power of their state in international competition. The industrial revolution also provided the material resources which allowed Western states to extend their dominance over other parts of the world.

The industrial revolution fed an increasing differentiation in the division of *labour.* Within industrializing states the wealth accumulated by the new industrial classes stood in sharp contrast with the living conditions of the new industrial proletariat. The transformation of the workforce from a primarily agricultural one to an industrial one and the changes in the gender division of labour were crucial features of economic, social and political change. The exploitation of the working classes and the conflict between capital and labour became the subject of political agitation and the domain of novelists and poets. At times it was feared by some social critics (and hoped for by others) that capitalist exploitation of the workforce would destroy the social and moral fabric of society.

The industrial revolution also sharpened the international division of labour between countries. Western states, led by Britain and then the US and Germany, raced ahead producing manufactured goods. Other parts of the world were increasingly incorporated into European colonial empires as the producers of raw materials for industrialized countries. For some countries this role continues today.

Finance played an important part in the construction of an international economy in the nineteenth century. It was important in the industrialization of all countries that managed to make the transition to self-sustaining economic growth. For example, the US used British capital to build its railroads. The export of capital is seen by many as a key instrument in the development of imperialism. During this period financial flows increased and the geographic spread of finance expanded. The interests of financiers and industrialists frequently came into conflict but in the latter half of the century in many centres, alliances developed between financial capital and industrial capital. Another major innovation in the development of market capitalism was the advent of the joint-stock corporation. The shift from family business as the main form of private enterprise to the modern corporation was attendant on the growth of the railways since the sums of money needed for investment were very large and the time frame for realizing profits was long term.

The states that were able to industrialize in the nineteenth century became the developed countries of the twentieth century while those that were unable to industrialize faced major *development* challenges in the twentieth and twenty-first centuries. The only Asian state able to take Western technology and successfully industrialize was Japan. Today, Japan is a leading advanced economy. The fate of non-industrializers was to fall behind their Western competitors. After keeping Western states at bay for hundreds of years India became a British colony while China was forced to grant spheres of influence to a series of Western powers. Today the information revolution may be playing a similar role in creating inequalities between different parts of the world.

The process of industrialization polluted the *environment* of the cities and countryside in Europe and Japan. A similar pattern occurred wherever industrialization took place. Globally, the process of industrialization changed the earth's ability to regulate the atmosphere because of the amount of carbon released into the air. The Kyoto Protocol is the legacy of the pollutants created by the industrial revolution.

In terms of national *governance*, this period saw the rise of the nation-state and the development of a liberal state. The liberal state presided over capital accumulation through its regulation of capital and labour. It was through the instrumentality of the liberal state that rights and responsibilities were assigned. The liberal state was essential to the growth of domestic capitalism and the emergence of an international economy through the role it played in increasing the power of markets and the formulation of policies designed to reward or punish behaviour which assisted or retarded the efforts of the emerging industrial capitalists.

In the area of international governance, the nineteenth century has often been seen as a period of relative peace. This, however, reflects a Eurocentric bias. Violence in the international system was endemic for many non-European peoples subject to various forms of European imperialism in Africa and Asia. In the Americas states were forged and domestic settlements made and rearranged through interstate and civil wars. Within Europe apart from some local wars peace was preserved through the operation of the balance of power. But it was this same balance of power system that exported European violence to the periphery.

The liberal state and Pax Britannica rested on a specific domestic political settlement in which the majority of the population was disenfranchized and played no role in policy making. As the century progressed working people began to agitate for increased access to political participation. One of the main differences between the nineteenth century and twentieth century international economic systems resides in the role played by the working class (and peasantry) in political decision-making. With the advent of the universal franchise greater attention was given by governments to the needs of workers. Of course, as detailed above there were gains and the domestic settlement in 1914 was different from that of 1815. Nevertheless, for most of this period governments represented elites and could ignore the demands of most of the population. Importantly this period saw increased conflict between the interests of rural landowners and industrialists. As the century progressed these conflicts tended to be resolved in favour of the industrial bourgeoisie. One way in which working-class agitation was quelled was through the rise of nationalism. Although socialist parties emerged committed to class struggle in which national borders were supposed to be transcended, the nationalist myth proved more potent as an organizing device.

Ideas and knowledge were essential to the evolution of the world economy in the nineteenth century. We can see three different ways in which ideas were critical to the evolution of the global economy in the nineteenth century. First, in a technical sense the industrial revolution was based on scientific and technological innovation. The series of events we refer to as the industrial revolution is thus inconceivable without reference to the development of scientific and technological expertise. In short, the industrial revolution involved the application of scientific and technological developments to production, the introduction of new energy sources to power the machines, and this in turn was linked to the reorganization of the labour force into factories.

However, underlying the specific inventions and technological break-throughs were ideas about the science, technology and religion. In other words, the specific inventions depended on developments in underlying world views. At this second level of the impact of ideas, we can highlight the role of the Enlightenment which ushered in new ways of thinking about the natural and social worlds. The spirit of enquiry unleashed by the Enlightenment was critical to fostering change in the international economy. This was mainly through freeing intellectual enquiry from the theocratic straightjacket in which it had been encased. This growing autonomy of the mind to pursue intellectual enquiry ushered in a new way of scientific thinking and the development of modern scientific method with its emphasis on independent proof and verification.

A third set of ideas about the social world and social relations also helped to transform the international economy. Three ideologies – liber-alism, nationalism and racism – were especially important in this process. Liberal ideology and the rise of the liberal state underpinned an interna-tional economic system committed at least in principle to liberal economic values. At the domestic level liberal ideas supported the growth of capi-talism and the development of laissez-faire policies. At the heart of nine-teenth-century liberalism was the belief in progress. Nationalism was responsible both for redrawing the map of Europe and for stimulating the economic growth of countries determined to catch up with the leading states. On the one hand nationalism helped to maintain domestic stability as populations identified themselves with their (emerging) states but on the other it also led to a backlash against liberal economic ideology as some states resorted to economic nationalist policies in their drive for industrial-ization. Racist ideology was also crucial in shaping nineteenth-century developments as racist ideas permeated European imperial expansion. European imperialism was based on myths of European superiority and whether articulated in terms of the white man's burden to civilize inferior races or as the right of Europeans to rule lesser races, this racial ideology helped mould and shape relations between European states at the centre of the world economy and peoples on the periphery.

The following chapter outlines how we moved from the wreckage of the nineteenth century system to a twenty-first century global political economy which shares some of its predecessor's characteristics, but has many new dimensions.

Chapter 4

The Twentieth Century: World Wars and the Post-1945 Order

The nineteenth century liberal and imperialist order came to an end with the onset of the First World War in 1914. Over thirty years passed between the end of the nineteenth century system in 1914 and the beginning of a new world order in 1945. These three decades were marked by the two world wars and an inter-war economic collapse. The wars and economic turmoil had a profound impact on the nature of the post-1945 system in which we now live.

This chapter examines the impact of the turmoil from 1914–1945 on the post-war system and the nature of that system itself. The two world wars dramatically weakened Western Europe on the world stage and led to the creation of new forms of state in Europe and other continents. The economic turbulence of the inter-war years encouraged the US to play a prominent role in the post-1945 era and contributed to the creation of a series of international organization to monitor the global economy.

The era which stretches from 1945 until today has been marked by several developments. The first has been the dominant role played by the United States and the triumph of a Western centred political economy over the Soviet Union. A second development has been the political independence of former Western colonies and the struggle for development by most of the non-Western world. A third change has been the transformation of the role of the state in the developing and developed world to a more liberal and competitive entity. A fourth transformation has been the growth of international organizations in governing global affairs. A final noticeable change has been the advent of a revolution in information technologies and its impact upon social, political economic and military organization.

War and economic disorder

This section examines the impact of two world wars and years of economic dislocation on the international political economy. The painful lessons learned from these years were significant factors shaping the design of the post-1945 system.

The world wars

The First and Second World Wars were massive shocks to the international economy, forcing a retreat from liberal and imperial policies. The First World War disrupted trade and finance patterns, leaving European states much weaker in 1918 than they had been before the war. The pattern of international trade suffered two effects. First, there was a change in the direction of trade as countries switched trading partners. Secondly, there was a change in the composition of exports as domestic production was switched from the export sector to war production. Denied access to European goods many countries turned to domestic production or alternative suppliers. This allowed some areas of the world such as Latin America to accelerate their own industrialization. Following the war, the task of European reconstruction was thus made more difficult since old markets were no longer open.

Capital movements were also affected as the pre-war pattern of the export of capital to primary producing areas was reversed with capital directed to Europe to aid in the war effort. Moreover, the international gold standard was abandoned and international financial dealings became a destabilizing element. Some short-term investment was temporarily not recoverable and some previously attractive investments were no longer available. The war turned a number of debtor nations into creditors and some creditor nations into debtors. For example, the United States which had started the war as a debtor nation had a healthy surplus of over £1000 million by 1922 as a direct result of its role in financing the war in Europe. On the other hand, Germany entered the war as a creditor and emerged as a debtor. The major European belligerents (Britain, France, and Germany) ended the war with a vastly reduced stock of foreign investments.

The appalling destruction of the First World War discredited the balance of power, secret treaties, and power politics as tools of organizing the international system. After exacting revenge against Germany for beginning the war, the victorious powers attempted to create a security system which relied upon international law and international organizations. For various reasons, this system proved inadequate to maintain peace and the world was plunged into another war twenty years later. The economic roots of this failure are outlined below; this section considers the political framework that proved woefully inadequate.

Following the lead of US President Woodrow Wilson, the victorious allies outlined a more liberal system of peace and security which rested on free economic relations and international organization. President Wilson (1918/1986) outlined this liberal strategy in his famous Fourteen Points speech to the US Congress in January 1918. Wilson's Fourteen Points set the agenda for the inter-war international order. He called for the end of secret treaties, free trade, arms reduction, national self-determination and an international organization for settling disputes between states.

At the centre of this system was an international organization called the League of Nations (Bennett and Oliver, 2002, pp. 27–45). Most states belonged to the League, although ironically, the US did not join. The US Senate responded to isolationist pressure and refused to give the President permission to join the League. This weakened the institution, depriving it of the financial and military resources of the most powerful state in the international system.

The League's primary task was to keep the peace. The League had a system of negotiation, arbitration and adjudication to encourage states to resolve their conflicts peacefully. Member states agreed to respect each others' territorial integrity. In addition, they professed belief in a system of collective security. Any attack on a member state was to be considered an attack on the international community as a whole. The League had the ability (on paper) to institute immediate economic and political sanctions upon any aggressor state. They could also raise military forces from member states to repel the aggressor's military action.

A series of crises in 1930s demonstrated the Leagues' shortcomings in preventing and containing war. Its first major failure was in September 1931 when Japan invaded China and occupied Manchuria. Although Japan was criticized for its aggression, the League was unable to reverse its occupation. In 1935 the Fascist Italian government launched an invasion of Ethiopia. Ethiopia had already successful fended off European imperialism during the Great Scramble. Although Ethiopia appealed to the League for help and fought the invaders, it was conquered by Italian forces. League sanctions were half-hearted and temporary. Following failure against Japan and Italy, the League proved unable to halt Hitler's annexation of Austria and Czechoslovakia. It similarly proved incapable of preventing the outbreak of World War II as Japan renewed its invasion of China and Germany attacked Poland.

The most devastating criticism of this form of international order was provided by E.H. Carr (1939) on the eve of the outbreak of the Second World War. Carr argued that the liberal notion of harmony of interest was utopian. Peace was not a shared interest when some states were dissatisfied with the status quo and could benefit from war. Similarly, the notion of collective security is misleading because states that did not feel threatened by an aggressive act would not use force to repel it. Carr advanced a sound realist critique of the liberal naiveté of the dangers of aggressive states. However, he also warned that realism without some dose of utopianism was power without a purpose.

The Second World War produced greater change for the world economy than its predecessor. One result was that it fundamentally altered the balance of global economic power and effectively marked the shift of power from Europe to the United States. American supremacy was built on positive and negative outcomes during the war. The positive elements arose from the tremendous growth of the American economy. The war finally put an end to the depression in the US which through harnessing its full productive capacity significantly expanded it share of world output. Both the size of productive plant and the physical output of goods increased by more than 50 per cent. At the end of the war the US accounted for more than a half of the world's manufacturing output. Another important factor in the rise of the US was its dominance of international finance. The US lent enormous sums to the Allies during the course of the conflict. At the end of the war the Allied powers were thus heavily indebted to the US.

A second development was the creation or elaboration of welfare states in Western Europe. Within Europe, leftist groups such as the communists and labour parties emerged with massive electoral support because of their opposition to Fascism. Conservative and business parties were placed on the defensive as large numbers of people demanded a redistribution of resources as their right following the defeat of Germany, Italy and their collaborators in other states. The result was that European states were forced to put a priority on building domestic economies and introducing legislation which distributed benefits more broadly than before the war.

A third impact of the war was the vast scale of destruction caused especially in Europe and Asia. Physical destruction and consequent social and administrative chaos resulted in a loss of production and export capacity. Key economic actors such as Germany and Japan ended the war unable to play the role they had performed in the pre-war economy. Moreover, they became a burden on the victorious coalition. The scale of devastation was such that it posed a serious problem for post-war reorganization. With the destruction of physical plant and the shortage of capital, not only were these countries and regions devastated it also contributed to US relative economic dominance.

A fourth impact was the shift in relative power between Europe and the societies in its colonies. Similar to 1918, European states emerged economically drained from world war. Japanese wartime victories in Asia highlighted the vulnerability of European colonial armies. The end of the Second World War also marked the beginning of the end for most of Europe's colonies.

Inter-war economic failure

The inter-war period of international economic relations was marked by change, uncertainty, erratic growth and depression. Leading states were unable to reestablish a stable international economic order. In Western states the era was divided into three phases. The first phase lasted from the end of the war until the mid-1920s. Domestically, states struggled to revive their economies. Internationally the value of currencies floated freely against each other and states attempted to liberalize economic relations between themselves. In some countries, such as Germany, this was the period of the great inflation. The second phase was characterized by a return to the gold standard and rising unemployment in many states. This period stretched from the mid-1920s until the early 1930s. The third phase occurred from 1932 until the outbreak of the Second World War and was marked by retreat from the international economy to regional economies as states attempted to deal with economic problems on a unilateral basis.

Following the First World War, elites in the victorious countries were eager to re-establish a liberal trading and financial system. Their failure to acknowledge the changed reality of the international political economy led to financial disaster and eventually war. There were several problems with the attempt to re-establish open economic relations. First, in creating rigid and punitive international monetary and credit systems, leading states failed to recognize the economic damage caused by the war and the heavy burden of war reparations on the system. This weakened already damaged economies. Secondly, international economic arrangements did not take into account the views and interests of the mass societies mobilized by the First World War. As a result, there was a popular backlash against liberal policies and a movement to state-led development. Finally, the largest power in the system was not fully committed to making the sacrifices needed to maintain an open international economy. The lack of US support weakened the system as it headed into crisis. We will consider these problems in turn.

Rigid monetary and financial systems. There are two aspects of the international monetary and financial system that proved to be very problematic. The first was the decision to re-establish the gold standard at pre-war levels and the second was the system of war reparations from Germany to France in compensation for the First World War.

States were eager to move back to the security of the gold standard which would give people confidence in the value of their currency and facilitate international trade. A problem emerged when states were so committed to the gold standard that they disregarded the harm it caused to their national economies. Several states fixed their currency to gold in ways that damaged their national economies. For example, Britain fixed its currency to gold at the same rate as it was before the war even though the economy was weaker. This meant that the British currency was overvalued and its exports were expensive for other states. This reduced employment as British exporters lost business and jobs. In Germany, the government eventually succeeded in curbing runaway inflation, but restricted the money supply until the economy ground to a halt, causing a massive increase in unemployment. The fixation with monetary stability and unwillingness to adjust the value of currencies and money supply to boost economic growth prevented governments from responding positively to recession and depression.

The punitive side of the international economic system can be seen in the Treaty of Versailles which ended the First World War. It stipulated that Germany make reparation payments to the victorious countries because it was guilty of starting the war. This, in turn, created some of the conditions for the financial crisis of 1931 and the collapse of the liberal international economic order. This political decision was taken without serious reflection on its impact on the international economy. The reparations issue became an important one in immediate post-war European economic and political relations.

International financial crisis broke out in 1931. In May of 1931, Austria's largest bank (the Creditanstalt) was discovered to be insolvent partly as a result of depreciation of its assets and partly because of the withdrawal of foreign funds. Because the German and Austrian financial systems were relatively close, the crisis spread to Germany. Britain wanted to aid Germany, but needed US financial assistance to do so. The US would only help if the French also contributed. The French government would only help Germany if it granted further political concessions to France. The German government, already under pressure from the National Socialist Party (Nazis) for being too weak was unable to accommodate the French government. Rather than face the possibility that their currency would collapse, the German government instituted capital controls (prevented people from selling German currency) and began to close their economy to the outside world. The events in Germany put pressure on other states and eventually both Britain and the United States left the gold standard and concentrated on improving their domestic economies. By 1932 major states had retreated into economic relations with states that used a common currency. Thus, Germany traded with its neighbours in central Europe in the mark zone, Britain concentrated its trade with the Empire in the Sterling area, the Americans operated in the dollar zone and French worked in the Franc zone.

As states restricted economic relations with each other the world tumbled into recession. Kindleberger (1986) suggests that the world depression of the 1930s was widespread, deep and long because Britain and the United States failed to undertake several key tasks of international economic management. In addition to failing to keep an open market for goods through free-trade policies, the states were unable to provide credit to countries in need. There was no lender of last resort. When financial crisis hit the international system, there was no lender who could step in with capital to stabilize the system. Domestically, the lender of last resort is the central bank. Britain played this role in the international system of the nineteenth century, but the isolationist US refused to play a similar role in the inter-war system.

Popular mobilization and new forms of state. The inter-war period is a good example of how a particular form of international order rests upon the balance of social forces between and across states (Cox, 1986). Karl Polanyi (1957) used the phrase 'double movement' to describe the dynamic at work in the early twentieth century. The first part of this movement was the attempt to create a liberal market system. This involved the creation of a labour market where people sold their labour for wages with little welfare protection, some degree of free trade and adherence to the gold standard. The second part of the double movement was the political reaction to the suffering caused by this liberal market. Social groups mobilized and put pressure on governments to protect them from the ravages of the market.

What was the problem with the liberal market? The main problem was the assumption that people were a commodity adjusting to the supply and demand of the market in the same way that commodities such as land or capital might adjust. People were viewed as 'labour' and policies assumed that they would freely participate in lowering their wages and income according to the economic models. However, the adjustments demanded by the market were so great and so brutal that people refused to accept lower standards of living and demanded governments take action to protect them.

Several alternatives emerged to the nineteenth century economic liberal state that limited economic and political participation by the majority of its citizens (Cox, 1987, pp. 164–209). During the First World War, a major challenger emerged in the form of Communism. Taking advantage of Russia's disastrous performance in the War, the Bolsheviks were able to seize power in Russia. They began a process of seizing the means of production (factories, farms) and turning them into state-run economic enterprises. Russia became a command economy where products were produced according to a series of government plans which set targets and dictated what should be produced. The free market of supply and demand was extinguished. The communist form of organization was popular among many of the workers who had been excluded from the benefits of capitalist production. Later in the century, communism was taken up by many peasant based societies in the developing world such as China, Vietnam and Cuba.

A second alternative to the liberal system was Fascism. Fascism came to power after 1930 when the market system was in crisis (Polanyi, 1957, pp. 237–48). The Fascist solution to the difficulties of re-establishing liberal economies was to keep a market economy, but to eliminate all democratic institutions in the industrial and political realms. Fascist strongmen offered their services to conservative forces threatened by the rise of socialism and communism. Capitalists were protected from leftists in the parliament and in the streets in return for handing the political realm over to Fascist parties. This appeal was particularly powerful in states such as Germany and Italy where Fascism used unsolved national issues to gain power.

Because of the horror of war and genocide unleashed by Fascism in the 1930s and 1940s, it is possible to overlook just how successful Nazism was in dealing with economic challenges. Contrary to liberal prescriptions, the Nazis instituted strict exchange controls and signed bilateral trading arrangements to create a restricted trading zone. Also contrary to liberal opinion at the time, the Nazis undertook massive spending on public works and armaments. Between and 1933 and 1938 they were able to send an estimated 6–7 million Germans back to work, virtually eliminating unemployment. To most Germans this appeared to be a vast improvement upon the economic chaos of the 1920s.

Finally, in the liberal states themselves, governments were pushed towards taking a greater role in the economy and responsibility for the economic welfare of their citizens. Both the United States and Britain experimented with what would later be called Keynesian policies. These were policies advocated by the British economist John Maynard Keynes (1936). Keynes suggested that when businesses lost confidence in the economy and refused to invest, governments should spend money to ensure economic growth. After 1933 the US took some steps in this direction by expanding credit, increasing payments to the unemployed and raising public investment through Roosevelt's New Deal policies. The British cheapened credit and protected their home market, but did not engage in large public works. The real success of the Keynesian policy would not come until the allied countries inflated their economies by preparing for war in the late 1930s and early 1940s.

US role. The United States played a critical role in the establishment of the international financial system and its unravelling in the 1930s. Within the United States the financial community argued strongly for US financial leadership in international affairs, the reconstruction of Europe, free trade and the League of Nations (Frieden, 1987). They helped found professional schools such as Columbia's School of International Affairs and Princeton's Woodrow Wilson School. Bankers took the lead in institutions such as the Carnegie Endowment for International Peace and the Council of Foreign Relations, as well as the new journal *Foreign Affairs*. All of this was done to help spread the message that the United States needed an activist foreign policy.

Internationalist forces, led by the financial community, had some success in extending finance to Europe in the 1920s. However, they suffered a series of defeats on issues such as the League of Nations, freer trade and the cancelling of war debts. A coalition of manufacturers, some trade-sensitive agricultural interests and the isolationist Republican Party proved too strong. The internationalism of the banking community was out of step with most Americans who were repelled by the European war and entanglement. When the international financial crisis struck in the early 1930s the United States raised its trade barriers even further in the Smoot-Hawley Tariff of 1930. This worsened the economy within the US and in other countries. Rather than showing leadership by leading coordinated action against the Depression, the US retreated within its own borders. This economic isolationism was matched by political isolationism.

Some international relations theorists have been so influenced by the contrasting role of Britain and the United States in the nineteenth and early twentieth centuries that they developed a theory of international stability from these cases (Krasner, 1976). The theory is called hegemonic stability theory. It suggests that a superpower or hegemonic power is required for the maintenance of an international liberal economic system. Economic openness is most likely to occur when a hegemonic state is in the ascendancy and the system is likely to become less liberal as that state's power decreases relative to other states (Krasner, 1976). Advocates of this view point to the fact that the liberal economic system of the mid-nineteenth century was backed by British financial and military might. During the inter-war years, Britain no longer exercized the same degree of dominance and the United States was unwilling to commit itself to system maintenance. While the US had the power, it lacked the will. The result was a slide to rival economic areas and eventually war. Following the Second World War the United States took up the role of hegemonic power and created a liberal international economic system.

Surveying the wreckage of the inter-war years, allied planners of the post-1945 era drew five lessons:

- International financial chaos played a key role in facilitating the rise of Fascism in Germany leading to a breakdown in the international system. Some mechanism would be needed to maintain a stable international monetary system and to facilitate the flow of liquidity. This view led to the creation of the International Monetary Fund, the World Bank, and the Marshall Plan.
- An economic system divided into competing regions could prove dangerous. Some effort would need to be made to liberalize trade between

states. After a failed attempt at creating an International Trade Organization (ITO) the response was the establishment of a multilateral trading system in the form of the General Agreement on Tariffs and Trade (GATT).

- The power of the masses and workers would need to be accommodated in some form or another. Leftist political forces could only be blunted if some of the concerns of their constituents were taken into account. The answer to this problem was the Keynesian state which redistributed income to the broad population.
- These economic arrangements would require more robust security arrangements than had existed under the League of Nations. States would need to be prepared to fight at an early stage in order to prevent a larger war at a later date. The post-1945 period saw the emergence of the Cold War, a series of military alliances such as NATO and reliance upon nuclear weapons to prevent wars between the superpowers.
- The above four points could only be implemented if the US played a more active international role than it had in the 1920s and 30s. Contrary to the inter-war period, the internationalists won the battle within the US and it assumed a role as major international power and leader of the western bloc. Indeed the period from the mid twentieth until the mid twenty-first century may well be remembered as the American Century.

The post-1945 order

This section outlines the post-1945 political economy. During this era US economic, political, military and cultural power has expanded beyond that of any other state. The United States stood astride the post-war world in a position of dominance unrivalled in the modern world. US firms dominated world production, technological growth, and US financiers controlled international finance. In the early years of the twenty-first century, although American power relative to other states is much less than the superiority it achieved at the height of its pre-eminence, it still remains significantly the most powerful state in the world.

The themes of this era that we will be examining are: growth in US power and dominance of a Western liberal economic order; decolonization and the struggle for development; transformation of the role of the state; the rise of international organizations; and the information technology revolution. Many of the issues we raise in this chapter will be examined in much more detail when we move into an analysis of key frameworks of the global economy in Part II of the book.

It is common to refer to the Cold War system of 1945–1989 as being composed of three worlds. The First World contained the US and its allies in Western Europe, Canada, Australia, New Zealand and later Japan. The Second World was composed of the communist states of Eastern Europe and the Soviet Union. The Third World was the term used for the rest of the world's states which were occupied with the process of development. Some countries such as China might fall into two camps – the Second and Third Worlds. The next two sections examine the relationship between these three worlds.

The US and the Western economic system

In retrospect we can see the US transition from superpower to hyperpower or sole primary power as developing in a series of steps. The confrontation with the Soviet Union required a military shield to protect the US and its allies. Western states were then bound together by a series of economic institutions which facilitated integration and cooperation. Finally, with the end of the Cold War, the US and other states have been adjusting themselves to a new distribution of power.

Cold War confrontation. The wartime alliance between the Western Allies and the Soviet Union was already under strain as Germany and Japan were in the process of being defeated. Indeed, it had always been a temporary alliance subject to rivalry and tension (Thorne, 1978). Following the war, Europe was divided between the two camps and a lukewarm alliance turned into a cold war. The Soviet Union placed friendly regimes in power in Eastern Europe and the United States led Western states in the creation of economic and military alliances against the Soviet Union.

The US pledged both economic and military resources to the confrontation with the Soviet Union. In the economic realm, US funds helped with the reconstruction of Western Europe, and Japan. In military affairs, the US stationed troops in foreign countries and agreed to the creation of a Western military alliance – the North Atlantic Treaty Organization (NATO). At the heart of NATO was the threat that the US would use nuclear weapons to deter Soviet aggression in Europe. Canada and the US stationed troops in Europe so that any Soviet invasion would force a united defence. Once the Soviet Union also developed nuclear weapons, a balance of terror called MAD (Mutual Assured Destruction) froze confrontation in Europe and made the prospect of direct conflict between the USSR and the US daunting (Freedman, 1985). Colonial powers France and Britain maintained the ability to intervene around the world and also developed nuclear weapons.

One of the effects of a relatively stable confrontation between the Soviet Union and the US was that conflict between the superpowers was played out in other parts of the world for example, when the United States supplied arms to Israel, Saudi Arabia and Iran (before the revolution of 1979) the USSR supplied Syria, Iraq and Egypt. The Soviet Union supplied arms to the Vietnamese in their struggle against the US and the Americans funded Afghan Islamic guerrillas against the Soviet Union. In Southern Africa, the United States supported the racist government of South Africa which was engaged in fighting Cuban-backed forces in Angola. In Central America the US backed right-wing governments against left-wing insurgent movements. The US and the Soviet Union became involved in a series of national revolutions and wars of independence, greatly exacerbating local conflicts (Halliday, 1983).

The impact of this global competition varied across countries. Some East Asian states benefited from US attention and aid. For example, Japan, South Korea and Taiwan were able to use US investment and the security umbrella to develop their economies (Stubbs, 1999). However, in many other countries, Cold War rivalry fed the flames of local conflicts, contributing to escalating violence and increasing poverty. Southern Africa, Central America, and Indo-china bore the brunt of Cold War conflict between the US and the USSR. In addition, authoritarian regimes of the left and right were able to maintain power to the detriment of their population due to sponsorship of one or the other of the superpowers. These proxy wars and other violent conflict led to death, destruction, devastation and famine for millions of poor people while maintaining the semblance of a peaceful world in Western countries.

Post-Cold War security. The demise of the Soviet Union and end of the Cold War in 1989 had a major impact upon the global political economy. In security terms the end of Soviet–US rivalry changed the face of global conflict. Some regional confrontations were moderated by the ending of superpower confrontation and UN peacekeeping was bolstered. Some parts of the world saw new conflicts emerge as Soviet power retreated (former Yugoslavia) while other parts of the world were ignored as their societies teetered on civil war (Rwanda). Conflict was much more likely to have an ethnic dimension and take place within or across states than between the professional armies of established states (Kaldor, 1997).

In economic terms new parts of the world were opened to capitalist activity as the post-Soviet states entered a period of transition to new economic and political systems. Along with China's opening to foreign investment that dated back to the late 1970s, this meant that nearly the whole world was once again actively seeking economic ties with foreigners. This offered considerable opportunities for investors, but raised some concern in developing states that badly needed investment and trade would be diverted from developing states to Eastern Europe and Russia.

In the realm of ideology it appeared for a time that the end of the Cold War had ended the battle of conflicting ideas about how society should be organized. Capitalism had triumphed over communism. Fukuyama (1992) suggested that history had ended in the sense that there would be no new models for society, only people converging upon the liberal democratic ideal. Such a view soon gave way to new debates and a resumption of ideological struggle. In the US, some analysts (Huntington, 1993) raised the threat of conflict between civilizations as the successor to the Cold War. By the end of the decade, the triumph of liberal capitalism was also being resisted by citizen groups from environmental, feminist and labour fields advocating more equity-based arrangements.

Heading into the twenty-first century, some claimed that the era of two superpowers had been replaced by one hyperpower. The US was seen to be a military giant and economic powerhouse that dominated the world. It possessed the armed forces with the longest reach and most devastating arsenal on the planet. The US was also home to the largest number of transnational corporations that exercized tremendous influence in manufacturing, financial, service and high technology industries. In cultural terms the US reached out through music, television, film and sporting events to spread a vision of its way of life around the world.

The view of the US as a hyperpower overstates the American role just as talk of a Pax Britannica overstated Britain's role in the nineteenth century. In Europe, the European Union is busy tying itself into a more social democratic political economy. In Asia, China is preparing for a world leadership role and Japan is attempting to regain its strength. The populous states of India and Brazil can be pressured by the US, but American influence is limited. However, while the US cannot force all other actors to follow its wishes, American participation is needed for effective global governance. As US President George Bush Jr. demonstrated with his refusal to respect the Kyoto Protocol to reduce global warming, an agreement without the US was not much of an agreement.

The simultaneous strength and weakness of US power was illustrated on the 11th September 2001 when four US passenger airplanes were highjacked and aimed at centres of US power. Two planes destroyed the World Trade Centre towers in New York, one hit the Pentagon and one crashed into a field. A transnational network of extremists was able to inflict thousands of civilian casualties on US centres of financial and military power for the first time in its history. The vulnerabilities brought about by sophisticated networks using public technologies against the world's greatest power was shocking to most observers.

US power following the attack was also evident as it mobilized an international coalition in a 'war against terror'. The US was able to use its military forces to topple the Islamic fundamentalist government in Afghanistan which sheltered the al-Qaida network accused of organizing the bombing. The US also applied diplomatic pressure to numerous states to participate in the campaign or provide support for American efforts.

In March and April 2003 the US and Britain launched an invasion of Iraq and toppled its government. They claimed the action was justified as self-defence, but were unable to convince the UN Security Council that Iraq posed an immediate danger. In addition to facing opposition from France, Russia and Germany, the American government was unable to secure the support of trade dependent allies in the Americas such as Chile, Mexico and Canada.

The Anglo-American invasion rekindled memories of nineteenth century imperialism. The US and Britain were able to harness their technological superiority to overwhelm a non-Western state and established an interim American controlled administration. The US government used Iraqi oil revenues to rebuild infrastructure destroyed by the invasion and granted contracts for reconstruction to US and British companies. In addition, American evangelical Christians mobilized to provide aid and convert the locals in another echo of past imperialist practice.

The long-term effect of US invasion and seizure of a country with the second largest oil reserves is unclear. American soldiers face an uncertain period of occupying Iraq and stability in several other Arab regimes is in question. At their most ambitious, some voices in the US government and beyond are calling for a reworking of the Middle East and an aggressive foreign policy to guarantee US dominance for another century. At home, the US military posture is likely to contribute to record budget deficits and stall economic growth. A unilateralist US is likely to increase uncertainty in the global economy.

The Western economic system. The US used its unparalleled economic and military dominance to construct a set of institutions to manage the world economy. The international trade and payments order constructed as World War II drew to a close was in theory a negotiated order with the principal participants, the US and the UK. However, in reality the order was largely shaped by American power and thus reflected American interests. Unlike the economic nationalism of the 1930s this system involved numerous countries. It was based on multilateral principles and rejected bilateralism. The key features of the order were liberalism, legalism, and multilateralism. The new order was based on liberal economic principles but not the laissez-faire liberalism that had characterized the nineteenth century international economic order. In the wake of the political mobilization of the working class and the experiences of the depression, policy makers attempted to balance social welfare concerns with a commitment to market principles. This multilateralism rested upon domestic political economies that were interventionist. There was no automatic adjustment as in the gold standard nor was free trade unrestricted. The goal was to create a system that had liberal attributes, but did not undermine domestic stability. Ruggie (1982) termed this order based on Keynesian principles one of 'embedded liberalism' to denote both the underlying liberal principles and the historic compromise with labour that permitted state intervention to secure domestic interests.

Western states participated in a number of economic institutions designed to free economic exchange. Three international organizations were created to oversee the liberal international economic order. While ostensibly committed to universal membership the International Monetary Fund (IMF), the International Bank for Reconstruction and Development (IBRD), otherwise known as the World Bank, and the General Agreement on Tariffs and Trade (GATT) restricted membership to countries committed to following free-market principles in their domestic economic management. The IMF and IBRD were both created as the war neared its end while the GATT arose in the early post-war years. The IMF and World Bank were designed in 1944 to support a stable monetary system and fund post-war reconstruction. Additional funding to aid reconstruction was provided by the US in the form of the Marshall Plan. The attempt to create an International Trade Organization failed, but the GATT served as a framework for gradually liberalizing trade. Both the IMF and World Bank were created to overcome the persistent economic problems that had arisen in the 1930s.

An important development in the post-war global political economy has been the development of regional economic institutions. The most advanced of these regional organizations arose and matured in Western Europe. Sheltering behind the security umbrella of the US and NATO, European states created the European Economic Community (EEC) through the Treaty of Rome in 1957 to assist with economic integration. This was the continuation of a process of closer cooperation initiated by the European Coal and Steel Community (ECSC) in 1951. The EEC evolved into the European Union (EU) and in the process brought European states much closer to political union. The unprecedented levels of economic cooperation leading to monetary union have not translated into effective harmonization of foreign and security policies, but EU states collectively have emerged as rivals to US dominance in a number of issue areas.

Sheltered by the nuclear umbrella and supported by sympathetic economic institutions, the US, Western Europe and Japan followed policies of economic growth in the post-war era. Government policy redistributed income, supported industry and maintained full employment. The provision of credit and a series of technical innovations facilitated a golden era of economic growth in Western states from the 1950s until the early 1970s. This system then came under strain as inflation from US spending on the Vietnam War and rising oil prices caused inflation and recession.

The struggle for development

As the Soviet Union and the US struggled for advantage in the Cold War, another historic process was taking place. This was the decolonization process and emergence of the 'Third World' as a political and economic actor. The states of the Third World embarked upon a struggle for development that has had, to this day, only limited success.

Decolonization. The post-1945 period saw an impressive process of decolonization as the European empires discussed in Chapters 2–3 crumbled. In some cases, European states recognized the difficulty of continuing to rule foreign countries while in other cases local populations had to wage violent campaigns to force the colonialists to relinquish control.

The French were much more willing than the British to use force to maintain their empire (Chamberlain, 1985, pp. 55–72). France waged long, bloody and ultimately futile wars in Vietnam and Algeria. In Vietnam, nationalists defeated the French at Dien Bien Phu in 1954. The Algerians secured their independence in 1962 after years of fighting. French retreat in sub-Saharan Africa proceeded more peacefully as states were granted independence, but kept close economic and political ties with France.

The US played a complex role in the process of decolonization. It granted the Philippines independence in 1946 and urged its European allies to abandon their empires. During the Suez crisis of 1956 it opposed the British/French/Israeli invasion of Egypt. However, as the Cold War

---

Box 4.1 Decolonization and violence

The effects of violence on the colonizer and the colonized were starkly illustrated by Frantz Fanon in the early 1960s. Writing in the shadow of Algeria's brutal struggle for independence from France, Fanon (1963, p. 94) argued that the use of violence against the colonizer served to cleanse the colonized from years of humiliation and oppression. What Fanon did not anticipate was that once independence was won, it was often difficult for independence leaders to abandon the use of violence in ruling their new countries.

intensified, the US itself became involved in old colonial struggles, such as preventing the reunification of Vietnam.

There are a number of competing explanations for the onset of decolonization. The Second World War was a major factor (Abernethy, 2000, pp. 345–60). For the second time in thirty years European states inflicted huge losses on each other's productive and military capacities. France, Britain and Holland emerged in a greatly weakened condition, much less able to hold on to territory by force. At the same time, Japanese success early in the war against the US and Europeans in Asia revealed the vulnerability of their empires. The war itself had the effect of mobilizing and uprooting millions of people in the colonies. Similar to the European masses after World War I, these people were not willing to return to the pre-war status quo.

Another important explanation is the growth of nationalist movements within the colonies and the increasing economic drain that colonies posed for European states (Darwin, 1988, pp. 17–24). Within countries such as India, Vietnam, and Indonesia educated local leaderships mobilized local populations to change the calculus of empire. Through a variety of means they demonstrated to the European colonizers that the project of empire was no longer sustainable. In the case of India, Gandhi's campaign of nonviolent resistance highlighted the potential ungovernability of South Asia. In the cases of Vietnam, Indonesia and Algeria, wars of independence were required.

The impact of decolonization was dramatic. A large number of new states came into being, shifting the balance in international institutions such as the General Assembly. In some cases new organizations such as the United Nations Conference on Trade and Development (UNCTAD) were created to serve the interest of developing countries. In the 1970s, developing countries pushed for a change in the rules governing the global economy which was called the New International Economic Order. Many of the new states, although formerly independent were highly dependent on their former metropoles for economic ties. In the security field, many of the newly independent states tried to steer a third way in the Cold War between USSR and the US. This initiative was called the Non-Aligned Movement (NAM) and was led by India, Indonesia, Ghana and Yugoslavia in the 1960s and 1970s. Finally, decolonization pushed the question of development onto the international agenda where it continues to be a significant issue.

Development success and failures. The issue of development and growth will be examined in a separate chapter in the second section of the book, but a brief overview is required here. Some states have experienced success in their attempts to develop their economies in the post-1945 period. Japan was able to rebuild its economy after US occupation while the four

Asian Tigers of South Korea, Taiwan, Hong Kong and Singapore achieved incredible progress in terms of growth rates, education levels and advances in particular economic sectors. The rise of these centres of economic power and the oil-producing states in the 1970s was so dramatic that some analysts in the US feared that American dominance or hegemony was in decline (Keohane, 1984; Gilpin, 1987). Some Asian leaders also began to believe that they had developed a political economy superior to the US and began to advance the notion of a distinct and better set of Asian values as the explanation for their success (Zakaria, 1994). Both of these trends were diminished by renewed US growth in the 1990s and the Asian financial crisis of 1997.

In contrast to some Asian success stories, many of the world's most populous states such as China, India, Indonesia, Brazil and most of Africa have suffered a series of setbacks in their pursuit of development. In some cases, such as China, until the reform process embarked upon in the 1970s, disastrous central planning destroyed agricultural and industrial productivity. In other cases such as sub-Saharan Africa, countries were trapped into producing products that declined in value over time (coffee, tin, etc.). Insecurity within and between states led to resources being diverted to fighting other states or internal guerrilla movements. In many instances, the debt crisis of the 1980s halted development projects and forced states into a series of structural adjustment programs that opened and undermined local economies.

State transformation

The function and nature of states at the beginning of the twenty-first century are different from their nature in the middle of the twentieth century. In the 1950s, states in the First World were characterized by Keynesianism or Fordism. They were committed to fostering full employment and cushioning economic turbulence within their borders. In the Second World, Soviet-command economies marshalled resources to feed industrialization and competition with the West. In much of the Third World, developmental states intervened in the economy to protect infant industries and begin the process of industrialization. By the year 2000 most of the centrally planned states had disappeared, while the welfare and developmental states had given way to different versions of the competition state.

From welfare to competition in the North. In advanced industrialized countries considerable concern has been expressed that the nature of the state has changed from providing welfare to its citizens to preparing both citizens and corporations for international competition. The idea of a 'competition state' captures this dynamic.

Cerny (2000) suggests that the transformation of the state's role includes several major policy changes. One change is that rather than supporting particular industries or sectors, states are more likely to ensure that national economies provide a competitive environment. This involves initiatives at the macro- and micro-economic levels. At the macro-level, states put a priority on low inflation to attract investment. At the micro or firm level, steps are taken to increase competition and flexibility. This might include deregulating or privatizing industries or changing labour legislation to permit more flexible (and less secure) employment practices. Finally, governments increasingly shift from maximizing general welfare through policies such as full employment and universal social programs to target programs designed to increase citizens' employability such as training or reducing welfare benefits to encourage work at lower wage levels.

Liberal and authoritarian competition in the South. States outside of the developed world have not been immune from the pressures of the global marketplace. Two developments dating back to the late 1970s and early 1980s have increased economic competition in developing states. One development was the unilateral decision by the government of China that it would begin opening to Western states by seeking trade and foreign direct investment. Although this was a slow process at the beginning, China grew to become the major recipient of foreign direct investment in the 1990s. This diverted investment from other developing countries and resulted in the growth of exports that competed with the products of other developing countries. For example, China, India and Indonesia might all be trying to sell the same product in the US market.

The second development was the debt crisis which forced many states to abandon inward-looking development strategies in search of finding a niche in the global market. Biersteker (1992) refers to developing states turning towards liberal economic policies as 'the triumph of neoclassical economics'. From a different perspective, McMichael (1996) describes the change as the abandonment of a national development project for a globalization project of fitting into the global economy. The crucial point is that this turn toward increased openness and economic competition is taking place under a variety of political frameworks. Communist China is aggressively courting foreign investment and trade, but retains an authoritarian state system which suppresses dissent and independent trade unions. In the 1970s Chile began its liberalization under the right-wing authoritarian rule of Augusto Pinochet. However, the 1990s also saw a number of Southern states which democratized (South Korea, South Africa, Brazil,

Mexico) and continued the pursuit of a policy of insertion into the global economy.

The rise of offshore. Another striking development in the state system was the growth of offshore regulation. The term 'offshore' refers to areas of the global economy where states create territorial or juridical enclaves characterized by a reduction in regulation (Palan, 1998, p. 626). One of the most significant developments in the offshore world has been the growth of tax havens. Tax havens are usually located in small states such as the Cayman Islands. They allow companies and banks to move large sums of money through paper companies to avoid taxation and regulation. Some estimate that half of the world's money resides in or passes through tax havens (Palan, 2002, p. 151).

Similar offshore developments can be seen in other economic sectors. Different forms of regulation have been applied to specific territories within states to foster investment and economic growth. For example, China has created special economic zones to attract foreign direct investment. Many developing and developed states have created export processing zones or tax-free zones. In developed states these zones are likely to be in depressed areas desperate for economic growth such as inner cities. What all of these areas share is that a different type of economic regulation is applied to these geographic spaces than in the rest of the economy. In some cases the zones may give companies tax holidays for a number of years in return for investment. In other cases, the main attraction may be the prohibition of independent trade unions from production in the zones.

The rise of offshore provides some business actors with increased economic flexibility to increase profits by reducing the costs of complying with regulation. Some states have benefited from offshore because it has allowed them to attract investment to their territory. However, other states have lost investment and the ability to tax or regulate in the public interest.

International organizations and governance

A striking feature of the global political economy has been the rise in international organizations in the second half of the twentieth century. The number of international organizations has grown, and so has their importance in organizing the global economy. In this section we'll briefly examine three sets of organizations – the UN, international economic organizations, corporate and civic associations.

The UN. The United Nations was created in 1945 as a successor to the League of Nations. There are two elements that have particular significance for the global political economy. The first is the Security Council and the second are the UN's specialized agencies. The UN's Security Council is composed of five permanent members and ten rotating members who are elected for two-year terms. The Security Council can make international law, compelling states to respond to its wishes. The permanent members each have a veto over proposals before the Security Council. The Security Council does not usually address strictly economic affairs, but it does influence the security structure and can authorize the employment of economic sanctions against states. Since the end of the Cold-War rivalry between the United States and the Soviet Union, the Security Council has taken a more active role in peacekeeping and monitoring elections (Weiss *et al.*, 2001, pp. 65–110).

The United Nations contains a host of specialized agencies designed to promote cooperation and address particular issues. The World Health Organization (WHO) attempts to improve global public health, United Nations Children's Fund (UNICEF) concentrates on improving the welfare of children and the United Nations High Commissioner for Refugees (UNHCR) provides assistance to refugees. In general these agencies attempt to cope with the casualties of the global political economy. While doing excellent work they have relatively less power to influence overall economic structures than international economic institutions.

International economic organizations. The multilateral framework created after World War II has proved remarkably resilient in the half century plus since it was constructed. Because a number of chapters in Part 2 explore the role of these organizations in the context of money, trade, and development, we will only provide a brief review of the continued relevance of the multilateral framework at this point. Three themes have dominated the post-war multilateral framework – adaptation, challenge and expansion. International economic institutions have taken on increased significance in world affairs, especially since the 1980s. These institutions influence behaviour by providing advice on economic policy, demanding policy change in return for financing or settling economic disputes between actors.

In the wake of the debt crisis in the 1980s, the IMF and the World Bank have taken on enlarged roles in the global economy. Their financial assistance and policy advice have been critical in dealing with states in financial crisis. In return for assistance the institutions have demanded that states adopt structural adjustment policies by liberalizing their economies and opening up to trade and foreign investment.

In the trade area, the World Trade Organization (WTO) was created in 1995. The WTO is a significant change from the GATT because it provides the trade regime with a permanent institution, opens up new areas of economic activity (e.g. services) to liberalization, and provides a strong dispute settlement mechanism. This last feature means that states are much more likely to be bound by trade rules after the creation of the WTO than before.

How do we explain the longevity of these institutions? For most of this period these organizations have enjoyed the support of the leading states within the global economy. Successive US administrations, EU countries, and Japan may at times push specific agendas that weaken one or other of these regimes but they have consistently provided support for a renewed and reinvigorated multilateralism. In other words, the post-war consensus concerning the necessity for an open, multilateral economic system has not been eroded despite shifts in economic policy. The close fit between knowledge and power has remained undisturbed in this period. The increased influence of these institutions has sparked a debate concerning their relevance and legitimacy with many civil society groups claiming that they are too powerful.

The IMF, World Bank and WTO are the most visible international economic institutions, but there are many others. The G-8 brings together the seven most advanced industrialized economies and Russia to discuss economic management of the global economy. The Group of 20 (G-20) focuses on financial issues such as financial stability. It includes the G-8 plus a number of prominent developing countries. The Bank for International Settlements (BIS) located in Geneva is the forum for central bankers. The Organisation for Economic Co-operation and Development (OECD) is an advisory organization that brings together the industrialized countries of the world. Alongside these organizations can be added the numerous regional groupings such as the European Union, North American Free Trade Agreement (NAFTA) and Asia–Pacific Economic Cooperation (APEC).

The multiplication of interstate organizations means that states, corporations and citizens are increasingly governed through international organizations. In some cases the impact is slight. For example, the OECD might publish a report urging a particular economy to spend more money on training. In other cases the impact is greater. For example, the IMF may demand that a country cut the amount it spends in its budget before giving desperately needed loans. Alternatively, the WTO might rule a domestic environmental regulation violates trade law and must be modified.

Corporate and civic associations. Both the for-profit and not-for-profit sectors have also been busy expanding their international contacts and forming international or transnational organizations. Boli and Thomas estimate that almost 60 per cent of international non-governmental organizations (NGOs) are concentrated in the economic or scientific fields (Boli and Thomas, 1999, p. 41). NGOs have been particularly active in international development. Although most publicity is given to the advocacy role of many of these organizations as they lobby governments and international organizations, NGOs have become increasingly important in the implementation of development projects (Sklias, 1999). In the 1980s Western governments increasingly used development NGOs as a channel for the provision of economic aid (Gordenker and Weiss, 1999, p. 25). Not-for-profit citizens organizations have also increased their international presence, and have created transnational advocacy networks to lobby transnational corporations, multilateral economic institutions and the governments of nation-states (Keck and Sikkink, 1998). This activity has been enhanced by the revolution in communications which enables activists to build networks at relative low costs. The anti-globalization protests at meetings of the WTO, World Bank, IMF, and G-8 summits provide evidence of non-state actors attempting to influence international economic policy-making. NGOs and citizen groups have thus become important as actors in the normative and material structures of the global political economy.

In some areas where states have not set up appropriate regulatory frameworks, industries have formed their own associations and brought in rules or norms. For example in the area of environmental standards, leading transnational companies have established the ISO 14000 set of regulations (Clapp 1998). The role of industry associations in the construction and maintenance of global governance structures is becoming increasingly visible. While industry associations have long played a part at the domestic level in influencing national legislation, as the appropriate levels of decision-making move beyond the state so national and transnational industry bodies have sought to influence global policy-making (Sell, 2000; Smythe, 2000).

The information revolution

In Chapter 3 we examined the advent of the industrial revolution and how this changed the course of history. The last decades of the twentieth century have witnessed another dramatic technological revolution. This time it is based upon information rather than machine power. Some have suggested that we are experiencing the third great wave of human progress (Toffler, 1980). The first wave was the agricultural revolution and the second was the industrial revolution. We are too close to the beginning of the information revolution to determine its final form and implications, but some initial points can be developed.

Technological. Most readers of this text will be familiar with the information revolution because it has become an everyday part of their lives.

Western university students may not be able to imagine a world without personal computers, cellular phones and the internet. Yet, these communication and information technologies only began their diffusion in the 1970s with the invention of the microprocessor (computer chip). In 1977 the first personal computer was introduced by Apple and user friendly software was soon marketed by Microsoft.

Since the mid-1970s the application of information and knowledge to innovation and production has accelerated technological change. Computers have become smaller and more powerful. The Internet has broadened the number of people exchanging information, products and entertainment. Digital technology has allowed for improved communications through voice (phones, radio) and visual devices (television, film).

Economic. The economic impacts of the information revolution are still working their way through the global political economy. Information technology has certainly facilitated the globalization of economic activity. For example, financial transactions such as foreign exchange or the purchase or sale of stocks and bonds can take place 24 hours a day almost instantaneously. Improved communication between different parts of corporations allows for production to be dispersed across a wide geographical area.

The information revolution offers the prospects of increasing productivity as information and computers are applied to the production process. New economic sectors are being created with the advent of new forms of consumer electronics, medicine and agriculture. The ability to map and track genes holds out the possibility of new medical cures for diseases. Genetic manipulation has led to the creation of genetically modified crops which are more productive and more resistant to disease and insects. However, the advent of these technologies has also brought about ethical and political controversies. Concerns have been raised about the ethical implications of human cloning or using genetic tests to select designer babies. In food production, popular fears have been expressed at the dangers of genetic modification of foods and plants.

In some cases new technology may allow some countries to leapfrog development stages. For example, cellular phones allow developing countries to create a telephone network without the cost of laying cables. Despite such optimism, concerns have been expressed about the digital divide (Norris, 2001). Advanced industrialized societies are rapidly diffusing the technology among their citizens, but many developing countries face the prospect of being left even further behind. While a country such as Canada may be worrying about how they can bring the internet to rural populations, some countries in Africa are still struggling to provide electricity or safe drinking water. The danger is that rather than allowing disadvantaged groups to catch up with developed countries, the gaps grow wider.

Table 4.1   *Decline in value of selective high technology stocks 2000–2003*

	10 March 2000	7 March 2003
Yahoo Inc	$178.06	$19.62
Intel	$120.19	$16.01
Nortel Networks	$180.5*	$ 3.20
724 Solutions	$304.90*	$ 0.55

*Canadian Dollars

Source: Data from *Globe and Mail* 10 March 2003, B10.

The enthusiasm for the information revolution created a bubble in the stock market in the late 1990s. Investors poured money into a wide range of information technology firms, inflating the stock market and creating instant paper fortunes for some entrepreneurs. Like all bubbles, this one burst leaving a wreckage of sour investors and broken companies (Table 4.1). The revolution continues, but with a more realistic appraisal of the time it will take for changes to work their way through the economy.

Social. Manuel Castells (1996) has suggested that the advent of the information revolution is having profound effects on social life. He argues that new forms of communication allow people to organize themselves through networks rather than hierarchies. In the network society, people build direct links with each other rather than working through institutions that have layers of authority. For example, people concerned about the environment may form a small environmental group rather than work through a political party. Companies may opt for flexible work teams rather a workforce divided into rigid roles and tasks. Universities might turn to distance learning rather than gather students in a classroom.

The advent of the internet and e-mail has certainly provided the tools for groups of people to form networks around the world in order to advance their views about how society should be ordered. Citizen associations in the fields of environment, women's issues, peace campaigners, development advocates and labour groups have used the new technology to share information and mobilize support.

Military. The information age is also thought to be creating a revolution in warfare (Cohen, 1996). The US has harnessed information technology to bolster its surveillance and attack capabilities. The American military is better able to identify targets and strike them from a distance than any of its opponents. The advantage might be compared to European use of cannon or repeating rifles against locals in the wars of empire in the nineteenth century. US success in the Persian Gulf wars of 1991 and 2003 as well as Afghanistan in 2001–2 indicates that a combination of new technologies and new tactics has made American military power much more effective. It is not invulnerable, but the US certainly has an edge over any possible contender.

Conclusion

The key frameworks of the post-1945 era will be dealt with in more detail in part 2 of this book. For now we will provide an overview of their evolution and contrast them with the historical eras examined in Chapters 2 and 3.

The post-1945 era saw an increase in both the volume and type of *trade*. Trade liberalization took place under a series of negotiating rounds of the GATT. Tariffs were gradually reduced and in the 1970s an effort was made to address non-tariff barriers to trade. In 1995 the creation of the WTO marked the next step in trade as countries began to liberalize trade in services and agriculture, as well as agreeing to submit their disputes to a binding dispute-settlement mechanism. Alongside these multilateral trade initiatives a series of regional agreements were created to facilitate the movement of goods and services among neighbouring countries. The most significant of these were in Europe (European Union), North America (NAFTA), South America (MERCOSUR) and South-east Asia (ASEAN). As trade agreements intruded more directly upon national political economies, trade initiatives became the subject of extensive national and international debate. Concern has been expressed about their economic, environmental and social impacts. Unlike earlier eras, trade and investment take place under an elaborate system of rules and formal international organizations.

The most visible development in the area of *production* has been the growth of transnational corporations. TNCs account for the majority of the global production structure and 50 per cent of world trade. In 1998, 53 000 TNCs with 450 000 foreign subsidiaries had total sales of $9.5 trillion. The largest TNCs have annual sales greater than the GDP of most countries. This results in the investment decisions of TNCs having great impacts upon the economic fortunes of particular states. The influence of these corporations has led to suggestions that the state is losing power to economic actors and that democracy is threatened by their growing power. Since most large TNCs originate in and invest in developed states, the problem of development continues to plague many countries.

Another significant trend has been the increasing importance of East and

South-east Asia as a site for international production. The development of the four tigers has been followed by the industrialization of the coastal Chinese mainland. China's government created special economic zones to lure foreign investment and build its export base. If it can maintain its political integrity and manage the inequalities brought about by industrialization, China has the potential to become a leading international power. Indeed, some analysts suggest that after a two-hundred-year interlude the centre of economic gravity is once again returning to China.

The years since the Second World War have seen a shift from an international to a more global division of *labour*. The concept of a global division of labour captures a form of organization which reaches around the planet, but where work is not confined to particular states. In a global division of labour you find activities that in the past might have been thought of as being confined to particular states existing in very different types of states. Labour that one might associate with a developing country flourishes in a developed state and jobs thought to be the preserve of advanced industrialized countries exist alongside very labour-intensive jobs in developing states. For example, an expanding computer software industry develops in India alongside the majority of the population that lives in subsistence agriculture. The distinctive feature of these jobs is that they are plugged into a transnational production process and that they are not confined to particular parts of the globe, although they may be more concentrated in some areas rather than others.

The *financial* field has witnessed a transition from the immediate post-war period where markets were restricted and government actors played a large role to today's global system where capital is extremely mobile and private firms take the lead role. The international monetary system has moved from a system of fixed exchange rates to a system of fluctuating rates. Thus, we have a system of capital mobility and floating exchange rates, but the currencies are not tied to an accepted commodity such as gold. The openness of the global financial field is not unprecedented, but its particular form has not been seen before. Information technologies allow for a much more rapid movement of funds across state boundaries while the flow of news sends markets moving on the latest current events. Financial crisis in one country can spill over into neighbouring countries and around the globe in a matter of days.

Development has become a significant issue in the post-1945 era with the process of decolonization. Although a large number of countries gained their independence in the post-war period, the struggle for development has been much more difficult. With the exception of some countries in East and South-east Asia, much of the world continues to lose ground relative to advanced industrialized countries. After a period of state-led development in the 1950s, 60s and 70s, developing countries are much more dependent upon private capital flows for investment. Some countries still struggle to industrialize while others attempt to make the jump from newly industrializing countries to advanced industrialized countries.

Environmental degradation became a large issue in the latter part of the twentieth century. One of the consequences of European, North American, Japanese and Soviet industrialization programmes has been the poisoning of the natural environment. Issues such as global warming have become prominent. The proposed solutions, such as the Kyoto Protocol have sparked heated debate within developed states and between developed and developing states. In the developing world poverty has led to economic practices which contribute to deforestation and pollution.

There are several *governance* developments that set this era apart from its predecessors. One element has been the proliferation of formal international organizations dedicated to coordinating policy on a wide range of issues. Institutions such as the IMF, World Bank and WTO exercise considerable influence over policy formation in the areas of trade, finance and development.

A second feature has been the democratization of state institutions. Greater public influence over decision makers (compared to previous eras), complicates foreign economic and diplomatic policies. Economic issues such as NAFTA and the operation of the WTO have become issues for debate in many states. This indicates that global structures of governance increasingly need to be rooted in the politics of democratic states. The automatic adjustment of the gold standard era governance is no longer possible.

A third feature has been the transition from a bipolar world in which two great military powers threatened each other (USSR and US) to an environment where there is only one military superpower – the US. The US continues to build its military advantage by applying technological innovation to its armed forces. Increasingly, the developed world is characterized as a zone of peace (with the exception of occasional terror attacks) while much of the developing world lives with the prospect of interstate or civil war.

In the realm of *ideas*, the post-1945 era has seen a prolonged struggle over the superior method of organizing domestic political economies. In Western states Kenysian welfare states dominated. Central planning in the Soviet model offered an alternative vision of society until the end of the Cold War in 1989. Although the capitalist system emerged triumphant in 1989, vigorous debates continue about what form of capitalism is appropriate for any particular economy. Usually the liberal Anglo-American systems are contrasted against more welfare-centred European arrangements or Asia corporatist practices which integrate business, government and subordinate labour organizations.

Another significant development in thinking has been the rise of the concept of globalization. Over the last quarter of the twentieth century the term 'global' was increasingly used to describe a range of activities in the cultural, economic and political realms. 'Global' seemed to capture the growth in volume and speed of activities across state borders. As the use of the word 'global' proliferated, so did the different ways in which people used the term. It has been used by different people to mean international-ization, liberalization, universalization, westernization, and deterritorial-ization.

Only the last of these concepts, deterritorialization adequately captures what is new about globalization. Similarly to Scholte (2000a) we view globalization as a process of relative deterritorialization. This means that territorial location becomes less important to a particular activity. It con-cerns the growth of supraterritorial relations between people. These rela-tions can be found in engagement and response to mass media (that is, pressure for humanitarian intervention following a CNN broadcast), developed through economic structures (global production and finance) or aroused in response to shifting centres of authority. These relations do not eliminate the importance of the state or replace important local social rela-tions. However, they do add another layer to some people's social, eco-nomic and political lives. Globalization is an uneven process whereby the barriers of time and space are reduced, new social relations between distant people are fostered and new centres of authority are created.

Finally, a noteworthy development has been the acceptance, as least in rhetoric, of basic universal human rights. This is in contrast to earlier eras where legal discrimination based on race was seen as legitimate. The norm of human rights puts pressure on states and corporations to adhere to an ideal and improve their practices.

The second section of the book examines these frameworks and prac-tices in more detail.

Part II

Dynamics

Chapter 5

International Trade

Trade across borders seems to inflame passions and create controversies that are absent in discussions of trade within countries. Early chapters of this book demonstrated the importance of trade in the evolution of the contemporary global economic system, and this chapter will not repeat those arguments. Instead it will provide an introduction to understanding the political economy of the global trading system. One striking feature of the contemporary international trading system arises from the conflict between the continuing political importance of the national border and its declining economic relevance. Political conflicts over trade exist simultaneously with the growth of transnational production (see Chapter 6) wherein production by firms is less restricted by national frontiers than at any time in history.

This chapter provides an introduction to international trade through an examination of the material and normative structures that constitute the international trading system. It begins with a brief definition of certain key terms, and an introduction to the importance of the means of exchange. In the theoretical perspectives section we discuss some of the more important theoretical disputes and examine empirical claims made by various proponents in key debates concerning the evolution and impact of trade. The third section examines the major developments in the post-war international trading system. These include the tremendous expansion in trade, the development of new forms of protectionism, and the emergence and development of the regulation of trade through first, the General Agreement on Tariffs and Trade (GATT) and latterly, the World Trade Organization (WTO). The key issues considered in this chapter are the special needs of developing countries, the growth of regionalism, and the debate over the legitimacy of the trading system.

Definitions

Simply speaking, trade refers to the exchange of one commodity for another. Whenever two or more individuals exchange goods and services they are engaged in trade. We can thus see that trade has been a feature of all civilizations. Trade as an activity takes place domestically when two or more individuals exchange goods and services. International trade arises when the exchange is conducted across national borders. In any discussion of international trade, two issues are of importance. These issues are the existence of barriers or restrictions to trade, and the medium of exchange in which trade is conducted. There are a number of different kinds of barriers to trade and we will be concerned here with political barriers rather than technical barriers such as travel and distance. Political barriers to trade are erected wherever different political authorities decide to prohibit or restrict their citizens' access to foreign goods and services. In other words, for a variety of reasons the goods and services from one political region may be prohibited from entering, or leaving for, another region; or they may be made more costly for citizens of a country in comparison with similar domestic goods and services. Within the global political economy, therefore, the national border has added significance in so far as different national authorities may attempt to control the activities of their citizens in making transactions across borders. Protectionism refers to policies designed to restrict the import of goods and services. In recent history discussions of protectionism have referred to national forms of protection, but this need not be the case. For example, until Federation in 1901, the Australian colonies had systems of protection against imports from each other. Protection can take many forms, the most common of which are tariffs, quotas, subsidies, currency controls, administrative regulations, and voluntary export restraints.

A tariff refers to the application of a duty (denominated in monetary terms) against goods and services from a foreign supplier: in other words, a tax on the price of imports which raises their price to consumers (see Table 5.1 for selected industrial tariffs). The effect of a tariff is to reduce profits in the export market, but this loss can be outweighed by gains in the domestic market. Quotas refer to the application of a quantitative restriction against goods and services from another country or region, as well as health and safety requirements. That is, quotas are specific limits on the quantity of imports or on their value. Subsidies are made to particular industries to help them to be competitive on the international market. Examples of subsidies include depreciation allowances, cash grants and tax holidays. Currency controls limit the availability of foreign currency for the purchase of foreign goods. Administrative regulations include bureaucratic procedures, systems of advance payment, minimal domestic content rules, special marketing standards and health and safety provisions. Voluntary export restraints refer to the situation whereby one country agrees to limit its exports to a third country (or countries). This agreement is usually made because the importing country (countries) threatens to place barriers against the goods of the exporting country.

Table 5.1 *Tariff rates on industrial products for selected WTO members*

(Average applied rate)

Import markets	Level (%)	Year
North America		
Canada	4.4	2000
United States	4.1	2000
Latin America		
Argentina	13.4	2000
Chile	9	2000
Colombia	11.2	2000
Costa Rica	4.7	2000
Mexico	15.6	2000
Peru	13	1998
Western Europe		
European Union	4.5	2000
Iceland	2.5	1998
Norway	3.3	1998
Switzerland	2.3	2000
Turkey	8	1999
Central and Eastern Europe		
Czech Republic	4.8	1998
Hungary	7.4	2001
Slovak Republic	4.4	2000
Asia		
Australia	4.7	2001
Hong Kong, China	0	2001
Japan	3.9	2000
Korea, Republic of	7.5	2000
Macao, China	0	1997
Philippines	6.7	2001
Singapore	0	2000
Africa		
Cameroon	17.6	1999
Chad	17.6	1999
Gabon	17.6	1999

Source: Data from WTO (2002) p. 32.

When two or more parties decide to engage in trade they have to agree on a medium of exchange. There are essentially two means of facilitating exchange – barter and money. As described in Chapter 2, under a barter system a direct exchange of commodities takes place. For example, person A swaps cows for goats with person B. When trade becomes more complex either through the number of traders involved or because of the range of commodities traded money tends to replace barter as the most efficient means of exchange. Money need not take the form we know today: historically many commodities, including cowrie shells, and gold have played the role of money, that is, a store of value and a means of exchange. In Chapter 8 we will consider how different international monetary systems facilitate or hinder international economic activity such as trade.

Theoretical perspectives: free trade and protectionism

Is trade beneficial or harmful? Should traders be free to move goods and services across national frontiers? And if trade is to be subject to restrictions, what kinds of barriers should be imposed and for what reasons? These questions have confronted policy-makers, citizens, business people and scholars for centuries. And in the era of globalization these questions take on an increased relevance.

Within the contemporary global economy international trade touches many societies and communities through direct and indirect effects. It reaches into our homes, places of work and recreational venues. Depending on where we live and how deeply our society is integrated into the global economy we can find daily reminders of the importance of international trade through the consumption patterns of our families and friends. At its simplest level the food we eat and the clothes we wear provide evidence of the tremendous importance of trade across national frontiers. But despite the importance of international trade there is no consensus concerning the costs and benefits to countries from engaging in the pursuit of trade. Perhaps we should say that conflicting views exist because of the salience of trade! Given the conflicting values and interests in this structure of the global political economy it is not surprising to discover the absence of agreement on the answers to these questions.

We will now explore contrasting perspectives on the costs and benefits of international trade beginning with arguments that emphasize the benefits of trade before moving on to examine perspectives critical of trade. Liberal political economy emphasizes the benefits of trade. For liberals, free trade benefits everyone, increases efficiency and raises productivity. In sharp contrast, nationalist and radical critics argue that free trade can undermine national economies, create uneven development, and damage the environment.

Within academic and policy contexts, liberal trade theory provides the framework for the analysis of international trade. This is a sophisticated and substantial body of work which has emerged since its tentative origins in the nineteenth century. Liberal trade theory appears counter-intuitive since it propounds a positive-sum view of something that most people perceive as being zero-sum. A common sense view of transactions sees one side as gaining while the other one loses. Many people are sceptical of the notion that both sides to a transaction can make a profit. The liberal case for free trade, that is, a situation in which all can gain, is based on the theory of comparative advantage. According to the theory of comparative advantage countries should specialize and produce goods and services for which they possess a comparative advantage.

The theory of comparative advantage thus lies at the centre of neoclassical trade theory. Prior to the development of the theory of comparative advantage (or comparative costs, as it is sometimes known) by the British political economist David Ricardo in the nineteenth century, the dominant approach to trade focused on absolute advantage. Mercantilist theories argued that the aim of a country was to increase its trade relative to that of its rivals thus increasing its wealth. For mercantilists, trade was a zero-sum game with one country's gain equivalent to a loss sustained by its trading partner. Since mercantilists believed there was a fixed amount of gold in the world it therefore followed that a country with a trade surplus received more gold and hence an increase in its wealth. Adam Smith had provided an answer to mercantilist theorists with his concept of absolute advantage. Smith argued that two countries can benefit from trade if they specialized in the goods they produced best and traded with each other. Smith's theory of absolute advantage was an advance on mercantilist thought but Ricardo's singular achievement was to demonstrate that trade was a positive-sum game in which all parties benefited even if one party had an absolute advantage in the production of all goods and services. Stated simply the theory of comparative advantage shows that if a country specialized in the production of those goods and services in which it is relatively efficient (or alternatively, relatively less inefficient) compared to its competitors it would be better off. As illustrated in Chapter 2, Ricardo's model discussed two countries and two products and showed how given different cost structures of production trade was beneficial for both countries since it enabled them to consume more than they would be able to without trade.

Under a liberal trading order, trade would be undertaken by countries according to their comparative advantage. Countries would improve their economic growth, become more stable, powerful and efficient since they would be specializing in the production of goods and services in which they are most efficient producers and enabling their consumers to buy foreign goods at the lowest prices. Specialization in accordance with comparative advantage promotes efficiency since by definition a small market is an obstacle to growth. Ricardo's theory provides the basic principles underlying modern trade theory. However, its assumption that differences in labour productivity was the sole determinant of comparative advantage is too limiting and modern trade theory focuses on factor endowments (capital and labour). Developed by Eli Heckscher (1919) and Bertil Ohlin (1933) the factor endowment theory states that comparative advantage arises from the different relative factor endowments of countries. In other words, a country will have a comparative advantage in the production of those goods that uses intensively the factor it has most in abundance. Thus a country will export those goods which are relatively intensive in their most abundant factor. For example, if sheep farming is relatively intensive in land compared with textile production which is labour-intensive and Australia is land-abundant compared with Bangladesh which is labour-abundant the Hecksher–Ohlin theorem predicts that Australia will export sheep to Bangladesh in exchange for textiles.

Liberal trade theory has been further refined to take account of the growth of intra-firm and intra-industry trade but these refinements do not challenge the basic underlying assumptions of the liberal paradigm. Liberal trade theory does not enquire into the origin of comparative advantage, that is, it does not ask how the different cost structures were established initially. It is also prescriptive since it suggests that the welfare of an individual country and that of the world as a whole will be improved if countries specialized according to their comparative advantage. This theory therefore prescribes free trade and warns of the dangers of protection (see Box 5.1). From a liberal perspective, protectionism is inefficient since it reduces competition, and increases the monopoly power and thus the profits of the industries (or companies) which benefit from protection. On the other hand, free trade increases the degree of products available to consumers although ultimately it will reduce the degree of product differentiation in each country. The gains from trade come partly from the greater degree of product variety and partly from the lower price per product.

Free trade theory emphasises the gains or benefits from trade for a nation. There are two aspects to the gains from trade: the static benefits deriving from specialization according to comparative advantage, and those deriving from and contributing to the process of economic growth and development over time. Trade in this view is an engine of growth and generates a number of dynamic, educative effects. These include the diffusion of knowledge of production and organizational techniques, and

Box 5.1 The costs of protectionism: a liberal perspective

Many opponents of liberal trade argue that further liberalization damages the interests of people in poor countries. However, the liberal theories examined above suggest the reverse. That is, it is protectionism rather than free trade that hurt the global poor in both developing and developed states. Protectionism may be in the interests of some producers but overall it has a negative impact on consumers in rich and poor countries.

Concerning the impact of rich country protectionism on the developing world, it has been estimated that such policies costs developing countries around $1000 billion a year. Protectionism or unfair trade practices hit precisely those sectors where poor countries have the greatest potential to reap gains from trade. For example, on average farmers in the European Union receive $16 000 per annum in subsidies under the Common Agricultural Policy. Surplus milk and sugar are often dumped in developing countries forcing poor farmers out of business. The gender dimension of such policies is also noticeable. Restrictions on the import of textiles to Western markets effectively limit the potential earning power of millions of poor (mainly women) workers in the developing world.

Moreover, protectionism in OECD countries also has a detrimental effect on the host country. For example, it has been estimated that American protectionist policies costs consumers in the United States around $32 billion annually. And, in Japan economic progress in the 1990s suffocated under the weight of heavy protection. In Japan 60 per cent of companies are based in construction, distribution, property and financial services but these companies generate just 32 per cent of the nation's income. The protection that allows for the survival of such inefficiency adversely impacts on Japanese consumption.

changed patterns of demand. Specialization leads to an increase in productivity and economic growth. The theory of comparative advantage, it is argued, is relevant for all countries, and indeed, provides hope for low-income countries. Liberal trade theorists argue that specialization brings the likelihood of an improvement in skills and an increase in the productivity of the workforce. They contend that since the export sector can act as a stimulus to the economy as a whole, and foreign investment accompanies increased trade, developing countries will be better off under a free trade regime. Liberal economists argue that the evidence shows that technological progress has been faster, all other things being equal, for countries that have been increasing their openness to the international flow of goods, services, capital, labour, technology and ideas. Low-income, developing countries can import technologies and information at virtually zero cost, whether explicitly (the actual process or plan), or implicitly (through the goods themselves). They insist that the process of innovation and the diffusion of knowledge is linked to international trade and is crucial for growth.

Despite its theoretical elegance the theory of comparative advantage has consistently been attacked by critics, but has been sufficiently robust to withstand these various critiques. We will now discuss two schools of thought critical of the liberal arguments in support of free trade. First, we will examine the approaches of writers who can, broadly speaking, be grouped together under the umbrella of mercantilism and neo-mercantilism.

Mercantilist and neo-mercantilist writers advocate the regulation of economic life in order to enhance state power or to protect a variety of national groups from competition. Support for protection comes from groups who argue that protection of local production increases national economic welfare. Many people are willing to forego absolute gain for relative gain. That is, in an anarchical international system states in pursuit of power may give primacy to the relative gains from trade and adopt protectionist measures in order to stabilize their economies even though it diminishes their absolute gains from trade.

Some state-based critiques of liberal trade theory have focused on the prescriptive power of the theory and others on the accuracy of its empirical claims. Two arguments have been made consistently since the nineteenth century concerning the desirability of free trade. The first argument is the so-called infant industry case. Supporters of industrialization argue that predominantly agricultural countries will experience obstacles in their attempts to industrialize since comparative advantage dictates that they continue to import industrial products whereas they may well have a future comparative advantage in the production of industrial products. The infant industry argument argues for temporary protection for industries likely to become competitive on the world stage. This perspective is not simply about individual industries but is tied to a wider societal vision. The process of industrialization, in this view, will be hindered in the absence of effective protection of fledgling local industries thus providing support for a policy of tariff and other protection for new domestic industries. In other words, protection should be given to these industries until they become competitive and can reap the benefits of comparative advantage. Historically, protectionist policies, by providing the opportunity to develop economies of scale and domestic market stability, have been important and perhaps necessary components of government-led strategies of economic growth and restructuring in countries such as Germany and the United States. According to advocates of this form of protection, governments should intervene to protect those industries that have the potential to develop efficient production but which at the moment would be destroyed by fierce international competition. Some liberal theorists are willing to accept the infant industry argument as an exception to standard comparative advantage theory. However, while providing support for temporary forms of protection they, nevertheless, recognize that there is an inherent problem with the infant industry argument. Domestic producers are unlikely to willingly renounce the protection from which they benefit, and therefore the agreement on the point at which protection is to be discontinued may prove politically difficult even though the economic arguments are compelling.

The second historical argument against free trade is that which claims that the dictates of national security take precedence over trade. In other words, countries need to be self-sufficient in the production of certain strategic industries. These may be related directly to the waging of war or they may refer to foodstuffs. Whether items are necessary for the direct defence of the nation or food security, dependence on external markets can threaten a nation's security. In the interests of national security countries are urged to temper support for free trade with policies protective of national security. It is widely accepted that if free trade jeopardizes other non-economic objectives such as national security it is necessary for governments to impose restrictions in order to protect society. From this perspective the real income gains that motivate free trade cannot be separated from the security externalities that can either impede or facilitate it. Trade with an adversary can be harmful to a nation's security; trade with an ally can support a nation's security. Although states resort to economic warfare and use economic sanctions in cases of conflict it can be argued that the security dimension of trade is always present.

The infant industry argument and the national security argument have a long historical pedigree. Recently, two further arguments for protection have emerged to lend support to opponents of the state-based critique of free trade. First, strategic trade theory (Krugman, 1987) argues that countries should pursue competitive advantage in those industries of future economic benefit to the nation where the economic and social costs of falling behind competitors are huge. Secondly, a number of governments and domestic groups concerned about the impact of globalization on their culture have argued that protectionist measures should be implemented to protect the national culture. In the face of globalization many analysts warn that distinctive cultural practices will be swamped by the import of goods and ideas from abroad. Cultural protection in relation to film, media and communications technologies is therefore supported by those who want to resist what they see as undesirable consequences of globalization.

We can identify three different strands of the radical critique of free trade. The one with the longest historical legacy we call the unequal exchange perspective. Writers in this perspective have a Marxist heritage and they provide a powerful social justice critique of liberal trade principles. Although a single unequal exchange perspective does not exist, broadly speaking, we can discern three main parts to this critique. First, these writers stress the importance of historical power relations in the creation of comparative advantage (Frank, 1967). Unlike liberal analysts who take comparative advantage as a given, unequal exchange theorists enquire into the construction of different cost structures across national borders and argue that many have been determined by imperialist plunder. The second aspect of the unequal exchange perspective is an emphasis on the redistributional benefits of free trade. They emphasize the unequal gains to participants in international exchange which they argue freezes the status quo and makes it difficult for poorer countries to develop, and also the concentration of economic power in the hands of the wealthy (Coote, 1992). Within the current world order trade from this perspective sustains the activities of transnational corporations and large bureaucracies (government departments or regional organizations) at the expense of peasants and workers (Madeley, 1992). A third variant of this perspective was developed by Arghiri Emmanuel (1972), an Italian Marxist, in his unequal exchange theory in which he argued that trade systematically discriminated against developing countries because of the lower wage rates in developing countries. Emmanuel assumed that labour productivity did not vary between rich and poor countries and therefore the product of labour was equal in rich and poor countries. But since the prices of goods produced by rich countries reflected their high wages and those produced by poor countries reflected their low wages the exchange was inherently unequal since goods produced by rich countries commanded a higher price internationally.

Another radical argument in favour of protection is made by environmental activists (Ekins, 1989; Morris, 1989) who claim that free trade contributes to environmental degradation. They argue that the externalities of trade are omitted from standard trade theory. Environmentalists contend that current trading practices are unsustainable and they campaign for a return to local trade (Shrybman, 1990). This is discussed in more detail later in Chapter 10. Finally, feminist scholars have recently turned their attention to the gendered nature of trade, arguing that trade is not gender-neutral. In common with human rights and environmental activists, feminists argue that trade theory has ignored the social costs of trade (Fontana *et al.*, 1998). Proponents of fair trade or those wanting the incorporation of labour rights and human rights issues into trade claim that the prevailing trade paradigm signally fails to address these issues and as such promotes the continuation of unequal relations.

In this section we have examined competing perspectives on the relationship between free trade and national and/or world welfare. We have argued that modern international trade theory provides a normative framework for the conduct of international trade. It furnishes both an explanation of, and justification for, trade. Trade theory is thus, despite the claims of standard neo-classical economics, ideological and political. This does not mean that its analytical tools, prescriptions and conclusions are to be rejected as biased and unscientific. Rather, this recognition brings to the fore the fact that trade theory is not only socially constructed but is the subject and object of its own analysis. A vulgar way of making this point would be to claim that actors in the trading system are influenced by the writings of trade theorists. While this captures part of the argument being made here it fails to fully extend its implications. The crucial point is that the 'reality' examined by trade theory is itself partly constructed by trade theory.

Moreover, it is arguable that even if the principle of comparative advantage is applied on a global basis the gains from trade will not be evenly distributed. In the short-term it is likely that free trade will result in an unequal distribution of costs and benefits thus undermining the basis for adherence to free-trade policies since those countries losing out will resort to protectionist measures such as tariffs or subsidies.

Major developments

There have been two notable developments in the world trading system since the end of World War II. One development has been a large increase in the volume of world trade. This has been accompanied by changing forms of protectionism as states struggle to cushion the dislocations caused by trade liberalization. The second development has been the transformation of the institutional arrangements governing world trade. The failure of states to create an International Trade Organization (ITO) after World War II left the General Agreement on Tariffs and Trade as the primary international framework governing trade relations. In 1995 the GATT gave way to the new World Trade Organization, an indication of a further institutionalization of trade rules.

Growth and protectionism

Since the end of World War II, trade has increased more rapidly than production which is a clear indicator of the increased internationalization of economic activities and of the greater interconnectedness which has come to characterize the world economy. Since 1945, growth in world trade has consistently outstripped growth in world production. World production has doubled but international trade has grown more than fourfold since 1945. There are certain noticeable features of this growth and these will be discussed below. We will focus on the magnitude of trade, its geographical concentration, the commodity composition of trade, and the growth in intra-industry and intra-firm trade.

The growth in trade has been uneven and there have been periods of recession when trade growth slowed, but overall the trend has been positive. The WTO calculates that merchandise exports grew on average six per cent per annum between 1947 and 1997, and that total trade in 1997 was fourteen times the level of 1950 (WTO, 1998). This suggests that trade has been an important sector in the contemporary global economy and a main agent of economic growth. The relationship between trade and growth has been intensely debated during this period especially since it is an important consideration for countries trying to promote economic development. The consensus among economists is that trade promotes growth. That is, countries with an open economy engaging in international trade have performed better than those countries where policy has restricted domestic markets to foreign products. The relation between trade and economic growth is twofold. First, trade acts as a stimulus to the local economy providing it with resources cheaper than it would cost to produce domestically. Trade thus raises the production possibility frontier enabling countries to consume more than they would have done in the absence of trade. The relationship between consumption and growth will be discussed below where we will show the importance of consumption to contemporary economic growth. Secondly, trade forces domestic producers to manufacture goods to world market standards thus increasing productivity, and product quality. This leads to a more efficient use of resources. In the light of these arguments it is possible to see one of the reasons for the failure of Soviet-style communism. Instead of embracing trade, communist authorities approached trade with suspicion viewing it as a source of economic leakage rather than, as it turned out, a source of economic strength. Trade remained a residual element in national economic plans where the drive was for self-sufficiency. Even the attempt at integration through the Soviet dominated trading organization, the Council for Mutual Economic Assistance (COMECON) was predicated less on exploring dynamic comparative advantage through the benefits of specialization than on protecting what were perceived to be national interests.

Not only has overall trade growth been uneven it has also been so in respect of different countries and regions. The majority of transactions in world trade is restricted to the advanced industrial countries, and the fastest growth in trade occurred among these countries (see Table 5.2).

Table 5.2 *The value of world merchandise trade by region*
2000 and 2001

(Billion of dollars; percentage in parentheses)

Exports		Region	Imports	
2000	*2001*	*Region*	*2000*	*2001*
6186	6192	World	6490	6439
1058 (17.1)	994 (16.0)	North America	1504 (23.2)	1410 (21.9)
359 (5.8)	349 (5.6)	Latin America	388 (6)	381 (5.9)
2441 (39.5)	2484 (40.1)	Western Europe	2567 (39.6)	2527 (39.2)
145 (2.3)	141 (2.3)	Africa	137 (2.1)	134 (2.1)
263 (4.3)	239 (3.9)	Middle East	171 (2.6)	174 (2.7)
1649 (26.7)	1671 (26.9)	Asia	1481 (22.8)	1544 (23.9)

NB: excludes the transition economies.

Sources: Data from WTO International Trade Statistics (2001) p. 20; WTO Annual Report (2002) p. 13.

The share of the developed countries in world trade has consistently remained around the 80 per cent mark. Whereas the theory of comparative advantage predicts that trade will grow fastest between unlike economies, post-war trade growth has seen the reverse of this proposition

In the 1950s and 1960s trade grew fastest in manufactured products. In 1945 the commodity composition of international trade reflected the sectoral composition of output in the leading economies and was therefore mainly composed of merchandise trade. But as services became the dominant sector in industrialized economies so the trade in services has expanded with the result that one of the major developments in the international trading system has been the rise of trade in services. While trade in services is not the largest sector in world trade it has been the fastest growing sector.

The term intra-industry trade refers to the situation where trade occurs within the same industry rather than between industries. One of the main features of post-war trade growth has been the phenomenon of intra-industry trade. Countries have exchanged like products where price and product differentiation have played important parts. In consumer goods we have seen the exchange of consumer durables so that although the UK, for example, produces motor vehicles and washing machines, it has also imported these items from other OECD member countries. International trade has supported both horizontal and vertical integration. Horizontal integration refers to the exchange of like products, for example video recorders, whereas vertical integration refers to the exchange of components in a single production process, for example making a motor vehicle. The growth of intra-industry trade has also been matched by the growth of intra-firm trade. The rise of the transnational corporation and a global production system (see Chapter 6) has stimulated intra-firm trade. An increasing percentage of world trade takes place within firms rather than between separate, individual firms. One of the crucial implications for trade theory and for national governments is that if trade takes place within a transnational corporation pricing policies will not reflect real costs. In such cases trade is driven not by comparative costs but by the management decisions of the firm.

The period from 1947 to 1973 was one of unprecedented expansion for the world economy with output and trade growing faster than in any previously recorded period. Global output expanded at an annual average of five per cent while exports grew at seven per cent per annum. This provided an economic climate conducive to trade liberalization, and it was against this background that protectionism was reduced on manufactured products. A number of significant structural changes took place between 1947 and 1973. The most important change in the context of the trading system was the shift away from a traditional dependence on the export of primary commodities to the increasing specialization in labour-intensive, low technology manufactured products by a number of developing countries such as India, Brazil and the East Asian NICs. These developing country exporters took advantage of expanding markets in the developed economies and the contraction of productive capacity in some sectors in the OECD countries as the dynamic comparative advantage of developing countries became evident. Industries such as textiles and footwear were initially developed in the industrialized countries but during this period the technological know-how associated with these activities were diffused to some developing countries.

During the long boom (1947–73) it was relatively easy for developed countries to make the necessary adjustments to imports of manufactures from the developing world because the employment-creating effects of international trade were outweighing the employment-displacing effects. The outcome of these developments was that the benefits of trade were obvious and by and large consumers and producers willingly acquiesced in the trade liberalization process. Thus protectionist pressures were specific rather than general.

With the downturn in the world economy following the first oil crisis in 1973–74 unemployment grew and became a critical political issue in the industrialized world. The importance of the recession between 1973–77 was to focus the attention of various pressure groups on the perceived connection between foreign trade and domestic employment, that is, on the link between employment displacement and import penetration. Employment preservation through the restriction of imports became an acceptable means of preventing unemployment from rising to unacceptable levels. What characterizes this period was the resort to non-tariff instruments of policy. Countries abandoned the use of old protectionism in the form of tariffs for new protectionism using non-tariff barriers (NTBs). And because they were the most vulnerable, discrimination against developing countries grew at an alarming rate. As an OECD report declared, 'developing countries have in practice been most exposed to discriminatory export restraint agreements and other trade distorting measures, with the incidence of this discrimination being greatest in those sectors in which they have a comparative advantage' (Goldin *et al.*, 1993, p. 22).

If structural change accounted for the onset of protectionism it was the existence of the GATT that shaped the forms the new protectionism would take. The GATT Articles do provide for the introduction of restraints under certain designated circumstances. For example, Article XIX condones the use of import controls for the emergency protection of domestic industry. Recourse to these escape clauses became increasingly prevalent in the 1970s, as the major developed countries made more frequent usage of the protectionist option. However, recourse to Article XIX was rather limited since many countries taking protectionist action preferred to evade GATT stipulations on non-discrimination and reciprocity and therefore turned to extra-legal alternatives which suited their purposes better than Article XIX. These provisions are central to the explanation of a reluctance to use Article XIX and a willingness to look for alternatives outside the GATT framework. The most widely used NTBs were voluntary export restraints, import quotas, product standards including regulations pertaining to health and technical safeguards, and anti-dumping measures and countervailing duties, which are still drawn upon today. An example of the use of health standards to discriminate against imports is given in Box 5.2. The negotiation of a voluntary export restraint allowed action to be taken on a discriminatory basis, a facility unavailable under Article XIX. In order to appease pressure groups at home while at the same time doing little to impair export prospects, governments followed the path of least resistance. This period also saw the mushrooming of administrative controls such as the use of health, safety and environmental standards. Protectionism also took the form of subsidies, and government procurement policies. This move from GATT's rule of law brought with it a heightened absence of transparency given that non-transparency is a property of NTBs.

The rise of new protectionism and the failure of the GATT to remedy these developments contributed to dissatisfaction with the organization's performance. This issue will be addressed in the next section. While the

---

Box 5.2 Health risks and hormone-treated beef

The European Union first banned the importation of hormone-treated meat in 1989, arguing that injecting livestock with bovine somatropin (BST) posed a health risk to humans. BST, a growth hormone produced by beef cattle was in use by major meat-producing countries including Canada, and the United States. Scientists from meat exporting countries that used BST argued that it was safe but consumer groups in the EU and the European farm lobby protested that hormonal irregularities or cancer would result from its consumption. Was this a genuine health issue or a form of disguised protectionism? The EU claimed it was a health issue but producers affected by the ban argued that it reflected an attempt to protect the inefficient EU meat industry.

Codex Alimenatrius the international food standards agency of the Food and Agricultural Organization and the World Health Organization announced in 1995 that no link existed between hormone-treated meat and human health problems. This ruling supported the contention of meat exporters to the EU who had lost revenue as a result of the EU ban. For example, US red meat exports to the EU fell from $231 million in 1988 (a year before the ban) to $98 million in 1994. Despite this ruling, deep scepticism remains among EU consumers.

---

new protectionism is no longer a major issue since the creation of the World Trade Organization (WTO) (see p. 154) gave a boost to liberalising forces, the confrontation between advocates of trade liberalization and those of protection remains an important issue in the contemporary global economy.

The growth in world trade in the 1990s and the early years of the twenty-first century has been uneven reflecting the global economic cycle. Some major developments with an impact on world trade growth include the IT bubble and burst, the entry of former command economy countries fully into the international trading regime, the rise in regionalism, the uncertain economic performance of the OECD countries, and the Asian financial crisis. World trade is as susceptible as ever to changes in world politics, and the economic trends in leading industrial states.

Changing institutional arrangements

The origins of the post-World War II international trade regime are to be found in Anglo-American cooperation during the Second World War. The liberal trade regime that was created reflected primarily American interests. American preference for open-market arrangements and for the imposition of a multilateral rule-based system to limit national action is at the centre of the regime. Two particular issues were of concern to American policy-makers – British Imperial preferences and the system of protection that had developed in Latin America during the war. The US therefore proposed a non-discriminatory, multilateral system of trade and payments. This meant in practice provision for reciprocity, international supervision of tariff and exchange rates, outlawing of quantitative restrictions, freely convertible currencies and the generalization of tariff reductions to all members of the regime. The trade regime is, to use a term coined by Ruggie (1982), one of 'embedded liberalism'. That is, its main features subscribe to liberal trade principles but nevertheless recognition is made for deviations from the standard principles. The international trade regime is not a laissez-faire system but rather one of managed trade. The trading regime is based on four key principles, namely, non-discrimination, reciprocity, transparency and multilateralism. These have been the guiding principles for a series of international institutions designed to govern post-war international trade.

Non-discrimination is enshrined in the Most Favoured Nation (MFN) clause. The MFN principle ensures that any concession granted to one member must be extended to all other members. Under MFN provisions all members of the GATT/WTO are treated in a non-discriminatory manner. A tariff on an import from a GATT/WTO member had to be placed on all other GATT/WTO members in a similar manner with the exception of customs unions, or free trade areas. This principle is therefore at the centre of the multilateral trading system. Reciprocity is intended to ensure that when one country lowers its tariffs against the exports of another country it will in turn be granted equal trade concessions. The principle of reciprocity applied through multilateral bargaining means that in theory one country's concessions are paid for by a third country which then passes it on to another country and the process repeats itself. Transparency refers to the fact that any discrimination must be clearly visible. The system is based on the principle that tariffs are the only permissible form of discrimination. Non-tariff barriers such as import quotas are banned and countries are urged to replace non-tariff barriers with tariffs. Finally the system is based on multilateralism which implies and reflects the commitment to the creation of a multilateral trade regime, multilateral cooperation in maintaining a rule-based system, and engaging in periodic rounds of tariff cutting.

The Conference on Trade and Employment held in Havana, Cuba in 1948 created the International Trade Organization (ITO) as the institutional framework of the post-war international trading system. However, opposition to the proposed ITO, especially in the United States, resulted in non-ratification of the treaty creating the ITO. Given the preponderant position of the United States in the world economy at this time most governments delayed ratification until the US Congress gave its assent, but in 1951 President Truman aware of widespread hostility to the ITO decided not to seek Congressional assent thus consigning the ITO to history. With the failure of the ITO, the General Agreement on Tariffs and Trade (GATT) became the institutional focus of the world trading system. GATT was the result of a tariff-cutting exercise by 23 nations prior to the Havana Conference. Meeting in Geneva in March 1947 these delegates decided on a series of tariff reductions, and a temporary mechanism to oversee these cuts. Instead of withering away as initially envisaged the GATT was given permanence. GATT provided a code of rules, a dispute-settlement mechanism and a forum for trade negotiations. Its main importance lay in its role as a forum for trade negotiations. In eight rounds (see table 5.3) of multilateral trade negotiations (MTNs) between 1947 and 1994 it presided over a period of unprecedented growth in world trade.

Until the Kennedy Round, negotiations were conducted on an item-by-item basis but in this round the negotiators moved to an across-the-board approach. The GATT enjoyed uneven success in its quest to reduce trade barriers. It was most successful in tackling barriers to manufactured goods but less so in preventing agricultural protectionism. Three main features of trade liberalization are visible in the GATT period.

At the Geneva Conference in 1947 significant tariff reductions were negotiated in successive multilateral trade reductions on some 45 000 products constituting approximately half of world trade at that stage (Williams, 1994, p. 150). Progress slowed somewhat between this first conference and the Kennedy Round but substantial tariff reductions were

Table 5.3   *GATT negotiating rounds*

Name	Dates	Number of countries participating
Geneva	1947	23
Annecy	1949	13
Torquay	1951	38
Geneva	1956	26
Dillon	1960–61	26
Kennedy	1964–67	62
Tokyo	1973–79	102
Uruguay	1986–93	123

achieved. The new approach used in the Kennedy Round yielded average tariff reductions of between 36–39 per cent, and despite the unfavourable economic circumstances, tariff cuts in the Tokyo Round averaged between 33 and 38 per cent.

Secondly, the process of trade liberalization under GATT was uneven. Trade liberalization was almost solely confined to manufactured products – the most dominant growth sector. In 1947 at the first round of GATT negotiations, the average tariff on manufactured goods was around 40 per cent. By the end of the Kennedy Round these tariffs had been lowered to an average of 10 per cent. The tariffs of the industrial countries were reduced by a further 35 per cent as a result of the Tokyo Round (Winham, 1986, p. 17). To illustrate the significance of tariff reductions to the industrial countries we note that tariffs on industrial products in the United States declined from around 50 per cent in 1947 to about 4 per cent in 1979, and those in the United Kingdom moved from around 40 per cent to about 4 per cent in the same period (Greenaway and Hine, 1991). Industrial countries were willing to liberalize in sectors that were expanding but reluctant to do so in those in which they had lost or were losing comparative advantage and felt most under threat. Agricultural protection continued unchecked until the Uruguay Round where a start was made on phasing out the protection afforded to farmers in the developed world. But reform of agricultural trade has proved difficult and will continue to be a sensitive political issue in future trade talks. Developed countries also devised a series of restrictive measures in relation to textiles and clothing. Under the guise of ensuring orderly market behaviour the GATT sanctioned the Multi-Fibre Agreement (MFA) to regulate trade in textiles and clothing. This was in effect a protectionist device. The Uruguay Round Agreements have committed governments to a phasing out of the MFA.

Thirdly, whereas trade liberalization was initially limited solely to trade in merchandise goods, beginning with the Tokyo Round, additional issues have been placed on the agenda. The Tokyo Round negotiations were conducted during the period known as the new protectionism where states prohibited from a recourse to tariff barriers through their GATT commitments began to impose significant non-tariff barriers. At the conclusion of the Tokyo Round negotiators agreed six voluntary codes to prohibit the use of NTBs but implementation was poor. They also attempted to develop a framework to regulate anti-dumping measures. During the Uruguay Round, the agenda of the world trading system was further expanded to include services, intellectual property rights, investment, environment, labour standards, and domestic (non-trade) policies.

GATT also provided a normative framework, and a dispute settlement mechanism. Assessment of GATT's impact as a normative framework is difficult but two issues can be examined. It is undeniable that GATT made a major contribution to the development of international economic law (Kock, 1969; Jackson, 1969). The GATT treaty is a legal document, and it provided a code of rules that set the framework for international commercial transactions. Additionally governments used the existence of GATT disciplines as a mechanism to resist demands for protection. One of GATT's major failures was its dispute settlement mechanism. Because the recommendations of the dispute panel required consent, contracting parties could block the decisions of GATT panels.

At the end of the Uruguay Round of negotiations a new trade organization, the World Trade Organization (WTO) was created. The WTO is the successor to the GATT and owes its existence to perceived deficiencies of GATT. Dissatisfaction with GATT grew because of the organization's failure to reverse the growth of protectionism, the weakness of its dispute settlement procedures, and the uneven nature of its trade liberalization process. The WTO created to remedy these perceived weaknesses is therefore an international organization with greater powers than the one it replaced. First, in an effort to reverse protectionism and bolster trade liberalization the WTO was created as a permanent international organization with greater scope than the GATT. The WTO consists of a set of legal codes which members must accept as a single undertaking. On accession to the WTO a state must adhere to the following agreements:

- the Agreement establishing the WTO;
- GATT 1994 and other multilateral trade agreements for goods including Sanitary and Phytosanitary Measures (SPS), the agreement on technical barriers to trade (TBT), and the agreement on Trade-Related Investment Measures (TRIMs);
- the General Agreement on Trade in Services (GATS);
- the agreement on Trade-Related Intellectual Property Rights measures (TRIPs);
- the Understanding on Rules and Procedures Governing the Settlement of Disputes;
- the Trade Policy Review Mechanism (TPRM).

The WTO also consists of Plurilateral Agreements governing civil aircraft, government procurement, and dairy and bovine meat but the acceptance of these agreements is not mandatory for membership.

Secondly, the dispute settlement mechanism was considerably strengthened. The Dispute Settlement Understanding (DSU) provides the machinery for settling members' differences on their rights and obligations. It consists of a first-stage panel adjudication followed by an appeals process (the Appellate Body), and a clear schedule for the processing of disputes. Moreover, decisions from the dispute settlement process are based on a negative consensus. That is, they can only be overturned by the General Council if all members are in agreement. As a centre for the settlement of disputes, the WTO contributes to the stability and further evolution of the world trading system since liberalization will not take place in the absence of effective dispute settlement procedures.

Thirdly, compared with the GATT, the WTO has transformed the management of world trade in three crucial respects. It engineered a shift from trade liberalization based on tariff concessions (shallow or negative integration) to discussions of domestic policies, institutional practices and regulations (deep or positive integration). It also constructed a new agenda expanding the scope (through the inclusion of services, trade-related intellectual property rights, and domestic [non–trade] policies), and changing the character of negotiations from a focus on bargaining over products to negotiations over policies that shape the conditions of competition. Finally, it initiated a movement towards policy harmonization, for example in the areas of subsidies, trade related investment measures, and services. The WTO's extensive powers has given it a much higher profile than its predecessor.

Trade liberalization has been accompanied by a rise in international trade (see Table 5.5) which supporters of further liberalization claim is a result of the process of removing restrictions to trade. They argue that the institutional framework creates liberalization and this in turn enhances increased trade (Finlayson and Zacher, 1981). Structuralist critics, on the contrary claim that trade expansion would have taken place without these governing arrangements since the growth of trade has principally been a response to structural change in the world economy (Strange, 1985).

The debate concerning trade expansion and the institutional structure of world trade can be illuminated through another examination of the rise of

Table 5.4 *World merchandise trade, 1948–2000*
(Billions of US dollars)

	1948	1953	1963	1973	1983	1993	2000
Exports							
World	58	84	157	579	1835	3641	6186
Imports							
World	66	84	163	589	1881	3752	6490

Source: Data from WTO (2001), p. 30.

so-called New Protectionism in the 1970s. Old protectionism refers to the use of tariffs and quotas by states to protect vulnerable sectors from foreign competition, to avoid unemployment, and to stimulate their economies. However, GATT rounds and GATT discipline between 1947 and 1973 reduced the tariffs on industrial products to negligible levels. The success of GATT was not only in reducing barriers to trade but also through the practice of binding tariffs ensuring that once lowered a tariff could not subsequently be raised again. Thus the commitments entered into by states both secured increased trade liberalization and also constrained the recourse to traditional mechanisms of protection. The response to the recession and consequent rise in unemployment after the end of the long boom was the development of new forms of protectionism. After 1973 governments increasingly turned to the use of NTBs. These included voluntary export restraints (VERs), the recourse to anti-dumping and countervailing duties, health, technical and other product standards. The new protectionist measures possessed limited transparency, were generally sector specific, and were lacking in uniform application. In a retreat from multilateralism, governments used NTBs to target specific industries in major competitor nations.

Key issues

There are numerous trade issues that spring onto the international agenda. We have chosen to focus on three broad issues that cover many specific trade disputes. One issue is the place of developing countries in the world trading system. A second issue concerns the significance of regional trading agreements. A third issue is the question of the legitimacy of liberal trade agreements which ignore the social and environmental dimensions to trade.

Developing country interests

Although the economic structure of developing countries are diverse, a set of interests specific to developing countries have emerged within the world trading system. This was recently reaffirmed by the Doha Ministerial Declaration at the conclusion of the 2001 Ministerial Meeting of the World Trade Organization. Central to this development has been the self-identification of developing countries, and the limited political influence they exert in international trade negotiations. Two issues have consistently emerged at the centre of the debate. The first concerns the benefits of a liberal trading order, and the second relates to the continuation of protectionist forces in the post-war trading system. In relation to the first issue a debate exists between those who contend that trade promotes development and those who maintain that industrialization is best achieved behind protectionist barriers. A related debate exists between those who argue that reform of trading arrangements will benefit developing countries and those who contend that the trading system is inherently exploitative. We will not revisit these debates here. Instead we will examine a number of current issues.

Table 5.5   *GDP composition by sector – agriculture 2001* (%)

Country	Share of GDP in agriculture (2001)
Liberia	60
Somalia	60
Afghanistan	53
Laos	51
Ethiopia	46
Nepal	41
Bhutan	38
Korea, North	30
India	25
Iran	21
Indonesia	21
China	15
Brazil	9.7
Greece	8.3
New Zealand	8
Russia	7
Ireland	4
Spain	4
France	3.3
Australia	3
Canada	3
Japan	2
United States	2
United Kingdom	1.7
Germany	1.2
Kuwait	0
Singapore	0

Source: CIA World Factbook (2001); available online at http://www.globastat.com

Many developing countries remain dependent on the export of agricultural commodities, and even in those countries in which agriculture is not the major export sector, agriculture remains a significant employer of labour (see Table 5.5). Whereas the industrialized countries have embraced liberalization in manufactured products, they have been reluctant to fully liberalize agricultural trade. Indeed, until the Uruguay Round, agriculture was kept off the negotiating agenda. Despite the progress made during the Uruguay Round agriculture in the industrialized countries continues to enjoy high levels of protection. The agricultural support policies of the developed countries have an overall negative impact on developing countries. This is an area in which the developed world abandons its support of comparative advantage and for a number of economic, political and social reasons implements discriminatory policies. When protection leads to excess domestic production this results in lower world prices, thus reducing the incomes of producers in the developing world. Protection in the form of import levies and quotas in removing a large part of agricultural trade from the world market increases the volatility of international prices. The persistence of impediments to market access in agriculture therefore remains a major policy concern of developing countries. The persistence of subsidies on major agricultural exports from the developed countries, continued domestic support to agriculture and high tariffs resulting from tariffication (the process whereby NTBs are converted to tariffs) have conspired to restrict the gains made by developing countries. The issue of agricultural protection is also of interest to some developed country exporters and has given rise to a grouping of developed and developing country producers. The Cairns Group (see Box 5.3) is an intergovernmental pressure group for agricultural reform linking developing countries and developed countries.

Box 5.3   The Cairns Group

Largely an Australian invention under the Hawke Government, the Cairns Group comprises 17 agricultural exporting countries. Formed in 1986 the Cairns Group has effectively put agriculture on the multilateral trade agenda after decades of stalemate over reduction in the protection received by agricultural products. It was largely as a result of the Group's efforts that a framework for reform in farm products trade was established in the Uruguay Round and agriculture was, for the first time, subject to trade liberalization rules. These are set out in the WTO Agreement on Agriculture.

Membership: Argentina, Australia, Bolivia, Brazil, Canada, Chile, Colombia, Costa Rica, Guatemala, Indonesia, Malaysia, New Zealand, Paraguay, the Philippines, South Africa, Thailand and Uruguay.

The failure of the developed world to live up to the rhetoric of free trade is also evident in textiles and clothing. From the early 1960s the developed countries attempted to control the export of textiles from the developing world. These efforts culminated in the Multi-Fibre Agreement first signed in 1974. The MFA was justified as an attempt to prevent market disruption in importing countries but its main aim was to protect jobs in the textile and clothing sector in the developed world. Despite evidence showing that imports of textiles from the developing world have a small impact on unemployment in textile and clothing industries in the developed world, developed countries, nevertheless, initiated and applied these restrictive measures. Once again the Uruguay Round agreements promised an end to this form of discrimination but implementation has been very slow. Although implementation of the agreement to phase out the MFA may have met the letter of the law it has not, to date, led to commercially meaningful liberalization because quotas which have been removed account for an insignificant share of restrained imports. Additionally, burdensome administrative and customs procedures, changes to rules of origin and frequent use of safeguard measures are adversely affecting exports of textiles and clothing.

Agriculture and textiles are issues that have been of concern to developing countries since the 1950s and the fact that they remain of concern is indicative of the limited influence developing countries exercise over international trade negotiations. The inclusion of these sectors in the Uruguay Round negotiations was a concession necessary to get developing countries to agree to the expansion of the multilateral trade agenda to include new issues. Three of these new issues were at the forefront of controversy during the negotiations and have remained so ever since. The first issue concerns services covered under the General Agreement on Trade in Services (GATS). The most frequently discussed services – tourism, business services, and finance – provide greater returns for the developed world but in some business services, for example, in publishing and data processing, developing countries have been able to build up exportable services. While developing countries were able to safeguard some of their interests by insisting that the GATS be based on a positive list (that is, countries must list services to be liberalized) the impact of the liberalization in services on developing countries remains a hotly debated topic.

The issue of intellectual property rights is also of great importance to developing countries. Until the Uruguay Round copyrights, patents and other forms of intellectual property were not treated as trade or even trade-related issues. They were brought into the Uruguay Round on the insistence of American transnational companies who insisted that exports of counterfeit goods, especially from South-east Asia, were responsible for large revenue and profit losses (Sell, 2000). Moreover, pharmaceutical companies had long campaigned that their profits and research and development were harmed by the local production of their products without payment of a license, and usually justified under national health guidelines. The Trade-Related Intellectual Property Rights (TRIPS) agreement gives increased influence to foreign investors and provides increased international patent protection to a range of products and processes previously exempt from patent protection (Hoogvelt, 1997, p. 136). It requires countries to accept the substance of existing international conventions on copyright (Berne Convention) and on patents (Paris Convention). But bringing these agreements under the WTO subjects them to WTO dispute settlement procedures and enforcement mechanisms. The agreement enforces two kinds of extra costs. The costs of being forced to pay for technology will fall principally on low- to middle-income countries since the higher income countries are approaching the point at which they will have the technology to export and protect. The likely detrimental impact of the TRIPS agreement has been most clearly visible in the pharmaceutical industry where drug companies holding the patents to medicines can dictate the price of essential drugs. In 2001 a huge controversy erupted over this issue with a focus on the legal battle between the South African government and makers of drugs to treat patients with HIV. This case attracted worldwide attention and was eventually settled in favour of the South African government. Moreover, pharmaceutical companies can take out patents and thus rob developing country producers. That is, local knowledge that is currently free will cease to be so if a foreign company takes out a patent on that knowledge. The costs of introducing the required legal and administrative mechanisms will be highest for least developed countries. It has been claimed that 'the main beneficiaries will be the core group of less than a dozen seeds and pharmaceuticals companies which control over 70% of the world's seeds trade' (Hoogvelt, 1997, p. 136).

Some critics are worried that the move towards giving foreign investors unfettered access to global markets will undermine the sovereignty of host governments. The issue surfaced in the negotiations on Trade-Related Investment Measures (TRIMS). Although an agreement with the potential to override national law does not exist it is believed by many that it is only a matter of time before such an agreement is signed. The attempt to create a regulatory code for foreign investment in the OECD met vociferous opposition from critics in the developed world, and also from groups claiming to speak for the developing world. Opposition to the Multilateral Agreement on Investment (MAI) from social movement activists was instrumental in the failure by governments to agree on the MAI (Goodman and Ranald, 2000).

Another issue of interest to developing countries concerns their special status in trade negotiations. Developing countries in the 1960s launched a campaign for special and differential treatment (S&D). The demand for S&D was based on the claim that the demands of development are incompatible with the free operation of market forces. The demand for S&D was first formally accepted in 1965 with the addition of a new chapter to the GATT. Part IV of the GATT entitled Trade and Development gave legal sanction to the principle of special and differential treatment and provided the developing countries with a specific focus from which to mount further campaigns for reform. While the Tokyo Round extended S&D, the creation of the WTO has seen a move away from treating developing countries as a special case. Within the WTO increased emphasis is given to the trade needs of the least developed countries; and developing countries, while given some concessions, are expected to conform to the general rules. Special and differential treatment under the WTO can be classified into five main groups:

- provisions aimed at increasing trade opportunity through market access;
- provisions requiring WTO members to safeguard the interests of the developing countries;
- provisions allowing flexibility to developing countries in rules and disciplines governing trade measures;
- provisions allowing longer transitional periods to developing countries;
- and provisions for technical assistance.

Within each of these groups additional provisions are made specifically for the least developed countries. The aim of the WTO is to include developing countries as full participants in the system, that is, to move to a position where it will be possible to withdraw any special and differential status. The provisions noted above with regard to the special and differential treatment of developing countries have largely been ineffectual. For example, the developed countries are not taking the special needs of developing countries into account in preparing and applying sanitary and phytosanitary measures, technical regulations, standards and conformity assessment procedure. Moreover, the transitional periods do not always give sufficient time to deal with specific shortfalls in capacity that are faced by individual members or with precise development needs. And finally, many developing countries emphasize the critical and continued need for technical assistance. They call for better coordination of technical assistance from all sources, and have asked for increased funding of technical assistance in the core WTO budget. Taking cases before the dispute settlement mechanism requires the payment usually of large fees for specialist legal advice.

Regionalism

One of the most important developments in the international trading system has been the creation of regional economic organizations. Regional economic organizations have multiple objectives of which the promotion of trade liberalization is frequently only one aim. Other aims can include investment liberalization, the managing of economic conflict, domestic economic restructuring, political integration. Nevertheless, whether trade liberalization is a central objective or the means towards an end, the development of regionalism is a crucial feature of the trading system. Analysts tend to periodize the development of regionalism into two phases. It is widely agreed that the creation of the European Economic Community (EEC) in 1957 initiated the first phase. The second period is dated from the mid-1990s. The impact of the two phases of regionalism on world trade is different.

In the first phase regionalism was relatively inward. In the developing world the aim of regional economic arrangements was to stimulate industrialization which meant that such organizations were more concerned with trade diversion than trade creation. Trade diversion refers to the process where low-cost suppliers from outside the union are replaced by high-cost suppliers within the regional grouping. Trade creation refers to the situation where, as a result of dismantling barriers within the region, trade is stimulated. In Europe, the scene of the two most successful early attempts at regional integration – the European Free Trade Area (EFTA), and the EEC, regionalism was concerned with dismantling barriers among the participants. In the second phase of regionalism many of the new associations have adopted a policy of open regionalism making the reductions to trade more compatible with multilateral commitments.

Although regionalism can be seen in most parts of the world, specific regional agreements vary greatly in their goals and terms. This has led to some debate about the internal nature of regions and the relationship between regions. Internally, political struggles have been waged over the degree to which specific regions should have strong or weak institutions and the scope of policy-making that should be considered at the regional level. These struggles have influenced the different nature of the regions. For example, the European Union has some supranational institutions which oversee common rules. It also has provisions for regional development funding and labour rights. Most of its members have gone even further and adopted a single currency. In contrast, the North American Free Trade Agreement (NAFTA) tends to enforce existing national legislation, has no development funding and very weak provisions for the respect of labour and environmental standards. Whereas in Europe there is discussion about eventual political union, this subject is of little interest in North America.

Moving to the Asia–Pacific area we encounter an even looser regional organization – APEC (Asia–Pacific Economic Cooperation). APEC is more of a coordinating body between countries on the Pacific Rim than an attempt to build strong regional ties with robust institutions. Asian fears that the US would use the body to influence their domestic economies or political regimes have led to a minimalist structure and trade liberalization agenda.

Some economists have raised fears that increasing regionalization will undermine the multilateral trading system. They worry that regions will erect barriers to products from other regions and divert the natural flow of free trade. This could cause economic damage and undermine political support for a multilateral system. Other observers have noted how regions which espouse different values systems can clash with other regions. For example, Europeans and Americans disagree about how much risk should be accepted in the production of food. This has led to conflicts at the WTO over the EU banning the imports of products such as cattle that the Americans have injected with growth hormones.

A final issue is the fate of those areas of the world that are left out of the prominent regional trading areas. Regional integration is proceeding with some speed in Europe, North America and in East Asia through the activity of government and firms. This excludes large areas of the world such as Africa, Latin America and South Asia. There have been several responses. In Latin America, Chile has lobbied for admission to NAFTA. In contrast Brazil has put its energy into building MERCOSUR, the common market of several South American countries. Sub-Saharan Africa and South Asia have a series of regional agreements, but these are underdeveloped because they lack a powerful motor economy such as Germany, the US or Japan. Their efforts at successful regional integration face large obstacles.

Legitimacy

As trade agreements at the multilateral and regional level have proliferated and influenced domestic political economies, increasing concern has been voiced by various segments of civil society in many states. There are a wide range of issues that have attracted attention. Some groups worry that regional and global institutions are insulated from democratic control. They contend that business and political elites have considerable input into the structure of such agreements, but citizens find it difficult to hold their governments accountable for the decision-making authority transferred to international institutions. It should be noted, however, that firms are also formally excluded from the WTO. The influence of the corporate sector comes from their influence at the national level (and inclusion on national delegations) rather than directly at the multilateral level. At issue are the democratic credentials of the WTO and regional trade agreements. It has become widely accepted that democracy is a universal norm and in the context of a debate on democratization a focus has arisen concerning the representative nature of multilateral trade agreements.

Box 5.4   Democracy and the WTO

Is the WTO an undemocratic organization? The scale and ferocity of protests against the international trading regime in general and the WTO in particular suggest that the organization is undemocratic and therefore illegitimate. What are we to make of such claims? First we can observe that no consensus exists on the definition, meaning or practice of democracy.

It can be argued that the WTO is one of the most democratic international organizations. First, its large and diverse membership represents most of the trading nations in the world and a variety of economic and political systems (no major country is currently excluded from membership). Secondly, the consensus method of decision-making in the WTO gives each country a voice, and goes some way towards providing small, poorer countries with some source of influence. Thirdly, the WTO is relatively transparent in terms of making access to its documents easy to obtain. In so far as negotiations are conducted in secret, it should be recalled that trade negotiations do involve complex and often controversial trade-offs.

The critics of the WTO reject the arguments made above and argue that the organization fails to provide sufficient access for civil society groups in its deliberations. Increased participation of social movement representatives will, it is claimed, provide high quality information; balanced input into policy-making; educate the public; and increase public support for the organization. These steps are needed to counter the alleged influence of transnational capital.

At the centre of the debate is, therefore, the intergovernmental nature of the WTO. But the solution is not a simple one. On one hand, if we accept the intergovernmental character of the WTO, the representative nature of national governments can be questioned. On the other hand, if we agree that an intergovernmental organization fails to capture the range of stakeholders affected by developments in the global trade regime, it does not follow that increased representation of NGOs necessarily makes the WTO more democratic since it cannot be assumed that NGOs are more representative than national governments. Indeed, developing countries remain hostile to increased representation of (largely Northern) NGOs from social movements.

This issue has been raised most vociferously in relation to the WTO but it has also surfaced in the European Union and NAFTA. At the European level, support for further integration has been diminished in a number of member countries, and nationalist sentiments gathered around right-wing parties have made some electoral gains. The so-called democratic deficit in the European Union became a topical issue in the mid-1990s and has remained so ever since. The debate on the WTO has focused on issues related to transparency, accountability and participation (Williams, 1999, pp. 158–60). Essential features of this debate are summarized in Box 5.4. The WTO has been responsive to criticism but this has not silenced its critics. In efforts to bolster its legitimacy, the WTO has derestricted documents, held consultations with NGOs, and accepted amicae briefs. Nevertheless, critics maintain the WTO is undemocratic, claiming that decisions are frequently made in secret and that the visible part of proceedings are a mere masquerade with little relation to the real exercise of power that takes place outside the public gaze. Moreover, they argue that access to information on which decisions are made should be more readily available. In response supporters of the WTO point out that the organization is an intergovernmental forum in which decisions are based on consensus, and subject to ratification by national parliaments. In this sense the organization is fully representative of its membership. A recent report by an independent British NGO on the accountability practices of five intergovernmental organizations, six TNCs, and seven NGOs investigated the decision-making practices of the WTO. Although the report placed the WTO second in its category, it argued that 'the reality is that some members lack the capacity to engage meaningfully in decision-making' (Kovach *et al.*, 2002/2003, p. 14). In respect to access to information the report noted that 'Information on the WTO's trade activities is excellent' (ibid., p. 15).

Other groups concern themselves with the detrimental effects of these agreements on social policies, environmental degradation and labour standards. Attention to global and regional trade organizations has developed as citizen attention has turned to the increasingly influential role these organizations play in a globalized world economy. The opposition to international economic agreements (including trade agreements) grew in the late 1990s and the first two years of the twenty-first century. The 1997 APEC meeting in Vancouver was marked by Canadian police pepper-spraying protesters while the 1999 Seattle WTO ministerial meeting was also disrupted by public protests. As one activist noted in the wake of the Seattle protests, 'What civil society, North and South, should be doing at this point is either pushing for the abolition of the WTO or overloading or jamming it so that it cannot function effectively' (Bello, 2000). In Europe, citizens expressed concern about the direction of integration through a number of referenda and in support given to nationalist, especially right-wing political parties. In the United States, President Clinton and initially President Bush found it difficult to secure negotiating authority from the US Congress to continue the liberalization process.

Increasingly, publics are concerned about further economic integration and trade agreements. They face a legitimacy problem because they are seen to place the values of liberalizing economic activity or protecting private interests above other values and interests. Some critics perceive the projects sponsored by such bodies as promoting economic globalization and social injustice. We will return to such issues in Chapter 11 which examines governance in the global economy.

Conclusion

Experience with tariff negotiations has led to the observation that most countries favour trade liberalization in principle but are reluctant to undertake unilateral reduction of trade barriers because it would open their markets leaving them vulnerable to international forms. Therefore protectionism remains a prominent issue in the world economy. Protectionism is an attractive policy to domestic markets, and it is here that pressing demands originate. The demands for protection reflect structural changes bound up with the growth of transnational capitalism. It can also be seen a part of a process of structural change in the global economy which may reinforce the strength of social forces favourable to the maintenance of open trade. The demand for protection comes from rational actors in the economic process that are concerned with the nations' interests that would suffer from free trade. The most obvious reason why protectionism remains a central feature of the world economy is that all economies need some degree of protectionism in order to develop.

Chapter 6

Transnational Production

Hundreds of books, theses, government reports, and thousands of papers in academic and professional journals have been written on the subject of transnational production, on the causes of foreign direct investment, and also on the costs and benefits of inbound foreign investment for a host country. Scarcely a day goes by without a newspaper or magazine article praising or blaming what is now often referred to as the globalization of business activity. Despite, or perhaps because of, the extensive literature on transnational production no consensus exists on either the causes or impact of this phenomenon, although the growth of transnational production, it is widely agreed, has profoundly shaped the evolution of the global economy. For example, the current rhetoric of globalization assigns a crucial role to changes in the global production structure. However, it should also be noted that attention to the role of large international firms first arose in the 1960s. Prior to the current obsession with globalization, students of the global political economy had developed an awareness of the impact of the changing production structure on international relations.

The global production system is a complex process with millions of workers, and workplaces integrated into diverse local, national, regional and global systems. The relationship between discrete centres of production and the global economy cannot be captured through any simple model. The link between sites of production, and wider patterns of social, political and economic integration forming part of the global economy raises problems of comprehension for the student of international political economy. One way of trying to provide an entry to understanding the global production structure is by focusing on the role of the principal agents of this process, namely the large international firm, hereinafter referred to as the transnational corporation (TNC). The literature on transnational production tends to focus on the role of the large international firm as the key agent in this process and this chapter will adopt this standard approach. The transnational corporation is one of the defining features of economic life in the contemporary global economy. TNCs account for the major part of the global production structure, and approximately 50 per cent of world trade. (See Table 6.1 for figures on global trade and production.) In 1999, total global flows of foreign direct investment was estimated to be $200 billion (UNCTAD, 2000).

Table 6.1   *Growth in the volume of world trade and production by major product groups, 1990–2001 (Annual percentage change)*

	1990–01	1996	1997	1998	1999	2000	2001
World merchandise exports	5.5	6.0	10.5	4.5	4.5	11.0	–1.5
Agricultural products	3.5	4.0	5.5	2.0	1.0	4.5	1.5
Mining products	3.5	5.5	9.0	5.5	–2.0	3.0	1.5
Manufactures	6.0	6.0	11.5	4.5	5.0	13.5	–2.5
World merchandise production	2.0	3.0	4.5	2.0	3.0	4.5	–1.0
Agriculture	2.0	3.5	2.5	1.5	3.0	1.0	0.5
Mining	1.5	2.5	3.5	1.0	–1.0	3.5	0.0
Manufacturing	2.5	3.5	5.5	2.5	3.5	6.0	–1.5
World GDP	2.0	3.0	3.5	2.5	3.5	6.0	–1.5

NB: World merchandise production differs from world GDP in that it excludes services and construction.

Sources: Data from WTO (2000) p. 17, and WTO (2002) p. 23.

We will begin this chapter with a discussion of the various terms such as transnational corporation or multinational corporation that have been used to describe large international firms. In the theoretical perspectives section we consider competing explanations for the emergence and growth of transnational production, and the impact of TNCs on national societies. The third section outlines the globalization of production. The final section examines three key issues addressed in the contemporary global production system. These issues are the benefits and costs of TNCs especially for developing countries, the changing relationship between the state and the firm, and the international regulation of TNCs.

Definitions

Economists distinguish between two types of foreign investment – foreign direct investment (FDI) and indirect foreign investment, also termed portfolio investment. The transformation of the global production system has been brought about by rising levels of FDI. Foreign direct investment refers to investment made outside the home country of the investing company in which control over the resources transferred remains with the investor. It consists of a package of assets and intermediate goods such as capital, technology, management skills, access to markets and entrepreneurship. Foreign indirect (portfolio) investment refers to specific assets and intermediate products (for example, capital, debt or equity, technology) which are separately transferred between two independent economic agents through the modality of the market. In this instance, control over the resources is relinquished by the seller to the buyer. Only financial resources are transferred. We will follow conventional usage and use FDI as an indicator of the growth of international production.

Before 1914, long-term portfolio investment was more important than FDI. In that period FDI was relatively short-term. FDI began to grow extensively after the Second World War. In the 1950s and 1960s FDI was predominantly in the manufacturing sector, and the largest amount of FDI flowed from the US (Vernon, 1977). As a consequence of post-war recovery and the attainment of high productivity, the growth of the Euro-currency market and improvements in transport and communications, FDI flows from Europe and Japan began to grow. FDI continued to grow rapidly in the 1980s and 1990s (Julius, 1990; UNCTAD, 1999). For example, in the early 1980s the annual growth rate of FDI was approximately 14 per cent and between 1986 and 1996, FDI rose 350 per cent. This growth was fuelled by investment in services as well as manufacturing (see Table 6.2).

While the distinction between foreign direct investment and indirect foreign investment is relatively non-contentious, no agreement exists on the term to be applied to firms engaging in transnational production or FDI. These firms are variously called multinational, international, transna-

Table 6.2   *Growth in foreign direct investment (FDI – million of US dollars)*

Region	1990	1998
East Asia and Pacific	11 135	64 162
Europe and Central Asia	1 051	24 350
Latin America and the Caribbean	8 188	69 323
Middle East and North Africa	2 458	5 054
South Asia	464	3 659
Sub-Saharan Africa	834	4 364
Europe EMU	53 165	116 849
World	193 382	619 258

Sources: Data from World Bank (2000/2001) p. 315 and World Bank (2000) p. 336.

tional or global. It is now common to speak of multinational corporations (MNCs), or multinational enterprises (MNEs), international firms, transnational corporations (TNCs) or transnational enterprises (TNEs), and global corporations. Most writers make no distinction between these terms and have settled for one terminology rather than another without any seeming reflection on the implications of these terms. The most commonly used term is MNC but this chapter will refer to these economic agents as TNCs for reasons that will be explained below.

Serious attention was first given to the rise of transnational production in the late-1960s and early 19790s. At this stage both political and popular interest (Servan Schreiber, 1968; Bannock, 1971) and academic attention (Kindleberger, 1969; Vernon, 1971) turned to describing and assessing the importance of what was perceived as a new international actor although large international firms had existed for centuries. The term multinational enterprise was first given prominence by the Harvard Multinational Project which produced a number of important studies including Mira Wilkins's analyses of the growth of American business (1970). These studies did much to establish the term 'multinational' to describe this new phenomenon. At the same time others, from various perspectives preferred to use the term international corporation, for example, Edith Penrose (1968) in her magisterial study of the oil industry. Raymond Vernon in his widely influential book, *Sovereignty at Bay* (1971), although based at Harvard, followed Penrose in using the term international corporation, as did Hugo Radice (1975) in an influential collection of critical essays.

While the term multinational first gained widespread usage to describe large international firms, it was challenged from the mid-1970s by the term transnational corporation or transnational enterprise (Vaitsos, 1975; Lall and Streeten, 1977). The term transnational reflected UN usage, and proponents of its use argued that whereas multinational suggested a merger of capital from more than one nation-state, with a few notable exceptions (for example, Royal Dutch Shell and Unilever), most large international firms are owned and controlled by nationals of one country and conduct activities across national borders. The term transnational corporation (or transnational enterprise) more accurately reflects the fact that these firms are usually owned and controlled by the nationals of one country and enter into direct productive activities abroad. The term multinational corporation thus appears inappropriate, and that of transnational corporation more accurate since these firms operate trans (that its, across) borders thus giving greater weight to that term than international. Another term sometimes used to refer to these large firms is global corporation. The term global corporation was popularized in the 1970s by Richard Barnett (Barnett and Müller, 1975). His central concern was the global reach of these firms and he coined the term to reflect the impact of their activities.

In reality these choices revealed no essential differences in the operation of the firms so described. The distinctions arise from those who want to emphasize the issue of ownership and those analysts who prefer to stress the reach of these actors. Despite the differences in nomenclature most analysts would agree that the firm they are describing could be defined as one with production facilities in two or more countries. Thus in reality a single definition can suffice whether these firms were called multinational, international, transnational or global. That is, a TNC is a firm that owns and controls production (value-added) facilities in two or more countries. It follows that all TNCs are not huge, uncontrollable firms, and TNCs will vary in size, resources, and influence potential. Furthermore we believe that the estimation of the size, resources, and power wielded by a TNC will vary depending on the standpoint of the analyst.

Theoretical perspectives: explaining the growth of TNCs

Two issues have dominated discussions of transnational production, namely the growth of the TNC and its impact on sovereign states. In this section we begin by reviewing some of the most influential theories devised to explain the growth of transnational production. In the second part of this section we provide a brief introduction to competing perspectives on the impact of TNCs. The three perspectives on IPE discussed in Chapter 1 provide broad interpretations of the issues discussed below. Economic nationalist perspectives emphasize the importance of state behaviour in creating the conditions necessary for the emergence of global production and focus on the ability of states to control the activity of TNCs. Liberal theory gives greater weight to the relevance of the market both in terms of explaining the growth of transnational production and in assessing the impact of TNCs on the state. Radical theorists emphasize the changing nature of capitalist relations and retain a scepticism concerning the impact of TNCs on host economies.

The growth of transnational production has attracted attention across the spectrum of the social sciences with contributions from economics, geography, political science, sociology, and business studies. Within the array of studies emanating from this profusion of disciplinary, inter-disciplinary and cross-disciplinary research, three approaches (economic, organizational and motivational) to the study of TNCs are discernible. Economic approaches tend to emphasize the market characteristics that have given rise to the decision to invest abroad. Organizational perspectives give more emphasis to the internal structure of the corporation and seek explanations in terms of the decision-making structure of the firm. And motivational perspectives provide explanations in terms of the individuals and the belief systems they hold. It is not our intention to examine the wide range of theories that have been developed. Instead we will briefly outline some of the theories that have been most influential in the study of international political economy. These can be classified as liberal, structuralist and radical.

Two of the most important liberal theories were proposed by Raymond Vernon and John Dunning. The first widely cited theory was the product-cycle model developed by Raymond Vernon which provided an explanation for the expansion of American business overseas (Vernon, 1966). Vernon argued that companies through advances in technology are able to gain competitive advantages in the American domestic market. In the initial stage these firms are content to sell their products abroad. However, the importers of American products begin to acquire the appropriate technology and start producing these goods domestically thus providing products at a cheaper rate than the imported goods since they do not face transport costs. In order to protect their markets American producers are forced to establish factories abroad. The third stage of the product cycle occurs when foreign firms begin producing the product cheaper than US companies and begin exporting to the US. According to this model the main motivation for FDI arises from the desire to exploit technological comparative advantage and maintain market share. Critics of the product-cycle theory pointed to its inability to explain non-American FDI (Caves, 1974). Another liberal theory has been developed by John Dunning, one of the most prolific writers on the TNC. Dunning, drawing on economic and managerial factors, has developed a comprehensive theory (see, for example, Dunning, 1973, 1981 and 1988). His ownership, location, internationalization (OLI) model focuses on the decision to invest abroad with emphasis on ownership characteristics, and the desirability of the foreign location.

Susan Strange has provided a structuralist alternative to the liberal theories which shifts the emphasis from the decisions of firms to major structural change in the global economy (Strange, 1991 and 1994a). Strange lists three key structural changes that have accelerated transnational production – falling real costs of transport and communication; development of new technologies; and the creation of new financial instruments. She argues that structural changes in technology, communications, and finance created the conditions for the growth of TNCs. She claims that a rapid increase in technology spurred by the revolution in information technology has quickened the pace of globalized production; increased capital mobility has facilitated dispersion of industry, and changes in the knowledge structure has made trans-border communication and transportation cheaper and faster.

Marxist writers with their traditional focus on the centralization and concentration of capital were well placed to provide explanations for the growth of transnational production. An interesting contribution to the radical literature was made by Stephen Hymer. In his seminal study *The International Operation of National Firms* (1976) he argued that the dominance of American business ventures abroad arose from the oligoplistic business structure. In later works such as *The Multinational Corporation: A Radical Approach* (1979) he drew on Lenin's theory of imperialism and gave more attention to systemic factors and emphasized the uneven development of capital.

The theoretical dispute over the causes of transnational production is mirrored in the conflict concerning the impact of this activity on the nation-state and on national societies. Two broad positions are discernible – the positive and negative. Some analysts have developed arguments that emphasize the positive results of direct foreign investment but these findings are disputed by those who claim that on balance the net effect of TNC investment is negative for host countries. The positive case stresses the net positive benefits of FDI. For the most part it can recognize the possibility of costs but tends to put the emphasis on the favourable aspects of foreign investment. The negative case coming out of radical and dependency analyses places the focus on the negative impact of foreign firms. Although some analysts in this tradition are willing to admit some gains from FDI others are unwilling to accept a positive role for transnational capital under any circumstances. These writers tend to stress the size of these firms vis-à-vis governments.

It is not surprising that it should be liberal economists and the business community who contend that the net impact of TNC activity is positive. These analysts argue that both the direct and indirect effects of FDI are on the whole beneficial for host countries. Four main positive direct effects are claimed in this literature. First, it is argued that FDI provides additional resources and capabilities, that is, capital, technology, access to markets and management skills. Furthermore, it provides additional tax revenues through the increase in economic activity in the host country. These analysts also contend that FDI increases GDP thus increasing the tax base. Moreover, by better linking the host economy with the global marketplace, TNCs help to advance economic growth by fostering a more efficient division of labour. And finally they assert that FDI improves the balance of payments through import substitution, export generation or efficiency-seeking investment.

It is claimed that FDI provides three positive indirect effects. First, TNCs bring new management styles and more dynamic competitive practices by injecting entrepreneurship, management styles, work cultures and more dynamic competitive practices. Secondly, TNCs bring more efficient resource allocation, and upgrade domestic resources and capabilities. By more efficient resource allocation, competitive stimulus and spillover effects on suppliers and/or consumers, TNCs can help upgrade the domestic resources and capabilities, and the productivity of local firms; and also foster clusters of related activities to the benefit of the participating firms. Thirdly, TNCs enhance national welfare by more directly exposing the host economy to the political and economic systems of other countries; the values and demand structures of foreign households; superior attitudes to work practices, incentives and industrial relations; and the many different customs and behavioural norms of foreign countries.

The critics document four main negative direct effects. They argue that TNCs transfer too few or the wrong kind of resources or assets. TNCs can cut off foreign markets (that is, those serviced by domestic firms); can fail to adjust to localized capabilities and needs; and may not provide an addition to capital at all. Secondly, TNCs use transfer pricing and other devices to lower taxes paid. Also by restricting growth there is an overall loss of tax revenue. Thirdly, FDI promotes a division of labour likely to be in the company's interests and this can be detrimental to the country's comparative advantage. The division of labour is likely to be based on what the firm perceives to be in its global interests which may be inconsistent with dynamic comparative advantage as perceived by the host country. Finally, TNCs worsen the balance of payments through limiting exports and promoting imports and outcompeting local firms which export more and import less.

The critics claim that TNCs bring three negative indirect effects. First, foreign entrepreneurship, management styles and working practices fail to accommodate to, or where appropriate, change local business cultures. The introduction of foreign industrial relations procedures may lead to industrial unrest. By the pursuit of anti-competitive practices, it may lead to an unacceptable degree of market concentration. Secondly, foreign firms can limit the upgrading of local resources and capabilities by restricting local production to low-value activities and importing the major proportion of higher value intermediate products. It may also reduce the opportunities for domestic economies of scale by confining its linkages to foreign suppliers and industrial concerns. Thirdly, TNCs may cause unrest by introducing conflicting values through advertising, business customs, labour practices, and environmental standards. Finally, TNCs may exercise direct interference in the political regime or electoral process of the host country.

Below we will argue that the rise and development of the TNC is to be understood as the result of a changing political, economic, technological and managerial context. We will also try to suggest a way not of reconciling competing views on the impact of TNCs but of going beyond them.

Instead of adhering to either a positive or negative overview this perspective recognizes that the costs and benefits of FDI will vary from case to case and also that what constitutes costs and benefits will vary depending on the values of the observer. Our intention in putting forward this perspective arises from what we see as key flaws in the competing approaches to state–firm relations. The pro-TNC approach fails to think about power in the market. In viewing TNCs as wholly beneficial these writers pay limited, if any, attention to non-economic factors, and minimize the role of market failure and market distortions. The anti-TNC perspective, in demonizing the firm, gives no credence to governments' ability to shape economic policy, and fails to appreciate fully the structural changes that have taken place in the world economy.

Major developments

There have been two major changes in the global production structure. The first has been the globalization of production. There has been a proliferation of corporate activity and business networks around the world. The second major development has been the change in the underlying principles of the organization of production, and key features of the global production system.

The globalization of production

The globalization of production is aptly captured by phrases such as 'from national production to global production', and 'from local markets to global markets'. It refers to the proliferation and stretching of corporate activity and business networks across the globe. The globalization of production is a consequence of structural change in the global economy, changing organizational forms and strategies of TNCs, and the policies of national governments. While initially the spread of transnational production was viewed as a distinctly American phenomenon, the overseas expansion of European and Japanese firms followed by TNCs originating from developing countries has demonstrated that it is a truly global event. For many analysts the creation of American hegemony in the aftermath of World War II brought with it the beginnings of globalized production 'based on offshore low-wage assembly' (Bernard, 1994. p. 221). This was also partly the consequence of American foreign policy which encouraged manufacturing firms to invest in anti-communist countries to support its position during the Cold War. In the past three decades, however, transnational production has escaped its early origins in US economic growth and policy choices and has become a driving force in the global economy. Major enterprises in industrialized countries have found that they have 'outgrown national markets, national laws and national financial markets' and in response have begun producing 'for a global market according to a global corporate strategy' (Strange, 1991, p. 246).

The spread of the capitalist mode of production and free trade following World War II has led to the development of a complex and highly integrated world economy in which international trade and investment flows occur on a massive scale at increasingly rapid rates. International economic structures based on finance and trade have led to increasing interdependence and closer ties between countries. An important part of this process is associated with the growth of transnational production, with the increasing ability of firms to locate parts of their production overseas, while still maintaining direct control over the activities of foreign subsidiaries. This move by many enterprises to spread their activities into other countries has bolstered the globalization process, broadening the links between countries. The organizational form of the transnational corporation has undergone extensive change leading to the development of deep integration (Dicken, 1992) and these developments will be discussed in the next section. In this section we will consider structural changes in technology, transport and communications, and finance, and the political conditions attendant on these developments.

Technological change. The global production system is dominated by rapid developments in the technological environment. New technologies have placed innovation at the centre of profitability, and the creation, implementation and diffusion of new technology is now critical to economic efficiency and international competitiveness. The new production techniques are characterized by cutting-edge technological innovation, sophisticated coordination of operations, and more efficient means of meeting the needs of customers. With these developments production has thus grown in scale and become more cost effective.

The accelerating pace of technological change has enhanced the capacity of successful producers to supply the market with new products and/or make them with new materials or new processes. At the same time the accelerating rate of technological change in the production process has been central to creating the world market system. Technological change has prompted the emergence of global markets for goods and services by contributing to greater homogeneity in consumer tastes worldwide, by causing firms to seek wider markets, and by making it easier for firms to produce and market products globally. Additionally new technology contributes to the processes whereby product and process lifetimes have shortened, sometimes dramatically. As companies are required to satisfy consumer demands and win strategic alliances, new technologies are being applied across a wider range of goods and services, making them easily available at more affordable prices. Technologies have been at the fore-front of the process whereby new products replace old ones at an alarming rate. This process can be illustrated through a brief overview of some of the developments in home entertainment for consumers around the globe but especially in advanced industrial countries. At the beginning of the twentieth century musical entertainment at home was produced by manual means with the use of piano, wind and string instruments. At the begin-ning of the twenty-first century we have access to electronic and digital technology to aid us in our production of music. The vinyl record and the cassette tape have been supplanted by the compact disc, and the video tape, a development which came into widespread usage less than twenty years ago, is now rapidly being replaced by the DVD.

Meanwhile the costs to the firm of investment in research and develop-ment, and therefore of innovation, has risen. The time it takes to recoup profits from national markets is too long to keep up with the costs of developing and installing new technology, products and processes. To keep products competitive, especially when other companies may already be transnational, firms are having to gain access to overseas markets to increase the volume of their sales. Despite the growth of liberal trade it can still be difficult to access foreign markets, and the risk that trade barriers may be raised is always a problem. To overcome this problem firms have directed their efforts toward producing locally in the markets it wishes to sell in, and this has proved to be more cost-effective (Strange, 1991, pp. 247–8).

Communications and transport. The steady and cumulative lowering of the real costs of trans-border transport and communications has been fre-quently overlooked in explanations of the growth of transnational produc-tion. But without these reduced costs, central strategic planning of far-flung affiliates would have been riskier and more difficult, and out-sourcing of components as in automobile manufacture would have been hampered. Reduced communications costs allow new systems of global information management to become feasible. Information and transport technologies lower the real costs and risks of management at a distance. Better communications networks which are reliable, fast and efficient have meant that TNCs can be in constant contact with all their subsidiaries and allow information to flow relatively freely within the firm despite geo-graphical distance. Transport systems are also faster and more reliable so resources and products can be moved cheaply and easily from primary extraction to processing plants to markets. In the mid-1980s, for example, Apple computers 'travelled' around two million miles before reaching the final customer (Kaplinsky, 1991). These global assembly lines are extremely fluid with the production organization being 'centrally coordinated' (McMichael, 1996, p. 89). Communications networks also give TNCs greater access to markets: televisions, radio, magazines, newspapers and the internet have allowed firms' advertising to reach millions of people around the world tapping into global markets at relatively low cost to the firm. Telecommunications technology allows firms to organize along global lines, moving components and software among offshore sites and selling products in world markets. As digital and communications technology has become more accessible and integrated into daily life it has become embedded in all areas of existence thus pushing us further towards a global marketplace.

Finance. Central to transnational investment is the acquisition and deployment of capital. Developments in international finance have created integrated financial markets (Stopford and Strange 1991) which facilitate global production. Firms have been able to finance their production operations overseas as a result of the internationalization of finance. This globalization in the financial market is the result of three factors. The first factor leading to an expansion in the availability of capital is technological innovation which has produced reductions in cross-border transaction costs and facilitated private international capital transactions. The second factor is the removal of governmental, legal and technical barriers to the movement of capital thus easing cross-border capital flows.

There has been a widespread liberalization of capital markets around the world. This partial and incomplete transformation begun with the creation of the Euro-currency market in the 1960s and continued with the deregulation initiated by the US in the mid-1970s and early 1980s. As barriers went down, the mobility of capital went up (see Table 6.3 for developments in the 1990s). The old difficulties of raising money for investment in offshore operations and moving it across the exchanges vanished. The third factor is the growth of innovation in financial instruments. A variety of financial instruments and capital mobility support the globalization of production and cross-border transactions of TNCs in global financial markets. Not surprisingly these developments have been most widely exploited among the developed countries where the barriers to integration have been the least. But they have also been important for developing countries. These instruments include interest rates, currency and stock market index futures and over-the counter instruments such as derivatives, swaps, options, futures, forward transactions, bond lending and reinsurance. As a result capital moves across borders and boundaries in places where previously it was difficult for it to do so. The impact of these developments transcends capital markets, in that capital mobility has intro-

Table 6.3   *Growth of global capital flows*

($US millions)	Net private capital flows	
	1990	1998
Low income	14 831	52 365
Middle income	27 775	215 336
Low and middle income	42 606	267 700
East Asia & Pacific	18 720	67 249
Europe & Central Asia	7 649	53 342
Latin America & Caribbean	12 411	126 854
Middle East & North Africa	369	9 223
South Asia	2 174	7 580
Sub-Saharan Africa	1 283	3 452

Source: Data from World Bank (2000) p. 336.

duced major changes in international trade and the organization of the TNC. This sustained growth of commerce and international investment is a central element in the globalization of production because it has provided the financing for the expansion of TNC operations.

The expansion of international finance has radically reshaped the structural and institutional composition of the world economy. The integration of capital markets into one worldwide market for savings and credit means that TNCs can enjoy far greater possibilities by raising money wherever they operate without having to transfer funds across frontiers and exchanges. It is either unnecessary for the TNCs to find new funds, or they could do so locally.

Attendant on these changes is the impact of capital flight on host countries. Short-term capital flows has caused instability in the international financial market and has played a part in the Mexican crisis of 1994, Asian financial crisis of 1997 and Argentinian crisis of 2001. The relationship between national governments and foreign investors can move from one of accommodation and cooperation to a hostile and adversarial one. Crucially capital does not operate in a vacuum and the determination of the impact of capital on nation-states is linked to government–business relations. See Box 6.1 for an exploration of one such relationship.

Political. The globalization of production has also been influenced by the policies of national governments. The policy decisions taken by states

---

Box 6.1   Government regulation, international capital and financial instabiltity: the case of South Korea

Until the late 1980s, government intervention in the economy, and in particular the financial sector, was important for Korea's development process. Interference in major financial activities including interest rates and credit allocations enabled the state to support growth in strategically chosen industries. Following partial deregulation of Korea's capital controls, the economy's exposure to unregulated international capital flows made it vulnerable to capital flight and the whims of foreign speculators. Direct financing includes issuing bonds and stocks and increased from 15 per cent of financing in 1970 to 45.2 per cent in 1990. The governments' deregulation of the short-term based commercial paper (CP) market moving faster than the long-term interest rates of the banks in the 1990s led to a large expansion of short-term borrowing. Between 1992 and 1996, these short-term liabilities accounted for a massive 84.4 per cent of total capital flows into Korea and by 1996 they amounted to one-third of its GDP. When economic growth is high this 'hot money' is useful for investments in capacity that gets used by buoyant demand. However, when demand becomes sluggish, the high level of investment becomes excess capacity and the loans, which require repayment in the short-term, become harder and harder to service. The increase in non-performing loans causes foreign investors to loose confidence in the economy and massive capital outflow ensures. Thus the Korean 'bubble economy', inflated by short-term investment, was at the mercy of world economic growth, in particular export demand, and the confidence of foreign investors. Short-term capital flows constituted a major destabilizing factor to the Korean economy in the mid-1990s.

---

cannot be seen simply as automatic reactions to structural change or as arising solely from competitive pressures. There are a mix of motives and pressures acting on national governments. We will mention three aspects in which political factors contributed to the globalization of production. First, we can see the influence of political factors in the construction and maintenance of the liberal system of trade and payments ushered in after World War II which formed the background of the early development of transnational production. We mentioned at the outset of this chapter the importance of American interests and US foreign policy in the outward expansion of American business enterprises. Of central importance in the development of transnational production was US military and political power underpinning the Bretton Woods system of liberal trade and payments, and American foreign policy supportive of an expansive capitalist system in the Cold War conflict with the Soviet Union. Secondly, we can note that the liberalization in financial markets that stimulated changes in the production structure after 1973 was the result of political decisions taken by states. The degree, content and timing of liberalization in the United States and Europe shows varying influences of competitive pressure rather than a necessary correspondence between structural change and governmental regulation.

Thirdly, we can note that the relocation of manufacturing production to Third World states during the 1960s and 1970s was in response to various nationalist projects. A major, and often overlooked reason for the shift in industrial production was the policies of developing countries governments to attract foreign investment. As some East Asian states embarked on their model of export-oriented industrialization they sought massive foreign investment. One such incentive was through the creation of export processing zones (EPZs). An EPZ is an estate created especially for industrial export production in which prevailing labour regulations and taxation laws did not normally apply. For example, in Mexico one investment firm was offered 100 per cent tax exemption for the first ten years, and 50 per cent exemption for the following ten years as an incentive to locate an EPZ near the border with the United States (McMichael, 1996, p. 94). EPZs are attractive to TNCs since they offer low-wage labour with minimal external costs, while governments reap the benefits of capital investment and foreign currency earnings from exports. Of course this was not the only determinant of these flows of investment. There were a number of other reasons. These included the desire of firms to break into growing markets. The best way to do this was to locate all or part of their production in these Third World countries. Moreover, at this point firms were also encountering market saturation and a reduction in profits in the industrial world.

EPZs remain controversial with supporters and critics engaged in dispute concerning their negative or positive impacts. For supporters they provide a link to the global markets and contribute to employment and income generation. For critics they are exploitative enclaves that fail to produce the hoped-for benefits and increase dependency on external agents. The impact of EPZs has been studied by governments, independent researchers and international organizations. Box 6.2 presents the findings of the International Labour Organization.

Changing organizational principles

The globalization of international production is as we have seen a response to structural change and governmental policies. It is also the consequence

---

Box 6.2 Export processing zones: an ILO perspective

The International Labour Organization (ILO) published a study, 'Labour and social issues relating to export processing zones' in 1999. The report noted the exponential growth in EPZs in the 1980s and 1990s, and the geographic spread of EPZs. The largest numbers of EPZs are in North America (320) and Asia (225). But the concentration of EPZs is rising in developing regions such as the Caribbean (51), Central America (41) and the Middle East (39) and the figures are likely to increase throughout the world. The report noted that while traditionally EPZs are associated with manufactured products, variations to this pattern have arisen in a number of places. For example, in Islamabad a number of Agri-Export Zones (AEZs) specializing in the export of cut flowers and rose onions had been established. On the central issue of the impact of EPZs on overall economic growth the report stated that, there is a 'pervasive absence of meaningful linkages between the EPZs and the domestic economies of most of the host countries'. Moreover, the principal author of the report, Mr. Auret Van Heedren, noted 'the frequent absence of minimal standards and poor labour-management relations have predictable outcomes, such as high labour turnover, absenteeism, stress and fatigue, low rates of productivity, excessive wastage of materials and labour unrest which are still too common in EPZs'. The report concluded that while some countries had capitalized on the presence of EPZs in their territory, others had not. Whether or not an EPZ had benefited its host country is related to the degree of sophistication of the goods produced in the Zone. Malaysia and Singapore attracted quality investment in high-tech manufactures and have utilized the presence of such industries to qualify their own workforce in highly skilled sectors. Other states, including Bangladesh, Pakistan and Sri Lanka, that host the more labour-intensive zones are finding that rather than increasing the quality of the workforce, EPZs are perpetuating a stagnant skill level in their workers. In the textiles, garment manufacturing and electronics assembly, women account for 90 per cent or more of the workers and it is in these processing and assembly operations where companies see labour as a cost to contain rather than an asset to develop.

of changing organizational patterns within firms, and changes in the wider system of production.

In the past each phase of the production process was completed by a different firm. Over time firms came to realize that by merging, so that one firm controlled several steps, they could reduce costs and improve production efficiency. Between each step of production there are transaction costs between firms. If these firms merged they could internalize these costs, resulting in an overall saving on external costs. Vertical integration or internalizing production flows is one of the major economic incentives that has led to the growth in TNCs. When a firm decides to move part of its production process overseas it retains control and reduces its costs by keeping the flows of 'globally-applicable technology and marketing expertise' (Casson, 1991, p. 271) within the company thus eliminating the necessity of licensing out to firms within the host country. This internal trade serves only to redistribute income between different divisions of the company eliminating the possibility that one parent of the transaction may default. This provides added security and control to the central managing body and prevents external forces from interrupting the production process. Much of the world's trade is now internalized in TNCs with the movement of components between foreign subsidiaries and parent companies during the production process. The benefits of internalizing transaction costs is an incentive for firms to transnationalize their production. The decision by one firm in an industry puts pressure on other firms to go global in order to remain competitive.

Another development has been in the creation of an integrated transborder production system. This arises when the entire production process is spread across widely dispersed locations within and between countries. Facilitated by supra-territorial coordination which links components, machinery, finance and services of a company anywhere in the world a global production operation emerges. The emphasis in this environment is the transfer of production to points of optimum conditions. Additionally, electronic networks have facilitated global alliances of manufacturing companies to allow more efficient outsourcing of production of parts or products to suppliers throughout the world.

From Fordist to post-Fordist production. The expansion of TNC activity in the 1950s and 1960s was in accordance with what has come to be called the Fordist production system. Named after the American industrialist Henry Ford production under a Fordist system conformed to two simple principles, namely, mass production and mass consumption. The standard system for production was the factory system based on semi-skilled labour using specialized equipment to mass produce standardized goods. Competitive advantage accrued from cutting costs and this was achieved through an assembly-line system. Firms achieved economies of scale through mass production and increased efficiency by training workers to perform routine tasks. Under this system workers earned sufficient wages to boost consumer demand thus ensuring factory production maintained a high rate of turnover. However, from the late 1970s there was a change in the organization of manufacturing activities which shifted the priorities of TNCs from labour costs and mass production to product innovation. Changes in the nature of consumer demand has meant that product innovation quality is more important than price competitiveness, although price is still an important factor. Companies now tend to look for flexible specialization, competitive differentiation and quality control as the main features of their production process. This means that mass production of goods which are very similar to the products of other companies will not necessarily give the competitive advantage required in today's market.

In the 1980s the Japanese automobile company, Toyota, developed the just-in-time (JIT) system in which component parts are delivered by Toyota's suppliers two hours before assembly – just in time. JIT permits Toyota to hold no inventory and allows design and production to be changed quickly in response to consumer demand and changes in the consumer market (McMichael, 1996, p. 107). These new systems of production reduce the ability of companies to mass produce goods which can then be stored until they are required on the market and the workers often need to be more skilled so that design and managerial decisions can be made on the factory floor. Furthermore, with the need to produce goods speedily in response to demands in the market, suppliers and assembly plants need to be in close geographical proximity. The advantage of low wages is not now as important in the location choice for production as it was under Fordist manufacturing systems. Factors that now affect location choice include proximity to suppliers and markets, and the availability of skilled labour and specialized technology. Post-Fordist production also has greater infrastructure requirements which many countries specializing in cheap labour are unable to meet. Under these new conditions, many TNCs need to have entire production chains occurring in one region. For example, this shift gives East Asia a competitive advantage over Africa. In East Asia tremendous efforts had been made to increase the skills of the labour force and much of the required infrastructure had been built during industrialization in the 1960s and 1970s, with large networks of firms established, mostly already within TNC production lines.

For much of Africa, however, these developments mean that it is unlikely that there will be a significant amount of investment by TNCs in the foreseeable future given the lack of infrastructure, geographical distance, and poorly educated population. While under post-Fordism the demand for mass-produced goods is still a feature of markets, the need for more flexible and innovative products has changed the direction of foreign investment.

Mergers, strategic alliances and joint ventures. If the shift from Fordist to post-Fordist production captures the key organizing principle of capitalist production in managerial terms there have also been changes in the ways in which TNCs organize in the emerging world market. The attitudes, organizational structures and behaviour of business corporations have adapted to changes in the global economy and the policies of governments. One development from the 1980s onwards has been the increase in mergers and acquisitions, joint ventures, and other strategic alliances. For example, in 1999, mergers and acquisitions accounted for 80 per cent of global FDI (UNCTAD, 2000). The creation of strategic alliances, joint ventures and the resort to increased incidence of mergers and acquisitions is partly a response to the impact of technological change on product life cycles (as discussed above), partly the result of the development of new markets and partly a consequence of the expansion in the services sector. A single firm lacks the combination of technological know-how, funds for research and development, local market knowledge, access to finance, and market share necessary to remain competitive in this rapidly changing environment. Thus firms have adapted organizationally to these developments.

Another development has been the emergence of new attitudes and strategies towards foreign investment. In the past firms tended to either increase investment or reduce investment sequentially. In the past 15 years or so, firms have used both investment and disinvestment strategies at the same time. They have expanded in one sector or territory while simultaneously contracting in another sector or territory. This is also a response to the rapid shortening of product cycles and the segmentation of market structures.

A third change has been the requirement under conditions of post-Fordist production to pay more attention to the relationship between market integration on one hand and the specialized nature of local markets on the other. For example, the global burger chain McDonald's while serving standard fare in most of its global outlets also develops products specifically designed for the local market. Firms are aware that they possess certain advantages or core competencies that have given them a competitive advantage but that these general characteristics are likely to be of limited utility unless their production is sensitive to the demands of consumers, and the shifting cultural context in which they operate.

Key issues

This section examines three key issues surrounding TNCs. The first issue concerns the evaluation of the benefits of FDI and we argue that this needs to be done on a case-by-case basis. Secondly, we will examine the continuing debate over state–firm interactions before turning to look at the problems involved in regulating capital.

Re-evaluating the benefits of FDI

As we pointed out in the section exploring theoretical perspectives there are competing views concerning the impact of TNCs on national societies. We are not concerned in this section with a repetition of those arguments. These debates between supporters and opponents of foreign direct investment erupted in the 1960s and continue today. During the 1970s when the Third World's demand for a New International Economic Order was at its peak, and dependency analyses were fashionable, the views of the critics were given greater prominence. But with the triumph of neo-liberalism and the imposition of adjustment policies in the developing world it is the views of the proponents of FDI that have been in the ascendancy. It is difficult to reconcile these contrasting views, and analysts use selective statistics and case studies to support their respective arguments.

The approach taken in this text rejects the over-generalization of both perspectives. Instead it begins from the observation that FDI can have negative or beneficial impacts but that this is essentially an empirical question which can only be answered in relation to concrete circumstances. This requires analysis to focus on specific country and firm characteristics rather than assuming a general orientation of firms and countries. In this section we will consider the ways in which governments may seek to increase the benefits for their societies from inward foreign direct investment. In other words, we raise some of the key issues that should be examined in the context of specific case studies through an exploration of the interactions between governments and TNCs.

It is not always apparent if many of the objections to TNCs stem from their size and control over economic resources or whether the main objections are made in respect of the foreign ownership of productive assets. The benefits and costs of FDI have been assessed through the use of economic, political and cultural criteria. Economic criteria include the balance of payments, economic growth, and tax revenues; political issues include interference in domestic politics, and the effect on sovereignty; crucial cultural issues focus on taste transfer and protecting traditional national culture. The evaluation of the costs and benefits of TNC investment in a host country will therefore vary depending on which of these criteria the analyst thinks is most important. Different conclusions will be reached depending on the starting point of the observer. For example, if the main objection is to foreign ownership then even if it can be shown that economic growth has been positive, the critique of TNC involvement still retains its force.

What determines the net benefits of FDI? What can governments do to ensure that such investment best contributes to economic growth and development? The answer to these questions depend on the policies followed by host governments, the economic and social context of investment, the type of firm and the sector in which the investment is located.

The impacts that TNCs have on their host countries will be strongly influenced by the host government's policies. While we recognize that the impact of FDI is also dependent on a range of economic and societal variables not necessarily subject to governmental control we will for illustrative purposes focus on governmental policies. In deciding to welcome FDI, unless states promote policies designed towards achieving greater economic and social welfare for their citizens from the activities of TNCs, they will fail to reap sufficient benefits. This is not solely an issue of governments becoming more accommodating to the needs of foreign firms. States need to maintain a certain level of control and input into the activities of foreign investors to ensure that they maximize the benefits to the host country. The different results available from studies of the impact of FDI, especially in developing countries, reflect the success or failure of governments to direct foreign investment to productive activity (Stopford and Strange 1991). While in some countries little attention has been paid to this issue, others have made consistent efforts to direct the activities of TNCs in fulfilment of their national development plans. In Singapore, for example, TNCs have been directed towards investing in 'higher than average value-added activities' and upgrading 'the quality of labour' (Dunning, 1985, p. 415). This has resulted in greater levels of development and economic growth in Singapore and has now allowed it to develop stronger national industries with a more skilled labour force to draw on. While some countries have actively promoted export processing zones (EPZs) to attract foreign investment, others are careful to avoid export enclaves by ensuring that at least a proportion of the sales are produced or sub-contracted locally (Ibid., p. 418). The nature of the host government's policies towards TNCs is thus a crucial factor in determining if a TNC enhances or inhibits the development of local industries.

One of the major points of contention over the net benefits of FDI for developing countries concerns the transfer of technology. Indeed, this is one of the main reasons why many governments allow greater foreign investment, as they realize that in the absence of the finance and knowledge provided by TNCs, it would be much harder, and in many cases almost impossible, for them to gain access to industrial technologies. While in some cases this transfer of technology by TNCs has led to much faster diffusion of technology than would otherwise have been the case, it is unlikely to achieve maximum impact unless governments upgrade human and technological capabilities. However, as will be discussed below, government policies are only one side of the picture. No amount of regulation by a government or national policies to enhance the technological capability of the population will help to provide value-added FDI if the technology transferred is less advanced compared to the technology which is being developed and used in home countries at any given time. Studies have shown that the technology frequently transferred from industrial countries to developing countries is designed to maintain low-level productive activities in developing countries (Bernard, 1994, p. 251). On the other hand, in advanced countries, the transfer of technology tends to be more effective with their better capabilities allowing them to 'absorb leading edge technologies' from foreign investors (Lall, 1991, p. 251).

The overall economic impact of TNCs through provision of additional capital, a positive impact on the balance of payments, increased tax revenue, and diffusion of skills and technology is dependent on governmental policies. Governments can devise a broad macro-economic framework, and institute legal and administrative reforms that ensure positive linkages between local firms and foreign capital. Within the developing world there exists a vast array of governmental attitudes, skills and ability to design and implement the requisite changes. In these circumstances the impact of FDI is likely to vary depending on the country in question. We do not intend to imply that the implementation of effective policies is a simple matter and that governments that fail to do so are simply incompetent. On the contrary, we recognize that the domestic political economy of reform is a complex and difficult process. We do not have the time or space to explore the economic, political, cultural, and institutional dimensions of domestic policy reform. In the context of this chapter the important point we are making is that the benefits of FDI will vary depending on the local context.

The evidence does seem to suggest that those developing countries that have been open to foreign investment and allowed TNCs to establish export-oriented plants have generally industrialized at much greater rates than their more restrictive counterparts (Lall, 1991, p. 251) This is supported by figures on international trade which show that between 1960 and 1979, Third World countries increased their share of world trade from six per cent to ten percent (McMichael, 1996, p. 86) most of which was due to the export of manufactured goods produced by TNCs; evidence from post-communist economies also supports these findings. As previously mentioned, above, government policies also play an important role in this industrializing process. It is vital that the state promotes integration with global structures by creating the necessary infrastructure thus ensuring that even if the TNCs were to withdraw from the country, domestic firms would have sufficiently developed the capabilities for continued participation in world trade and production.

While the above suggests that the net effects of TNCs participation in the local economy can contribute positively to development with relevant government policies, the likelihood that governments will be in a position to maximize bargaining with the firm has also to be discussed. The structural power of TNCs can lead to situations where sound macro-economic policies followed by governments may not always produce positive net benefits. For example, while export levels and visible industrialization may take place, the actual development of the host country may be inhibited. There is concern in both developed and developing countries that the plants established by TNCs in host countries serve only as 'offshore satellites for the main activities' in home countries (Dunning, 1985, p. 415). The result is that few benefits accrue to the host country since the profits are, for the most part, returned to the parent company. Even more importantly, high value-added activities, research and development activities for example, tend to remain concentrated in home countries and few of the cutting-edge technologies are transferred to foreign subsidiaries, limiting the opportunities for host governments to establish industries capable of producing high-end exports, or in some cases moving beyond basic component manufacture. It has been argued, for example, that the export-oriented industrialization achieved by some Third World countries was more a result of the First World 'shedding the production of consumer goods' (McMichael, 1996, p. 86) rather than a positive attempt to assist developing countries along the path of industrialization.

Research and development (R&D) within enterprises has also tended to remain in home countries. A study of TNCs from Japan, Germany and the United States, the three largest sources of foreign investment, showed that 'an overwhelming share of their R&D spending' is maintained at home (Pauly and Reich, 1997, p. 22). Any R&D that does occur overseas is generally directed towards studies of the local markets for the customization of products or to collect knowledge which is then sent back to the home country (Ibid., p. 12). The Nike Corporation, for example, produces most of its shoes in Asia but all product design and sales promotion is done at the company's headquarters in the United States (McMichael, 1996, p. 98). As Lall puts it, by receiving the know-how (operational procedures) but not the know why (research and innovation capabilities), combined with the internalization of technology markets within TNCs, developing countries are restricted from moving their own technological base 'beyond that needed for adaptive activity . . . and research' (1991, p. 253). Lall further claims that evidence from Taiwan and Korea has shown that know-how has developed far more in industries in which TNC entry has been restricted. In short, there is compelling evidence to suggest that TNCs from the advanced industrial countries continue to exercise a tight rein over their technological knowledge (Mudzafar, 2001).

Moreover, from a nationalist perspective, if the entry of foreign firms into local markets results in local firms being squeezed out despite an improvement in efficiency, this will be seen as a negative development which will ultimately undermine the economic development of the country. During the industrialization of the West, infant industries were often given the benefit of protectionist government policies to allow them to establish themselves before they faced competition. With the involvement of TNCs and the liberalization of international trade however, new local industries in developing countries are not provided with similar opportunities. By the early 1970s the amount of manufacturing exports that was controlled by TNCs ranged from 20 per cent in Taiwan, to 43 per cent in Brazil to 90 per cent in Singapore (McMichael, 1996, p. 82). Without careful management and policies by the host government, the technological transfer and industrializing promises of TNCs do not actually help developing countries come any closer to catching up with industrialized states. While some benefits have accrued to developing countries from investment by TNCs it has been argued by many critics that this is only a by-product of the move away from manufacturing and unskilled production by the advanced industrial countries. The Third World thus became an inexpensive source of consumer goods that are no longer viable to produce in highly industrialized nations.

State–firm interactions

The growth of transnational production does not only have implications for government policies as they relate to foreign investment but also state–firm relations as a whole and the nature of sovereignty within the international system. The issue of the net impact of FDI on host societies is intimately connected with the wider question of the changing relations between the state and the firm. The central issue often debated here concerns the relative power of the state and the TNC. A number of commentators and social groups are concerned that the globalization of production has created or is creating a situation in which the state is losing some of its authority and power and is being replaced by the TNC in many areas.

TNCs act as the producers of wealth within the international political economy and as such have increased their ability to influence political systems. When firms were generally confined within national borders they relied on the state to represent their interests at the international level. Now, however, TNCs are becoming important actors within the global political economy (Stopford and Strange, 1991) and it is arguable that at times their influence can be greater than that of states. States are increasingly involved in bargaining with TNCs in order to attract foreign investment (Strange 1994a). Increasingly in both developed and developing countries states need to cooperate with TNCs to achieve economic, political and social goals. Trying to control the activities of many large firms through regulatory policies can be difficult and risky considering that the opportunities offered by foreign investment can be an important part of economic planning and growth. States have therefore moved into a new policy environment in which they must try to find a balance between attracting and encouraging investment while still maintaining a range of social goals and promoting the so-called national interest. Within this new environment states still retain territorial control and firms require access to territory in order to conduct their business activities. As such, states enjoy a degree of legitimacy that is denied to firms. The changing context of state–firm interactions has raised a number of issues. In this section we will focus on four: changing attitudes of governments towards TNCs; decision-making and national autonomy; the transformation of state policies; and the impact on labour.

Changing attitudes. An important factor in determining the evolution of state–firm interactions is the views and attitudes held by the political elite concerning the net benefits of FDI. The attitudes of governments to TNCs have changed considerably over the last forty years. With the onset of the North–South dialogue in the 1960s many Third World governments were highly critical if not downright hostile to foreign investment. Attitudes began to change in the 1980s with most governments in the developing world acclaiming FDI as good news. In the earlier period it was generally believed that the economic power of TNCs and their affiliates had adverse effects on national economies through such practices as transfer pricing and restrictions on the sources of imported components (Dunning, 1991, p. 231). In response government policies attempted to bolster domestic industries while restricting the activities of foreign firms. Governments also used planning to allocate resources rather than markets.

There are a number of reasons for this change of heart. The first is the triumph of neo-liberal economic ideology and the resort to neo-liberal economic policies by most governments. The renewed faith of most countries in the workings of the market economy is demonstrated, for example, in the wholesale privatization of state-owned assets and the deregulation and liberalization of markets over the past 15–20 years. The move to remove structural market distortions has been played out all over the developing world, and was initiated in the United States and Western Europe. For some analysts this development arises from the proven superiority of the liberal order while for others this is the result of the imposition of structural adjustment policies by international financial institutions and multilateral development banks.

The second explanation is the increasing globalization of economic activity and the integration of international production and cross-border markets by TNCs. This has led many countries to re-evaluate the costs and benefits of FDI and the opportunities provided by TNCs for increased participation in international trade and labour markets. In the Third World, in particular, industrialization policies based on import substitution were replaced with export-oriented policies based on TNC systems of production and distribution. The third reason is that the key ingredients of contemporary economic growth of created assets, such as technology, intellectual capital, learning experience and organizational competence, are not only becoming more mobile across national boundaries, but becoming increasingly housed in TNC systems.

The fourth reason why governments have modified their attitudes towards FDI is the successful industrialization of a number of countries particularly in East Asia. As a result the competition for the world's scarce resources of capital, technology and organizational skills is becoming increasingly intensive. The fifth is that the economic structures of the major industrialized countries are converging, one result of which is that competition between firms from these nations is becoming more intra-industry and more pronounced.

The sixth explanation is that the criterion for judging the success of FDI by host governments has changed over the years, and changed in a way which has made for a less confrontational and more cooperative stance between themselves and foreign investors. More particularly the emphasis of evaluating inbound TNC activity over the past two decades has switched from the direct contributions of foreign affiliates to its wider impact on the upgrading of the competitiveness of a host country's dynamic comparative advantage. And finally, the learning experience of countries about what TNCs can and cannot do for host countries has created a belief in many governments that they can take action to ensure they more efficiently promote their economic and social goals. This appears to be a belief that has limited application in reality and many governments in the developed world find it difficult to fulfil these goals. For example, in 2001 the British government was confronted with its abject failure to protect jobs after two TNCs – Corus and Motorola – decided to disinvest. This happened despite the fact that investment was in depressed regions of the UK and the government tried to persuade the companies to maintain production.

Decision-making and national autonomy The ability of TNCs to transfer resources abroad in response to changing national and international conditions affects the autonomy of state decision-making authorities. An inherent conflict exists between the political organization of authority based on national governmental structures and the economic organization of value based on growing economic interdependence. The limits to effective public policy are partly determined by the capacity of a state to promote a climate for investment favourable to transnational capital.

The globalization of production presents extraordinary challenges to the economic management of a country. Economic development is no longer restricted to the national territorial forms that prevailed for most of the past two centuries. Instead national production is now located within world production systems. Countries can no longer rely on natural comparative advantage to win them a place in the global economy. Instead decisions are made on the basis of global production strategies and relative efficiency. The utilization of high levels of technology and policies that encourage efficiency and promote competition are the new imperatives to international competitiveness. Although most economic activity is not global in this sense, nevertheless, this is an emerging trend and governments are increasingly having to adjust to international demands and pressures. The innovation of financial instruments, the development of multinational banks and other financial institutions have made regulation of the economy more difficult. The integration of national economies and communication systems thus creates a global system of interaction in which the state is but one player amongst others and state borders are losing their significance.

Moreover, firms themselves often disregard the domestic regulation of governments. Given their global production and distribution systems firms are not dependent on governmental policy in a single state. They can, for example, evade restrictive credit policies by borrowing on international capital markets, and escape taxation of corporate profits through timely inter-firm transfers of resources. In so far as TNCs are no longer constrained by the regulation of particular states, they are effectively footloose.

This problem of diminished or diminishing national authority is particularly relevant in the developing world. The sheer size and resources of many TNCs in comparison to developing countries provides for an unequal relationship between the two. This predisposes developing states to modify the demands they make of TNCs. Additionally the capacity of firms to locate anywhere in the world exerts an inordinate amount of pressure on countries to acquiesce to their demands, or suffer negative consequences in their macroeconomic stability. The mobility of capital increases the alternatives available to firms while at the same time circumscribing those available to states. Thus, for many, the benefits developing countries derive from FDI will remain negligible given the structural imbalance between TNCs and Third World governments.

Transforming state policies. The globalization of production has altered the attitudes of governments, shifted the bargaining power between states and TNCs, and also transformed the nature of the state. This change is captured by the phrase 'the competition state' (Cerny, 1995). States have become increasingly compelled to liberalize because of competitive deregulation pressures resulting from the mobility of capital (Cerny 1993). Boundaries are shifting as resources are linked with indistinct borders, while industries shift and react to changed circumstances and new technologies. The threat of shifting production from one country to another causes countries to compete against each other. This has produced the phenomenon of competitive deregulation between states as they attempt to maintain their attractiveness to investors and to sustain global competitiveness. The competitive processes between states can lead to a situation in which wages, working conditions and environmental standards become depressed. This is a consequence of increased liberalization as states seek TNC investment.

The globalization of production and internationalization of finance has enhanced the capacity of the holders of capital to evade the jurisdiction of what is often perceived as hostile economic management. States must therefore be increasingly sensitive to the regulatory policies of their neighbours, since they are now effectively competing for the right to regulate investment. Further, this new competitive dynamic is propelling states to accommodate the preferences of market actors, and to actively court international investors by introducing more liberal regulatory standards (Andrews, 1994, pp. 193–218). States will only be able to influence this process, and to regulate foreign direct investment by assigning or delegating to supranational institutions some of their power and authority. The development of offshore markets is another instrument that has eroded national financial barriers. These changes provide investors with prospects for minimal levels of taxation and regulation, thereby allowing for the unconstrained movement of financial resources. These sources have also been critical in providing a wider source of funding for TNCs engaged in the process of globalizing their businesses.

Labour. The issue of the impact of transnational production on labour will be examined in Chapter 7. However, we cannot leave the topic of state–firm interactions without a brief mention of the debate concerning the state's role in protecting workers. Critics point to the massive profits TNCs can make as a result of transferring production from high-wage industrial countries to low-wage developing economies. Henderson calculated that in 1975, if one hour of electronics work in the United States was valued at 1000 then the equivalent work was worth twelve in Hong Kong, seven in Taiwan, and five in Indonesia and Thailand (1991, p. 54).

Consequently TNCs moved production processes using low-skilled and unskilled labour to developing countries to take advantage of these low wages. But they were not only escaping higher wage rates, they were also trying to circumvent minimum health and safety requirements and to reap the benefits of working with a largely non-unionized workforce. Instead of protecting their workers, many Third World governments colluded with transnational capital to maintain poor working conditions. In a recent popular study of the impact of transnational production, Klein argues that 'When the actual manufacturing process is so devalued, it stands to reason that the people doing the work of production are likely to be treated like detritus – the stuff left behind'. (2001, p. 217). She produces figures which show that while assembly-line workers in the United States and Germany are paid $18.50 per hour, the equivalent rate for the same work in China is $0.87. From the perspective of workers in advanced industrial countries, the shift of labour-intensive production overseas altered the economic structure causing economic and social decay in the wake of high levels of unemployment.

Regulating capital

The impact of TNCs on states and societies, and the difficulty that individual governments face in controlling these firms have led to calls for greater international regulation of the activities of international business. While civil society actors call for the regulation of international business, both government and private sector interests have been increasingly resistant to such demands. But private interests are interested in promoting forms of international regulation conducive to their interests.

There are two contentious issues, one on each side of the regulatory agenda, that encapsulates the current dilemmas. Those groups trying to subject the behaviour of TNCs to greater scrutiny and to impose state sovereignty on firms' taxation provide an interesting example of the failure of both domestic and international regulatory power. Through diverse accounting procedures, firms have devised strategies to evade taxation and as a result the corporate tax contribution to the finances of governments has been declining. There is an attempt to reduce the power of firms to evade taxation at the national level through the introduction of international surveillance and cooperation between national governments. This is not a radical proposal and is supported by many liberal and conservative governments in the OECD. However, the attempt in 2001 by the OECD to develop guidelines for international taxation policies was defeated through the lobbying efforts of TNCs. They were successful in persuading the US government to oppose the OECD guidelines. On the other hand, a contrasting OECD set of regulations favourable to the expansion of international business was defeated by a coalition of civil society groups who felt that it increased the power of firms relative to that of governments. The Multilateral Agreement on Investment (MAI) aimed to set standards that would further liberalize national investment regimes.

To some observers of the contemporary global economy, TNCs are increasingly exercising a parallel authority alongside governments in matters of economic management affecting the location of industry and investment, in the direction of technological innovation, and in the extraction of surplus value. Corporations have actively sought through industry associations and individual contacts with governments to influence the architecture of national, regional and global regulation. Firms have, to date, argued successfully for minimal regulation, and for self-regulation rather than public authority control in situations where some direct form of regulation is required. The TNC has become endowed with a greater political role as it uses more diverse means of achieving its objectives. Not only have TNCs resorted to using access to the highest levels of decision-making with national governments, but also access to the WTO and other multilateral institutions to ensure corporate agenda is prioritized everywhere (Sell, 2000; Smythe, 2000).

To some extent TNCs have joined states as the authorities exercising power (whether or not affirmed by them) over the course of national and global economic development. Moreover, companies exert considerable influence over the global economy as they account for an increasing proportion of international intercourse than do governments. This development facilitated by technological change has redefined state sovereignty by reducing the magnitude of authority claims asserted by the state. Despite this, governments remain the decisive holders of authority in regard to the territories over which other states recognize their supremacy, but are restrained in their capacity to affect economic decisions within their borders.

Conclusion

The spread of TNCs since the 1950s and the creation of a global production structure has had significant effects on international economic and trade structures, industrial development and government policies. The growth and nature of transnational production has changed over time, especially with the introduction of post-Fordist production systems, and TNCs have greatly affected national and regional developments around the world. Much of the uneven development and industrialization that occurred in the final years of the twentieth century can at least partly be explained by differences in TNC involvement and government policies towards foreign investment. The shift towards transnationalization by many enterprises has also changed traditional state–firm relations, with policies of cooperation essential to the economic planning of both actors. The large amounts of capital owned and controlled by TNCs combined with their participation in virtually every national economy in the world has given them a great deal of strategic power in the global political economy and their role in influencing international trade negotiations and other international agreements is an important issue in the contemporary global political economy.

The role of TNCs in creating a new international division of labour will be examined in the next chapter. It will discuss the ways in which transnational production has affected mature industrial economies and developing countries. TNCs have been the major actors organizing a shift of unskilled and semi-skilled manufacturing production from the advanced industrial countries to the semi-periphery. Many developing countries were integrated into global production systems because of their large pool of low-wage labour.

Chapter 7

Global Division of Labour

When studying international economics or global political economy it is easy to concentrate attention on the activity of corporations or states and lose sight of the fate of particular people or groups of people. This chapter focuses on how people are caught up in a division of labour created by the global political economy. Where a person fits in in this division of labour has a significant role in determining how long they will live and what their quality of life will be. The focus on the division of labour reveals gross inequalities and great injustices that may not be so visible when examining other aspects of the global political economy.

The chapter begins by outlining some of the variations in terms surrounding the division of labour such as the international, global, gendered and racial division of labour. In the theoretical perspectives section we consider the liberal theory of division of labour and objections to this from nationalist and critical perspectives. Under major developments we consider changes in the production process (how things are made) and the move from an international to a global division of labour. The key issues considered in the chapter are: the gendered division of labour; the global struggle for worker's rights; and the relationship between workers' rights and global stability.

Definitions

The division of labour refers to how people fit into the production process. Different societies and economic systems have different ways of organizing who does which particular job. Some societies have relatively simple divisions of labour where many people do similar tasks while other societies may have a detailed division of labour where people specialize in doing only one or two tasks. Take the example of the difference between people who live on farms and those who live in cities. Most farmers must take on a number of different jobs in order to survive. In addition to planting crops, they may have to be able to fix their machinery, preserve their own vegetables, bake their own bread and even take a second job in the city. Most city dwellers specialize in a particular job and then pay others to do tasks such as baking bread, growing crops, fixing machinery or even caring for children. In this case the city dwellers have a more specialized division of labour than the farmer.

There can also be different approaches to allocating tasks to particular individuals or groups. In some cases a division of labour may be based on race, such as in the apartheid era in South Africa or in the pre-civil war era in the southern US. In both of these examples violence was used to enforce the allocation of tasks. In other cases unofficial discrimination or lack of skills may maintain a racial division of labour. Many Western societies aspire to a division of labour based upon merit and operating in response to impartial market forces, but ethnic, racial, class and gender divisions continue.

Moving beyond local communities one can speak of an international division of labour. This refers to a process whereby people in particular countries build or make particular things for export. Your geographic location has a great influence upon what type of job you do in the international economy. For example, if you are participating in the global economy and happen to live in Honduras you would probably be involved in the export of bananas; if you lived in Bangladesh it would likely be textiles, in China it could be toys, in California it could be aerospace or the entertainment industry.

The concept of a global division of labour captures a form of organization which reaches around the planet, but where work is not confined to particular states. In a global division of labour you find activities that in the past might have been thought of as being confined to particular states existing in very different types of states. Labour one might associate with a developing country flourishes in a developed state and jobs thought to be the preserve of advanced industrialized countries exist alongside very labour-intensive jobs in developing states. For example, an expanding computer software industry is developing in India alongside the majority of the population that lives in subsistence agriculture. Alternatively, textile sweatshops thrive in Los Angles and New York. The distinctive feature of these jobs is that they are plugged into a transnational production process and they are not confined to particular parts of the globe, although they may be more concentrated in some areas rather than others. To return to the example, most computer software jobs are in advanced industrialized countries and the textile industry is a much greater presence in developing states. Yet, some developing countries have information technology jobs and developed countries have immigrants working in the textile industry.

There is another important aspect of the division of labour and that is its gendered character. Men tend to be grouped in different jobs from women. Gender refers to the ideas societies have about what social roles and forms of employment are most appropriate for men and women. For example, if you look around a university, it appears that most professors are men and most secretaries are women. In the global economy, women are the majority of workers in export-processing zones and men are the majority of the managers. In the finance industry, men are a majority of the stockbrokers, women the majority of bank tellers.

The interesting thing about the gendered division of labour is that it is not preordained or 'natural' but changes over time depending upon social and economic circumstances. For example, in Canada and the US before World War II, women were largely confined to domestic tasks. However, with the shortage of male workers during the Second World War, many women were called upon to work in factories where they were more than capable of doing 'male' work. Once the war ended, women were encouraged to return to the domestic role so that men could resume their 'natural' employment patterns.

There can also be a racial and ethnic division of labour. In these cases groups of people from particular ethnic backgrounds or with visible physical differences are confined or corralled into specific forms of labour. The racial division is used to justify the different legal status and economic exploitation of these groups of workers (Persaud, 2001). The practice of slavery in the Americas is a brutal example of a racial division of labour. However, racial divisions have also been crucial to the employment relations of Koreans in Japan, Indonesians in Malaysia, Mexicans and central Americans in the US, Turks in Germany, Algerians in France, West Indians in Britain, Indians and Chinese in many countries.

Theoretical perspectives: Adam Smith and his critics

The economic benefits of an advanced division of labour, both nationally and internationally are at the heart of liberal economic theory. The 'naturalness' of the existing division of labour has been criticized by those who highlight the role of power in creating and maintaining particular divisions of labour. Theorists and practitioners interested in the welfare of a particular state or nation have tried to influence the division of labour by supporting the development of particular forms of industry such as manufacturing or high technology. Feminist theorists have tried to undermine the gendered division of labour by revealing its manufactured nature.

We'll spend some time considering the liberal theory in detail before turning to alternative views. The liberal philosopher Adam Smith chose to begin his famous work, *The Wealth of Nations* by explaining the benefits of an increasing division of labour: 'The greatest improvement in the productive powers of labour and the greater part of skill, dexterity, and judgement with which it is anywhere directed or applied, seem to have been the effects of the division of labour' (1776/1983, p. 109). Smith illustrated his point by contrasting a system of production where individuals made pins versus a system where the various tasks of making pins were broken down between a group of people. He suggested that a single person may only be able to make one pin in a day. If they were especially skilled they might be able to make as many as twenty in a day. However, if the job was to be broken down into tasks and assigned to individuals, many more pins could be made. One person could draw out the wire, another could cut it, and yet another could make the points. Smith divided the task of pin-making into 18 distinct operations. Under his system 18 people could make 48 000 pins – the equivalent of one person making 4800. One can certainly doubt the various numbers that Smith used, but the point is significant. The division of labour increases productivity.

Smith attributed this increase in productivity to three factors. First, practice at a particular task increases dexterity which increases speed. The more someone does a task, the better and faster they can do it. Secondly, time is saved by eliminating the need to move from one job to another. Finally, by simplifying the production process through task specialization, machinery can be applied to the tasks. They can then be performed more quickly.

Smith also believed that the causes of the division of labour had three sources. The first was that brought about by what he saw as people's natural propensity to 'truck, barter and exchange'. He believed that it was part of people's nature to want new products and things that they could not provide for themselves. The second factor was 'self love'. People's interests in furthering their own position encouraged them to trade and engage in the division of labour. Finally, people were engaged in different activities due to 'to habit, custom and education'. Some people were more skilled in particular trades, others had better education and still others were raised in particular tasks.

Recognizing the benefits that could be derived from a division of labour, Smith and other liberals moved on to some other points. In general, they believed that the more advanced a society, the greater the division of labour. Thus, states should take steps to support the division of labour. One thing they could do was to enlarge the size of the market. The larger the market, the more different types of products would be created and the greater the division of labour. Local markets could be expanded to national markets which could then be expanded by engaging in an international market through international trade.

Central to Smith, and liberal ideology, is the idea that the benefits of the division of labour and liberal policies flowed down to the lowest members of society. Smith argued that the difference between a prince and a peasant in Europe is not as great as between a peasant and an African king. The debatable point he wanted to make was that the worst off in the most advanced society fared better than the best off in a less advanced society. While this is clearly untrue, one can see the link between Smith's view of the benefits of an international division of labour and David Ricardo's theories of comparative advantage discussed in Chapters 3 and 5. Ricardo's view was that if each country specialized in the product that it could produce best, all countries could benefit from international trade. These benefits flowed from shifting national resources into the most competitive industries, increasing the degree of specialization in the international division of labour.

Modern liberal economic theory and many international institutions propagate these views by suggesting that countries and peoples will prosper by engaging in free trade and tasks that the market rewards. Thus, one sees that structural adjustment programs of the IMF encourage developing states to open their economies and produce for the export market. The WTO was established to encourage states to reduce barriers to trade and facilitate an increasingly specialized division of labour.

Critiques of the liberal approach come from those who suggest that the division of labour is not natural and is shaped by power relations. There are three slightly different versions of this critique. Scholars working out of the dependency tradition note that countries are locked into particular forms of labour because their economies were the victims of imperialist expansion. A second set of theorists focusing primarily on advanced industrialized states argue that particular economic sectors are strategic and vital to state interests. States must shape the division of labour to ensure that they remain active in these areas. This second group shares some of the assumptions of the first about power relations shaping economic activity to the benefit of some states rather than others, but focuses on the struggle between advanced industrialized states rather than the gap between Northern and Southern states. Feminist scholars are the third group and they argue that the gendered division of labour is caused by patriarchy and the unequal distribution of power between men and women.

Looking back at history one finds considerable support for the claims of dependency theorists that the division of labour is not 'natural' but is based upon historical conflict which locks countries into particular roles (Dos Santos, 1970/1991). An examination of the international system in the nineteenth and early twentieth centuries reveals that there was a limited form of a division on an international basis with areas, countries or even continents specializing in particular tasks. In general, countries which had gone through the industrial revolution made manufactured goods and other states supplied raw materials or food. A crucial question is: when did the division of tasks begin and why? Was it, as Smith might have suggested, something natural? Or did force and conquest play a large role in establishing an international division of labour? Unlike liberal theory which suggests that the division is an outcome of some natural process,

French historian Braudel (1979, p. 50) argues that the 'past always counts'.

Let us review the fate of the triangular trade across the Atlantic and the resulting division of labour. Europeans exchanged manufactured textiles and guns for African slaves. These slaves were then forcefully transported to plantations in the Caribbean and the US. The products from the Caribbean and the southern US were then sold at immense profit in Europe and farther East. In the case of cotton, the raw material was transformed into textiles and sold on. This division of labour increased productivity and helped to feed the industrial revolution, but how did it come about? It is clear that the process which resulted in the African continent 'specialising' in slaves, the Americas specializing in raw materials and Europe in manufactures was not simply a product of different skills. America's resources were exploited through the use of force and slave labour. Many of the products in which the Caribbean and Latin America 'specialize' in (for example, sugar) were transplanted by European colonists from other parts of the world.

Another good example of force of arms shifting the division of labour is the textile industry in Britain and India in the eighteenth and nineteenth centuries. When Britain had the superior navy and inferior textiles, it managed to keep Indian textiles out of Britain. Both countries were able to produce textiles because British textiles could not compete in India and the Indian product was kept out of the British market. However, in later years when British textiles were superior (because of the industrial revolution) and India was held by force, Britain was able to destroy the Indian textile industry by selling its cheaper products in the Indian market.

One can conclude from such examples that the international division of labour was not an agreement between equal parties open to review. Economic patterns and power relations sometimes date back to an ancient state of affairs. The significance of this point is that political authorities in the form of states have a role in shaping where their population 'fit' in the division of labour.

Palan and Abbot (2000) have examined the various strategies that states have pursued in order to shape comparative advantage and their place in the division of labour. Depending upon their existing place in the global political economy and domestic political coalitions, some options are more feasible than others. Small to medium sized states bordering economic powerhouses might try a strategy of regional integration. Poor, small states could opt to fit into the division of labour by acting as tax havens or selling their flags to shipping lines who use them as flags of convenience. Some states can exploit their knowledge base and use social programs to shield their workers, while others attempt to gain a cost advantage by suppressing the cost of labour.

Feminists note that employment in the labour market is segregated by gender. Particular tasks are assigned to men and other tasks are assigned to women. Women are clustered in poorly paid, unpaid, insecure forms of work. They are rarely able to reach positions of power. An example of this glaring inequality can be seen in photographs of G7 finance ministers, heads of state or business leaders. A woman's face rarely appears among the pictures of men in dark suits. Women are noticeable by their absence. Women are excluded from many occupations by a variety of obstacles and tools. These tools include the law, tradition, unequal educational opportunities, lack of public services and violence. From a gender perspective the division of labour is created by unequal power relations and is reproduced on a worldwide basis (Peterson and Runyan, 1993).

Major developments

There have been two major developments in the division of labour. The first has been the change and spread of different production processes. The way that things are produced has gone through a number of changes and this influences how people fit into the work process. One major change was the introduction of Fordism in the early twentieth century while the second change occurred at the end of the century with the introduction of more flexible work organizations. The second major development has been the move from an international division of labour to a global division of labour. This has reduced, but not eliminated, the connection between type of work and geographical location.

Changes in the production process

Although the benefits of a division of labour were known before the 1800s it was the industrial revolution and the application of modern factory management techniques which greatly boosted productivity. One man, Fredrick Taylor had so much influence that they even named a form of production for him – Taylorism. Taylorism refers to the practice of scientific management (Braverman, 1974, pp. 85–137). Similar to Smith, Taylor advocated the breaking down of production into individual tasks. He conducted detailed studies on the factory process and then recommended particular changes. In a famous case Taylor used a stopwatch to time the shovelling of iron and made changes to improve the amount that could be shovelled by one person in a day by from 12 to 47 tons.

Key to Taylorism was management control over worker time. Managers concentrated knowledge and power in their hands. Workers were viewed as beasts of burden who had to be instructed in particular tasks and closely supervized. The result was that workers were increasingly deskilled as they fit into the factory system. Workers could be substituted into a series of simplified tasks.

The person most famous for successfully applying and elaborating upon Taylorism was the car maker Henry Ford. Ford engaged in the mass production of automobiles on factory lines. He standardized car models so that they could be made more quickly and cheaply. Advertisements for the Model T car promised customers they could have cars in any colour as long as it was black! The working conditions in Ford's factories were very difficult. He would often put the strongest workers at the beginning of the assembly line forcing all others to keep up to the fastest pace. On a more positive note, Ford introduced the $5 a day wage which was higher than what his competitors paid. The wage was designed to attract workers and also offered the possibility that workers might one day be able to afford the products they were producing. It opened up the door to mass consumption to go along with mass production.

Some approaches to political economy, such as the Regulation School, label the post-1945 economic system in the advanced industrialized countries 'Fordism' (Dunford, 2000). Fordism combined the model of mass production (the factory system) with mass consumption. Mass consumption was achieved by redistributing income from the wealthy to a broader base of citizens through programs such as progressive taxation, old-age benefits, public health care and education, and unemployment insurance. Organized labour played a role in the system as it negotiated wage increases for its members as productivity in the economy increased.

The Fordist system contributed to a boom in Western economies in the 1950s and 1960s as the volume of consumer products exploded. However, by the 1970s, Fordism came under increasing pressure from inflation and the emergence of a new international division of labour. Competition from new producers in industrializing countries put pressure upon national Fordist arrangements. In the 1980s the Fordist method of production was increasingly challenged by what was variously called flexible specialization, lean production or Toyotoism (after the Japanese car company). These new methods emphasized a form of production that was more flexible than Fordism. For example, just-in-time inventory systems meant that companies would not stockpile parts; they would order them and receive them just-in-time for production. Workers were encouraged to work in teams, learn a variety of skills and abandon traditional union structures in favour of work teams or company unions.

Today we have a mixture of production methods in the global economy. Many automobile manufactures have moved to Japanese production methods and more flexible specialization. However, the mass-production factory system is alive and well in many old industries such as textiles and some newer service industries. For example, call centres where workers are closely monitored and follow particular scripts operate on a rigid factory model.

From the new international to the global division of labour. Beginning in the 1970s, a number of people noticed a new international division of labour (Frobel *et al.*, 1980). This observation reflected the development of manufacturing in the newly industrializing countries (NICs) such as Brazil, Mexico, and the 'Four Tigers' – Hong Kong, Singapore, Taiwan and South Korea. It seemed to be reversing the historical trend where non-Western states supplied raw materials for Western states.

As discussed in Chapter 6, a combination of factors helps to explain the geographical dispersal of corporate activity to other parts of the world (Dicken, 1998). Technological change made it possible to split up the manufacturing process and locate different operations in different countries. Improved transport and communication systems allowed for better control of this diffusion of manufacturing. Another factor was the combination of growing costs in developed states and low production cost sited in developing states. The Fordist system in industrialized countries resulted in rising wage rates for labour. In industrializing states, labour costs were low and efforts were made to keep them low through labour suppression or the creation of export-processing zones. Many states in the developing world pursued an active policy of supporting industrialization and exporting to the developed world.

In advanced industrialized states, the growth of manufacturing in developing states caused some concern. The Fordist compromize of distributing benefits to workers came under increasing pressure. Locked in cost competition, some workers were forced to accept wage reductions and some manufacturing operations closed down. Workers were urged to be more flexible in terms of working longer or more varied hours. Factories closed in many industrial areas such as the northeast of the US and a vigorous debate was launched about whether countries were 'deindustrializing'.

By the beginning of the twenty-first century the process of globalization was facilitating the creation of a global division of labour. As outlined earlier in the chapter, geographic space was coming to be less and less a factor in determining what tasks were accomplished where. Patterns of inequality were still massive and growing, but pockets of different types of activity could be found in most parts of the world. To be clear, the concept of a global division of labour does not suggest that all the people of the world are involved in the same labour market. Indeed, even those sympathetic to the notion of global labour estimate that only 15 per cent of the world's population is actively engaged in such activity (Harrod and

O'Brien, 2002, p. 13). Yet, this is a significant and growing group. More and more people are influenced by the global economy and must adjust their behaviour to take account of forces beyond national borders. Some specific groups benefit greatly from this trend and push for more rapid liberal globalization (see Box 7.1)

One of the interesting elements of the global division of labour is the role played by migration. People have migrated for thousands of years, but new forms of transportation and communication make it easier to travel long distances and allow migrants to maintain contact with their home community. There are about 150 million people (three per cent of the world's population) living in countries other than the one of their birth (Stalker, 2001, p. 8). This includes people who have settled permanently in new countries, contract workers on limited stays, professionals working for TNCs, undocumented workers (illegal immigrants), refugees and asylum seekers. Although migrants are a small percentage of the world's population, they play a vital role in the global economy. In many developing states, the money that migrants send home from their employment in developed countries plays a significant economic role (see Figures 7.1 and 7.2). For example, it is estimated that Mexicans in the US send about

Box 7.1 Globalizing elites

A division of labour has implications for those people at the top of the income scale as well as the majority of people who live in poverty. Groups which benefit from a more liberal economic system and increasing capital mobility press for further liberalization and integration. A set of globalizing elites agitate for public policy which will allow them to continue to accumulate wealth at a rapid rate. They have political, economic and cultural orientations which favour global rather than national economic activity and lifestyles. Sklair (2001) has argued that groups of TNC executives, state and international bureaucrats, technical professionals, merchants and media officials form a transnational capitalist class. A major concern of these elites is to balance the continued opening of the global economy with the need for social stability (Gill 2003). Globalization processes highlight and reinforce inequality, but it also provides marginalized groups with the opportunities to build alliances and challenge their subordinated position. Thus, the World Economic Forum, which serves as a meeting place for globalizing elites, is now challenged by the presence of a World Social Forum inhabited by non-elites seeking different forms of globalization.

$3 billion a year back to relatives in Mexico (Ellwood, 1998, p. 172). In Egypt remittances from migrants have, in some years, exceeded revenues from the tourism, oil and the Suez Canal combined (Stalker, 2001, p. 109).

Developed countries are becoming more and more dependent upon migrant labour and immigration to fulfil their labour needs. Foreign workers are in demand because of two developments. First, the birth rate is so low in developed states that their population is shrinking. Secondly, the population is rapidly ageing which means that there will not be enough workers to pay for pensions and health care demanded by the older genera- tion. It is estimated that if Europe wants to retain a healthy ratio of workers to retired people it will need to allow almost 159 million new immigrants into its territory by 2025 (World Guide, 2001, p. 21). Without increased immigration almost 47 per cent of Europeans would be retired in 2025.

The increasing importance of migrant workers and immigration has raised a number of significant issues in the global political economy (Stalker, 2001). Migrant workers often have poor employment conditions and are subject to abuse or exploitation. Social tensions can arise in receiving states because native workers or citizens may feel themselves under economic or cultural threat from foreign workers. Since migrants

Figure 7.1   *Top ten developing country recipients of workers'*
remittances 2001

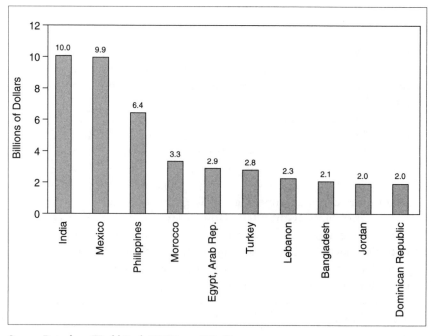

Source: Data from World Bank (2003) pp. 159–60.

Figure 7.2   *Top ten country sources of remittance payments 2001*

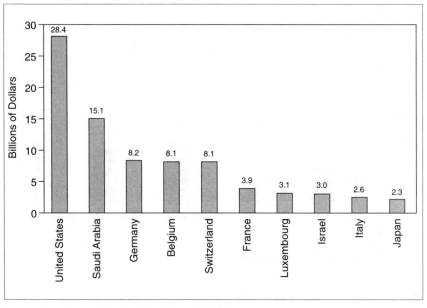

Source: Data from World Bank (2003) pp. 179–60.

play a crucial economic role in the states that they leave and the states that they work in, it is essential that mechanisms are developed to deal with such issues.

Key issues

Migration is just one of many pressing issues surrounding the global division of labour. In this section we will focus on three: the maintenance and transformation of the global gendered division of labour; the struggle over workers rights in the global economy; and the relationship between workers rights and global stability.

Continuity and transformation in the gendered division of labour

A major issue in the global division of labour is the fate of the gendered division of labour. In some states, considerable progress has been made to break down the barriers between 'women's' work and 'men's' work.

Figure 7.3   *Gender inequality in economic activity*

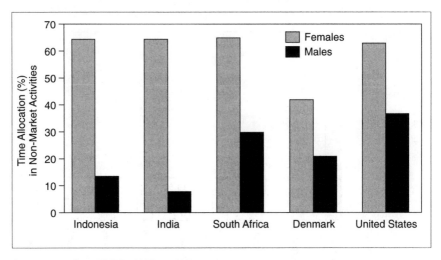

Source: Data from UNDP (2002) p. 238.

However, progress has been uneven and falls short in even the most progressive countries. On the global level, women occupy particular places in the division of labour and they are affected in particular ways. In this section we'll review this state of affairs and consider processes of change. What are the implications of this gendered division of labour and what changes can be made?

Every society has a particular pattern of gendered work. The tendency is for women's work to be less well paid than work dominated by men. Women are often concentrated in particular types of employment. Women are over represented in the 'caring' and support professions such as clerical, teaching, nursing, counselling, and childcare. Women usually combine this paid work with the unpaid work of maintaining the family home and childcare (see Figure 7.3). Finally, the vast majority of people engaged in prostitution are women or children. Being a woman in the global economy entails a much greater chance of being poorer, working harder and under worse conditions than a man.

In this section we'll survey three ways that women are incorporated into the global division of labour: providing personal services in the sex trade and as domestic workers; working in manufacturing plants of transnational corporations; acting as human shock absorbers for structural adjustment programs (SAPs).

Personal services: the sex trade and domestic workers. A large number of women from developing countries are engaging in providing personal services to men and families in wealthier states. This can range from prostitution for a male clientele to providing cleaning, childcare and health-care services in homes and institutions.

The global sex trade has expanded to include many women and children since the 1970s. Some are employed in their own countries servicing local and foreign men while others are exported to foreign countries. The large sex trade in South-east Asia has its origins in the Korean and Vietnamese wars. US and allied soldiers taking time off from the conflicts sought out sex workers in countries such as Thailand and the Philippines. Demand for prostitutes in these 'recreation' zones led to an upsurge in the sex trade. Once the Vietnam war ended in the mid-1970s, foreign tourists took the place of soldiers. These tourists tend to be Western and Japanese males who take advantage of the benefits of modern transportation to travel to other countries for sexual pleasure. The drawing power of prostitution for the tourist trade can be immense in some countries. For example, it is estimated that up to 73 per cent of tourists to Thailand are single males (not with female partner) and that up to 3 per cent of all Thai women are engaged in some form of prostitution (Peterson and Runyan, 1993, p. 98).

This is a global business overlaid with racial stereotypes and designed to benefit men in developing and developed countries. Men purchase the services and keep the vast majority of the profits. Western men engage in activities that would be unacceptable or certainly much less available in their home states. Some local men prosper as they secure revenues from pimping, through bribes to police, or from hotels and bars. For Western men visiting sex tourist countries, native women combine exotic cultural traits that make them the desired sexual partners. Asian women are stereotyped as being more submissive and responsive to Western men's needs than the women of their own cultures.

This trade exacts a devastating price on the women and children who are involved. One cost has been the spread of sexually transmitted diseases such as AIDS. This in turn drives a demand for younger and younger prostitutes in the mistaken view that customers will avoid the disease if they turn to younger victims. Physical and psychological damage to people engaged in the trade is also high. Those exported to other countries often live in conditions of slavery.

One can see efforts to address this problem in several sectors. For example, an organization called End Child Prostitution in Asian Tourism (ECPAT) was founded in Thailand to publicize the plight of child prostitutes, and lobby for change (O'Grady, 1994). In the area of child abuse by sex tourists, a number of Western states have introduced legislation to allow for such abusers to be prosecuted in their home countries. For example, a British citizen who has sex with a child while in South-east Asia may now be prosecuted in British courts.

Women are exported from one country to another in much the same way as one would export a commodity such as wheat. Much of this export is designed to alleviate poverty in the sending country as the worker sends part of her pay cheque home to support her family. In some cases, the exported women are forced into prostitution. Figures are difficult to come by, but an example is that in 1984 up to 16 000 Thai women were exported to the prostitution industry in Japan, Europe and the Middle East (Peterson and Runyan, 1993, p. 98). In recent years domestic work has also developed as a major international business. Women from developing countries are imported into Western Europe, Canada, the US and the Middle East to help provide childcare, do house work or to assist in nursing elderly people at home or in hospitals.

The numbers of women engaged in this activity are large and the amount of money they contribute to their home economies through remittances is significant. Reliable figures are difficult to find and often dated, but here are some estimates. In 1984, over 18 000 Sri Lankan women were working as domestic servants abroad. In 1988, 81 000 Filipino women serving as servants abroad earned an estimated $60–100 million in foreign exchange (ibid., p. 99). In the case of the Philippines, women make up almost half of the migrant labour force. Men usually work abroad in the construction industry. By 1994 it was estimated that Filipino workers sent home up to $7 billion dollars annually. This exceeded income from sugar or minerals and was close to 3.5 per cent of the value of all goods and services produced in the country (Chang, 2000, p. 130). It was also an amount large enough to cover the interest payments on the Philippines' massive foreign debt.

This form of activity creates contradictory links between women in developing and developed states. Many women in developed states have been able to pursue careers similar to men in recent decades. However, in countries where there has been a reduction in welfare services or the absence of affordable day care (as in the US), these women must seek out a private solution to the task of domestic work and childcare. One solution has been to hire foreign women to work as domestics. This can be done legally through employment agencies or illegally through less established channels.

The degree to which labour from developing countries facilitates the lifestyles of the middle and upper middle professional classes in some developed states was very publicly illustrated in 1993. US President Clinton was eager to bring women into his cabinet to show that he was reaching out to a wide group of Americans. However, his plans for diversity were upset by the fact that two of the professional women he approached (a corporate lawyer and a federal judge) had used 'illegal' immigrants for childcare (Marcus, 1993). Clinton's third woman candidate and eventual attorney-general, Janet Reno, was childless and did not face similar problems.

This example shows the tight connection between forms of labour in developing and developed states. Deprived of economic opportunity in their own countries, many women (and men) must migrate to earn money. They are often subject to physical and emotional abuse as they work in insecure and dangerous occupations. Some of the freedom from domestic labour enjoyed by Western women (and men) and the reduced cost of the welfare state have been achieved by relying on labour from developing countries desperate enough to leave their homes and families to earn a living.

Women and TNCs in developing countries. Women have increasingly been integrated into global production through labour in TNCs, especially in export processing zones (EPZs). EPZs are designated areas within a country which are designed to attract foreign investment by providing financial incentives or regulatory relief from national laws. On average, 80 per cent of the workforce in these zones are female. In China about 20 million people of which 70–80 per cent are female work in export processing zones or special economic zones (David, 1996, pp. 22–3). Why is this the case? Factory managers might suggest that women are chosen because they have smaller fingers and can do more intricate work at a faster pace. Many women may be more skilled at dextrous work because of having developed skills such as sewing, but this is interpreted as a biological difference rather than a skill difference. Since it is not seen as a skill it does not need to be rewarded by higher pay.

Another reason why women make up a large percentage of the workers in EPZs is because they are thought to be more compliant to manager's demands. Women have less of a history of unionization and are often willing to put up with very poor working conditions to support families. However, this impression of compliance is deceiving, as many women factory workers have been active in lobbying for better working conditions and the formation of independent trade unions.

The incorporation of women into export oriented work has had a number of contradictory outcomes. On the negative side, working conditions are often very difficult. Unions are often prohibited, working conditions and wages poor. Many workers are exposed to dangerous and unhealthy conditions as well as the threat of physical and sexual abuse (ICFTU, 1996a). In response to these issues, women have organized amongst themselves and participated in international campaigns to secure fair treatment from the multinational corporations that benefit from their labour.

Working conditions vary widely in TNCs and can often be better than in local firms, providing opportunity to local women. These forms of employment have sometimes challenged local gender roles and provided women with better alternatives than pre-existing work options. Some women are able to leave restrictive home environments and secure increased status and independence from the incomes that they earn in the factories.

There are, in fact, a number of different patterns of work relations between women and TNCs in developing countries and one needs to be sensitive to this variety. In some cases work may be relatively well paid, providing young women an opportunity to accumulate some wealth and education. In other cases working conditions are brutal and abuse is widespread. The challenge is to expand the first type of employment and battle the second form through greater worker rights and economic development.

SAPs and structural adjustment. A gender perspective on the global economy reveals that men and women are impacted in different ways by trade and development policies. While many men have suffered from structural adjustment, women have been systematically and more dramatically impoverished. A gendered division of labour ensures that crises in world economy are in great measure absorbed by poor and working-class women.

As governments attempt to balance budgets and engage in structural adjustment programs to make their economies more internationally competitive, women are often forced to pay the price by taking up tasks performed by the state or giving up their existing sources of income (Chang, 2000, p. 124–9). When food subsidies are cut, women often cut back on their own nutrition in order to feed their children. As health and education are cut back, women often take on the additional burden of nursing family members, or girls are kept at home to help in domestic tasks rather than be sent to school. The move to export agriculture for foreign currency can cause peasant women to lose their land or force them into becoming seasonal workers. In desperation, many women export their labour as outlined above.

Women have reacted to this situation of inequality by organizing themselves and engaging with states, international organizations and corporations to improve their living conditions. For example, women's groups have been in an extended dialogue with the World Bank (O'Brien *et al.*, 2000, pp. 24–66). They have had some success in convincing the Bank staff that development policies that ignore women are flawed. As a result, the Bank has supported basic education for girls and the channelling of credit to poor women. Women's groups in alliance with trade unions have also been able to bring women's issues on to the agenda of the International Labour Organization. In 1996 the ILO adopted guidelines for employment in home work (Prugl, 1999). Home work is not house work, but work that companies have labourers do in their home. It is populated by women working for very low pay. The fact that the ILO would examine home work is a sign that feminist views and women's issues are making inroads into mainstream institutions.

In response to the problems faced by many women in the global political economy some academic analysis has called for the 'ungendering' of labour (Peterson and Runyan, 1993, p. 160). This would involve creating an environment where gender did not play a role in the form of work one chose to do. Such a scenario would involve women increasing their presence in male dominated areas and men in female dominated areas such as nursing and teaching. Such a transformation would require a shift in the balance of power between men and women and an acknowledgement of the value of the vast amount of work conducted by women that goes unpaid. One way of approaching this goal is for proper value to be attached to women's reproductive labour in systems of national accounts. The true cost of policies need to be made visible. Another step would be for countries to support equal pay for equal or comparable work, national childcare policies and full reproductive rights.

The obstacles to change are great. Women must struggle against patriarchy in their own society, the strength of transnational corporations and the inequalities generated by capitalism and with the difficulties of reforming a global system. However, the struggle for greater gender equality is one of the central issues in the development of a global division of labour.

The struggle for workers' rights in a global economy

Over the past two decades most international economic agreements such as the revitalization of European integration through the Single Market project and monetary union, the North American Free Trade Agreement (NAFTA), the creation of the WTO and the attempt to negotiate a Multilateral Agreement on Investment at the OECD have been designed to liberalize economic activity. In each of these cases non-business social interests have attempted to influence the content of the agreements. However, the attempt to bolster labour rights in a globalizing and liberalizing economic world is extremely difficult. Although a wide range of groups have joined the struggle they face two difficult questions (O'Brien, 2002). The first question is: 'How do you regulate transnational capital?' The second question is 'What is the appropriate relationship between equity groups located in different areas of the world?'

The first question of how to regulate capital concerns how people can create rules which will place the activity of businesses that operate across state borders in a broader social context. How can they be prevented from undermining labour and environmental conditions? Corporate behaviour can be influenced through two different mechanisms. Firms can be regulated by states or by pressure in the market. With regard to state regulation, this can take place through the extraterritorial regulation of powerful states or the application of rules in multilateral institutions. Extraterritorial regulation involves a state demanding that corporations which have headquarters in their state or engaged in economic activity in their state conduct global business according to the home state's rules. It sets the preferences of a particular state as the benchmark for corporate behaviour in other countries. In practice this means that corporate activity must conform to the desires of particular interests in advanced industrialized states.

Depending upon one's position on a particular issue, extraterritorial jurisdiction can have negative or positive effects. Most people would agree that developed states which prosecuted their corporations for using slave labour in foreign countries were doing a good thing. However, other prohibitions are viewed more negatively. Numerous states have objected to such activity in measures such as the US Helms-Burton legislation forbidding trade with Cuba. Since the US is engaged in economic warfare with Cuba, it threatens corporations that do business in the US with penalties if they trade with Cuba. Some Canadian executives of Canadian companies cannot enter the US because they would be arrested for the economic activity of their companies in Cuba.

Extraterritorial rules reflect the balance of power within a particular state rather than a consensus of the international community. Since the rules are set nationally and not negotiated between a group of states they are idiosyncratic. The United States' single-minded pursuit of economic warfare against Cuba is incomprehensible to most other states. However, because the US is such a powerful actor, its particular views have considerable impact. This is not a recipe for a global system with common rules.

It is because of the negative implications in unilateral extraterritorial regulation that multilateral arrangements involving a negotiated standard between numerous states is often viewed as preferable. However, multilateral agreements are difficult to negotiate and suffer from the accusation that they also benefit the strongest powers. This is illustrated in the debate about linking labour standards to the operation of the WTO.

Following the creation of the WTO many elements of the international labour movement, such as the International Confederation of Free Trade Unions (ICFTU), sought to have their concerns addressed in the organization The international labour movement's goal (as represented by the main international confederations of trade unions) for WTO is to have core labour standards (or a social clause) brought into its purview (O'Brien *et al.*, 2000, pp. 67–108). The social clause would commit states to respect seven crucial conventions of the ILO (Conventions 87, 98, 29, 105, 100, 111, 138). These conventions provide for: freedom of association, the right to collective bargaining, abolition of forced labour, prevention of discrimination in employment, and a minimum age for employment. The key to having the conventions as part of the WTO is that for the first time they would become enforceable and not depend upon the whims of individual states. In contrast to the ILO's reliance on moral argument, the WTO has the ability to enforce compliance. In order to achieve this goal, groups such as the ICFTU and affiliates including the AFL–CIO have pressured the US and the European Union into raising the issue of core labour standards at the WTO. They argued that continued support for trade liberalization in developed states required a minimum floor for workers' rights.

The labour movement has been unable to secure enforceable labour rights in international institutions mainly because of the opposition of a combination of liberal states, developing countries and business associations. Leaders in many liberal states argue that economic growth raises labour standards and any interference in trade for labour reasons would lower the gains from trade. Many leaders in developing states have expressed a fear that labour standards would only be used as a form of protection by developed states against developing countries. Finally, businesses remain opposed, fearing both a rise in protectionism and a reduction in their profits.

In addition to resistance from state and corporate elites, there are elements of the labour movement which oppose both the idea that core labour standards should be part of the WTO and the existence of the WTO itself. For example, the linkage between labour standards and the WTO was rejected in two national conferences of Indian unions in March and October 1995. Delegates expressed fears that the social clause initiative was driven by protectionist desires in Northern countries. The Indian union suggestion was that rather than working through the WTO, workers should push for a United Nations Labour Rights Convention and the establishment of National Labour Rights Commissions (ALU, 1995).

The difficulty in achieving state regulation of corporations has led to attempts to influence corporate behaviour by introducing, monitoring and enforcing codes of conduct. In Western countries in recent years, there has been an increased consumer awareness and concern about the methods used in production. This has spawned a series of campaigns against particular corporations by consumer and union groups. Such activity is part of a civil society campaign to 'Think Globally and Punish Locally' (Rodman, 1998). In college campuses across the US, the largest student activist movement since the anti-Apartheid campaign has formed around the issue of sweatshop labour. A national movement, 'Students Against Sweatshops' has lobbied for improved working conditions and labour rights in companies that supply products to universities. It has also put the question of ethics and the possibility of profiting from an ethical policy on the agenda of many corporations and in business publications.

Codes of conduct are meant to set basic principles for the behaviour of TNCs (and their subcontractors) with respect to their labour practices and environmental policies. In some cases firms are willing partners in implementing such codes. For example, the Levi-Strauss Jean company's code of conduct is reproduced in union literature as an illustration of a TNC working with the union movement (ICFTU, 1996a, p. 59). Levi-Strauss is notable not just for its code of conduct banning labour exploitation, but for its withdrawal from states operating extreme forms of authoritarian industrial relations such as Burma and China in 1992.

One prominent union strategy is to select a particularly serious abuse of workers' rights, highlight the abuses in the media and attempt to pressure governments to legislate, consumers to boycott, and corporations to change behaviour. Good examples are the campaigns against child labour and labour conditions in Far Eastern toy factories (ICFTU, 1995a). Another example is the campaign against child labour in the manufacture of footballs (ICFTU, 1996b). Prior to the start of the 1996 European Football Championships, the ICFTU revealed that footballs endorsed by the governing football association, FIFA, were made in Pakistan using child labour. This involved cooperation between the ICFTU, Norwegian unions who supplied the camera crew, British unions in the country of the championships and Pakistani unions on site in the targeted country. The adverse publicity resulted in FIFA adopting a new code of practice and more attention being given to labour issues around a key social/sporting event.

The pressure from organized labour and consumer groups in developed countries has forced the hands of government and international organizations as well as TNCs. For example, in April 1995, US President Bill Clinton announced a voluntary code of conduct covering business ethics and workers' rights for US companies working abroad. In an attempt to reinvigorate its role in the labour standards issue, the ILO has announced its intention to push for a global social label. The proposal is in response to the numerous private initiatives at social labelling. The Secretary General of the United Nations has also become involved by bringing together selected corporations, NGOs and trade unions to agree to labour and environmental standards. His initiative is called the Global Compact.

Market-based solutions have recently been favoured because of the hurdles in establishing agreement between states. The proliferation of codes and the ensuing debate has focused a spotlight on the plight of workers in many countries (Pearson and Seyfang, 2001). Although one can point to achievements of such activity, the fact is that it is a second-best strategy. It occurs because state regulation has failed (Kearney, 1999). Market activity is not seen as sufficient in national societies because of the inefficiency of effort required to launch continuing citizen campaigns. There are problems with collecting and distributing information, mobilizing citizens and the need for constant vigilance. A legal process and institution is needed to regularize activity and enforce general rules. If market-based activity is seen as inadequate for domestic purposes, why would it prove sufficient on a global scale?

In practice, there are a multitude of strategies from market to state based initiatives seeking to address the labour standards issue. Some civil society actors have been successful in raising awareness, while the threat of state action (either unilaterally or multilaterally) has been useful to focus the minds of corporate and state elites. The challenge is to work out a suitable combination of these strategies (O'Brien, 2002).

The division of labour and global stability

It may seem strange to people living in the present era, but there was a time when the state of people's working conditions was thought to have an influence on international peace and security. Following the Russian Revolution and the end of World War I, Western leaders were so worried about labour unrest contributing to conflict between states that they created an international organization to deal with labour issues – the ILO. The goal of the ILO was to ameliorate working conditions so that labour unrest would subside and communist agitation would fall on infertile ground.

It is time to once again consider the relationship between labour unrest and global order. This can be done in both liberal and critical theoretical traditions. From a liberal perspective, labour can be viewed as one of many domestic interest groups that make international cooperation very difficult (Milner, 1997). From a critical perspective, labour is part of a broad social force that seeks to challenge the existing basis of international order (Cox, 1986). Numerous labour oriented groups are offering a challenge to the basic liberal principles that make up the global order. Here we'll consider just three groups of workers mobilizing to challenge the basis of global order: workers in the US, Newly Industrializing Countries and peasant farmers (O'Brien, 2000).

In the past thirty years, US labour has moved from being an unquestioning ally in the spread of US hegemony to being a growing obstacle to further liberalization and internationalization. US labour has not abandoned the state for worker internationalism, but it is rethinking its position. This raises doubts about the social base in the US for maintaining leadership in the liberalization process.

In the immediate post-war era, US labour was firmly engaged in the politics of productivity (Maier, 1977). The politics of productivity involved subsuming class conflict by ensuring that growth and productivity gains were distributed across the economy. It reflected a belief that proper technical management of the economy would create the conditions for prosperity which would eliminate the need for harmful distributional battles. It was a method of neutralizing labour opposition by integrating unionized workers into a division of economic spoils. Internationally, organized labour played a crucial part in laying the groundwork for today's process of neo-liberal globalization. US labour took a leading role in marginalizing radical workers organizations in Latin America, Asia and Western Europe (Cox, 1977; Radosh, 1969). This ground-clearing work facilitated the expansion of US business and resulted in labour becoming an actor in the globalization process (Herod, 1997).

However, the rise of neo-liberal governments in the US and Britain, accompanied by a business offensive against workers, led to the ejection of labour from the governing coalition (Rupert, 1995a, pp. 167–207). This marginalization of moderate worker organizations corresponded with a movement by US elites to separate their destiny from the rest of the nation (Lasch, 1995; Reich, 1992). As the polarization of US society continues and the revolt of the elites is clearer, it becomes more practical for workers to look to the international realm for solidarity and assistance. In the US context, Rupert (1995b) has argued that the NAFTA debate may be a watershed in organized labour's acceptance of the dominant brand of liberalism. Not only did labour break with US corporations over the issue of linking workers' rights to regional trade agreements, but it also openly opposed a Democratic Party leadership and a sitting Democratic President. A second notable change in the policies of organized labour was the attempt to work with environmental and consumer groups to forge a common position on this element of economic policy. Finally, the AFL–CIO was forced to cultivate relations with the emerging independent Mexican unions rather than rely on the Mexican government-sponsored CTM union. The CTM proved adequate for US workers' interest in the Cold War when the fight was against communism, but allies in the fight against transnational exploitation would have to be found in unions controlled by their members.

In what ways might a more oppositional US labour movement influence the global political economy? One method is by changing the agenda for international institution building. At the multilateral level, labour organizations have complicated the WTO's plan to extend liberalization into new sectors and regions as they press for inclusion of core labour standards

(O'Brien, 1998). Labour organizations are pushing the IMF and the World Bank to revise the neoliberal content of their structural adjustment lending (ICFTU, 1995b). In the case of the World Bank lending to South Korea, this has resulted in provisions aimed at offering unprecedented (if limited) protection for workers (World Bank, 1998). At the regional level, an alliance of convenience between labour and right-wing populism stalled US approval for the expansion of NAFTA. A second method is shaping the international economic environment through corporate policy. In concert with other social groups labour has increased pressure on multinationals to change their investment locations or method of conducting business. This is particularly evident in the campaigns for company codes of conduct to temper poor labour and environmental practices mentioned above.

The recent, hesitant transformation of US labour may be part of a new internationalism for a broad spectrum of groups concerned with labour issues. A number of authors (Waterman, 1998; Moody, 1997) have raised the possibility of a new internationalism based upon transnational networks of labour activists inside and outside unions. These networks form alliances with other social movements in the North and South to offer an alternative prescription for economic, political and social order.

In newly industrializing countries, the 1997 financial crisis in East and South-east Asia placed the issue of workers' rights and activities firmly on the analytical agenda. The Asian development model sometimes sympathetically described as paternalistic authoritarianism (Pye, 1988), was thought to prosper because, in contrast to Latin American authoritarian models, development was more egalitarian. Workers were often coerced, but they shared in the benefits of growth (in this view). Stability was ensured by growth. Suddenly, economic growth vanished, at least temporarily. Workers in South Korea faced the prospect of unemployment in a non-welfare state. The Korean state was forced to create new welfare provisions in order to deal with potential unrest in the new democracy (Huck-Ju, 2001). In Indonesia the economic collapse was more serious and eventually led to a transformation of the political system.

The social chaos arising from the financial meltdown in Asia and the reaction of workers to that chaos is a factor in determining regional and global stability. The World Bank recognized the danger of social disintegration when Bank President James Wolfensohn announced that approximately 60 per cent of the $16 billion it had promised in financial assistance would be directed to 'protecting the poor and providing a social safety net'. (IHT, 1998). Social unrest was viewed as an imminent danger to internationally backed plans for financial restructuring. The threat to the IMF's and World Bank's rescue packages did not come from the political and economic elites of the target states, but from those who bear the costs of such restructuring – the working population.

As important as the role of workers in Asian states may be, there is another significant labour issue confronting the global political economy. To use McMichael's (1997) terms, it is the 'agrarian question'. The agrarian question concerns the implications of replacing peasant based agriculture with capitalist agriculture. Although this was a subject of grave concern in Western states in the nineteenth century and attention to peasant affairs was also raised during social revolutions in China, Cuba and Vietnam in the middle of this century, the agrarian question has not been posed again until very recently. It has re-emerged in response to the threat that liberalization of agriculture poses to billions of peasants around the world.

Slowly, but surely, a global peasant alliance is emerging to challenge the dominant notions of liberalization, consumption and environmental destruction. The most dramatic event has been the peasant and aboriginal rebellion in the southern Mexican state of Chiapas (Reding, 1994). Although the rebellion draws upon a historical legacy of oppression, it was clearly linked to steps taken by the Mexican government to liberalize agricultural land holdings in the run-up to the NAFTA. Local concerns were linked to broader developments in IPE. The Zapatistas have been quick to exploit modern technology to broadcast their cause worldwide and have begun the task of forging links with similarly minded groups in other parts of the world (www.ezln.org).

The Peoples' Global Action against 'Free' Trade and the World Trade Organization (PGA) is another example of a peasant based anti-imperialist grouping. The PGA is an instrument for coordination which brings together people's movements to oppose trade liberalization (PGA, 1997). The PGA organizes conferences approximately three months before the biannual Ministerial Meetings of the World Trade Organization. Conferences are used to update the PGA manifesto and to coordinate global and local action against free trade. The conference committee for the February 1998 event included groups such as the Frente Zapatista de Liberacion Naciónal (FZLN) from Mexico, Karnataka State Farmer's Association (KRRS) from India, Movemento sem Terra (MST) from Brazil and the Peasant Movement of the Philippines (KMP). The PGA is committed to non-violent civil disobedience and a confrontational attitude in pursuit of its opposition to free trade. It represents a constituency firmly in opposition to dominant trends in the global political economy.

This analysis is not arguing that workers or peasants in the developing world will serve as the basis for a revolutionary movement to overthrow capitalism. There are certainly many peasants in the world, but the power they face in economic and military terms is immense. It is possible, however, to identify these groups as offering potentially significant resistance to the liberalization project. They represent a key force in world politics, but it is one usually hidden from view because of the standard IPE analytical categories. Analysis of the international order that ignores them would be incomplete and flawed.

Conclusion

A person's place in the global division of labour will have a great impact upon how long they will live, how much they consume and what kind of health they can enjoy. The existence and growth of massive inequalities around the world is literally a question of life and death to millions of people. At the same time that such problems proliferate, people are active in forming themselves into trade unions, community associations, political parties and non-governmental organizations to combat the negative effects of a growing global division of labour. They seek to increase equality and influence the division of labour to the benefit of the world's populations. Readers of this book are part of that process in their activity as citizens and consumers.

Chapter 8

The Global Financial System

This chapter considers the global financial framework by focusing on its two most significant parts. Although they will be treated separately for analytical purposes, they have evolved in tandem and influence each other. We will look at the system which governs how one national currency is exchanged for another (the international monetary system or IMS) and we will examine how credit is created and distributed across borders (the credit system).

Both of these systems have undergone dramatic changes since they were established in the mid-1940s. The IMS has evolved from a system of fixed exchange rates to one where many of the currencies float. Recently, a number of states have abandoned their national currencies in favour of regional currencies (for example, the Euro). In the global credit system, the creation and supply of credit has moved from being the responsibility of public authorities (governments) to being provided by corporations. In addition, advances in information technology and deregulation of financial flows have resulted in much more rapid transfer of capital across state boundaries. The consequence of these developments is that many states, even the most powerful, are increasingly sensitive to market fluctuations.

We'll begin the analysis by providing some definitions and background about transformations in the global financial system. The theoretical perspectives section outlines a key theory concerning the relationship between capital flows, exchange rates and domestic policy. This proposition is used to find our way through the rest of the chapter. The third section outlines three major developments in the global financial system since the Second World War. These are the move from fixed to floating exchange rates, financial innovation and the 1980s debt crisis. The final section provides readers with an overview of three key issues facing today's global financial system. These issues are the rise of regional currencies, dealing with global financial crisis and the debate over autonomy, convergence and democracy.

Definitions and background

In this section we consider the nature of the international monetary and credit systems as they were created after the Second World War. We begin by focusing on the IMS as a set of arrangements that govern the exchange of one nation's currency for another. A sound IMS is necessary if economic activity across state borders is to proceed smoothly. Importers and exporters need to be able to conduct business in their clients' currencies and be able to take profit in their own. The post-1945 IMS has undergone two dramatic changes. The biggest alteration was a move from fixed rates to floating rates. The second major change has been the growth of regional currencies gradually replacing national currencies. We'll examine the major developments in the next section.

Reviewing the turmoil of the inter-war period, US and British post-war planners were convinced of the need for a stable international monetary system for international economic activity and peace. The attempt to fix countries' currencies to gold proved disastrous following the First World War, but so did the system of competitive devaluation that followed the breakdown of the gold standard. Planners wanted a system that would provide stability in exchange rates, but would allow for some adjustment from time to time. Their solution was the gold exchange system of Bretton Woods.

The post-war IMS was negotiated in Bretton Woods in the US in 1944. The two most influential participants were the US and Great Britain. In general, the British favoured a system that would restrict capital flows and provide for strong international monetary institutions whereas the US pushed for a more liberal system with less regulation. Since the British were in debt to the US because of borrowing to finance their participation in the Second World War, the US was able to secure an agreement that fell closer to its desires (Block, 1977, pp. 32–69).

The core of the system was the US dollar which was fixed to gold at a rate of $35 to one ounce of gold. Similar to the classic gold standard discussed in Chapter 3, this would encourage people to have faith in the unchanging value of the key currency. However, in contrast to the gold standard, other currencies were not fixed to gold. They were fixed to the US dollar, but provisions were made to allow for their rate to be occasionally adjusted. The thinking behind this was that if the underlying productivity of the other country's economies changed, the value of their currency should also change. For example, if a country experienced a natural disaster which destroyed their industrial base, they should be allowed to lower the value of their currency. This would encourage exports and help rebuild the economy.

The Bretton Woods conference created two international institutions to help oversee the operation of the international financial system, the International Monetary Fund (IMF) and the International Bank for Reconstruction and Development (IBRD). The monetary system was to be supported by the IMF. Its purpose was to help countries that had temporary balance of payments problems. If for some reason a country was unable to pay for its imports, the Fund could loan money to help them through a temporary cash shortage. This money would be repaid when the difficulty had been overcome.

The Bretton Woods system relied upon people having faith that the US currency would be exchanged for gold at the fixed rate if there was a demand to do so. There was no reason to doubt this assumption in the 1950s. The US possessed large gold reserves as a result of its role as a safe haven and creditor during the First and Second World Wars. Many people and states wanted to hold US dollars because they were backed by gold, but were more valuable since you could earn interest on the dollars.

An economist named Robert Triffin noticed that there was a problem at the heart of this system (Eichengreen, 1996, p. 116). The problem was that as US dollars flooded out into the world through the Marshall Plan, US

Box 8.1   Balance of payments confusion

The balance of payments is a record of the economic transactions between one country and the outside world. It is composed of two parts – the current account and the capital account. The current account records the sum of the flow of goods and services between one country and the rest of the world. The capital account records the movement of short and long term capital. Any transaction that will lead to a payment to another country is registered as a debit. This includes purchasing imports and investing abroad. Any transaction that will lead to payment from another country is registered as a credit. Exports, inflow of foreign direct investment and profits on foreign investments all lead to credits. The balance of payments should always balance or be equal to zero because outflows of money to foreigners must be matched or financed by inflows. However, there are two complicating factors. First, no state is able to record all its transborder economic transactions so the national balance of payments accounts do not balance on paper – there is always an error factor.

Secondly, even though the payments balance, there is often reference to a balance of payments deficit when countries go through financial crisis. What does this mean? People are usually referring to a country being unable to pay for the goods and services it would like to import. In economic terms the current account is in deficit and can no longer be financed by the capital account. The country is using internal resources such as the money held at the central bank to finance its external activity. Since foreign activity cannot be financed solely from limited domestic resources, a long term balance of payment deficit requires some action to restore the balance such as reducing imports, devaluing the currency or structural adjustment.

defence spending and Americans buying foreign goods, the balance between dollars and gold was deteriorating. Eventually there would be more dollars outside the US than gold inside. At some point the US would be unable to honour its gold commitments. This was called Triffin's dilemma. The outflow of dollars was needed to provide money or liquidity to other parts of the world, but this would eventually undermine the US' attempts at keeping their currency fixed to gold. Foreigners would begin to worry that the US would run out of gold and would start to cash in dollars for gold to make sure that they secured full value for their currency. In 1960 US foreign monetary liabilities first exceeded US gold reserves. In 1971 the US broke the link with gold. This subject is taken up in the major developments section.

Turning to the issue of credit, readers will recall from the first section of this book that the credit mechanism is vital for economic growth and bestows a certain degree of power upon those who issue it. In 1945, war-torn countries needed credit to rebuild, so US and British planners devised a system to funnel money to Europe. The centrepiece was the IBRD (later known as the World Bank) which was designed to lend states money for long-term rebuilding projects. Despite these plans, the Western economies faced a serious problem. There was a severe liquidity shortage. The IBRD did not have enough funds to enable European states to rebuild and purchase goods, especially American goods that required US dollars. Other mechanisms would have to be found to transfer capital. The US ended up transferring money through three mechanisms: the Marshall Plan, military spending and foreign investment. The Marshall Plan transferred about $13 billion in grants from the US government to Western Europe. These loans were used to assist reconstruction and to bolster investor confidence.

The Marshall Plan was far more than a financial transaction as it was deeply rooted in Cold War politics. The US Congress was only persuaded to release the money for Europe following the communist coup in Czechoslovakia in 1948. The threat of a communist takeover in Europe was required before American legislators came to Europe's financial assistance. The strings attached to the grants were also influenced by Cold War rivalry. On the surface the grants were available to any European state, including the Soviet Union and communist East European states. However, a condition of disbursement was that the accepting state had to commit itself to liberalizing its economy and engaging in freer trade. This was impossible for any East European state to accept because their policy of a planned economy could not be combined with an open economy. As a result, Communist states were excluded from the inflow of liquidity that the US provided to its European allies. The United States also insisted that recipients cooperate in the administration and dispersal of US funds. A new organization, the Organization for European Economic Cooperation was created to manage Marshall funds. This was one of the first post-war organizations facilitating European cooperation and integration. It was later expanded to states outside of Europe and renamed the Organisation for Economic Co-operation and Development (OECD).

The immediate response to demands for reconstruction funds was met by public sources, primarily the US government. However, the trend until the end of the century would be for larger and larger percentages of international liquidity and credit to be distributed by private sources. A key element of this shift was the rise of the Euro-currency markets which will be examined further below. Before tracing the major developments in the monetary and credit systems we'll pause to consider the diverse theoretical approaches in the issue area.

Theoretical perspectives: the monetary policy–exchange rate–capital mobility trade-off

There are three primary approaches to understanding the global financial system. Many in the financial community subscribe to a liberal view of the way the system should operate. The liberal view is that the exchange of currencies and provision of credit should be determined by private actors in the marketplace. As described below, the liberal view has picked up the label of the 'Washington Consensus'. This consensus is sometimes challenged by a more social democratic view which attempts to temper market mechanisms, and build in safeguards for financial stability and redistribution. This might involve slowing down the rate at which financial transactions occur or regulating the behaviour of private firms. Outside the corridors of power, variations of neo-Marxist thought are highly critical of the liberal financial system because of instability and promotion of inequality between and within states. Dependency analysts focus on how Northern states are able to use the financial system to retain great influence in the economies of developing economies. For example, US companies made considerable progress in Asian markets following the 1997 Asian financial crisis.

These different understandings of how the financial system operates will be recalled in the following sections. However, for now, we will focus upon a theoretical proposition about the relationship between the ability of money to cross borders (capital mobility), the existence of fixed or floating currencies (stable exchange rates) and the ability of a country to set its own interest rates to influence domestic economic growth and employment (monetary policy). This relationship is important because it has implications for regional currencies, financial crisis and national autonomy which are all key issues of debate.

As far back as the 1960s it was theorized by two economists (Mundell and Flemming) that states could not simultaneously have an independent monetary policy (supply of money and interest rates), stable exchange rates (either fixed or with gradual movement) and free flows of capital in and out of the country. Two of these objectives might be pursued, but the third cannot be achieved for any length of time because it would violate the other two. Governments have to choose their priorities. For example, if a government favours capital mobility to attract investment, then it must choose between a fixed exchange rate which will facilitate trade and investment or an autonomous monetary policy which will support domestic economic conditions. If it chooses a fixed exchange rate, interest rates must support that policy by providing investors with returns which will keep their money in the country. If interest rates do not support the currency and target domestic concerns, such as unemployment, investors may move money out of the country, putting pressure on the exchange rate. The exchange rate comes under pressure because investors sell the currency as they move their money into other currencies and assets. This creates an excess demand for the currency, lowering its value and cost. If enough investors sell the currency it will be devalued, as happened in Britain in 1992, and Thailand in 1997 (more on this below).

Alternatively, if a state chooses to control its own interest rates based on the domestic economy in an environment of capital mobility, the exchange rate will fluctuate. This fluctuation in exchange rates may influence trade flows as the country's exports rise or fall in cost with the currency fluctuations. Countries such as Australia, Canada, the US and Great Britain have capital mobility, floating exchange rates and interest rates responding to the domestic economy. However, if a country wants an independent monetary policy and fixed exchange rate, it will have to reduce capital flows. After the 1997 Asian financial crisis Malaysia limited capital mobility by imposing capital controls so that it could pursue domestic monetary priorities and stabilize the exchange rate.

When we use the term 'monetary autonomy' we are referring to the ability of a country to control its own money supply and interest rates in response to domestic conditions. In the 1950s and 1960s the decision about interest rates and money supply was usually taken by central banks under the direction of national governments. In the 1980s and 1990s many states made their central banks independent of government instruction and directed them to achieve low inflation. In times of slow economic growth and low inflation, central banks would lower interest rates and raise them when inflation increased. Committing to a fixed exchange rate means abandoning this policy tool because interest rates must be high enough to prevent investors from selling the currency.

These theoretical observations have moved from the academic world into difficult policy decisions for state leaders. Many states welcome capital mobility because it allows them to access more funds for investment and economic growth. Some states (mainly developing countries) have pursued fixed or stable exchange rates in order to reassure investors that the value of their money will not be lost thorough a depreciating currency, while others have wanted to avoid the uncertainty of fluctuating currencies. States also like to be able to have interest rates that respond to their own economies so that rates will be lowered during recessions to fight unemployment. However, these policies cannot be pursued simultaneously. As capital mobility has increased, it has become much more difficult for states to stabilize exchange rates *and* pursue nationally focused monetary policies (Pauly, 2000). In practice, most governments have opted for freeing capital flows and then struggled to strike a balance between having some domestic autonomy and an exchange rate that is either fixed or does not fluctuate too greatly. The goal of capital mobility has been easier to achieve than either that of exchange rate stability or domestic autonomy. We'll see just how difficult it has been to manage this trinity of factors when we consider financial crisis below. In some cases this has led to increasing turbulence in financial markets, in others it has contributed to deflationary national policies. The contradictions radiating from an increasingly liberal and global financial system have led to an intense search for new methods and institutions to govern an increasingly volatile system.

Major devlopments

There have been dramatic changes in both the international monetary system and the provision of credit on a global basis since the post-war system was created. In this section we will highlight three major changes. The first change has been the move from fixed to floating exchange rates. We'll also look at an example of how one region has tried to adapt to the change in the 1970s and 1980s by reviewing the history of the European Monetary System. The second significant development has been financial innovation and liberalization. We'll chart the rise of the Euro-currency markets, the liberalization of capital controls and innovation of financial instruments. The third development was the debt crisis of the 1980s which devastated many developing countries and encouraged policy changes in many states.

The move to floating rates

The system of fixed exchange rates was eventually undermined by the Triffin dilemma and the failure of countries to voluntarily adjust their exchange rates. The excess of US dollars compared to gold made some states and investors nervous. The government of France insisted upon turning in its dollars for gold. Investors sold dollars for other currencies, fearing that the US would be forced to break its link with gold. The US increasingly relied upon foreign central banks to support the US currency by buying dollars and upon foreign governments to stimulate imports from US. One of the underlying problems was that even though European and Japanese economies were now much stronger they were unwilling to revalue their currency against the dollar. By keeping rates fixed their industries gained an advantage over US industries. The overvalued dollar meant that foreign products were cheap for US consumers and US products were expensive in other countries. This meant that the US trade balance was deteriorating.

In the summer of 1971 the US President, Richard Nixon, decided to unilaterally change the monetary system by ending the link between the US dollar and gold. He also imposed a temporary ten per cent tax on imports. This is sometimes called the 'Nixon Shock'. Cutting the link with gold resulted in a devaluation of the dollar as it began to float against other currencies. This was meant to restore the competitiveness of the US economy. Although there were attempts to reestablish a fixed system, it was clear by 1973 that currencies would float for the foreseeable future. Two lessons can be drawn from the ending of the system of fixed exchange rates (Eichengreen, 1996). The first is the difficulty of maintaining fixed or pegged exchange rates in the face of increasing capital mobility. The second is that a fixed system required considerable international cooperation, which had its limits.

No one was quite sure what the consequences of moving to floating rates might be. Some predicted that it would ease economic tensions because currencies would find their proper value in the market and adjustment would be automatic. Others feared chaos as fluctuating currencies made planning and trading more difficult. The result was somewhere in the middle. Exchange rates proved to be more volatile than advocates of floating rates suggested, but they did not result in immediate financial chaos. Governments intervened in the market by buying and selling currencies in an attempt to halt large swings.

Floating rates turned out to be more of a problem in the 1980s. In 1979 the US central bank (Federal Reserve) moved against rising domestic inflation by dramatically raising interest rates. The hope was that higher US interest rates would slow the economy and stop price rises (inflation). If credit was more expensive, people and industries would borrow less and spend less, reducing demand. This reduced demand would stop inflation because people would be less able and willing to pay higher prices.

The effects of this change on exchange rates was dramatic. The higher US interest rates attracted investors into the US dollar, causing its value to rise. Between 1980 and 1982 it rose in value compared to other currencies about 30 per cent. At the same time that the Federal Reserve tightened monetary policy through high interest rates, US President Ronald Reagan loosened fiscal (budgetary) policy by increasing military spending and cutting taxes. This gave Americans more money in their pockets to buy imports. President Reagan ignored the international consequences and pursued tight monetary and loose fiscal policy The implications for US trade were dramatic. Other countries were able to increase their exports to the United States and the US found it harder to sell its exports abroad. The result was a rising US trade deficit and calls for greater protectionism.

A system of ad hoc cooperation trying to coordinate the economies of Europe, North America and Japan emerged as a result of turbulence in the foreign exchange markets (Eichengreen, 1996, pp. 145–52). At the Plaza meeting in September 1985 the G5 (US, Japan, Germany, UK and France) agreed to take action to reduce the value of the dollar. All countries wanted to head off the threat of increasing protectionism in the US. The markets responded to this initiative and the dollar fell rapidly, losing 40 per cent from its peak against European and Japanese currencies. Two years later at the Louvre meeting of the G7 (add Canada and Italy), the Japanese agreed to stimulus measures, the Germans to tax cuts, and the US to stabilize dollar through adjustments in domestic policy. In the second half of 1988, dollar resumed its decline.

The West European response to increasing exchange rate volatility was to try and create their own zone of currency stability called the European Monetary System. Although the European Community had been unable to advance the cause of monetary union in the 1970s, there was support for taking some action to reduce currency fluctuations. In general, European leaders were dissatisfied with floating rates because of the problem of overshooting. When investors moved out of the dollar they tended to rush to the German Deutsche Mark (DM) knocking it out of line with European currencies. Appreciation made it difficult for Germany to export its goods while the depreciation of other currencies caused inflation in those states. The Germans wanted to take pressure off the DM. If there were fixed rates, an investor would be just as happy to hold French Francs as German Marks. It was also hoped that fixed rates would build confidence and investment, encouraging transnational European companies (Swann, 1992, pp. 181–220).

The response was to create the ECU and the exchange rate mechanism (ERM). The ECU was a composite currency for bookkeeping purposes. It was composed of the currencies of the members participating in the exchange rate mechanism and was weighted according to the country's share of the collective GNP, share of collective exports and size. Each national country's currency had a specified value in relation to one ECU.

States were committed to limiting the fluctuation of their exchange rate to the ECU by no more or less than a given percentage below the central rates. Once a currency reached its bilateral limit, the central banks of each country intervened in the foreign exchange markets by buying or selling currencies to support the one in difficulty. For example, if the Irish punt was about to fall out of the band, the Irish and other central banks would sell their foreign reserves to buy punts.

Originally the UK decided to stay out of the ERM. When it did join in 1990, its currency was fixed at a relatively high level compared to the other ERM countries. This hurt British exports to Europe and had a depressing effect on the British economy. In an environment of capital mobility Britain was forced to keep interest rates high to attract investors into the pound in order to maintain its level in the ERM. In the late summer and early autumn of 1992, investors began to doubt that the British government would be able to continue to support a high pound in the face of deepening recession in the UK. Investor concern about the willingness of the British people to sacrifice economic growth for a fixed exchange rate began when the Danish people voted to abstain from the monetary union project. Investors began to sell the pound for other currencies fearing that the UK government would eventually drop out of the ERM and their investments would decrease in value as the currency depreciated. Even though the government was committed to defending the pound and the British central bank depleted its reserves through buying pounds on the market, the currency was eventually forced out of the ECU band. So many investors were selling pounds that the British government was unable to buy them all.

The British government was committed to capital mobility and a fixed exchange rate. Recalling our trinity theory, this meant that it would have to let interest rates target the exchange rate rather than the domestic economy. In the end, the government was unable to do so because the political cost of having very high interest rates in the middle of a recession was unsustainable. Investors recognized this and sold the pound until the British government recognized the situation as well. To understand this we need to understand the link between exchange rates and capital mobility.

The evolution of the post-1945 monetary system has taken place in the context of increasing capital mobility. This means that it has been increasingly easier for individuals and corporations to move money across state borders. This will also be discussed in the next section. For now, our comments will be confined to capital mobility and the foreign exchange markets. The move to floating exchange rates, the easing or eliminating of restrictions on exchanging currencies and the information revolution have all led to increased activity in foreign exchange markets. The existence of floating rates has introduced the possibility of selling currencies while information technology has allowed traders to do this in greater amounts, in more ways and at greater speeds. Although the variations can be complicated, the underlying principle is simple. Profit can be made by selling a currency that will decline in value and then buying it back at a later time. For example, imagine that Susan sells her $1.00 (US) for 1.00 Euros. If by the next day the Euro rises in value or appreciates 10 per cent (10 cents) against the dollar, Susan can sell her 1 Euro for $1.10, making a profit of 10 cents. If Susan had bought 100 000 Euros, her profit would be $10 000 for less than a day's work. If these numbers are multiplied many times, the time period is shortened from a day to minutes, and losses as well as gains are factored in, one begins to get an idea of the frenzy of activity on foreign exchange markets.

In the case of the attack on the British pound, speculators were betting that the pound would fall by selling pounds for other currencies. In this case it was a very safe bet. If the government succeeded in keeping the pound in a narrow band through the ERM, the investors would only lose the money that it cost them to exchange currencies. However, if the pound did fall out of the ERM it could decline significantly and vast fortunes might be made. The most famous speculator in this event was George Soros who was rumoured to have made $1 billion by selling the pound.

This type of activity is interpreted in several different ways. For some it is damaging speculation. Wealth is created without anything actually being produced. Even more serious is the claim that flows of money in and out of countries can weaken otherwise healthy currencies and economies, creating economic hardship. An opposite, more liberal, view is that foreign exchange fluctuations serve a positive role by signalling when economies are pursuing harmful policies. This encourages governments to adopt corrective measures. A third position might hold that currencies react to real problems, but that because of the volume and speed at which they operate a herd mentality amongst investors can cause unnecessary economic damage.

The EMS enjoyed some success in bringing a degree of monetary stability to Europe and encouraging states to follow similar economic policies. However, the system was wounded by the attacks on several currencies in 1992. Rather than destroying the prospect of monetary cooperation, this incident illustrated the need to either let currencies float or to fix currencies on a permanent basis. Europeans were undeterred and pushed on with the creation of a single currency – the Euro.

Financial innovation

A remarkable feature of the global financial system has been the degree of innovation in the past fifty years. Advances in telecommunications such as fax, high-speed telephone lines, satellite connections and the internet have allowed financial transactions to take place at a much faster pace and greater volume. In addition, new types of financial products have been introduced to provide investors with more options. This section begins its consideration of financial innovations with the Euro-currency (or Eurodollar) markets.

Actually the term Euro-currency markets is a bit misleading. It does not refer to European currencies. It refers to a wide series of financial transactions that take place in currencies other than the currency of the state in which the business is being conducted. For example, the Euro-currency market was initially composed of the exchange of US dollars in London. The Euro-currency market in New York would operate in funds other than US dollars. The market in the Cayman Islands would operate in any currency other than the local one. The primary reason why financial operators did not use the local currency was because state authorities would not regulate their activity if they were working with foreign currencies.

The Euro-currency market began in London after the Second World War and met several needs. The British state supported its expansion because it brought financial business back to London and helped the city re-establish it role as an important financial centre. The Soviet Union made use of the market as a place where it could store and exchange US dollars beyond the reach of its Cold War rival, the US. US corporations investing in Europe increasingly used the market to escape restrictive US laws on banking activity. However, the big jump in the Euro-market's size came with the 1973 oil crisis and the increase in revenues flowing to OPEC states (Organization of Pertroleum Exporting Countries). Many of these states turned to the Euromarkets to conduct their banking. Estimates of the money put into the markets show it rising from $3 billion in 1960 to 75 in 1970, to 1000 billion by 1984 (Strange, 1988, p. 105).

Alongside the rise of currency markets, the 1970s and 1980s saw a global financial revolution. Capital was increasingly flowing between countries in larger volumes and at faster speeds. Technological advances allowed for cheap, instantaneous, constant communication. In the late 1970s and early 1980s a number of key states eliminated capital controls, allowing individuals and corporations to move their money freely in or out of their country. The US took this step in 1974 and the United Kingdom followed in 1979. In 1986 the UK increased liberalization in its financial industry through what was called the 'Big Bang'. This was the name given to financial deregulation in Britain. It involved two major elements. The first was allowing any foreign company to enter into the UK's stock market and foreign exchanges. The second step was to allow banks, stock-broking firms and insurance companies to compete in each other's industries. This broke down the barriers which had formerly stipulated that only banks engaged in banking, insurance companies in insurance and stockbrokers sold stocks. The advantage of this deregulation was that it increased competition in the financial industry. The disadvantage was that this competition might push some firms into more risky behaviour, possibly leading to financial crises.

The liberalization of financial activity resulted both in increased competition and in a series of financial crises. Financial products proliferated with a range of new instruments coming on to the market. These included currency swaps, futures, options and derivatives. However, financial problems also arose. In Great Britain an economic boom followed upon the creation of new wealth from the enlivened financial markets. However, the boom turned to bust in 1988 following the 1987 stock-market crash and the collapse in the housing market. Fuelled by the expansion in credit, many people bought houses at over-inflated prices and suffered the consequences when the economy slowed.

The financial liberalization and innovation of the 1980s accelerated in the 1990s. Large sums of money were expended to manage and profit from increasing risks of the volatile financial markets. An increasingly popular method of coping with the risk (the possibility that exchange rates, the rate of inflation or the price of commodities might change) was the use of *derivatives*. The term 'derivatives' is used for an array of financial instruments that are derived from more basic financial instruments. The two most common forms are futures and options. These are derived or spun off from stocks or bonds. A future commits someone to buying a stock or a commodity at a specified time in the future for a price set today. Futures have been very common in the agricultural field where someone would agree to buy a farmer's product six months before it was available. This gave the farmer a guaranteed price and some security against the risk of planting a crop and then receiving a low price during the harvest period. One might also buy oil futures if there was fear that oil prices would rise in the future. Futures can be bought on margin which means that the purchaser only has to put down a percentage of the purchase price when committing to the deal and the rest when the future comes due. An option requires someone to pay a small fee for the opportunity to buy a stock or bond at a specified price at a specified time. If the price of the commodity goes down, the trader can back out of the purchase, but loses their fee. If the price goes up they can buy the commodity and sell it for a profit.

Used wisely, derivatives can insure businesses and individuals from the risks of falling or rising prices. However, they are also used to make money in themselves. Traders and investors use them to make money by betting on the value of a product at some time in the future. If they are correct about the price movement, they can sell at a profit. If they are incorrect, they suffer a financial loss. Since these products can be bought on margin, large sums of money can be pledged without having the ability to pay for it at the time of purchase. This kind of a system encourages investors to take risks for potentially large pay-offs. We'll consider some of the dangers of rapid innovation in the key issues section.

The 1980s debt crisis

For developing states the liberalization of capital markets had far more serious consequences – the debt crisis of the1980s. A combination of supply and demand factors help us understand why developing countries became exposed to large debt (Lever and Huhne, 1986), but decisions about interest rates in developed states led to the onset of the crisis.

On the supply side, vast sums of money became available for lending purposes in the 1970s. The rise in oil prices had a dramatic effect on the international credit market. It caused a shift in wealth from oil consumers to oil producers. The producers, primarily members of (OPEC), invested some of their money in the Eurodollar markets. This money then had to be lent out if the banks were to turn a profit. Bankers were flooded with cash and eagerly looked around for potential customers.

Fortunately for the banks, there was a great demand for credit. Developing countries were desperate for funds to help them industrialize their economies. In some cases, developing countries were oil consumers and required loans to help pay for rising oil prices. In other cases, a decision had been made to follow a strategy of indebted industrialization (Frieden, 1981). This meant that states borrowed money to invest in industrialization and would pay off the loans from the profits of their new industries. Loans were an attractive option because they did not come with the influence of foreign transnational corporations that accompanied foreign direct investment and most states had few funds of their own to invest.

In the late 1960s and early 1970s developing states appeared to be a sound investment because many had indeed enjoyed high growth rates up to that point. The market appeared to be working well by bringing together the capital rich and the capital poor to the benefit of both. However, events at the end of the 1970s took a turn for the worse and the debt crisis erupted in 1982.

In 1979 the Ayatollah Khomeini was able to overthrow the Shah of Iran in the Iranian revolution. Not long afterwards war erupted as Iraq invaded Iran in a misjudged attempt to take advantage of political turmoil. The result was a second oil shock. The US response to this oil shock was considerably different from that in 1973. Rather than let the higher prices move through the US economy via inflation, a decision was taken by the chairman of the US Federal Reserve to fight inflation by raising interest rates. Interest rates would reduce the rise in prices because credit would be more expensive and people would have less money to spend or invest. This would reduce the amount of money chasing goods and services, reducing demand, leading to a slowdown in price rises (deflation).

The effect of this policy in the US was the onset of recession. The effects in other parts of the world were much more serious. The cost of international money went up, following the increase in US interest rates. Whereas interest rates on international loans were about 2 per cent in the early 1970s they rose to over 18 per cent in the early 1980s. This greatly increased the interest charges to developing states on their international loans. At the same time that developing states were facing higher interest charges it became more difficult for them to sell their products to developed states. The recession that swept the developed world reduced imports in two ways. Recession meant that demand for imports went down in general. In addition, recession fed protectionist forces in developed states, resulting in the restriction of imports to support domestic jobs.

The consequence for many developing countries was disastrous. Those states that were oil importers were faced with massive bills to cover their debts. Those developing states that were oil exporters (such as Mexico and Venezuela) were hurt because they had borrowed heavily to industrialize and were then caught as oil prices fell in response to lower demand during the recession.

In August 1982 Mexico announced that it could not longer service its debt. This meant that they could no longer cover the cost of interest payments, much less hope to repay its debt. Mexico's announcement burst the bubble and ushered in the debt crisis as banks recognized their exposure to a series of bad loans. Private funds into Mexico and some other states halted. Before long it was evident that states such as Brazil, Venezuela, Argentina, and many sub-Saharan African countries were in equally difficult financial positions.

It was in these circumstances that the IMF began to play a more prominent role. The Fund negotiated standby loans with debtors offering temporary assistance to states in need. In return for the loans states agreed to undertake structural adjustment programs (SAPs). These programs entailed the liberalization of economies to trade and foreign investment as well as the reduction of state subsidies and bureaucracies to balance national budgets.

The phrase 'Washington Consensus' was coined to capture the agreement upon economic policy that was shared between the two major international financial institutions in Washington (IMF and World Bank) and the US government itself. This consensus stipulated that the best path to economic development was through financial and trade liberalization and that international institutions should persuade countries to adopt such measures as quickly as possible. Although the 'Washington Consensus' refered to conventional wisdom, critics of the IMF and World Bank associate the term with all that is wrong with rapid economic liberalization. In their eyes it stands for harmful and arrogant policies determined by financial and Western elites imposed upon developing states.

The effects of these policies on the population in developing countries was devastating. The 1980s is known as the 'lost decade' of development. Many developing countries' economies were smaller and poorer in 1990 than in 1980. Over the 1980s and 1990s, debt in many developing countries was so great that governments had few resources to spend on social services and development (see Table 8.1).

The debt crisis sealed the 'triumph of neoclassical economics' in most developing countries (Biersteker, 1992). Starved of international finance,

Table 8.1   *National expenditure on social services vs. debt*

| | | Percentage of central government expenditure on | |
	Year(s)	Basic social services	Debt service
Africa			
Tanzania	1994–95	15	46
Kenya	1995	13	40
Uganda	1994–95	21	9
South Africa	1996–97	14	8
Asia			
Philippines	1992	8	31
Sri Lanka	1996	13	22
Nepal	1997	14	15
Thailand	1997	15	1
Latin America and Caribbean			
Jamaica	1996	10	31
Brazil	1995	9	20
Costa Rica	1996	13	13
Chile	1996	11	3

Source: Data from UNICEF (1999) p. 32.

Figure 8.1   *Developing country external debt as a percentage of GNP*

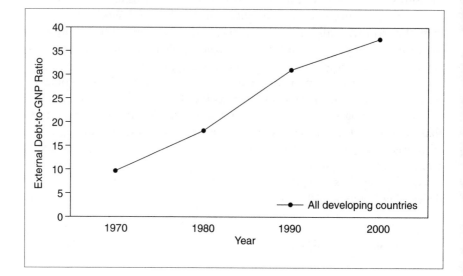

Source: Data from World Bank (2001) p. 246.

Figure 8.2   *Regional averages: external debt as a percentage of GNP*

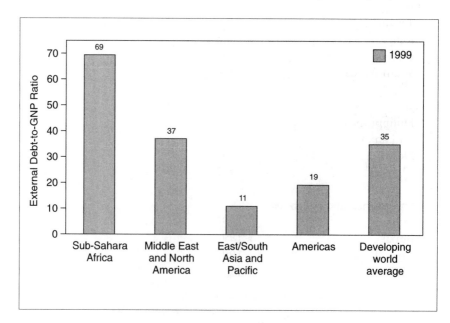

Source: Data from UNICEF (1999) pp. 30–1.

Box 8.2   Debt and AIDS

The effects of the debt crisis go well beyond financial indicators. In sub-Saharan Africa, debt burdens have greatly complicated responses to the AIDS crisis. Approximately 5000 people die every day from AIDS in Africa and the disease has rolled back previous gains in life expectancy and development. Structural adjustment programs designed to address debt problems have led to the downsizing or privatization of health and educational services (Cheru, 2002). This has weakened the ability of governments to provide health care and information about AIDS to their populations. Money that might go into public health campaigns has been diverted to pay off external debt. Efforts by the World Bank and IMF to reduce the debt loads of heavily indebted poor countries (HIPC initiative) have freed up some money for some countries. However, given the extreme health emergency, broader and more rapid cancellation of external debt may be required.

states had little choice but to open their economies to foreign investors and trade. Mexico is the most dramatic example. Following its revolution in the early part of the twentieth century, Mexico had tried to follow a development strategy which stressed the building of a national economy. It was a leading advocate of import-substitution industrialization. Mexico erected tariff barriers against imports and tried to produce its own goods behind these barriers. However, following the debt crisis, Mexican policy concentrated upon integrating itself in the international market. As the 1980s and 1990s progressed, more and more developing countries followed a similar path. McMichael (1996) has described this as a transition from a development model of national economic growth to a globalization model of searching for a 'niche' in the world market. The Mexican liberalization process was capped and solidified by its pursuit and achievement of the 1993 North American Free Trade Agreement. NAFTA locked in Mexico's liberal reforms because it acted as an economic constitution for North America. However, despite the policy changes in many developing states the burden of debt compared to domestic national product continued to grow in the 1980s and 1990s (see Figures 8.1 and 8.2).

Key issues

This section focuses on three key issues that have dominated the global financial system in the last decade of the twentieth century and the early years of the twenty-first. The three key issues are: the rise of regional currencies; financial crisis and international regulatory mechanisms; questions of autonomy, convergence and democracy.

The rise of regional currencies

The most recent change and pressing issue in the IMS has been the growth of regional currencies. In Europe many states have given up their own national currencies and adopted the Euro. In the Americas, there has been increasing discussion of unilateral adoption of the US dollar, called dollarization. First, we'll examine the Euro then turn to dollarization.

On 1 January 1999, eleven European countries fixed their exchange rates in preparation for monetary union. Many countries began to advertise prices in the local currency and the Euro so that customers could become used to the imminent currency. On 1 January 2002, the Euro appeared in physical form and the phase-out of national currencies began. This most recent attempt to create a single currency had started with the signing of the Maastricht Treaty in December 1990. The treaty had set out a list of qualifications required of countries wishing to join the new currency. These conditions were called the convergence requirements and stipulated that: countries had to have an inflation rate no more than 1.5 per cent above the average of the three EC states with the lowest rate; that long-term interest rates had to be within 2 per cent points of the average of the three members with the lowest inflation rates; that national budget deficit be less than 3 per cent of GDP; public debt ratio not be greater than 60 per cent of GDP and that the currency had been in the narrow band of the ERM and not devalued for the previous two years. The point of these criteria was to ensure that these economies would be in similar states of economic health before tying themselves to the same currency. States interested in joining the Euro would have to sacrifice national monetary autonomy.

The operation of the Euro is overseen by a new European Central Bank (ECB). After consultation with representatives from the national central banks, the ECB sets a single interest rate for all member states. It also manages the exchange rate between the Euro and other currencies. The primary goal of the ECB is price stability which means low inflation. In response to fears that some countries might not respect low inflation levels and might be tempted to run budget deficits, EU members agreed to a stability pact in June 1997. This stipulated that national governments must not run an annual budget deficit of more than 3 per cent of GDP. Fines could be applied to states who did not comply.

The British and Danish governments were not enthusiastic about the process and demanded an opt out which would allow them to avoid joining the currency. The decision about who could join the currency was taken in May 1998: Greece and Sweden were found not to have met the requirements while Britain and Denmark exercized their opt out. Eleven other states embarked upon the historic journey (Austria, Belgium, Finland, France, Germany, Ireland, Luxembourg, the Netherlands, Italy, Portugal, Spain). After a series of reforms Greece was also admitted.

The drive to adopt the Euro prompted considerable public debate. A number of objections were raised. One issue was that countries would lose the ability to devalue their currencies if there was an economic shock that hit their country. For example, a country reliant on oil exports such as Britain might be hit by low oil prices. With their own currency Britain would probably devalue, letting exports in other industries make up for employment losses in the oil industry. Under a single currency this would not be possible. The result might be that particular areas of the European Union could stagnate as they lose the ability to adjust their currencies.

A single monetary policy and interest rate may not suit such a diverse economy. For example, the Irish economy might expand while the German economy is stagnant. Because of the large size of the German economy, it is likely that in such a situation European interest rates would be lowered to boost German economic growth. This would help Germany, but hurt Ireland. The low interest rates in Ireland would fuel consumer and business spending and cause inflation.

Opponents argued that the mechanisms which allowed federal states such as the US to overcome these problems were absent in Europe (Feldstein, 1992). The lack of labour mobility and absence of transfer payments were striking. Because of language and cultural barriers, Europeans were much less likely to migrate to jobs in another part of Europe. Many would stay in a stagnant area rather than move. Another difference with federal states is that there was little transfer of funds from richer to poorer areas for development or equalization payments. In the end, although there were economic arguments in favour and against the Euro, the decision to push forward was taken by those wishing to form a closer political union. The single currency was seen as a way of increasing the bonds between European citizens in preparation for closer political ties.

The creation of the Euro was undertaken as much for its contribution to political union as its alleged economic benefits. In other parts of the world there is not the same desire for political union. Nevertheless, there have been moves by some states to reduce or eliminate their national currency in favour of a foreign currency. The general name for this trend is dollarization, although it can occur with a number of different currencies, not just the US dollar. In this section we will look at dollarization in the Americas where it does in fact occur through use of the US dollar.

Dollarization can take place in two ways and for two reasons (Dean and

Globerman, 2001). The two ways it can take place are de facto and de jure. De facto dollarization means that national currencies still exist, but a large number of people use the dollar in practice. It is dollarization in fact. De jure dollarization means dollarization in law. This occurs when the national currency is legally replaced with the US dollar. Since the 1980s, de facto dollarization has occurred in many countries of the Americas while de jure dollarization has occurred in Panama and Equador.

Why would a country give up or reduce the use of its own currency? One reason is that individuals and business may lose faith in their own currency. High inflation or repeated devaluations may encourage people to hold their money in foreign currency as a preferred store of wealth. This is known as asset substitution. Fearing that their money may lose its value they choose to hold a safer currency, in this case the US dollar.

A second reason for adopting another currency is to facilitate trade relations with a dominant economic partner. For example, Canada's economy is heavily reliant upon trade with the US. If Canada adopted the US dollar it would increase economic exchange and eliminate problems of fluctuating currencies. In this case, Canadians (especially businesses) might favour the US dollar as the best medium of exchange. This is known as currency substitution.

In the case of Latin American countries, dollarization would bring some economic benefits. Foreign investors would no longer fear that they would lose money when a currency declined. It would be less risky to invest in Latin America. This should lead to more foreign investment and growth. Money would also become cheaper in dollarized countries. At the moment, Latin American states must pay an interest premium when lending domestically. This means that they must pay higher interest rates than the US to encourage investors to buy government bonds and securities. This is necessary because their currency is a riskier investment. By adopting the US dollar this risk premium would disappear.

Despite obvious advantages, there are serious disadvantages to the dollarization process. Unlike the European example, there is no effort to make US monetary policy sensitive to the needs of other countries. There would be no central bank of the Americas similar to the ECB in Europe. Countries that enter into dollarization will have their money supply and interest rates controlled by the US. This may reduce economic growth if the US pursues a monetary policy that is contrary to the needs of the dollarized country. If a dollarized economy experiences some form of economic shock it will be unable to devalue its currency to restore competitiveness. Adjustment will have to take place by further depressing real wages and reducing incomes.

In a dollar bloc it is likely that most of the financial institutions will be from the US. These institutions may not have much interest in lending money to local small business, poorer individuals, farmers and local governments. Clients of the formerly national institutions could well be starved for credit, hampering economic growth. On the other hand, dollarization may feed speculative bubbles as funds flow into particular sectors and flow out again with similar ease.

In short, dollarization offers some advantages, but creates more restraints on state policies. It reduces their flexibility and policy levers. If there are no funds to help with the process of adjustment (none are proposed) the economic costs of dollarization could prove to be very high. This in turn would likely lead to increased domestic political conflict as the costs of adjustment are distributed unequally through the national economy.

The advent of the Euro and the dollarization process indicates several things about the international monetary system. First, many states are willing to consider the benefits of abandoning their national currency in favour of joining a currency bloc. In the European case, this is part of a deep process of economic and political integration. In the Americas, the motivation is primarily economic gain. Secondly, the existing international monetary system is not serving the interests of many of its members. Many developing countries cannot trade or borrow unless they do it in a major currency such as the US dollar. They must pay for goods in dollars and loans are denominated in dollars. Countries must continually earn more dollars to engage in international economic transactions. This means that they are very vulnerable to any shock that upsets their economic relationship with the outside world.

Financial crisis and international regulatory mechanisms

Even though the 1980s debt crisis was managed in such a way that financial collapse was prevented, many people are still worried about the stability of the financial system. In the late 1980s one leading observer of the operation of the global financial markets termed it 'Casino Capitalism' (Strange, 1986). Strange argued that the increased volatility in most markets and the lack of sensible regulation over transactions had turned the financial markets into one large casino. Investors placed bets on the future of company profits, commodity prices, exchange rates, interest rates and many other economic indicators. The large sums involved and the rapidity at which money travelled encouraged investors to take risks and increased the possibility that crisis would occur. Crucially, this casino has many involuntary players. People not placing the bets suffer the consequences when the financial wheel of fortune takes a bad turn. The citizens of developed states bear the cost of financial bailouts through their taxes and the population of developing states pay through reduced living standards and in some cases malnutrition and death. In this section we will review several of the financial crises of the 1990s that reinforce concern about the stability of the international financial system and consider the arrangements put in place to deal with them.

Two financial collapses of the 1990s illustrate that the proliferation of financial instruments is difficult to regulate through market mechanisms and risky to employ even for the most brilliant financial and mathematical minds. The case of the collapse of Barings Bank in 1995 demonstrates the difficulties that financial firms have in keeping track of the activity of their employees. Over the summer of 1995, Nick Leeson, an employee of Barings Bank in Singapore used derivatives to place a series of bets that the Japanese economy would prosper in the following years. Unfortunately for Japan and Barings Bank, economic recession continued and Japan was struck with a large earthquake. When the dust had settled and the margins were called, Barings could not cover its loses. The bank collapsed and Mr Leeson spent some time in prison in Singapore. Criminals can be found in any organization, but what is striking is that the bank was unable to monitor its employee's actions and that it gave so much financial power to individual traders.

Perhaps an even more cautionary tale is that of Long Term Capital Management. This was an investment firm set up by leaders in the financial field, including two economics Nobel Prize winners, numerous mathematics PhDs and people with backgrounds in Wall Street firms and the Federal Reserve. They created a hedge fund which used derivatives to make large sums of money for their wealthy clients and banks. All their mathematical models proved of no assistance when Russia experienced economic difficulty in 1998 and the fund's assets disappeared. The US financial system teetered on the brink of collapse before a number of private financial institutions stepped in to pick up the pieces at the urging of the US government (Blustein, 2001, pp. 305–36). A system that encourages financial risk led a group of talented financial minds to financial ruin and almost caused a national and international financial crisis.

Development groups and social democratic critics of the liberal global financial system have suggested that capital mobility needs to be slowed down to provide greater stability. One proposal to do this has been the Tobin Tax. The Tobin Tax would levy a charge on foreign exchange dealings. The idea is that the tax would discourage those people trading currencies just to make money, but would not deter foreign exchange transactions for purposes such as medium to long term investment, buying imports or tourism.

Although there are technical objections to the Tobin Tax and other measures to slow the flow of capital, the primary obstacles are political. Vast fortunes are generated by the free flow of capital. Those who benefit from the system are adept at using their influence to prevent measures which might reduce their potential for increased wealth. The beneficiaries of capital mobility are those who have money to invest. This includes wealthy individuals, the financial industry itself, and corporations with a need for investment or which are investing in financial instruments or the stock market.

Corporations and wealthy individuals have recently been joined by a large number of less wealthy individuals who have interests in the stock market. Over the past twenty years, large numbers of people from modest economic backgrounds in the developed world have had their pensions and savings invested in the stock market. As governments increasingly privatized the provision of pensions in the 1990s by scaling back state pensions, more people relied upon their own investments for retirement earnings. This has meant a large growth of individual investment in the stock market through mutual funds or unit trusts. In addition, employer pension funds of civil servants or teachers have become major stock market participants as they search for the best return for their customers. These organizations are called institutional investors and their investment decisions can move markets. The number of people in advanced industrialized countries committed to open financial markets has grown, making attempts to curb such openness much more politically difficult (Harmes, 1998). At the same time, the number of people vulnerable to a stock market slump has also grown. This opens the possibility of an anti-liberal backlash if a prolonged recession destroys millions of investors' retirement funds.

Turning to financial crises in states, we should consider the case of Mexico, a country which had undergone massive restructuring as a result of the 1980s debt crisis. Mexico plunged into another crisis in the mid-1990s. The decade had started well enough for Mexico. Its negotiation and signing of NAFTA had convinced investors that the government was committed to liberalization. Between 1990–1993, $91 billion flowed into Mexico, a fifth of all capital going to developing states (Strange, 1998, p. 103). Money flowed into the stock market boosting share prices and creating a sense of increasing wealth. However, a series of events including higher interest rates in the US, rebellion in the state of Chiapas, and the assassination of a presidential candidate caused investors to doubt whether Mexico could maintain its fixed exchange rate with the US dollar. In December 1994, investors sold the Mexican peso in quantities so large that the government ran down its foreign currency reserves and was forced to abandon the link with the dollar. Although Mexico was committed to capital mobility (to attract investment) and exchange rate stability (to keep the investment), it was unable to withstand the destruction caused by rapid capital flows. When it was over, the Mexican government owed over $55 billion, mostly to private foreign investors such as pension funds. The US government, over the objection of the Congress, committed $20 billion dollars to a rescue package and pressed the IMF and BIS to contribute another $32 billion. The effects of the crisis on Mexicans were disastrous as living standards were cut in half. The poor suffered enormously and the middle class faced huge debts because of skyrocketing interest rates and diminishing of their savings when the peso devalued.

The Mexican crisis was notable for several factors. First, it spilt into other countries such as Brazil and Argentine, forcing them to take defensive measures such as raising their interest rates to stop capital flight. This became known as the Tequila effect. Secondly, Mexico suffered a severe financial crisis despite having undergone over a decade of liberalization and economic restructuring after the first debt crisis. Thirdly, the dangers of the flow of short-term capital into and out of a developing country were highlighted by the Mexican events. Finally, the players on the creditor side had changed. In the 1982 crisis, it was banks that were involved and eventually had to accept some losses on their loans. In 1994 it was non-bank actors such as pension funds, mutual funds and stock market investors that pulled the money out. Thanks to the US/IMF/BIS loan investors escaped with relatively little financial loss. The Mexican people were not as fortunate.

Two-and-a-half years later an even more remarkable financial crisis occurred. It was remarkable because it hit a group of countries which had formerly been held out as success stories – the newly industrializing countries of East and South-east Asia. In 1997 South Korea, Malaysia, Thailand and Indonesia suffered serious financial crisis. Hong Kong, Taiwan and even China were threatened by turmoil as well. Yet, only a few years earlier the World Bank (1993) had issued a report praising the 'development miracles' of East Asia. How could this have come about?

In July 1997, investors started to have doubts about whether the government of Thailand would be able to maintain the value of its currency against the US dollar. Similar to events in Mexico in 1994 and Britain in 1992, they began to sell the local currency, betting that the government would eventually have to devalue. After defeating the Thai peg, attention turned to other countries in Asia. Successful speculative attacks were mounted against Indonesia, Malaysia, South Korea and unsuccessful attacks took place against China and Hong Kong. States formerly thought to be in good shape were forced to turn to the IMF for financial assistance

There are several interesting aspects of the Asian crisis. One is that it revealed the degree to which almost any developing state could be subject to a financial crisis in a very short period of time. A second point is that the states affected by capital outflows adopted very different policies. Thailand closely followed advice from the IMF, as did Indonesia and South Korea later. In contrast, the government of Malaysia blamed foreigners for provoking the crisis and instituted capital controls to prevent rapid inflows and outflows of funds. A third point is that although many in the US saw the reforms requested of states in crisis as natural and advisable, many in Asia saw them as an opportunity for US business and state elites to take advantage of Asian weakness (Higgott, 1998).

The series of financial crisis at the end of the twentieth century which included East Asia and Russia led many people to question the stability of the global financial system. Investors alarmed by crisis in one part of the world had the tendency to remove money from other parts of the world, spreading panic beyond the initial problem cases. This is known as contagion and is a considerable source of worry for money managers and state elites. The official response to these fears was to begin a discussion about new forms of governance in international finance. Hundreds of studies and many hours of meetings were devoted to the topic of a 'new financial architecture'. The two substantial institutional innovations that emerged out of this process were the Financial Stability Forum (FSF) and the Group of Twenty (G20).

The Financial Stability Forum brings together officials from the most industrialized countries (G7) with representatives of a wide range of international financial institutions and regulators. Representatives from the International Monetary Fund and World Bank are joined by the Organization for Economic Cooperation and Development, the Bank for International Settlements, the Basle Committee on Banking Supervision, the International Organization of Securities Commissions, the International Association of Insurance Supervisors, the Committee on the Global Financial System, and the Committee on Payments and Settlements. The FSF has concentrated its work on three issues: offshore financial centres, cross-border capital flows and highly leveraged institutions (hedge funds). Its investigation of offshore financial centres confirmed the view that these areas contributed to systemic instability. They proposed that more information about offshore centres should be gathered and that they be pressured to comply with international standards.

A more politically oriented body was created with the founding of the G20 in September 1999. The G20 is composed of the finance ministers and central bank governors of the G7 states plus Argentina, Australia, Brazil, China, India, Indonesia, South Korea, Mexico, Russia, Saudi Arabia, South Africa, and Turkey. It also includes representatives of the European Union, IMF and World Bank. As a group they account for over 85 per cent of the world's GDP and 65 per cent of the world's population. Whereas the FSF is essentially a gathering of the most economically developed states, the G20 includes several of the largest developing states (Brazil, China, India and Indonesia). This is an attempt to bolster the legitimacy of financial reforms by having a broader base of countries participate in decision-making. The G7 countries suffered from the accusation that they were a rich man's club.

Initially the G20 concentrated on reviewing codes and standards for financial transactions and exchange rates. It was thought that the institution could serve as an arena where policy could be formulated and implementation followed up. The larger multilateral institutions of the IMF and World Bank could take formal decisions after the G20 reached a consensus. At its second annual meeting in Montreal in October 2000, the G20 broadened its future agenda to include issues of social safety nets, infectious diseases, the environment and debt relief. (G20, 2000). It is doubtful whether the G20 framework has the resources to handle these issues, but public concern about the consequences of financial liberalization has forced them to take up a broader agenda.

A crucial aspect of the debate around the Asian financial crisis and the stability of the international financial system was whether the primary problem was with the units or the structure of the system. A problem with the units would mean that there was something wrong with the policies that individual states were following. They might be spending their money in a wasteful manner, following inefficient economic policies, borrowing excessively or have a financial system that lacked transparency. A system fault would mean that there was something wrong in how international finance was organized. This could stem from markets that moved too rapidly, or incentives to firms to engage in unwise lending, or a trading system that made it difficult for countries to earn sufficient resources. If the problem was at the unit level, the solution would be found in domestic reform. If the problem is at the systemic level, the solution would require changes to the rules governing the exchange and flow of money.

With few exceptions, creditors and advanced industrialized countries believe that the problem of financial stability arise because of poor policies at the unit level. Efforts to increase stability are therefore aimed at reforming developing countries (again!). During the 1980s, Latin American countries were faulted because their economies were not sufficiently export oriented. In the late 1990s, formerly successful Asian states are blamed for practising a corrupt form of capitalism – crony capitalism. In contrast, many developing countries and non-governmental organizations believe that the fault lies in a global financial system which rewards speculation and the rapid flow of capital.

Autonomy, convergence and democracy

Underlining many of the technical debates about the global financial system are the issues of autonomy, convergence and democracy. The openness of financial markets has sparked a debate about whether all states are being forced to pursue similar policies (convergence) or whether there is still room for different economic strategies (autonomy). Following on from this is the question of the tension between the demands for financial restructuring and policy preferences articulated through the democratic process. We'll briefly outline these positions before concluding the chapter.

The idea that governments and populations have lost power to the market and business leaders is captured by the phrase 'increased structural power of capital' (Gill and Law, 1993). This means that the organization, or the structure, of the financial system gives more power to those who posses wealth and those who can move their money around the global system. Because financial markets operate around the clock and transactions can take place almost instantaneously, investors can move their money out of countries that adopt policies which might threaten their profits. For example, a government that runs budget deficits to fund welfare policies may threaten the profits of investors. Investors may then transfer money out of that country, hurting businesses and the government's finances. Financial interests are not able to dictate policies, but they increase the cost to those pursuing policies that are seen to be against investors' profits. This reduces the autonomy of states and societies that have different priorities from investors. Although this line of argument started before discussion of globalization became fashionable, many people who discuss the power of globalization are referring to the power of financial markets.

One of the interesting organizations which has received more attention in this time of financial globalization is the bond rating agencies such as Moody's and Standard and Poors (Sinclair, 1994). These private firms rate the debt worthiness of governments and corporations. If your rating goes down, the price of money goes up. A government or firm with a low bond rating must pay investors higher interest to compensate them for risk. Governments need to pay attention to the judgement of these agencies because a poor rating will influence the terms upon which they can access money. They raise or lower the cost of certain policy options.

The notion that state policy has been restricted by mobile capital has been challenged by scholars who maintain that states may still make significant choices. They argue that policies are not converging upon a particular liberal financial model. Sturdy domestic institutions and the power of organized labour and leftist political parties are factors which blunt the power of investors (Garrett, 2000). Liberal financial policies are implemented by particular governments who must be held responsible for those policies. For these analysts, power still resides at the state level and the attempt to find the cause of changing state policies at the global level are mistaken.

The debate about convergence and the structural power of capital has important implications for the practice of democracy. If the structural power of capital perspective is correct, democracy can be undermined because financial interests are having an increasingly large say over public policies. Voters may elect a government on a program of economic growth and lowering unemployment, but the government may not follow these policies because of the financial implications. The will of the people is undermined by the power of the dollar. On the other hand, if analysts who discount the power of global financial markets are correct, then talk of globalization and structural power only serves to shift responsibility from governments to shadows beyond the state. Democracy can suffer because people give up trying to hold governments accountable for their actions. We will return to issues of governance and accountability in the final chapter of this book.

Conclusion

Although there are many debates surrounding the global financial system, it clearly is an important factor in the operation of the global economy. It channels credit to some of the actors that need capital for economic growth. It also places restrictions on those who are in debt or exposed to the shifting financial markets. A sound financial system will facilitate trade, growth and prosperity. A weak or faulty system will impede trade flows, slow growth and undermine prosperity. In the worst case scenario, a major financial crisis would result in a collapse of the global economy and political confrontation between states. It is a significant part of the policy environment facing states, corporations and citizens.

Chapter 9

Economic Development

Attention to economic growth and development springs from a number of different motives. These include the eradication of global poverty, a reduction in inequalities in living standards, and a lessening in global disparities of power and influence. A commitment to the pursuit of economic development as a means to eliminate poverty signals an aspiration that has been widely accepted by peoples and their governments around the globe. The World Bank's *Voices of the Poor* (Narayan *et al.*, 2000) provides an excellent introduction to the reality of poverty in its various manifestations as experienced by poor people from many countries. Although some agreement exists on these objectives, there is no consensus on the methods and strategies necessary for the achievement of these goals.

This chapter is centrally concerned with the global pursuit of economic development in the period since the end of the Second World War. It provides an introduction to a central issue in the contemporary global economy through an assessment of the ways in which states and other actors have engaged with the challenge of aspirations for material improvement in the context of persistent global inequality. Despite universal acceptance of, and support for, economic development, it nevertheless, remains a profoundly controversial concept. Proponents differ concerning its definition, and the policies likely to bring it about. Many of these debates concerning development are themselves linked to other debates surrounding capitalism and modernity. In this chapter we will be analysing development both as an aspiration or goal, and a concrete set of practices.

The late twentieth century's obsession with economic development (a fixation carried over to the twenty-first century) finds its roots in an earlier period. The origins of the quest for economic development is to be found in the onset of the era of modern economic growth begun in Western Europe with the industrial revolution in Britain in the eighteenth century. Since Britain's successful industrialization, modernizing elites around the globe have attempted to emulate this feat (Kemp, 1983, pp. 1–17). The linkages between industrialization and military power further fueled the drive for modernization (Sen, 1983). Until the Second World War, a country's industrialization was perceived almost solely as a national objective. This does not mean that there were no international implications but rather that economic growth, understood principally in terms of industrialization, proceeded without appeals for international assistance. This phase came to an end when in the post-war era, the promotion of economic growth in poorer countries became an international issue. The quest for economic development, as it was now called, has been a significant feature of the post World War II international system. A proclaimed objective of Third World elites, international organizations, and Western governments, economic development has become an indisputable and undeniable right of peoples living in poverty. It has been claimed that, 'The development project brought all nations into line with the idea of national economic growth, even across the Cold War divide' (McMichael, 1996, p. 243). This chapter begins by exploring the debates over several of the key terms encountered in discussions of international development. In the theoretical perspectives section we will explore two major debates that have taken place. Under major developments we discuss changes in approaches to development and development planning. The key issues considered in this chapter are: the organization of development; economic aid; and solidarity and fragmentation among developing countries.

Definitions

Like many concepts in the social sciences the concept of development remains ill-defined and contested. As Cherry Gertzl asserts, 'There is no consensus as to what development means or requires' (1995, p. 1). In this section we will discuss how people have interpreted the concept of development, and also controversies surrounding the terminology to be applied to countries that are in the process of overcoming mass poverty. Development as used in the literature suggests both a process and a condition. It is a process, in so far as attention is given to the means whereby a society may transform itself so that it achieves self-sustaining economic growth. In the words of Anna Dickson, development is 'an on-going process of qualitatively ameliorated social, political and economic change' (1997, p. 16). The term is also used to denote the condition reached by those societies that have made the successful transition to self-sustaining growth. It has also been seen as the condition in which 'individuals are more aware of, and have greater access to (such) new technologies, and are induced to take advantage of their possibilities through the working of market forces' (Sundrum, 1983, p. 15). The definition given by Thomas and Reader captures development seen as both process and condition. They define development as a 'multidimensional process involving change from a less to a more socially desirable state' (1997, p. 91).

As the result of an historical accident, modern economic growth developed in Western Europe and has been successfully exported almost exclusively to territories settled by Europeans. One unfortunate result of this historical accident has been a tendency to examine development as a process taking place almost exclusively in non-European areas of the globe. Thus although in 1948 the gap in living standards between some European societies (for example, Ireland, Portugal and Spain) and parts of the so-called developing world were reasonably close, economic growth in Europe was never seen in terms of development. And when, after the fall of communism in Eastern Europe, attention turned to economic growth in the post-Soviet empire, these countries were categorized as transitional economies (or sometimes emerging markets) rather than as developing countries. Development then is, or shall we say became, the province of Africa, Asia, Latin America and the Caribbean, and the Pacific. For some writers, this geographical limitation is part of Western control of colonial and post-colonial peoples and territories (Escobar, 1995). The concept of development in this view was created as a means of taming and controlling the Third World. This is an influential thesis but whether one is convinced by its claims rests on its further assertion that the development discourse is incapable of meeting its stated objective (that is, economic progress) since it is an instrument of control. We will return to this issue later.

In the immediate post-war period, development was defined in terms of economic growth, where the standard measure was the gross national product (GNP) of a country. This approach emphasized economic variables and gave little if any attention to sociological and cultural aspects of development. Moreover, because of its focus on aggregate growth, internal redistribution (that is, the different rates of growth of different regions) and the impact of growth on various social classes was not taken into account. Underlying this perspective was a naive faith in the so-called trickle-down effect. Redistributive issues were perceived as second-order concerns. In other words, overall economic growth was necessary before attention could be given to dealing with inequality. This view was given scientific support by the Kuznets curve which plotted the relationship between economic growth and equality (Kuznets, 1966). According to the Kuznets curve an inverse relationship existed between growth and equity at early levels of development with a more positive link developing as economic growth increased. This perspective which equated economic growth with development came increasingly under fire in the 1960s. When Dudley Seers (1969) published his 'The Meaning of Development' article in 1969, it provided the first comprehensive alternative to the traditional definition. Seers contended that the development as growth model was too restrictive, and failed to address the multi-faceted nature of development. He was particularly concerned with equity, and insisted that the definition of development should include social objectives such as employment, health, and shelter. Development in this perspective was concerned with decreasing poverty, and improving welfare indicators. Not only has the definition of development changed but the scope of traditional concerns has widened over time. Initially development policies failed to recognize the gender dimension but since the publication of Ester Boserup's pioneering study *Woman's Role in Economic Development* in 1970 (Boserup, 1989) increasing attention has been given to women's role in development. This is partly the result of academic research and writing and partly a response to grass-roots activism.

Many economists continue to measure development in terms of gross national product. This should not be seen as a refusal to update their methods but rather reflects the advantages in using a single measure. Despite the various deficiencies that have been raised concerning GNP as an indicator, it is a standard, well-known measure that allows cross-national comparisons to be made. But critics of an economic definition have also developed criteria with which to measure development. Perhaps the best-known such measure is the Human Development Index (HDI) pioneered by the United Nations Development Programme (UNDP). The HDI is based on a definition of development that takes account of social factors (see Table 9.1).

In 1990 the UNDP published its first Human Development Report. It argued that 'the real wealth of a nation is its people. And the purpose of development is to create an enabling environment for people to enjoy long, healthy creative lives' (UNDP 1990, p. 9) This focus on human development goes beyond income and the UNDP invented the Human Development Index as a basis for classifying countries. It is based on life expectancy, education (adult literacy and mean years of schooling) and income. The report ranks countries according to HDI and is published annually. The following statistics are taken from the Human Development Report 2001 (UNDP, 2002). The HDI then looks at data to find the current minimum value (for example life expectancy of 38.3 in Sierra Leone) and the current maximum value (a life expectancy of 80.8 in Japan). Each country is then ranked according to the distance travelled from the minimum towards the maximum (expressed as a percentage). Concentrating on the classification of countries, the Human Development Reports divides countries into three groups. The first group comprises those with high human development, with a HDI of 0.8000 and above. Its membership is currently 48 and it includes all developed countries and some developing countries such as Argentina, Costa Rica and Barbados. The category of medium human development, with a HDI of between 0.5000 and 0.799 is the second group. Currently comprizing 78 countries, it includes many middle-income developing countries, including some which are very well favoured in per capita income terms, such as Malaysia, Saudi Arabia, and Venezuela. The third group, with a HDI of below 0.500

currently comprises 36 countries. This groups together many of the poorest countries in the world and is heavily concentrated in Sub-Saharan Africa (for example, Mozambique, Sierra Leone and Zambia).

It is now widely agreed that development cannot be confined solely to economic growth. While there is agreement that development refers to economic, social and cultural variables, no consensus exits on either how we measure development or how it might be attained. To some extent the

Table 9.1   *Social indicators of development for selected countries, 1998*

HDI rank	Life expectancy at birth (years)	Adult literacy rate (%)	GDP/capita (PPP $US)	Human Development Index value
High human development				
1 Canada	79.1	99	23 582	0.935
2 Norway	78.3	99	26 342	0.934
3 United States	76.8	99	29 605	0.929
4 Australia	78.3	99	22 452	0.929
5 Iceland	79.1	99	25 110	0.927
Medium human development				
47 Saint Kitts & Nevis	70	90	10 672	0.798
48 Costa Rica	76.2	95.3	5 987	0.797
49 Croatia	72.8	98	6 749	0.795
50 Trinidad & Tobago	74	93.4	7 485	0.793
51 Dominica	76	94	5 102	0.793
Low human development				
140 Lao People's Dem. Rep.	53.7	46.1	1 734	0.484
141 Madagascar	57.9	64.9	756	0.483
142 Bhutan	61.2	42	1 536	0.483
143 Sudan	55.4	55.7	1 394	0.477
144 Nepal	57.8	39.2	1 157	0.474
145 Togo	49	55.2	1 372	0.471

Source: Data from UNDP (2000) pp. 157–9.

search for a consensual meaning is a fruitless one and we will conclude this discussion with two observations. First, development is more than mere economic growth and involves structural change and attitudinal change in a given society. It requires a structural transformation of the economy and a movement from a 'traditional' value system to a 'modern' one. Secondly, development consists of a set of material practices and a collection of ideas, and statements. This controversy concerning the term 'development' is mirrored in debates concerning the terminology and classification of countries seeking to make the transition to the ranks of the advanced industrial countries.

Immediately after the Second World War these countries were variously called underdeveloped, poor or backward. As more and more of these countries gained their independence these terms came to be seen as derogatory and offensive. By the early 1960s these terms were replaced by the term 'less developed country' but by the mid-1960s this term itself was held to be offensive and was replaced by the now ubiquitous term 'developing country'. Another term to describe a group of developing countries was coined in the 1950s and has also come under critical scrutiny. The term 'Third World' reflected more a political than an economic division in the world but came to be used interchangeably with that of developing country. Various critics have argued that the term Third World implies inferiority since third comes after first and second. But such criticism is misplaced and signally fails to acknowledge the origin of the term. When Alfred Sauvy first used the term in 1952, he was making an analogy with the Third Estate in French civil society and emphasizing the revolutionary potential of the countries so classified. Thus governments and many civil society organizations in the developing world have retained the use of this term since they do not attach negative connotation to it. In the 1970s it became fashionable to refer to the Third World as the South since most of these countries were in the southern hemisphere, and in the 1990s this terminology was replaced by that of Global South partly to indicate the fact that conditions of poverty and marginalization occurred in advanced industrial societies; thus the term referred to people regardless of their geographical location. However, the term has become popularized in a manner that makes its usage no different from the term it replaced. It thus appears to be useful for the geographically illiterate in that it reminds them that South does not mean the south of whatever country they found themselves in! But whether one uses developing, Third World, South or Global South, the grouping is invariably the same.

While debate about terminology is not substantive a further debate concerning divisions within this group of countries has greater political significance. The group defined as developing is large and heterogeneous as we will discuss below. The heterogeneity of the group has given rise to a debate on the criteria to be used in making divisions within the grouping, and the names to be given to these various sub-groups. Indeed, at various times it has been argued that instead of a singular category we should recognize a number of different types of countries that are not developed. We will not enter into this debate except to make the point that division into groups is an inherently subjective and political exercise. For example, following the first oil price rise in 1973 it became fashionable to talk about a Third World, a Fourth World and a Fifth World ostensibly on the basis of their access to petroleum resources but crucially this was an ideological intervention at a time when the solidarity of the developing world threatened Western interests. In a similar vein, when in the 1990s financial analysts began to refer to developing countries that offered the opportunity for profitable investment as 'emerging markets', this signified a positive evaluation and was designed to speed the transfer of funds to these countries.

Theoretical perspectives on growth and develoment

The political economy of development has initiated a number of theoretical debates and controversies. Instead of detailing these various debates and issues that have engendered such conflict, this section will instead examine two of the enduring schisms discernible in discussions on development and link them with historical debates. Theorists and practitioners interested in the economic development of a particular state or region can be divided according to their views on two issues. The first concerns the relative importance of internal or external factors for the failure of a society to achieve development. The second issue is related to the comparative roles of the state and the market in promoting development. As will become apparent, these debates reflect and replay the inter-paradigm debate in IPE. Liberal theorists have tended to emphasize the role of internal factors in the success or failure of a state to achieve development. Writers influenced by the economic nationalist tradition have no consistent approach to this issue with some agreeing with the liberal perspective and others agreeing with radical writers, who give greater weight to the role of external factors in inhibiting national development. It is not surprising that in the arguments concerning the relative importance of the state and market as agents of economic development that economic nationalist writers will emphasize the role of the state and liberal theorists will give more credence to market-related factors. Critical perspective writers, while focusing on the role of global capitalism, have tended to support state initiatives in this debate.

We will spend some time exploring the first of these two issues before turning to the second. Proponents of what we will term the internal causation theory begin from the assumption that the absence of development in a particular society results from that society's failure to harness its resources in a way relevant to the demands of modern economic growth. The causes of underdevelopment are to be found in the underdeveloped society and the solution to underdevelopment is therefore to be found at the domestic level. This view was first and most systematically articulated in modernization theory.

Modernization theory originated in American sociology and economics, and adopted an evolutionary perspective on social change taking the view that the currently underdeveloped societies were at an earlier stage of development from the advanced industrial countries. These poor countries could develop if they adopted similar attitudes, and social structures to the developed world. W.W. Rostow's *Stages of Economic Growth* (1960) presented the definitive statement of modernization theory's approach. He argued that there were five phases or stages of development through which a country had to pass through. The movement from one stage to the next depended on raising standards of living and adopting modern values.

In contrast to this focus on internal causes of and solutions to underdevelopment, a different approach which can be termed 'the external causation theory' is adopted by many practitioners and scholars. From this perspective underdevelopment is the result of external forces that constrain a society's efforts to develop. The most widely influential example of external causation theory is dependency theory which arose in the mid-1960s as a direct challenge to modernization theory. The dependency school began with analyses of Latin America (Frank, 1967, 1969; Dos Santos, 1970) but was extended to cover Africa (Amin, 1976) and the Caribbean (Beckford, 1972; Thomas, 1974). Dependency theorists argued that lack of development was not the result of poverty and the absence of modern values but instead was the direct consequence of economic exploitation. Whereas for modernization theorists development depended essentially on national efforts, for dependency theorists underdevelopment was the other side of development. In other words, underdevelopment was a condition historically created by development. Dependency theory argues that the development of some countries has resulted in the underdevelopment of others. That is, current advanced industrial societies only achieved this status through the expropriation of economic surplus from the currently underdeveloped societies. Moreover, whereas modernization theory predicted a successful transition to development for the underdeveloped world through the adaptation of specified practices, dependency theory argued that development was an impossibility within a capitalist international economic system. It was only by delinking or opting out that the poor would be able to prosper. Dependency theory contends that the developing countries do not have any meaningful choices since they are controlled directly or indirectly by external influences.

From the perspective taken in this book, both internal causation and external causation theories are flawed. A complex phenomenon such as development is not attributable to forces arising from a single level of analysis. National societies are, as we have demonstrated in Part 1 of this book, integrally linked to an emerging global political economy. This observation severely weakens the internal causation perspective which relegates external causes to an, at best, secondary role. Similarly we have presented evidence to show that external structures are mediated through internal processes in ways that are not automatic thus raising serious questions about the external causation approach. Moreover, the relationship between external and internal variables is not fixed and their relative importance will vary according to national society, and historical period.

Turning to the two variants of the approaches discussed, it should be clear that modernization theory in its failure to address external structural constraints omitted a crucial set of considerations. And, dependency theory was not only over-pessimistic but it overstated the impact of external conditions on domestic development, and could not account for differential rates of economic progress of countries faced with a similar external environment. While there are many cases in which developing countries have limited choice and are satellites or appendages of foreign companies or countries, one does not have to accept the simple dependency hypothesis since it overstates the constraints facing decision-makers.

In short, development is neither solely an internal affair nor driven relentlessly by external pressures. Furthermore, the distinction between domestic and external policy is an analytical convenience that cannot be sustained when examining policy-making and economic development in poor, weak states with open economies. For many governments in the Third World, blaming the external environment is an easy option when domestic reform proves difficult. For most developing countries, efforts to improve the external environment will not bring the hoped-for rewards unless at the same time efforts are made to change internal policy-making. The stress on external change can be misguided and is frequently employed in an effort to avoid dealing with domestic problems. A thoroughly benign external environment cannot assist a dysfunctional domestic system. And it is arguable that a malign external environment can do less damage to a country that has a degree of flexibility and efficiency in its decision-making.

On the other hand, attention to internal issues should not blind us to the fact that all problems are not domestic in origin. There have been and continue to be external forces over which poor countries have limited control. All developing countries can be injured or overwhelmed by external events and forces for which they bear no responsibility such as the oil crisis or global inflation. The international system imposes a hierarchy of hindrances and dangers that affect different countries in different ways but nevertheless do create barriers of injustice. However, there are many cases where the choices for Third World nations are not completely determined by outside forces, and these choices are neither trivial nor meaningless. The available choices may be sharply circumscribed by the weakness and poverty of the Third World and the options available may be heavily conditioned by the attitudes and assumptions of the advanced industrial countries, but even within these boundaries the possibility of better or worse decisions for each country has frequently remained open. Moreover, the persistent impact of nationalism, the growth of indigenous capacities, and the impact of international organizations have increased the desire and ability of developing countries' elites to make their own decisions.

As enduring as the debate on the relative impact of external and internal variables is the debate between proponents of the market and those of the state as the critical actors in promoting development. While the debate concerning the relative merits of the state and the market continues to engage adversaries concerned with promoting development, we will illustrate the key issues involved in the debate through an examination of a specific moment in the debate.

The success of the Asian Newly Industrializing Countries (NICs) – Singapore, Taiwan, South Korea and Hong Kong, collectively known as the Four Tigers – spurred a debate concerning the reasons for their success. Between 1965 and 1980 these countries achieved impressive levels of economic performance characterized by fast growth, low inflation, macroeconomic stability and strong fiscal position, high savings rates, open economies and thriving export sectors allied with improvement in welfare indicators such as life expectancy and literacy (see Table 9.2). In the 1980s and early 1990s a second tier of East Asian countries – Indonesia, Malaysia, the Philippines and Thailand appeared poised to repeat this success.

Two competing schools of thought developed – the neo-liberal school which emphasized the export oriented industrialization policies adopted by these states, and the developmental state school which put most stress on the ability of the state to intervene successfully in the economy. Neo-liberal scholars argued that the success of the NICs derived from their adherence to market discipline, and promotion of export-led growth. Unlike the majority of developing countries, which developed highly interventionist policies, the NICs, in pursuing growth, had chosen to deregulate their economies. Success was the result of the pursuit of liberal economic policies, a climate conducive to foreign investment and a minimal role for the state (Hughes, 1988, 1989; World Bank, 1993). For successful industrialization the government's role should be limited to the promotion of free trade, the provision of free labour markets, high interest rates to encourage

Table 9.2   *Economic and welfare indicators for Asian NICs*

Economic indicators

	GNP/ capita	Average annual CPI (%)	Export of goods & services % of GDP		Gross domestic saving % of GDP	
	1960–78	1970–78	1960	1978	1960	1978
Korea,	6.9	19.3	3	34	1	28
Rep. of Taiwan	6.6	10.3	11	59	13	33
Hong Kong	6.5	7.7	79	98	1	15
Singapore	7.4	6.1	163	164	3	27

Welfare indicators

	Adult literacy (%)		Life expectancy	
	1975	1998	1978	1998
Korea	93	97.5	63	72.6
Rep. of Taiwan	82	..	72	..
Hong Kong	90	92.9	72	78.6
Singapore	75	91.8	70	77.3

Sources: Data from World Bank (1980) p. 11; UNDP (2000) p. 157.

savings, and conservative budgets. Neo-liberals criticized the suspicious and at times hostile attitude to the international economy taken by most developing countries. These countries tried to limit interaction with external actors and promoted industrialization through a process of import substitution. Import substitution industrialization (ISI) denotes a high-tariff policy in which the aim is to keep foreign products out, develop domestic infant industries, and industrialize behind these high protectionist barriers. ISI policies tended to run into bottlenecks unless the developing country had a sufficiently large market. The costs of industrialization were immense, and the costs of imported technology, and intermediate goods meant that far from saving foreign exchange, the country was still running a large import bill. Neo-liberal theorists argued that successful industrialization in the NICs was based on a diametrically opposed strategy to ISI (See Table 9.3 for statistical support of the superiority of the NICs export-led growth compared to Latin America's ISI growth). Instead of protecting the domestic market these countries had taken an open view towards foreign capital and had promoted industrialization through exports rather than import substitution.

Proponents of the developmental state perspective (Amsden, 1989; Wade, 1990; White, 1988) did not dispute the export orientation of the NICs but argued that the state had played a crucial and determining role

Table 9.3   *Comparison of Latin American and East Asian economies: 1965–80*

(per cent)	Annual rate of growth of real GDP		Annual rate of growth of manufacturing		Annual rate of growth of exports	
	1965–80	1980–89	1965–80	1980–89	1965–80	1980–89
Latin American countries						
Argentina	3.5	–0.3	2.7	–0.6	4.7	0.6
Brazil	8.8	3	9.8	2.2	9.3	5.6
Chile	1.9	2.7	0.6	2.9	7.9	4.9
Colombia	5.8	3.5	6.4	3.1	1.4	9.8
Mexico	6.5	0.7	7.4	0.7	7.6	3.7
Peru	3.9	0.4	3.8	0.4	1.6	0.4
Venezuela	3.7	1	5.8	4.9	–9.5	11.3
Latin America & Caribbean (Ave)	6	1.6	7	1.5	–1	3.6
East Asian Countries						
Hong Kong	8.6	7.1	n.a.	n.a.	9.5	6.3
Indonesia	8	5.3	12	12.7	9.6	2.4
Korea	9.6	9.7	18.7	13.1	27.2	13.8
Malaysia	7.3	4.9	–	8	4.4	9.8
Singapore	10.1	6.1	13.2	5.9	4.7	8.1
Thailand	7.2	7	11.2	8.1	8.5	12.8
East Asian (Ave)	7.2	7.9	10.6	12.6	10	10

Sources: Data from World Bank (1989), (1990).

in East Asian industrialization. In the first place these countries did not begin with a process of export oriented industrialization (EOI) but had undergone an ISI phase first. The crucial issue was not ISI versus EOI but rather the point at which governments switched from ISI to EOI. Moreover, EOI was not as was claimed by neo-liberal apologists, a recipe for laissez-faire economics: on the contrary governments had been active in promoting EOI. In this perspective the quality of government intervention and the choice of industrial policies and strategies was critical to economic success. With the exception of Hong Kong, governmental intervention was extensive in East Asia. Successful government intervention was based on a powerful set of policy instruments, a corporatist/authoritarian model of the state, and the ability to restructure the economy towards high-technology production. That is, the success of the NICs was the result of strong states governing the market. In other words, government intervention was vital in promoting economic development.

The strength of the neo-liberal approach lies in its critique of ISI, and its weakness arises from its failure to give sufficient attention to historical factors. The strength of the developmental state model arises from its comparative analysis of political factors in the success or failure of economic policy, and its weakness lies in the difficulty of assessing the effectiveness of government intervention on development policy. It is worth noting a third approach to explaining East Asian development. This is the cultural approach which emphasizes the role of Asian values. According to this perspective, the NICs succeeded because of the impact of Confucianism on their societies (see Box 9.1). What this argument fails to confront is the many centuries in which Confucianism appeared to be an obstacle on economic progress. It isn't clear how or why centuries of stagnation were suddenly transformed into economic success when the cultural component remained the same.

This debate between competing schools of thought was of profound importance to other developing countries since the various perspectives had implicit or indeed, explicit assumptions concerning the relevance (lessons) of East Asian success for their economies. The liberal laissez-faire model was the easiest to follow and partly accounts for its success/emulation by many developing countries. This required countries to deregulate, privatize, and dismantle governmental controls. Although this was not easy to do in societies where vested interests supported protectionism, and governments depended on these vested interests, theoretically, it was the easiest of the options. The second option required changes in governance structures, and more fundamental societal change. The conditions for the creation of a developmental state were far from obvious. The third approach was the most pessimistic since Asian cultural values could not easily be transferred to Africa, Latin America, the Caribbean or the Pacific.

Box: 9.1   Confucianism and economic development

The core values of Confucianism are derived from the concept of *ren*. *Ren* (goodness, humanity) describes the highest human achievement reached through moral self cultivation. The implications for the individual include a collective orientation, reciprocity, and knowledge through intuition. One result of the high priority given to these values in the business environment is a focus on the social and relational aspects of the business transaction. Trust developed through interaction in the public and private lives of partners is built to ensure the long-term nature of business relationships. Decision-making is less confrontational and involves consensus and cooperation with mutual benefits being a high priority of all business deals. The importance of the family to Confucianism permeates into business life with companies becoming the second family of individuals. Paternalistic leadership encourages respect and long-term commitment on the part of employees.

Major developments

From the foregoing it should be obvious that the pursuit of economic development has excited passions, aroused debate, and affected billions of people in the post-war era. While each society will have its own periodization based on political and economic indicators we will outline two broad historical periods in the evolution of development as an issue in the global political economy. Undoubtedly views about development and development practices have altered many times in the past five decades in response to the experiences of developing countries and a changing global economy. Arguably, however, a major change occurred at the beginning of the 1980s when in McMichael's (1996) terminology, the development project was discarded in favour of the globalization project. The first period we will discuss is one in which the nation-state was perceived as a key instrument in the search for economic growth and development, and development was conceived principally in national terms. In the second period far greater emphasis has been given to the importance of market forces, and development has been conceived primarily in terms of the world market.

Development and national capitalism, 1947–1981

Development in this period was conceived principally as a project of a strong and active government. States were expected in the Keynesian post-war compromize to establish a balance between supply and demand for goods; to encourage consumption; to promote growth of domestic industries; and to provide a safety net for its citizens in the form of social welfare. Keynesian economic theory sought a balance between non-intervention in the market by the state and guided control.

The political conditions for the nationalist development project were laid by the post-independence modernizing elites who were intent on securing economic growth as a mechanism to bolster their legitimacy. At the same time many of these regimes were weak or corrupt or both. They thus pursued policies that supported their continued hold on power rather than those most likely to lift the majority of their population from poverty. In a bid to protect both the regime and sovereignty many governments devised measures to increase the power of the state. A belief that the external environment was not conducive to development led, on one hand, to criticism of the international economy and the major international economic organizations, and, on the other, to domestic policies of import substitution.

The quest for economic development was shaped and moulded by developments in the world economy and by the attitudes and actions of governments and international organizations. A number of changes in the international economy were to have a profound impact on the prospects for development in this first period. A striking characteristic of the international economy for most of this period was economic recovery and strong growth trends especially among the advanced industrial countries. Between 1947 and 1971 the world economy experienced a period of unprecedented growth. This growth began to falter in 1971 with the collapse of the Bretton Woods system of monetary management and came to an end after the first oil crisis of 1973–74. During this period although many developing countries experienced high growth rates most of this increase was consumed by high population growth. Moreover, the benefits from the post-war long boom of economic growth were limited for the developing countries. The post-war boom was based on the growth of manufactured exports and since most developing countries relied on primary commodities the dynamism of the world economy was irrelevant to their prospects. But if their gains from post-war growth were meagre the downturn in the world economy in the mid-1970s created an unfavourable economic climate. The first oil shock triggered, but was not solely responsible for, the onset of global recession in 1974. Non-oil exporting developing countries were faced with severely deteriorating balance of payments. It was in this period that Third World debt began to grow as governments borrowed to meet their obligations. The second oil shock of 1979 plunged many countries into severe balance of payments problems, and heralded the difficult times ahead. These events exposed the vulnerability of Third

World economies, and opened up divisions among them as the pace of growth between the middle-income and low-income countries widened.

The practice of development was also shaped by changing ideas about development. Early theories of economic development were concerned with establishing the characteristics of underdevelopment. Studies such as Gunnar Myrdal's *Asian Drama* (1968) helped to demonstrate the differences between the industrial world and the underdeveloped one. Without resorting to caricature the standard view of an underdeveloped country saw it as one with a predominantly large population characterized by the absence of modern values. The theory of economic dualism developed in the 1950s asserted that developing countries were characterized by a modern, dynamic and a traditional, stagnant sector. The task was to expand the small modern sector through investment. To the early development economists it seemed that development was a relatively simple matter of the application of certain techniques. At the beginning of this period there was also a naive belief in trickle-down economics. It was believed that economic growth would trickle-down from the rich to the poor within societies. Over time it became increasingly apparent that this optimism was ill-founded. During the 1960s these views became increasingly under challenge as some analysts shifted the focus from the internal problems of developing countries to the negative impact of the external environment.

The orthodox position held at the beginning of this period came under sustained attack from a number of sources. Although in agreement with the dominant position that industrialization provided the path to development, the view that underdevelopment arose from domestic failings was challenged by dependency theory. However, from the perspective of policy-making it was the terms of trade argument that made most impression. Simply put, the terms of trade thesis alleges that there is a persistent tendency for the terms of trade of primary commodities to fall vis à vis manufactured exports. This thesis was propounded by Raul Prebisch, the first Secretary-General of UNCTAD, and was influential with policy makers in the developing world. The terms of trade thesis led to export pessimism and supported ISI policies but it also led to two specific campaigns. First, it provided the economic rationale for preferential access for the manufactured exports of developing countries. If dependence on primary commodities condemned developing countries to a foreign exchange gap it was logical to support their diversification into manufactured exports. Similarly, the terms of trade thesis provided the rationale for international commodity agreements as a mechanism to halt the decline in export earnings.

The downturn in the world economy in the mid-1970s and the failure of industrialization and trickle-down policies led to a new approach. The Basic Needs approach which gained support from the ILO and World Bank in the mid-1970s rejected trickle-down policies and argued for redistribution with growth, and also replaced the focus on industrialization with one giving greater attention to agriculture and the rural sector. Furthermore, gender considerations had been absent from orthodox development theory. During this period, research on gender and development began to show the necessity to bring such considerations to the forefront.

Another crucial feature of this period was the development of a Third World coalition to campaign for change in the international economic order. Modernizing Third World elites began to articulate a distinctive set of interests within the global economy. Although divided by levels of economic development, ideology, political systems, culture, and amazing diversity of domestic economic policies, the governing elites of developing countries were united in their demand for additional resources and reform of the international economic order. In the post-independence world, Third World elites were willing to assert their own vision of development. They did so through two main organizations. The Non-Aligned Movement (NAM) created in 1960, although mainly concerned with political issues, progressively addressed what it saw as the failures of the post-war liberal international economic order, and was instrumental in making reform of this order a key diplomatic issue in the 1970s. The second organization, the Group of 77 (G77) became the chief vehicle through which Third World demands were aggregated and articulated (See Box 9.2 for membership). The developing countries, grouped together as the G77, lobbied UN organizations, and as the Group of 24, brought a collective Third World voice to the World Bank and IMF. During this period the most intense and politically significant campaign occurred over proposals for a New International Economic Order (NIEO) and this will be discussed below.

The international political environment, and specifically the Cold War context, was also significant for most of this period. Western and communist states competed for the allegiance of Third World states and this competition was not solely political or strategic. It was also an engagement over economic ideology, markets and access to resources. Was capitalism superior to communism as the economic system likely to bring prosperity? Which side would have access to the strategic minerals in the developing world? Which side would find a lucrative market for its products? These questions framed the pursuit of development. Moreover, the Sino-Soviet split brought competition between Moscow and Beijing for Third World support. The West responded to the perceived threat of communism with reform of the World Bank and the GATT, and in Latin America, the US sponsored the Alliance for Progress. But at the same time that limited reform efforts were underway, and support was given for land reform, Western policy supported anti-communist governments rather than those

---

Box 9.2   Group of 77 membership (2002)

Islamic Republic of Afghanistan, Algeria, Angola, Antigua and Barbuda, Argentina, The Bahamas, Bahrain, Bangladesh, Barbados, Belize, Benin, Bhutan, Bolivia, Bosnia & Herzegovina, Botswana, Brazil, Brunei, Darussalam, Burkina Faso, Burundi, Cambodia, Cameroon, Cape Verde, Central African Republic, Chad, Chile, China, Colombia, Comoros, Democratic Republic of the Congo, Republic of the Congo, Costa Rica, Cote d'Ivoire, Cuba, Cyprus, Djibouti, Dominica, Dominican Republic, Ecuador, Egypt, El Salvador, Equatorial Guinea, Ethiopia, Fiji, Gabon, The Gambia, Ghana, Grenada, Guatemala, Guinea, Guinea Bissau, Guyana, Haiti, Honduras, India, Indonesia, Islamic Republic of Iran, Iraq, Jamaica, Jordan, Kenya, Democratic People's Republic of Korea, Republic of Korea, Kuwait, Lao People's Democratic Republic, Lebanon, Lesotho, Liberia, Socialist People's Libyan Arab Jamahiriya, Madagascar, Malawi, Malaysia, Maldives, Mali, Malta, Marshall Islands, Mauritania, Mauritius, Federated States of Micronesia, Mongolia, Morocco, Mozambique, Myanmar, Namibia, Nepal, Nicaragua, Niger, Nigeria, Oman, Pakistan, Panama, Papua New Guinea, Paraguay, Peru, Philippines, Qatar, Romania, Rwanda, St. Kitts & Nevis, St. Lucia, St. Vincent & the Grenadines, Sao Tome & Principe, Saudi Arabia, Senegal, Seychelles, Sierra Leone, Singapore, Solomon Islands, Somalia, South Africa, Sri Lanka, Sudan, Suriname, Swaziland, Syrian Arab Republic, Tanzania, Thailand, Togo, Tonga, Trinidad & Tobago, Tunisia, Uganda, The United Arab Emirates, Uruguay, Vanuatu, Venezuela, Vietnam, Western Samoa, Yemen, Yugoslavia, Zambia, Zimbabwe, Palestinian Liberation Organization.

Source: Group of 77 at the United Nations, World Wide Web, http://www.g77.org/.

committed to development. That is, the containment of communism was more important than the eradication of poverty. This support for the security state apparatus resulted in the squandering of economic resources.

Development and neo-liberalism 1982–2002

The eruption of the Mexican debt crisis in 1982 signalled a shift in the development project. Importantly, it changed relations between developing countries and industrial countries, between developing countries and international organizations, and among developing countries. At the end of the

1970s the second oil crisis and consequent recession hit many developing countries hard. It was apparent to astute commentators that development strategies at the end of the second Development Decade had failed. The World Bank began the process of structural adjustment lending in 1980 but it was the conditions created by the debt crisis that brought adjustment lending to the fore since it strengthened the conditionality imposed by the Bank and the IMF.

In August 1982 the Mexican government announced that it was unable to service its debt thus bringing into the spotlight the severely indebted nature of many developing economies. The debt crisis was not only a problem for the international economy, it had fundamental implications for the distribution of power and for ways of thinking about development. The debt crisis initially challenged not only developing economies but also the Western banking system. During this period the debt crisis was the main issue in the international economy of importance to the development prospects of the developing countries. The economic consequences of the debt crisis were disastrous for most of the developing world. The 1980s have become known as the lost decade because of the overall decline in living standards, and the increased numbers of people living in poverty. The debt crisis also led to a fall of investment in the developing world and a sharper concentration of investment in a limited number of countries. It contributed to widening income gaps domestically and internationally, increased differentiation among the developing countries, and reversed many of the gains made in the previous decade. Politically the debt crisis put the Third World coalition under severe strain partly because of the different levels of indebtedness, partly because of the uneven development which arose, and partly because the response of Western creditors favoured the more politically and strategically important states. The debt crisis was also politically important since it increased the leverage of the multilateral financial institutions. The World Bank and IMF were given prominent roles in finding solutions to the crisis, and as lenders of the last resort were able to impose stringent disciplines on Third World debtors.

The debt crisis also heralded a major shift in the development paradigm. It swept away basic needs and poverty alleviation approaches and replaced them with the neo-liberal policy of structural adjustment (see Box 9.3) Although no single template exists for structural adjustment programmes they do have certain features in common. These include a curtailment of the role of the state in the economy, a bias toward the export sector, and a penchant for free markets. Adjustment programmes sought to shift developing countries from a reliance on ISI to one on export oriented industrialization (EOI). As a consequence of the emphasis on rolling back the state, NGOs were given a greater role in development. An intense debate that remains unresolved arose concerning the impact of adjustment programmes on the economy, the poor, and women. Critics allege that structural adjustment programmes hurt the poorest, increase women's burdens and provide no effective solution to debt (Bangura and Beckman, 1991; Pio, 1994; Sahn, 1994). Supporters have acknowledged negative impacts of structural adjustment programmes but have argued that these can be addressed (Kahn and Knight, 1986; Sisson, 1986). Their main contention is that countries undergoing adjustment have performed better economically than those without adjustment programmes.

Box 9.3   Structural adjustment: the case of Mexico

Following the financial crisis in 1994 the Mexican government and the IMF agreed a structural adjustment programme. This was the second time in just over a decade that Mexico had sought the assistance of the IMF. The Mexican debt crisis in 1982 had ushered in an adjustment package.

On February 1, 1995, the International Monetary Fund approved an 18-month standby credit for Mexico of up to the equivalent of SDR 12070.2 million (about US$17.8 billion) in support of the Government's 1995–96 economic and financial programme. The SAP attached to this loan has short and long term conditions. Structural adjustment is the long-term condition. In relation to its Mexican program, the IMF stated, 'The domestic adjustment package, combining prudent fiscal and strong monetary and credit policies, a disciplined incomes policy, and further structural reforms, provides an appropriate policy response to current circumstances.'

IMF's adjustment programmes have a number of common features. These include trade liberalization, privatization, deregulation, credit reduction, and wage suppression. Critics of the programme argue that growing poverty, unemployment, depression of wages, the undermining of rural livelihoods, and the disintegration of societies are also common to the programmes. The 1995 agreement consolidated and extended progress made in the area of IMF imposed structural reform since 1982. It provided a reinforcement of the government's strategy for privatization, including privatization of basic infrastructure (rail, ports, airports, electricity generation, and radio and telecommunications). Critics point to the adverse social effects that the programmes had on Mexico, including over 50 per cent of all Mexicans living in poverty, more than a quarter of a million people losing their jobs by May 1995, a sharp decline in real wages, and the government's banning of free wage negotiation. Some even claim that economic policies are the cause of the Chiapas uprising.

The failure of the demand for the NIEO suggested the difficulty faced by the Third World coalition as a force for change but the impact of the debt crisis challenged its very *raison d'état*. The coalition survived the fragmentation and forces of disintegration and has re-emerged, although not as powerfully as in the 1970s, as the instrument through which a collective voice can be heard. It continues to insist that global inequalities remain relevant, and to coordinate positions before major conferences. Instead of arguing against the liberal system as it did in the 1970s, it now seeks to ensure that developing countries are not discriminated against.

Until the end of the Cold War in 1990, the international political system was marked by continuing East–West tension and Sino-Soviet rivalry. And, development needs were once again sacrificed to political ends. The end of the Cold War in 1990 brought East–West competition in the developing world to a close. The end of communism has resulted in competition for investment and aid between former communist countries and traditional Third World countries. The end of communism also brought with it the end of the Soviet-style model, and given that China had since the onset of the Four Modernizations programme in 1979 effectively abandoned socialism, development was now cast firmly in capitalist terms. But the dangers of an open world market were all too visibly brought to the fore by the Asian financial crisis that erupted in mid-1997. It showed again how vulnerable developing countries were, and how shallow much economic growth can be. The core Asian Tigers were not as hard hit as the second-tier countries especially Thailand and Indonesia.

This post-Cold War period has been noticeable for a modification in the neo-liberal development paradigm. The Rio Conference in 1992 officially established sustainable development as the new approach to development. Although no agreed definition of sustainable development exists, that of the Brundtland Commission (World Commission, 1987) is most widely used. The Brundtland Commission defined sustainable development as development that meets the needs of the present generation without jeopardizing the resources available to future generations. The end of the Cold War and the movement to sustainable development were important in the new focus given to governance issues. It is now widely accepted that governance is an important component of the search for development, and in this pursuit democracy and democratization have come to occupy centre stage. This is a view of development far removed from the simple economic input model with which we began in the 1940s. Views have changed as the complexity of the task has become more apparent. But these changing views also represent the triumph of certain interests.

Key issues

Developing countries continue to face a large number of issues in their quest for economic development. We raised the issue of developing countries and the trade regime in Chapter 5, bargaining with TNCs in Chapter 6, the division of labour in Chapter 7, and the debt crisis in Chapter 8 and we will discuss the challenge of sustainable development in the next chapter. This section will focus on three key issues that have dominated the global debate on development in the last decade of the twentieth century and will continue to do so in the immediate future. The three key issues are: the organization of development; economic aid; and the North–South conflict.

The organization of development

Although the dominant view is that development will largely arise from national efforts, it is evident, as the previous section has shown, that development is also a process that is organized internationally. That is to say, national development aspirations and efforts are shaped by international organizations, the policies of donor states, and ideas concerning the meaning and practice of development. A major issue in the global political economy of development is the role of international organizations in this process. There are a number of controversies concerning the specific policies and general impact of multilateral development agencies and international financial institutions. In this section we will provide a brief introduction to the role of the World Bank in the international organization of development.

Table 9.4 *IBRD lending by region, fiscal year 2000*

Share of total lending of $11.5 billion	
Region	*Percentage share of lending*
Europe and Central Asia	42
Latin America & the Caribbean	37
East Asia & Pacific	9
South Asia	8
Middle East & North Africa	4
Africa	1

Source: Data from World Bank (2002) p. 27.

The World Bank. The World Bank is the world's premier multilateral development agency. It consists of five organizations – the International Bank for Reconstruction and Development (IBRD), International Development Association (IDA), International Finance Corporation (IFC), Multilateral Investment Guarantee Agency (MIGA) and the International Centre for the Settlement of Investment Disputes (ICSID). The Bank fulfils three main roles: it provides loans to countries; develops international norms; and resolves disputes. The most visible of these functions is that of the provision of loans to its member states. The IBRD provides loans and development assistance to middle-income countries and credit-worthy poorer countries (see Tables 9.4–9.6), and the IDA provides long-term loans at zero interest to the poorest countries. Through its research and development activities, and the conditions it attaches to its loans the World Bank contributes to the normative framework of international development. The Bank also tries to resolve disputes between its members and between its members and private creditors.

While the Bank has attracted some form of critical scrutiny from the outset of its operations, in the past thirty years it has been in the forefront of controversy. This is the result of a number of factors of which the most important are the impact of its adjustment policies on poorer countries in the 1980s and the impact of its policies on the environment. When the World Bank abandoned its Basic Needs approach in the early 1980s and,

Table 9.5   *IBRD lending by theme, fiscal year 2000*

Share of total lending of $11.5 billion	
Theme	*Percentage share of lending*
Financial & private sector development	30
Public sector governance	24
Economic management	9
Urban development	8
Human development	7
Social protection & risk management	6
Rural development	5
Environmental & natural resource management	4
Social development, gender & inclusion	4
Trade & integration	2
Rule of law	1

Source: Data from World Bank (2002) p.27.

Table 9.6   *IBRD lending by sector, fiscal 2000*

Share of total lending of $11.5 billion

Sector	Percentage share of lending
Law & justice & public administration	31
Finance	18
Transportation	13
Health & other social services	12
Education	7
Energy and mining	6
Agriculture, fishing & forestry	5
Industry and trade	5
Water, sanitation & flood protection	2
Information & communication	1

Source: Data from World Bank (2002) p.27.

in tandem with the International Monetary Fund, began to focus on structural adjustment lending, it ignited a debate on its lending policies that has still not lessened even though the Bank's lending policies have shifted significantly since these policies were first instituted. Adjustment policies pushed recipient countries to liberalize their economies, and to reduce the role of state intervention in economic management. Whether these were necessary reforms to counter decades of poor economic policies or were irrelevant and misguided policies that made poor countries even more vulnerable to external shocks remains an issue of debate between supporters and critics of these policies. All sides are, however, agreed that the initial policies had consequences that were detrimental to the poorest and most marginalized sections of societies undergoing adjustment. Adjustment policies, for example, increased the burdens on women. By the mid-1990s the Bank had come to accept many of the criticisms of these policies, and began designing safety nets for the most vulnerable groups in society (World Bank, 1998). The Bank also began to shift its lending priorities away from adjustment and towards the new goal of sustainable development. Under adjustment lending, it was believed that macro-economic growth was the main target and that poverty reduction would follow from a general improvement in the economy. The move to sustainable development lending has seen a greater focus on poverty reduction strategies but this is also coupled with an increased emphasis on the role of the private sector in the promotion of development.

The role of World Bank lending remains controversial. Supporters of the

Bank argue that it provides developing countries with much needed capital and they maintain that the projects it supports are vital in the fight against world poverty. In their view these resources provide important supplementary assistance for the governments of developing countries and enhance the perceived stability of the economy to international investors. Supporters of World Bank policies think that the conditions it attaches to its loans provide a framework of sound financial management for the governments of its borrower nations. On the other hand, critics accuse the Bank of putting profits before people, and of distorting development. To the critics these resources are often insufficient, inadequate and ineffective. Critics contend that the specific conditionality imposed by the Bank privileges external interests over those of the recipients and is focused on repayment of the loan rather than improving welfare.

The World Bank espouses a liberal economic vision and it was conceived as an important instrument in the construction of a liberal economic order. As such, the Bank's policy prescriptions support the maintenance of liberal economic values. Over time there has been a shift from a Keynesian liberalism to a neo-liberal vision. And it is this liberal ideology that remains contested today. The Bank's normative framework of market principles and economic growth is opposed by radical critics and environmentalists who believe that the market-based approaches cannot effectively contribute to development and/or promote sustainability. In the 1970s and 1980s, Bank lending received stringent criticism for the laxity of its environmental controls which resulted in its funding projects such as hydro-electric dams that were environmentally disastrous (Rich, 1994). Although the Bank has developed an environmental portfolio (World Bank, 1995) its policies continue to be criticized by a number of social movement groups.

Another critical issue in terms of the organization of development concerns the democratic nature of the process. This is an issue that can also be illustrated through reference to the World Bank. In the context of the Bank this issue is seen in two ways. First, democracy is discussed in relation to the formal decision-making provisions of the organization. The highest decision-making authority in the Bank is the Board of Governors consisting of a representative from each member country. The Board of Governors meets annually and its functions are carried out by the Executive Board consisting of 24 Executive Directors that meets twice a week. Voting power in both the Board of Governors and the Executive Board is based on weighted voting with each member's votes dependent on their economic contribution to the organization. Thus decisions in the Bank are biased in favour of its major shareholders (US, Japan, Germany, France and the UK). Critics of this system argue that the weighted voting mechanism should be replaced by a 'one state, one vote' rule but the current holders of power are unlikely to continue to fund an organization over which they have limited control.

A second aspect of the debate on the democratization of the Bank refers to the openness of the Bank to influence from civil society groups and the populations subject to its policies. In the 1980s, development, environmental and women's groups launched a series of campaigns to make the Bank's decision-making more transparent and more accountable for the policies it implemented. While the Bank has not responded in a manner that satisfies all its critics, it has become more open to scrutiny by external groups and has increasingly engaged in consultative processes to discuss its policies and proposed changes in its programs. For example, the Bank has created an Inspection Panel to hear complaints, and has engaged in wide-ranging dialogues with civil society groups concerning the content of its annual World Development Reports. The World Development Report has an enormous impact in the field of development policy.

As the above has demonstrated there are conflicting views on the World Bank's role as a development agency. While the Bank has been the target of criticism from the right of the political spectrum (Bauer, 1984), it has attracted most criticism from the left as detailed above. Is it possible to adjudicate between the Bank and its critics? To a large extent the perspective one takes on the Bank is linked with the standpoint taken on economic aid (see below), capitalism and government intervention in the economy. Secondly, as the world's largest multilateral development agency, the Bank's profile means that it inevitably receives a significant amount of criticism. Thus in assessing the importance to be given to any critique it is necessary to probe the existence of alternatives. That is, what are the feasible alternatives of organizing the specific aspect of development? Thirdly, much criticism of the Bank is often out of date. Many critics appear unaware of the adaptability of the Bank and produce critiques of policies or programs that are no longer current. Therefore in assessing any criticism of the Bank it is important to ascertain its current relevance to Bank operations. Fourthly, it is important to distinguish between the Bank's bureaucracy and its members. Criticism should be sensitive to the relationship between the Bank staff and its more influential members. Finally, it is important to recognize that the World Bank is a financial institution and any effective criticism must recognize the financial constraints under which the Bank operates.

Economic aid

The centrality of economic aid in the development regime has ensured that it has remained a subject of major dispute. Economic aid has been one of the most prominent, persistent and enduring features of international development policy. Originating in the development activities of the colonial powers in their overseas territories, the period since the end of the Second World War has witnessed the institution of programs of economic cooperation by United Nations agencies, other multilateral organizations, and national governments. Although no accepted definition exists most writers would agree that to qualify as aid or official development assistance (ODA) transfers, two criteria must be met – the flows should be primarily for development purposes and must be concessional (that is, below market interest rates). A number of issues relating to aid remain of crucial importance in the contemporary global economy and we will examine three of them in this section: motivation, effectiveness, and conditionality.

Motivation. One of the reasons for the controversy generated by aid arises from conflicting interpretations concerning the motivation of aid givers. Aid agencies and politicians have variously cited humanitarian reasons as the main motivation for giving aid. An influential report into international development assistance published at the end of the 1960s asserted, 'The simplest answer to the question [why aid] is the moral one: that it is only right for those who have to share with those who have not' (Pearson, 1969, p. 8). And this view remains strong today. However, the assertion of a moral case for aid has ensured continued political attention to aid since critics on the right have argued that no moral basis exists for aid giving (Bauer, 1971) and that Western governments have a responsibility to their domestic constituents and not the elites of the developing world since aid invariably ends up in the pockets of the rich in poor countries (Bauer, 1981, 1984). Left-wing commentators have argued that the moral argument is decidedly hypocritical since the main motivation for aid giving is to maintain the economic and political power of the donor countries (Hayter, 1971).

From an economic point of view a case has been developed in support of aid giving. While the economic arguments underlying the provision of external assistance by donors has changed over time a central focus has been on the impact of external resources on local savings and growth. The two gap model developed by Chenery and Strout (1966) provided the economic rationale for early aid policies. In this model economic growth is constrained by two gaps – a savings gap and a foreign exchange gap. Aid fills both gaps by adding to the total resources for investment or savings and through the provision of foreign exchange. Currently aid policy focuses on a number of economic goals including protecting the consumption of the poor; improving economic policies and resource allocation; and increasing the efficiency of capital.

The most widely cited motive for the provision of aid is that of support for political goals. For some analysts the political goals are related to the preservation of order, stability and peace in the international system (Brandt Commission, 1983) while for others the main motive is more closely related to the national interests of donor states.

Any search for a single motive is likely to prove illusive since the aid programmes of most countries are the result of different pressures. Aid is given for political, economic and humanitarian motives. Analysis of the allocation of aid shows conclusively the importance of political concerns in donors' motives (Maizels and Nisanke, 1984). Politically motivated aid is viewed by donors within the overall context of their foreign relations with recipient countries and other potentially affected countries. During the era of the Cold War, Western countries' aid programmes were devised to support anti-communist regimes, and aid from the Soviet Union and its allies attempted to support anti-Western sentiment in the Third World. And, discussion of aid fatigue in the post-Cold War period emphasizes the political content in aid giving. Politically motivated aid may be given for ideological purposes; to maintain post-colonial spheres of influence; promote culture; the strategic importance of the recipient; or to win votes in international organizations. While the political interests of donors clearly play a large part in aid allocation we cannot discount economic motives. Both types of economic motives mentioned above are apparent in the history of official development assistance. Aid is disbursed in an attempt to improve economic growth and economic development but it is also given by particular states in order to secure commercial benefits for their industries. Although it is fashionable to deride humanitarian motives for aid giving it is too overtly cynical to conclude that humanitarian motives play no part in governmental decision-making on aid allocation. An appeal to morality has played an important role in Western aid programmes from the outset.

Aid effectiveness. The impact of aid on recipients cannot be fully divorced from arguments concerning the motivations of donors and it is not surprising that most of the critics of aid effectiveness are those writers who are suspicious of the motivations of aid donors. Aid continues to be attacked from both the right and the left of the political spectrum. In general terms, the right-wing critics claim that aid is neither necessary nor essential for development; it is frequently given to corrupt governments and most aid is wasteful expenditure. From the left, critics argue that since aid is part of a structure of dominance and dependence, it fosters debt and is therefore incapable of generating either growth or development.

The ability of aid to meet any or all of its economic goals remains the subject of much debate with some authors claiming that aid decreases savings (Griffin, 1970; Griffin and Enos, 1970) and others arguing that the

Box 9.4   The 'Pacific Paradox'

There are 24 Pacific Islands nations. These are conventionally sub-divided into Micronesia, Polynesia, and Melanesia. The core group of islands includes Papua New Guinea, Solomon Islands, Vanuatu, Fiji, Nauru, Kiribati, Tuvalu, Tonga, Western Samoa, Niue, and the Cook Islands. The 'Pacific paradox' is the continued slow growth and underdevelopment of these islands despite: receiving a disproportionate share of global official development assistance (ODA); relatively high levels of investment; plentiful natural resources; sensible macroeconomic management; and few trade distortions. Despite accounting for only 0.14 per cent of the population of all developing nations, the Pacific islands receive 3.5 per cent of all ODA flows. Most of these countries attained little or no growth in per capita income over the last few decades, with Fiji, Kiribati, Solomon Islands, and Vanuatu recording negative growth in the 1980s. While the World Bank report (1991), *Pacific Island Economies: Towards Higher Growth in the 1990s*, attributed the 'Pacific paradox' to the dominant role of the public sector, an inability to adopt needed structural reforms, a general lack of competition, and weak financial sectors, critics of this view point to institutional and cultural constraints, political instability, the difficulties of nation building, and lack of infrastructure and clear property rights.

real economic motivation is not an improvement in the living standards of recipient countries but rather it is a mechanism for assisting firms in donor countries to create or maintain market share in recipient countries (Hayter, 1971). The continuing debate over aid effectiveness can be illustrated through the examination of a case study. See Box 9.4 for a brief résumé of aid and the Pacific.

Conditionality. Perhaps, the most intense conflict today concerns the conditions attached to aid. While the governments of recipient countries have from the outset of the aid regime resisted the political and economic conditions attached to aid, the donors have tended to insist on these conditions for a variety of reasons. Economic conditions are attached either to ensure repayment or to support the exporters of the donor states. Political conditions vary from the pursuit of specific foreign policy goals to more general systemic objectives. Bilateral donors have always attached some form of policy measures to aid packages reflecting their political or economic interests. Such strings were usually seen as an integral part of aid.

The current controversy over conditionality has developed as a result of practices followed by bilateral and multilateral agencies from the 1980s onwards when access to aid was made increasingly subject to the fulfilment of certain policy conditions. After the end of the Cold War, Western donors developed political conditionality in relation to the objective of good governance. In this context conditionality is designed to support democratic reform or to encourage respect for human rights in recipient countries. Two issues exercise governments and civil society groups – Should donors attach political conditions? And will they work?

While it is unlikely that any serious commentator would not subscribe to the idea of good governance, it is by no means clear that political conditionality is the most effective or appropriate mechanism for promoting the governance agenda. Good governance refers to a set of policies intended to reform domestic politics in many developing states (Burnell, 1993). Many developing societies have to contend with arbitrary policy-making, an unaccountable bureaucracy, an unenforced legal system, the arbitrary use of executive powers and widespread corruption. In such circumstances the level of civil society participation is low. Good governance priorities include reform of the state (competent government and efficient public administration), pluralist politics (multi-party systems), the promotion and protection of human rights, and conditions enabling effective civil society participation in policy-making. The extent to which external agencies can promote democracy remains unclear. And, for some, political conditionality is an exercise in neo-imperialism, especially in a context where democracy remains an essentially contested concept.

North–South conflict

It should be apparent from the arguments in this chapter that the practice of international development is a distinctly political process in which consideration of power is central. In contrast to a liberal perspective that emphasizes the mutuality of interests between developed and developing countries, we perceive the simultaneous existence of common and competing interests. An integral feature of the international political economy of development, therefore, is constituted by what is termed the North–South conflict. This refers to the existence of political differences and a diplomatic conflict between the governments of advanced industrial countries and the governments of developing countries. We have alluded to this conflict above and in this section we will explore certain aspects of the historical evolution and contemporary manifestation of this aspect of international development. Within the global political economy, issues of dominance and dependence remain important and the answer to questions concerning who gets what, when, and why is linked to the different ways in which interests are articulated. The answer to fundamental questions such as 'What is development? What are the best methods for promoting development?' cannot be divorced from the issue of exactly who gets to frame the answers to such questions. In other words, the central problem concerns the issue of who speaks for whom. This is a complex issue in which it is possible to identify a number of potential stakeholders. Although civil society groups involved in the promotion of economic development cannot be left out of any comprehensive answer to these questions, we will focus our discussion at the level of official policy-making. States remain the key instruments of legitimacy in the global political order and development policies are officially implemented through agencies of the state. In this section we will focus on the North–South conflict as an integral part of the international political economy of development through a brief exploration of its historical evolution. The ability of developing countries to exercise influence over international negotiations depends on the degree of solidarity they can achieve and therefore we will assess the extent to which divisions among developing countries means that they will be incapable of presenting a united front to the holders of power in the world economy.

The North–South conflict in an historical perspective. The dissatisfaction of developing countries with the liberal international economic order first surfaced in the 1950s with demands for reform of the international trading order, and calls for increased economic aid. These demands were made with increasing stridency within the United Nations system after developing countries gained the majority in the United Nations General Assembly in 1960. A concerted demand for additional financial resources and increased market access for their exports followed the creation of the United Nations Conference on Trade and Development (UNCTAD) in 1964 in Geneva. As part of the UN system, it became the principal forum for North–South confrontation over economic issues, and the instrument through which the developing countries hoped reform would be undertaken. Between 1964 and 1973, UNCTAD spearheaded campaigns for increased market access for Third World manufactured exports, stabilization of international commodity prices, and additional development assistance. UNCTAD's record during this period was mixed, with very limited gains.

The North–South conflict was given increased prominence in the 1970s with debate over a New International Economic Order (NIEO). Between 1973 and 1979 the NIEO dominated North–South discussions. Indeed, it can be argued that this period saw development with its highest international political profile. At the centre of NIEO demands were those pertaining to international commodity markets. The NIEO also encompassed reform of the GATT, IMF and World Bank. Developing countries argued that these organizations were controlled by the advanced industrial countries and failed to support their interests. A number of resolutions were passed by the UN General Assembly of which the most important were the Declaration on the Establishment of a New International Economic Order (1974), the Programme of Action on the Establishment of a New International Economic Order (1974), and the Charter of Economic Rights and Duties of States (1975) creating the framework for the NIEO. These UN resolutions were seen by some scholars as important legal documents. They set out the mutual responsibilities of states, established a framework of action and the justification for a new order. The negotiations leading to the creation of a NIEO ended in failure. No single event or factor was responsible for the failure of the NIEO. However, the refusal of Western states to enter into serious negotiation was the most important reason for the collapse of the North–South dialogue.

For some analysts the fragmentation of the Third World coalition in the 1980s led to the demise of the North–South conflict but this is a limited and limiting view that fails to situate North–South conflict as a structure of the international political economy of development. The North-South conflict arises from a real disparity in power and resources between rich and poor states. The gap between the richest and poorest countries of the world has increased rather than diminished in the past three decades (Hoogvelt, 1997, p. xi). As Thomas and Reader state, 'almost a third of humanity still lives in conditions of dire poverty, and 14 million people die of hunger annually' (1997, p. 90). For example, the International Commission on Peace and Food stated in 1990 that in a world population of 5.3 billion nearly 2 billion people lived in poverty; and in 1994 over 40 000 people died of malnutrition daily (1994, p. 106).

Third World solidarity and fragmentation. The above discussion has not assumed commonality among developing countries but has noted the existence of a common bargaining platform. We have already noted the existence of significant differences among developing countries and the three main regions – Africa, Asia and Latin America. The concern of an international political economy of development is not with any organic unity but rather with the political expressions of unity and discord. Unity does not in itself lead to specific gains but it is an indicator of the extent to which the developing countries can articulate a distinct vision in the global political economy. The historical record shows that Third World solidarity responds to changes in the global political economy and is not static.

Third World solidarity began to fragment in the 1980s primarily as the result of two developments. The debt crisis had a two-fold impact on the coalition. First, it created a range of special interests as countries sought to battle their specific debt burdens and were given differential treatment within the international financial system. For example, while some countries welcomed wholesale debt reduction, others were concerned that such a strategy would undermine their creditworthiness. Secondly, the structural adjustment policies imposed by the World Bank and IMF in promoting liberal economic thought severely curtailed the independence of developing countries. The severely indebted countries, as supplicants of Western economic assistance, were in no position to demand change in the international economic order. The second major development in the international system of the 1980s with an impact on the Third World coalition was the success of the NICs since it exacerbated the differences among developing countries. But the scale of fragmentation is somewhat exaggerated and we still see and hear the collective voice of the developing world in many international negotiations. The important point is the extent to which they can articulate a different view.

Third World solidarity in this context refers solely to the joint efforts by countries that identify as developing countries. In this sense we can make two observations. A Third World coalition remains a part of the international debate on development. At all major international conferences, developing countries continue to try to present a common position, and a common Third World response to developments in the world economy or proposals by the G8 is a feature of contemporary economic diplomacy. Apart from the continuing existence of poverty and inequality, many countries identify with a collective Third World voice because of their lack of influence in international organizations. This inability to influence the international agenda is most starkly seen in the decision-making process of the International Monetary Fund and World Bank with their decision-making systems of weighted voting. But it is also perceived in institutions such as the G8 leading industrial countries that meet periodically to make decisions concerning the future of the global economy. The G8 is a constant reminder that Third World governments do not shape the international agenda.

Secondly, the historical record shows that as a counter-hegemonic force the Third World coalition has been most important in presenting an alternative vision of development and a critique of the liberal economic order. It has not achieved important gains in material terms. Thus we should not expect in the future that there will be any change in the ability of poor countries to wrest concessions from the richer nations.

Conclusion

In a powerful and influential critique of post-war development policy, Arturo Escobar argues that the development discourse began in 1949 with

President Truman's inaugural Presidential address in which he enunciated large-scale support for development. This perspective usefully alerts us to the role of external powers in constructing development and the importance of the international political climate. Escobar's view is, however, a limited one since it removes autonomy from developing countries, and makes them solely passive recipients of Western policy.

As we have seen, development is centrally concerned with material and normative issues. Whether the focus is on absolute poverty, or relative poverty it is apparent that poverty shapes the life chances of millions of individuals around the globe, constraining access to material and non-material goods and services. While development remains principally a national concern it has from the outset of the development assistance regime at the end of the Second World War been inscribed on the international agenda. There have been at least two major phases in international concern with development. The national development model based on a Keynesian consensus was replaced in the 1980s with a neo-liberal vision often referred to as the Washington Consensus. The conception, organization, promotion and execution of national and international development policies is the result of structural change in the global political economy and the adaptation of state and non-state actors to these changes.

Chapter 10

Global Environmental Change

The study of international political economy has only recently incorporated the environment as one of its concerns (Helleiner, 1996). There are two principal aspects to the integration of environmental concerns in IPE. First, a number of environmental problems have an impact on the global political economy, and some form of international agreement is necessary to cope with these problems. As Hurrell and Kingsbury note, 'international co-operation is required both to manage global environmental problems and to deal with domestic environmental problems in ways that do not place individual states at a political or competitive disadvantage' (1992, p. 5). This intersection of environmental concerns and the international political economy can be termed the problem of international or global governance.

Secondly, global environmental change is intimately linked to national and international systems of production, distribution and consumption. 'The . . . most important aspect of increased globalization derives from the complex but close relationship between the generation of environmental problems and the workings of the effectively globalized world economy' (Ibid., p. 3). This can be characterized as the problem of sustainability. The historical process of capital accumulation and the pursuit of economic growth has contributed to current environmental degradation. Key issues concerning growth and development strategies, industrialization, international trade, and North–South relations, for example, all require re-examination in the current historical conjuncture. In this context, it can be argued that modern global environmental challenges are characterized by three main features that is, uncertainty, irreversibility, and uniqueness or non-substitutability (Pearce, 1990, p. 366). Since the 1992 United Nations Conference on Environment and Development in Rio, local and national authorities as well as international organizations, firms, and non-governmental organizations have all in their various ways pledged allegiance in various forms to the concept of sustainable development. That is, they have made numerous commitments to preserving environmental quality and to combating environmental degradation. While it is not surprising that the rhetoric has surpassed the reality, this result nevertheless has to be explained rather than taken for granted. This chapter explores the interface between environmental issues and the international economy. It looks at the ways in which attention to environmental issues alters perceptions of and actions within the global political economy. The chapter begins by discussing some of the terms used in analysing the political economy of the environment. In the theoretical perspectives section we consider rival IPE explanations of environmental degradation. Under major developments we trace the evolution of the environment as an important issue in international economic discussions. The key issues considered in this chapter are: sustainable development, trade and the environment, and international environmental agreements.

Definitions and background

Right at the outset we are faced with the far from simple issue concerning whether the focus should be on environment or ecology. Without seeking to prejudge the issue we will use the term 'environment' to discuss the issues with which we are concerned rather than ecology. Within the literature these terms are sometimes used synonymously and at other times they are used in order to distinguish anthropocentric approaches from those that reject species hierarchy.

Although used in various ways by different writers the central difference between the terms appears to rest between an approach – environmentalism – that retains humans at the centre of its analysis and another – ecologism – that focuses on the interrelationship between humans and nature in a non-hierarchical manner. Given the widespread usage of the term 'environmentalism' to refer to the interactions between humans and the natural environment, this chapter will adopt the terms 'environment' and 'environmental' to denote the subject under scrutiny. At its simplest, environment simply refers to the surroundings of a specific unit, that is, a unit or a system exists within a context and it is the context (that which surrounds the unit or system) to which the term 'environment' refers. In the context of the study of political economy, concern with the environment focuses on the impact of human activity on the natural environment. In other words, attention is given to the use and misuse of natural resources and nature by humans. Environmental degradation therefore occurs when humans (ab)use nature in ways that threaten both the sustainability of the natural resource base and creates unwanted problems such as pollution for human societies.

Defining environmentalism is difficult since it houses a variety of perspectives rather than a single approach. It has become standard to distinguish between two broad strands (or ideologies) of environmentalism although no agreement exists on the terminology to be used for this purpose. One useful and often cited distinction in the literature is that between 'light Green' and 'dark Green' perspectives where the term Green refers to a positive and supportive attitude towards the protection and preservation of the environment. A light Green approach is essentially reformist accepting the major institutions of capitalist society and seeking to engender respect for the environment and preservation of the environment through strategies that do not disrupt modern economic growth and industrial society. On the other hand, the dark Green or radical environmental approach begins from the assumption that fundamental practices will have consequences for future generations.

Other writers maintain a distinction between two main strands of environmentalism but use different terms to convey the central distinction. One author distinguishes between technocentric and ecocentric positions (O'Riordan, 1976) where technocentric refers to approaches that attempt to accommodate sustainable development in the context of market incentives whereas ecocentric positions challenge conventional economic goals and models. And Dobson (1990), for example, distinguishes between environmentalism and ecologism. Environmentalism is characterized as 'a managerial approach to the environment within the context of present political and economic practices' (Dobson, 1990, p. 35). Ecologism on the other hand, 'presupposes radical changes' in humanity's relationship with the environment in order to care for it. Goodin makes a similar point when he distinguishes between an environmentalist posture which is concerned with making environmental choices serve human interests and a Green approach which refuses to reduce nature to human or divine interests, and posits an independent role for nature in the creation of value (1992, pp. 7–8). For Eckersley, the key division is between anthropocentric and ecocentric approaches. Anthropocentric thinking 'offers opportunities for *human* emancipation and fulfilment in an ecologically sustainable society' (1992, p. 26). On the other hand, ecocentric theory is one which 'pursues these goals in the context of a broader notion of emancipation that also recognizes the moral standing of the non human world' (ibid., p. 26).

Moving beyond approaches to environmentalism, we can recognize the existence of different ways of classifying issues of environmental concern. There are different approaches to classifying environmental problem sets. We can distinguish between physical changes, for example, atmospheric pollution, ozone depletion, climate change, marine pollution, loss of biodiversity; development activities, for example, energy production and use, tourism, agricultural production; and the human condition and well-being, for example, population growth, health, and security. A different classification distinguishes between problems arising directly from human activity on the land (for example, deforestation, top soil erosion, watershed failure), and those arising as the indirect result of waste (for example, greenhouse gases, ozone depleting gases, nuclear contamination, and toxic waste). The first set of problems are relatively localized in their consequences, whereas the latter have direct global reach.

Furthermore, we can also distinguish environmental problems in terms of the situations faced by actors as they pursue cooperative or conflictual strategies, for example, global commons, shared natural resources, transboundary externalities or linked issues (Young, 1994). Problems such as the depletion of the ozone layer, the potential for climate change as a result of the greenhouse effect, the loss of biodiversity, and deforestation and desertification are well documented. It is important to recognize that the impact of these trends and events on the physical fabric of the planet cannot be limited to environmental or technical considerations but are to be seen as essentially political in character since 'the globality of environmental problems stems not merely from the replicated institutions which create them and the spread of environmental activism, but also from both the very transboundary nature of pollution and depletion problems and the reliance on co-operative mechanisms for problem solving' (Laferrière 1994, p. 95).

There are five commonly accepted features of environmentalism:

- Environmental degradation is global in the sense that it affects everyone, and can only be managed effectively through global cooperation.
- Environmental degradation can exacerbate intra-state and inter-state tensions.
- There are complex linkages between the environment and the global economy.
- Environmental issues are distinguished by uncertainty, that is, there is no guarantee that sometime in the future a finite natural resource will be replaced by technology.
- Irreversibility is a key feature of environmental politics, for example, once a species is extinct it is impossible to make it appear again.

However, the environmental problematique is a complex and multi-faceted one, with diverse political, social, economic and ethical dimensions and these common features provide a starting point for analysis rather than settled conclusions. For example, while many environmental problems are indeed global in scope, it is an overstatement and a mistake to assume that all environmental problems possess this quality. To assume that all environmental problems are global can lead to the erroneous conclusion that environmental degradation translates into shared concerns, that we share a common future, and that we have a common interest in combating environmental destruction. Such a conclusion is apolitical and abstracts from the power relations inherent in both the causation of ecological harm and the steps necessary to provide workable solutions.

Theoretical perspecitives: IPE and environmental studies

The recent upsurge of interest in the environment has resulted in the publication of numerous studies as analysts have explored the causal relationship between human practices and environmental degradation. These studies draw upon differing understanding of the causes of environmental degradation and propose a range of appropriate responses to address the problems that have arisen. Theorists and practitioners interested in global environmental politics have conflicting views on the causes of and solutions to environmental degradation. In this section we will explore two theoretical debates: one that has arisen in International Relations and IPE, and a second that is more familiar to students of environmental economics and environmental studies. We will spend some time examining the debate between rival schools of thought in IPE (economic nationalism/realism, liberalism and Marxism) before turning to look at a debate based on differing conceptions of the relationship between humans and the environment (anthropocentric, environmental and ecocentric perspectives).

IPE debates

The traditional approaches to IPE, that is, economic nationalism, liberalism and Marxism historically paid little or no attention to environmental issues. However, the emergence of the environment as an international political issue and the evident linkages between global environmental change and national and international systems of production, distribution, and consumption have seen scholars working within these paradigms turn their attention to the analysis of global environmental politics. Most attention has been paid to the creation and maintenance of international cooperation on the environment, and the relationship between the global economy and the causes of environmental degradation. We will first review the debate on international environmental cooperation before turning our attention to the political economy of sustainability.

The economic nationalist or realist approach to international environmental cooperation is based on two main assumptions. Realists assume that states act in terms of their national interest and that international cooperation is difficult to achieve and sustain, given the existence of competing national interests in an anarchical international system. With each state attempting to maximize its military and economic power, international cooperation on the environment, like any form of international cooperation, is inherently difficult since environmental interests will be subsumed to traditional political power goals.

The realist assumption that states are rational, self-interested utility maximizers leads to the conclusion that international cooperation on the environment will only be possible in situations where states perceive such cooperation to be in their interests. Moreover, realists contend that in an anarchical international system, cooperation on the environment will only be feasible on those issues and in specific situations that support and maintain the interests of dominant states. Realist approaches are therefore sceptical about the possibility of extensive cooperation on environmental issues (Blackhurst and Subramanian, 1992; Barrett, 1993). There are, of course, many examples in environmental politics where states have either failed to establish a basis for cooperation or where a cooperative arrangement has broken down that provide support for the realist perspective. For example, the refusal of the United States to ratify the Kyoto Protocol lends support to the realist argument. However, realist political economy is less well placed to explain why in the absence of the dominant power in the world economy (the United States) so many other states have been willing to ratify the Kyoto Protocol.

The willingness of many states to ratify the Kyoto Protocol in the absence of the United States is better explained by liberal IPE theories. Liberal IPE theories, although using the state as a key unit of analysis, begin from a recognition of the demands of interdependence. For liberal theorists international environmental cooperation arises from the recognition of mutual or shared interests. A globalizing world economy creates networks of interdependencies and bonds of common interests among the various actors thus facilitating international cooperation. Although states remain important actors they are enmeshed in a network of transactions and interdependencies which limit and constrain their authority. Furthermore, environmental cooperation is made more feasible through the activities on non-state actors such as intergovernmental organizations, NGOs, scientific networks and firms.

There are a number of diverse radical approaches to international environmental cooperation. Some radical writers argue that the rivalry between capitalist states makes international environmental cooperation unlikely. Whereas realist writers emphasize the interests of states in maximizing power, and liberal theorists show how interdependence creates mutual bonds of interest, radical scholars focus on inequality and dominance in the international system. In this perspective international cooperation is subsumed to the economic interests of dominant states and the capitalist class. International environmental cooperation is likely, but the forms of cooperation and the institutions created, since they are based on capitalism, will be incapable of providing effective solutions to environmental degradation. Some radical writers argue that in a hierarchical international power structure, the developed countries of the North dominate international decision-making, thus maintaining the historically established pattern of exploitation of Southern countries. Negotiations on international environmental issues will therefore reflect Northern interests and Southern concerns will be marginalized (Haas, 1990b, pp. 47–52).

While all three perspectives appear to have something useful to contribute to analyses of international environmental cooperation, each perspective on its own will be incapable of providing satisfactory answers to the range of issues and cooperative arrangements that arise in global environmental politics. The realist approach, for example, is flawed because its focus on states and emphasis on power is empirically unsustainable. A focus on states seriously limits analysis and omits consideration of important actors in the global political economy. Many analyses of global environmental politics have documented the critical roles played by international organizations, firms and NGOs.

Moreover, a number of studies have clearly demonstrated that international cooperation is possible and regimes can be created and maintained in the absence of a hegemon (Keohane, 1984; Axelrod and Keohane, 1986; Young, 1994). While liberal analysis, in admitting the importance of non-state actors, provides a more realistic account of environmental politics, liberal theories have a tendency to neglect the role of power in shaping institutions in the first place. In other words, liberal theories fail to give sufficient attention to considerations of structural inequalities. While radical theories show awareness of the importance of structural patterns on dominance and dependence, they frequently underestimate the importance of international actors. For example, international organizations are not mere epiphenomena with negligible impact on international relations, and the forms of bargaining that take place within such organizations do not merely reflect the distribution of power in the global system.

The second area of contention between the perspectives concerns the relationship between the global economy and environmental degradation. Since the issue of sustainable development will be discussed further below, at this point we will only highlight some important differences between the three approaches. From an economic nationalist perspective sustainable development will only arise if states perceive such policies to be in their interests. Since states exert control over national economies the pursuit of sustainable development is dependent on states identifying this as a key goal. However, efforts to promote sustainability are likely to founder if economic growth remains the primary goal of political elites. As long as the elements of power are constituted through practices that degrade the environment, sustainable development will remain an aspiration rather than a reality.

In a liberal perspective, environmental degradation arises because of market failure, specifically the absence of mechanisms to provide a proper valuation of natural resources. The extension of market principles to the environment through, for example, the allocation of property rights, and the inclusion of environmental values in pricing policies will lead to a more efficient allocation of resources and environmental protection. Sustainable economic policies in this view are dependent on increased economic growth rather than its retardation. The problem is not growth per se but rather the forms that growth has taken to date. Indeed, economic growth and proper environmental assessments are crucial strategies for the promotion of sustainability.

Radical theorists locate the cause of environmental degradation in the development of capitalism. Radical critics argue that environmental degradation arises from capitalism and that current economic practices and value systems cannot promote sustainable policies since the capitalist system is inherently exploitative. As Michael Redclift has claimed, 'The concentration on "growth" has served to obscure the fact that resource depletion and unsustainable development are a direct consequence of growth itself' (1987, p. 56).

Once again we can see that none of the perspectives provides a convincing explanation of the political economy of sustainability. First, the ahistorical approach of realist IPE ignores the causes of environmental degradation since it fails to enquire into the ways in which historically constructed patterns of production and consumption have created current environmental problems. Such an approach is incapable of challenging the processes of accumulation, production and reproduction central to capitalism and responsible for creating the environmental problems in the first place. Liberal theories are deficient because they fail to deal adequately with power and power relations. Specifically, they are unable to represent structural forms of power. Neo-Marxist analysis with its emphasis on the structural relationship between labour and capital, and its location of environmental degradation in the political and economic structures of capitalist societies, does appear to represent an advance. But the historical evidence clearly shows that both capitalist and socialist regimes failed to protect the environment. The failure to implicate socialist development strategies in environmental degradation arises from a continued attachment to economic growth, and a failure to recognize the ecological limits to growth. Another weakness of radical theories lies in the tendency to equate capitalism with industrialization.

This debate between the three traditional IPE paradigms serves to show the limitations of the traditional paradigms when applied to the study of the environment. While realists, liberals and Marxists do, as we have seen, have different foundations, they nevertheless all share a paradigmatic assumption of, and commitment to, the necessity and desirability of economic growth.

Environmental studies debates

At this stage it is necessary to move away from the established way of conceptualising IPE as a contest between three perspectives to focus on a different set of values at the heart of environmentalism. The shared commitment to anthropocentrism of the three IPE paradigms results in their failure to engage with debates in environmental studies between proponents of technocentric solutions on one hand and supporters of ecocentric goals on the other. In this section we will examine the contestation between environmentalism (technocentrism) and ecologism (ecocentrism) since it extends analysis of environmental degradation and sustainability.

The technocentric perspective is based on the assumption that the central objective of economic growth is to satisfy the needs of humans. This perspective is based on the superiority of Western cultural values, and the transformational capacity of capitalism. Two variants of technocentrism can be identified – conservative and reformist. From the viewpoint of conservative technocentrism, modern economic growth is the basis for personal liberation and capitalism is the driving force for change. In this perspective, ecological change is necessarily attendant on economic growth but this does not mean that such change is negative. Writers in this perspective tend to emphasize the positive impact of economic growth and to argue that humans have in the past found solutions to impending environmental problems. Capitalism, it is claimed is an ingenious system that through the search for profit will naturally find market-based solutions to environmental problems. Indeed, some economists have argued that concern with environmental issues is misplaced, and any attempt to hold back progress in the name of environmentalism will result in economic catastrophe. Wilfred Beckerman in a polemical text, *Small is Stupid* (1995) has presented a fierce attack on controls on economic growth.

While the conservative technocentric position contests the claim that modern economic growth is responsible for environmental degradation, reformist technocentric writers have, principally through the development of the sub-field of environmental economics, tried to demonstrate the continued relevance of conventional economic theory to the study of environmental change. The reformist technocentric approach is rooted in environmental economics and begins from the assumption that environmental degradation is an accidental outcome of modern economic growth. It is thus a reformist rather than a radical position and argues that if the environment is fully priced, environmental degradation would be reduced.

In other words, from this perspective environmental degradation arises from market failure. In order to protect the environment it is essential to value the environment through determining the 'real costs' of resource use, and then proposing the most efficient solutions. A tension exists among environmental economists between those who prefer the use of incentives and market-based solutions and those who argue in support of regulation, and command and control measures. This tension can be perceived in discussions on global warming. Proponents of market-based solutions argue in support of tradable permits whereas those who prefer interventionist solutions propose legislation restricting emission levels. Current national and international solutions to environmental change are largely based on this reformist perspective, and the policy debate is usually constructed in terms of market versus interventionist solutions.

This policy approach has been termed managerial environmentalism (Levy, 1997). It recognizes the link between human activity and the environment but believes that accommodation can be found between current economic activity and the long-term goal of sustainable development. Central to environmental managerialism are two features, the first is a commitment to business and the belief that capitalism and the environment are not antithetical, the second includes a liberal internationalist belief in multilateral co-operation. This technocentric approach contrasts sharply with more radical ecocentric approaches (see Box 10.1).

The reformist technocentric approach has become an important part of contemporary discourse through the development of environmental economics. This is not to claim that concern about ecological limits to growth arose in this period for the first time. In the 1960s a self-conscious sub-discipline of environmental economics began to emerge. At the centre of environmental economics is the idea that the economy is an open system. Environmental economics is based on a materials balance view of the economy which begins from the assumption that the economy is an open system with three basic processes – extraction, processing and consumption. Resources (renewable and non-renewable) are extracted from the environment and processed for consumption. All economic activities create waste which must either be recycled in the economic process or absorbed in the environment. The central issue therefore becomes that of maintaining economic growth without decreasing the assimilative capacity of the environment to absorb wastes. Environmental economics builds on the insights of neoclassical economics, and has successfully incorporated the environment into standard economic theory. It has moved from a position in which the economy is seen as closed to one which stresses the open nature of the system. But the overall assumptions are similar to those of its parent discipline. The objective of the economy is still to maximize the welfare of society. The fundamental economic problem remains the efficient organization of production and consumption.

An ecological focus forces us to confront the changing relationships that have developed between human activity, natural systems and the built environment. Social systems and natural systems exist in a dynamic inter-

---

Box 10.1   Technocentric and ecocentric approaches to sustainability

The ecocentric approach to sustainable development recognizes the environment as central to survival and progress. This can be compared to a technocentric approach, which is centred around humans and views nature merely as an instrument in sustaining human life. They can be compared in relation to a number of issues. These include:

Primary economic objectives – economic growth (technocentric) vs zero economic growth (ecocentric).
Economic organization – large scale (technocentric); small scale (ecocentric)
Market incentives – green consumerism; eonomic instruments to regulate production (technocentric); limited consumerism; strong regulation of the economy
Attitude to resource management – conservationist (technocentric); preservationist (ecocentric)
Attitude to trade – reconciliation of trade and environmental standards (technocentric); anti-trade and promotion of self-sufficiency (ecocentric)
Political project – maintenance of nation-states and the status quo (technocentric); creation of small-scale communities as the basis of political authority (ecocentric)
Global governance – reform of the existing international economic order (technocentric); resistance to industrialism, capitalism and modernity (ecocentric)
Ethical standards – intergenerational and intragenerational equity (technocentric); ecological justice; equality for all life forms (ecocentric)

---

active context and interdependencies between the two systems mirror developments in both. From the work of anthropologists we have extensive evidence of the myriad ways in which cultural beliefs, cultural artefacts, social structure and type of technology are intimately connected.

Unlike the technocentric perspective an ecocentric perspective is founded on a rejection of continued economic growth and a critique of global capitalism. Writers within this approach are questioning of modern industrial growth and modern institutions. They reject anthropocentrism and argue instead for an ecological approach in which human needs are balanced by concern for all living organisms. Ecocentric theorists contend that the current emphasis in the organization of society is on human wants rather than human needs (Pepper, 1996, pp. 69–70). Human wants are socially derived and reflect the materialistic values of society whereas human needs combine spiritual and material values to arrive at a balance between humans and the environment.

Ecological critiques of conventional economic theory point to a number of omissions in neoclassical economics, which render it incapable of providing solutions to global environmental degradation. According to ecologists one key reason for the failure of neoclassical economics to provide a convincing analysis of environmental change stems from the omission of the fundamental laws of thermodynamics and ecology from its basic assumptions. Moreover, unlike conventional economics, the ecocentric perspective views the natural world and the environment as subsystems of society and the economy rather than vice versa. Conventional economics tends to view the economy as a closed system but ecologists see it as an open system.

Ecologists also object to what they perceive as the obsession with the short-term and marginal analysis of neoclassical economics. Instead of focusing on the short term, ecologists insist that we need to give more attention to the long run. This critique is related to the issue of discounting for the future, and ecologists argue that the future discounting assumptions of conventional economics are seriously flawed. Furthermore, in common with other radical critiques, the ecological perspective rejects the sterile, abstract reasoning of conventional economics and its embrace of arid mathematics. Conventional economic theory is based on constructing theorems based on questionable assumptions about human nature instead of integrating observed human or organizational behaviour into its analyses.

Although there are a number of strands of ecological economics, they all share two central ideas. These are a commitment to restricting or imposing limits to growth because of a belief that natural or ecological limitations to the earth's carrying capacity are real, and a rejection of anthropocentrism, that is, a belief in holism and an interactive relationship between all species. Three strands of ecological economics have made important contributions to the theorization of global environmental degradation. Steady-state approaches focus on the issue of scale and attempt to maintain a link between the size of the economy and the overall system. Central to steady-state theory is a determination to maintain the natural resource base for future generations. Radical ecology is indebted to Marxist insights and emphasizes the ways in which capitalism leads to over-production and hence environmental degradation. Co-evolutionary approaches attempt to combine knowledge, values, social organization, technology and ecosystems. In this view environmental degradation arises from the failure to respect the equilibrium of natural ecosystems and the neglect of the human/nature equilibrium.

Major developments

This section focuses on the evolution of the environment as an issue in the global political economy and the forms it has since taken. Over the past four decades increased attention has been given to global environmental issues, and there has been a proliferation of initiatives in the global political economy to address environmental degradation. The modern concern for the environment has gone through two phases. The first phase corresponds to the emergence of a new wave of environmentalism beginning in the 1960s. The second phase is marked by the United Nations Conference on Environment and Development (UNCED) in 1992 and ushers in the mainstreaming of environmental issues on national and international agendas.

Bringing the environment in

Lynton Caldwell (1988) notes that there were three types of international environmental agreements in the first part of the twentieth century. The first category relates to wilderness and wildlife conservation and included agreements such as the Pacific Fur Treaty (1911), and the International Convention for the Regulation of Whaling (1946). A second type of environmental agreement was developed to govern maritime pollution and included the International Convention for the Prevention of the Pollution of the Sea by Oil (1954), and the Convention on the High Seas (1958). Agreements limiting the spread of nuclear weapons such as the Antarctic Treaty (1959), and the Treaty Banning Nuclear Weapons Tests in the Atmosphere, Outer Space and Under Water (1963) formed a third category. These efforts are important but they were not seen as part of an integrated concern with the environment.

Global concern with environmental degradation is a relatively recent phenomenon and stems from three sources. The first lies in international conferences convened by the United Nations. These conferences were notable for their preparatory process, the resolutions passed, and the follow-up process. The first significant conference was the United Nations Conference on the Human Environment (UNCHE) convened in Stockholm in 1972 (see Box 10.2). Called in response to lobbying by Scandinavian countries concerned by pollution, the agenda of the conference extended discussion beyond pollution. During the preparatory phase the developing countries emphasized the link between development and the environment laying the basis for the process that culminated in the Rio Conference twenty years later. UNCHE recognized the environmental consequences of modern economic growth and these linkages were enshrined in the conference recommendations. Although these were subsequently ignored by gov-

---

Box 10.2 Advancing environmentalism: the United Nations conference on the human environment (UNCHE)

Preparatory phase
1971 – Founex meeting – 27 experts gathered by Maurice Strong, Secretary-General of UNCHE. Establishes, for the first time, a clear link between environment and development.

The Conference
First major conference to bring governments together to discuss variety of environmental issues. Attended by 1200 representatives from 114 states; parallel formal NGO conference and an informal People's Forum.

Outcomes
Stockholm Declaration of 26 principles;
Action Plan of 109 recommendations;
creation of the United Nations Environment Program (UNEP).

---

ernments, one notable impact of the conference was the creation of the United Nations Environment Programme (UNEP), a permanent bureaucracy in the UN system to champion environmental issues.

The process began in Stockholm culminated in 1992 when the United Nations Conference on Environment and Development (UNCED) held in Rio legitimized the environment as a concern for international economic diplomacy (see Box 10.3). The preparatory phase of the Rio Conference attracted significant attention from governmental and non-governmental actors. Also, the high political profile of the disputes during the preparatory phase ensured maximum visibility for the conference proceedings. This became the largest conference ever held, in terms of the number of delegates present, and it also attracted the largest number of world leaders ever to convene in one place. The wide-ranging agenda gave rise to heated debate and produced Agenda 21, a document designed to provide a framework for future actions to halt environmental degradation. Agenda 21 also included a monitoring and implementation process. At the centre of the deliberations and conclusions of the Rio Conference was the concept of sustainable development. The assembled delegates reached agreement that environmental degradation potentially could have profound ramifications for economic growth and prosperity.

The second factor contributing to the emergence of the environment as an international issue was scientific knowledge. Probably the most significant advance here was the discovery of a hole in the ozone layer above

---

Box 10.3   Advancing environmentalism: the United Nations Conference on Environment and Development (UNCED)

Preparatory Phase
Preparatory committee – established as a committee of the United Nations General Assembly.
Three preparatory committee meetings – three working groups established a framework for negotiation and draft declaration of principles (representing 85 per cent of the conference program).

Conference
Attended by governmental representatives from 178 countries; including 114 heads of state or government.
Global Forum – 7892 NGO delegates from 167 countries.

Outcomes
Rio Declaration on Environment and Development;
Agenda 21;
Statement of Forest Principles;
UN Framework Convention on Climate Change;
Convention on Biological Diversity.

Antarctica by a team of British scientists in 1985. The health implications of the ozone hole shocked populations and galvanized governments to act. In one sense the image of the ozone hole was stark and readily comprehensible, and in another sense the solution was reasonably straightforward. In saying this we do not imply that it was easy to agree a treaty but rather that it did not involve a series of complicated linkages. But if the discovery of the ozone hole was part of a process of the expansion of knowledge, not all of this process was consensual. Peter Haas developed the concept of epistemic community to describe a collection of scientists and decision makers sharing a knowledge base. Epistemic communities have played a part in providing solutions to environmental problems (Haas, 1990a).

But of equal importance to epistemic communities are the seminal books and articles that challenge conventional wisdom and alert publics to the linkages between environmental degradation and society. The publication in 1972 of *The Limits to Growth* by Dennis and Donella Meadows (1972) is one such contribution. Its controversial thesis was that the earth's finite resources would soon run out unless steps were taken to conserve energy use. Even though the projections made by the Meadows were subject to exhaustive tests and refuted by a range of experts, *The Limits to Growth* controversy was important in placing ecology on the agenda. A later report (Meadows *et al.*, 1993) published after sustainable development had become a major feature of contemporary political debate maintained a pessimistic vision of the earth's future.

A third factor contributing to awareness of the linkages between environment and the economy was a series of environmental mishaps in the 1960s, 1970s, and 1980s. These included the Torrey Canyon disaster, Seveso, Bhopal (see Box 10.3) and Chernobyl. These incidents served to underline the fragility of human and marine life in the face of modern industrialization. These disasters showed that modern production methods, industrialization and transport systems threatened health and safety rather than provide a welcome release from poverty. These disasters did not lead, except among a small group of people, to calls for abandoning economic growth but to a desire to find ways to reconcile both growth and environmental sustainability.

These developments were given impetus by two political developments. In chronological terms the first was the development of the second wave of environmentalism in the United States and Western Europe in the 1960s. Some have argued that growing affluence among the middle classes contributed to the growth of an environmental movement in the West. While this is part of the explanation, environmentalism was also spurred by the

---

Box 10.4   Bhopal

In December 1984 a gas leak occurred in one of three of Union Carbide's pesticide tanks in Bhopal, India. An investigation revealed that a large amount of water was introduced into the tank where methyl isocyanate (MIC) was stored. This caused a reaction that ultimately released a vapour cloud, which infiltrated homes overnight and within days, killed 3000 people. Over the next few years, 2000 deaths were attributed to the 'irrespirable gases'. An estimated 150 000 people directly affected by the gas leak now live with chronic illnesses such as fibrosis, bronchial asthma, chronic obstructive airways disease, emphysema, and recurrent chest infections. Pulmonary tuberculosis among the exposed population is notably higher than India's national average. Over 578 000 people have been affected and have received some form of compensation. Union Carbide paid $US 470 million to the Indian Government to settle the victims' claims. Yet only about half of it has been distributed, in most cases at $550 per recipient.

disasters described above, and increasing scientific knowledge. Affluence, however, played a central role in the ability of these groups to organize effectively. Possessing unprecedented material resources and high levels of education, the diverse environmental movement spawned effective advocacy and lobbying organizations and political parties that were in a position to influence the agenda of politics in Western Europe and the United States. The second development concerned the end of the Cold War, and the removal of the straightjacket of East–West tensions from international discussions of the environment. From the period of Gorbachev's glasnost it became progressively easier to address environmental issues in a mature manner in the international arena.

Mainstreaming environmentalism

Following the Rio Conference, environmental issues definitively moved from the margins to the centre of politics at domestic and international levels. This is not to say that politicians, the public, and academics necessarily engaged with environmental issues in a manner likely to halt unsustainable practices. Rather it signals a salience given to environmental issues in the sense that the environment became normalized in political discourse. The concerns of Green parties and environmental activists are no longer regarded as outlandish or silly but have instead been co-opted to the orthodox political agenda. This enables a form of environmental management to become the standard approach in which politicians, business groups and social movement activists are accorded the same legitimacy. More fundamental questions regarding the nature of economic growth in a world of finite resources are not addressed in this new approach to the environment. There are three main features that characterize the current mainstreaming of the environment.

The first feature of the mainstreaming of the environment lies in the development of environmental regulation at the domestic level. States in both the North and the South have established ministries wholly or partly responsible for the environment. These ministries have ushered in legislation (see Table 10.1) to define acceptable limits of pollution, manage resources in a sustainable manner, and prescribe penalties for activities that contribute to environmental legislation. There are, of course, disputes at the domestic level concerning the best mix of policies to be followed, and there are still groups that oppose environmental legislation. Nevertheless, it has become commonplace in many states to initiate environmental impact assessments as routine measures when planning new projects.

Secondly, environmental issues have been mainstreamed within many international organizations. To many critics the so-called greening of inter-

Table 10.1 *Sample of environmental legislation in Australia*

- Removal of Prisoners (Territories) Act 1923, in so far as it relates to the Territory of Heard Island and McDonald Islands and the Australian Antarctic Territory
- Heard Island and MacDonald Islands Act 1953
- Captains Flat (Abatement of Pollution) Agreement Act 1975
- Historic Shipwrecks Act 1976
- Environment Protection (Alligator Rivers Region) Act 1978
- Environment Protection (Sea Dumping) Act 1981
- Koongarra Project Area Act 1981
- Wildlife Protection (Regulation of Exports and Imports) Act 1982
- Aboriginal and Torres Strait Islander Heritage Protection Act 1984
- Protection of Movable Cultural Heritage Act 1986
- Sea Installations Act 1987
- Sea Installations Levy Act 1987
- Hazardous Waste (Regulation of Exports and Imports) Act 1989
- Ozone Protection Act 1989
- National Environment Protection Council Act 1994
- Wet Tropics of Queensland World Heritage Area Conservation Act 1994
- Ozone Protection (Licence Fees–Imports) Act 1995
- Ozone Protection (Licence Fees–Manufacture) Act 1995
- Hindmarsh Island Bridge Act 1997
- Natural Heritage Trust of Australia Act 1997
- National Environment Protection Measures (Implementation) Act 1998
- Environment Protection and Biodiversity Conservation Act 1999
- Environmental Reform (Consequential Provisions) Act 1999
- Fuel Quality Standards Act 2000
- Product Stewardship (Oil) Act 2000
- Renewable Energy (Electricity) Act 2000
- Renewable Energy (Electricity) (Charge) Act 2000
- Environment Protection and Biodiversity Conservation Amendment (Wildlife Protection) Act 2001
- Lake Eyre Basin Intergovernmental Agreement Act 2001

Source: Data from Environment Australia, http://www.ea.gov.au.

national institutions offers little if any real contribution to environmental sustainability. But that is a moot point in this context. For example the World Bank's approach to the environment has undergone significant change (World Bank, 1995). Whereas once the Bank ignored environmental issues and made no attempt to assess the environmental consequences of its loans, the post-UNCED World Bank has consciously attempted to develop a green portfolio. It has adopted two different strategies to achieve its goal of sustainable development: instituted mandatory environmental assessments, and systematic and routine environmental monitoring; and now disburses environmental loans. Its lending practices include one set of policies aimed at urban renewal and pollution control and another set of policies designed to promote biodiversity and reforestation.

The third feature of a mainstreaming of the environment in the global political economy can be seen in the behaviour of major firms. In response to the actions of environmental activists and the policies of governmental departments, business has shifted its profile and adopted an approach that emphasizes the sustainability of resources (Schmidheiny, 1992). Even those firms engaged in practices that at face value appear to be far removed from sustainable practices, such as mining and oil exploration and production, have embraced the concept of sustainable development. However, not all corporations have adopted this approach and many continue to find ways to oppose and denigrate the efforts of environmentalists.

Key issues

The extent to which the efforts of national governments, international organizations and firms seriously address the environmental crisis remains the subject of fierce debate. Within the contemporary global political economy the politics of sustainability generates debate on various issues. Conflicts arising from international trade, pollution control, the preservation of biodiversity, and sustainable development have all figured prominently on the international agenda. This section focuses on three significant environmental issues: sustainable development, the relationship between trade and the environment; and global environmental governance. All three issues are at the centre of the debate between proponents of environmental management and its critics.

Sustainable development

The problem with the term 'sustainable development' is its vagueness. It has proved very difficult to formulate a definition that is comprehensible while retaining analytical precision. Sustainable development has been the subject of diverse definitions from a number of commentators (Pearce *et al.*, 1989, pp. 173–85). As a result it has come to mean very different things to ecologists, economists, planners and politicians. In its favour is the positive connotation implicit in the term. It is unlikely that any sane person or organization would willingly endorse unsustainable development or sustainable impoverishment if that is not an oxymoron. Sustainable development is not necessarily identified with increased consumption and production but with an improved quality of life where the state of the natural environment is taken into consideration.

Of the many issues debated in the political economy of global environmental change, sustainable development is perhaps the most urgent. Sustainable development has become within a very short time a term to which everyone can subscribe but also attach a different meaning. The concept of sustainable development, like that of globalization, is hotly contested with views ranging from those who reject the term as meaningless to others for whom it expresses the current development paradigm.

For some, sustainable development implies a commitment to sustainability with a consequent reduction in economic growth while for others the concept of sustainable development is seen as integral to a new era of economic growth. While some analysts question the utility of a concept subject to multiple meanings it should be pointed out that contestation over its meaning is not unique to sustainable development. This is a normal state of affairs regarding important concepts in the social sciences. In looking at the concept of sustainable development it is vital that analysis moves beyond the clever but simplistic observation that sustainable development is a contradiction in terms. Without definitions of development or sustainability such a conclusion is facile and incapable of wrestling with the core issues raised by sustainable development. In its various conceptualizations, sustainable development is a serious attempt to reconcile what at first sight appears to be contradictory objectives, and to meet the urgent test of fulfilling the needs of developing countries in their drive to eradicate poverty, and reducing the damage caused to the planet by unsustainable modes of production and consumption.

Different conceptions of development contribute to contending perspectives on sustainable development. Radical approaches reject capitalist development and argue that capitalism is responsible for both the creation and perpetuation of poverty and environmental degradation (Saurin, 1996). Thus from this perspective development requires rejection of the current international economic order, and a search for development models that emphasize small-scale, participatory development. In this view the pursuit of economic growth can be counter-productive since such growth frequently stimulates policies which degrade the environment.

On the other hand, the dominant conception of sustainable development accepts the prevailing global political–economic structure, and locates development within the capitalist political economy. Within the dominant approach, economic growth per se is not a problem but an inescapable starting point. The report by the Trilateral Commission, *Beyond Interdependence* states: 'Given the growth imperative evident in the material poverty of much of human kind, the only reasonable alternative is sustainable development' (McNeil *et al.*, 1991, p. v). As this report suggests economic growth is necessary in order to eradicate poverty. The World Bank, which has adopted sustainable development as its goal, has argued that it is poverty which is responsible for environmental degradation. In this view economic growth provides the instruments through which societies can address environmental degradation.

In this debate between different approaches to development, history has shown convincingly that it is not the economic system, as such, but the importance attached to environmental values, that is central. The radical critique is on firm ground when it draws connections between capitalist development and unsustainable modes of production and consumption. But it is surely on shaky ground when it assumes that a socialist (or non-capitalist) economic system automatically provides the conditions for sustainable practices. The evidence of the environmental disasters created by the communist regimes in Central and Eastern Europe are stark reminders of the fact that environmental pollution was in many cases far worse under these regimes than in the capitalist West. The objection that these were not true communist states is irrelevant. It is irrelevant because one can equally claim that Western states are not examples of true capitalism. But more importantly these regimes provide a counter to the claim that capitalism creates environmental degradation since whatever we call their economic systems, they were certainly not capitalist.

Differing conceptions of sustainable development also arise from contending views on the meaning of sustainability, and the measures by which sustainability is to be achieved. Crucial questions include the following: Should sustainability be conceived in terms of a renewal of resources? How do we measure sustainability in relation to the needs of future generations? Should we use market-based solutions or command and control measures?

One of the sources of conceptual confusion surrounding the term is that no agreement exists regarding exactly what is to be sustained. The goal of sustainability sometimes refers to the resource base itself, and sometimes to the livelihoods which are derived from it. Some commentators refer to sustaining levels of production while others emphasize sustaining levels of consumption. This difference is important since development at the global level has become unsustainable largely due to the patterns of overconsumption and irresponsible production in the major developed countries. However, policies for sustainable development that have been put forward to date are essentially production oriented.

Despite the controversy surrounding the term a dominant approach to sustainable development is discernible in national and international policy-making circles. That is, current solutions to the problems of environmental degradation and poverty are framed according to a consensual definition which ignores alternative conceptualizations. The dominant discourse has its origins in the Brundtland Commission. The Commission's Report *Our Common Future* defines sustainable development as 'development that meets the needs of the present without compromising the ability of future generations to meet their own needs', where 'needs' is defined as the essential needs particularly of the world's poor, and 'development' is vaguely defined as the 'progressive transformation of economy and society' (World Commission, 1987, p. 43). The Brundtland Commission's definition of sustainable development has become, if not the standard definition, the one that is most widely used in policy-making circles. The evidence on critical thresholds (natural parameters) raised by reports such as *The Limits to Growth* is barely acknowledged, and the main limitations acknowledged are the 'present state of technology and social organization' (ibid., p. 43).

A number of common themes emerge in the debate on sustainable development. First, sustainable development appears to require an inescapable commitment to equity, specifically, intergenerational equity. There is general agreement on the principle of intergenerational equity. In other words, sustainable development policies should ensure that the welfare of future generations is no lower than our own. Secondly, sustainable development requires an entrenchment of environmental considerations in policy-making and proponents of sustainable development focus on efficiency in resource use.

Efficiency in resource use entails the internalization of environmental costs in pricing decisions. Looking more closely at the use of natural resources, and the pollution created as a result of economic production, efficiency is defined so that the full social costs of goods and services are reflected in the price of production inputs and consumer goods. Thirdly, the literature on sustainable development has been concerned with the inter-country and intra-country effects of changes in economic policies. In the context of the global political economy, equity is normally discussed in relation to North–South issues. The advanced industrial states achieved their current living standards through a process of industrialization which resulted in untold environmental degradation. This option is now closed to the developing countries. However, the adoption of sustainable policies will be costly, and unless the advanced industrial countries are willing to provide major transfers of resources, the necessary policies are unlikely to be implemented. Finally, a focus on sustainable development shifts the narrow focus on growth and obsession with GNP per capita and replaces it with greater attention to social aspects of development.

Sustainable development is the current dominant solution to development. It seeks to combine the right to development with sustainability objectives. Politically, it is imperative that sustainable development is focused on economic growth since to argue for a steady state in the developing world is unacceptable to the elites and masses in Africa, Asia and Latin America. The concept is a delicate balancing act and does not in itself suggest how one can reconcile these objectives should they come into conflict.

But progress has been made in the implementation of sustainable development. One major development has been in the mainstreaming of environmental assessments especially in aid projects. It has become commonplace to give importance to the environmental consequences of new projects. But the rhetoric of sustainable development should not be confused with the reality of effective implementation. Independent assessments of lending by multilateral agencies counsel caution in the depth of commitment to meeting environmental objectives. Moreover, most private sector investment is exempt from such scrutiny since, although environmental ministries have mushroomed in the developing world, many of these agencies lack the resources and power to intervene effectively in support of environmental objectives.

A second major development has been increasing attention to participatory development. In the absence of genuine participation by stakeholders affected by development schemes and projects, it is highly likely that old-fashioned unsustainable development practices will remain and may even be reinforced. In situations where the population has a clear stake in the programme or project sustainability, concerns are more likely to be implemented. Sustainable development has provided a site of contention and major policy initiative as governments have tried to address environmental issues in the global economy.

Trade and environmental degradation

A second key issue concerns the relationship between international trade and environmental degradation. Unsurprisingly, this is an issue of contention between various actors in the global political economy. In broad terms, some observers and participants contend that trade and environmental protection are perfectly compatible and that the pursuit of trade liberalization will enhance rather than destroy environmental sustainability, while others maintain that free trade promotes unsustainable patterns of production and consumption (Williams, 1993). These conflicting views have been evident in the search for regulatory polices linking trade and the environment. We will discuss two issues that have arisen and continue to be controversial in this issue area.

Does trade liberalization promote a 'race to the bottom', and does it lead to the creation of pollution havens? Many critics of free trade assert that unfettered trade has a deleterious impact on the environment through these two outcomes. Stated simply, in a competitive world in which firms are seeking to cut costs, they will move production from those countries that have high environmental standards to those with lower environmental standards. Given the importance of transnational corporations in world trade and the transnationalization of production, countries are, it is claimed, reducing their environmental laws in attempts to lure foreign investment. Since some countries will reap a competitive advantage through lax environmental standards, this will force others to abandon stronger environmental protection laws in order to remain competitive.

Another related point is that concerning pollution havens. The claim here is that as a result of these lax environmental standards, some countries will become major recipients of pollution while others can enjoy the benefits of the products produced in ways detrimental to the natural environment without suffering any of the costs. To date, international regulation has not been developed in response to these fears. Governments have tended to support the contention that no conflict exists between free trade and environmental regulation. In this view they are supported by mainstream economists who argue that the 'race to the bottom' is not a universal feature. Economists contend that environmental costs are not the major determinant of the location of investment. Given the low priority given to environmental costs in the cost structure of most transnational corporations, it is unlikely that production will be located in any massive way to take advantage of lower standards. Indeed, it has been claimed that countries may indeed reap competitive advantages through higher environmental standards (Nordstrom and Vaughan, 1999). The pollution haven hypothesis is also rejected since it is only relevant in situations where environmental costs outweigh other locational advantages (Letuchamanan, 2000).

A second policy issue concerns what are called process and production methods (PPMs). At the moment, WTO rules oblige members to treat domestic and foreign goods alike irrespective of the manner in which they have been produced, whereas for environmentalists this decision leads to unsustainable production, trade and consumption. That is, current WTO regulations are based on product standards, and governments can legitimately restrict imports on the basis of a product's characteristics but not on the basis of the process used to produce the product.

This issue can be illustrated through a specific example. Suppose you wanted to buy a car and you were trying to decide between two different makes of car produced in two separate countries. Suppose that you were provided with information which proved conclusively that the production methods in one country harmed the surrounding environment but this was not the case in the second country. You may decide to buy the car from the country whose car manufacturing operations were not harmful to the environment because you supported environmental sustainability. On the other hand, if your value system was different and if the car made with polluting technology cost considerably less than the other car you would be tempted to buy that one irrespective of the production method. The dilemma is therefore whether we treat products on the basis of the finished article that is, a car is a car, or whether we create policy to distinguish between how the cars were made so that the one made with polluting technology could be subject to some form of restriction in our domestic market.

From an environmentalist perspective the production process used is crucial to determining the environmental degradation arising from trade. Thus environmentalists have been campaigning for the incorporation of PPMs into the trade rules, and supporters of the status quo are opposed because they believe that discriminating on the basis of process rather than product will foster discriminatory tendencies in the world trading system (Williams, 2001, p. 5).

This issue raises the possible inconsistency between implementing domestic environmental reform and international environmental policy in the failure of the WTO to accept PPM-based environmental trade measures. But there are a number of problems inherent in a move to PPM-based environmental trade measures. One crucial issue concerns the fact that countries vary in their ability, and willingness to absorb pollution. They possess different absorptive capacities and differing environmental values. If environmental regulations designed for more advanced industrialized countries are forced on developing nations, surely this is an example of eco-imperialism.

Furthermore, any imposition of global standards will erode the comparative advantage of some states. Another problem with enforcing PPMs resides in difficulties inherent in devising monitoring and compliance systems during production processes. Notwithstanding these difficulties, PPM measures cannot be easily dismissed partly because they are vital for the development of sustainability, and partly because it is becoming increasingly difficult to maintain a distinction between production processes and products. For example, a focus on sustainable energy draws attention not to the product but to the production process. Furthermore, life-cycle approaches have demonstrated the importance of assessing the production process as well as the product.

Environmental governance: international environmental agreements

The WTO Ministerial Meeting in Doha in November 2001 concluded with a decision to give greater attention to the subject of multilateral environmental agreements (MEAs). This is a continuation of a positive approach to MEAs noted since the Rio Conference. Governments have enthusiastically adopted multilateral environmental agreements as one response to transboundary environmental problems.

From a political economy perspective, one crucial issue concerns the negotiation and implementation of these agreements. The failures to successfully conclude an agreement on climate change has tended to draw attention away from the proliferation of treaties covering a range of international environmental problems. Regimes have been established for common pool problems (for example, ozone depletion), those related to transboundary externalities (for example, hazardous waste) and shared resources (for example, rivers). Various theories have been put forward to explain the ability of governments to negotiate environmental treaties. These focus on, among other things, the role of knowledge, the importance of institutions and the rational pursuit of interest. Attention to international environmental agreements has reinforced the multiple levels of governance and the range of actors within the global political economy. Firms, states and NGOs are all important in the search for regulation, and environmental degradation requires action at national, regional and international decision-making levels.

Another issue arising in the context of international environmental agreements relates to the possible conflict between multilateral environmental agreements (MEAs) and WTO rules and obligations. Some of these agreements, for example, the Convention on Biological Diversity, the Montreal Protocol on Substances that deplete the Ozone Layer, the Basel Convention on the Control of Transboundary Movement of Hazardous Wastes and their Disposal, and the UN Framework Convention on Climate Change, contain trade provisions. Although to date no dispute involving the trade-related provisions of an MEA and WTO rules has been brought to the WTO, nevertheless, some governments have sought clarification of the potential impact of MEAs on the WTO. Those governments seeking clarification of the WTO–MEA interface argue that they want to prevent potential conflicts, create a policy-making environment conducive to MEA negotiations, and to confirm the legal relationship between MEAs and the WTO.

One proposal to advance these goals concerns the creation of a consultative mechanism in the WTO to ensure consultation between countries prior to the use of trade measures under MEAs. Another proposal that has been put forward is the creation of an 'interpretative understanding' which would define the framework under which trade measures taken under an MEA may be deemed compatible with GATT Article XX. This movement has alarmed environmentalists and those governments who believe that such requests have disrupted the existing consensus regarding the relationship between MEAs and the WTO, and threatened the autonomy of MEAs. They think that such measures seek to replace the current norm of separate but equal status for MEAs and the WTO with oversight by the WTO. This would enable some WTO members to resort to the WTO's dispute settlement procedures in order to overturn MEA trade-related provisions.

Conclusion

Given the extensive nature of the social, economic and political impact of environmental degradation, ecological concerns form a central role in the study of the global political economy. The connections between economics and the environment, combined with the necessity of collective action to counter common resource problems place contemporary environmental concerns at the centre of international relations. The causes of environmental degradation are complex and require careful understanding of the ways in which economic systems interact with the ecosystem.

This chapter has shown that no consensus exists on how we might best understand the processes of environmental degradation, and the solutions to the environmental crisis. At one end of the spectrum, neoclassical environmental economics requires the extension of market-based principles to areas of economic activity previously exempt. At the other end, radical ecological approaches to economic activity are based on the necessity for fundamental changes in economic structures, value systems and social behaviour.

The introduction of environmental issues to IPE poses questions concerning the adequacy of the three IPE approaches to adequately explain environmental sustainability and environmental cooperation. In the absence of a specific green international political economy perspective (Dryzek, 1996), this chapter has examined the emergence of environmental problems, the different perspectives on the environment and various solutions to environmental problems. It has argued that global environmental issues which the existing IPE perspectives have should be supplemented through attention to debates in environmental economics and ecological economics.

The interaction of social systems, natural systems and the built environment are features of human history and it would be pointless to search for a position from which environmental degradation began. What we conceive as environmental degradation is essentially social, and one generation may accept something as natural that a subsequent generation may find unacceptable. A minor but pertinent example is that of cigarette smoke, which as little as 30 years ago in much of North America and Western Europe was not seen as harmful to non-smokers. However, today it is generally accepted that secondary or passive smoking is detrimental to those who suffer its effects.

Chapter 11

Governing the Global Political Economy

The subject of this chapter is global governance. While previous parts of the book have given some attention to global governance, this chapter explores the concept in greater detail. Specific attention is given to current understandings of governance, contemporary issues facing the global political economy, and the attendant challenges ahead for global managers and citizens. We paint a picture of increasingly global political economic relations with states, firms and citizens struggling to create, manage and distribute wealth and power. The first section of this chapter outlines how governance is accomplished in such a widespread and multilevel system. The focus is on the issue of how rules are created and maintained. In order to understand the phenomenon of global governance it is necessary to explore the complex relationship between state, corporate and civil society actors (O'Brien, 2003). Or to put this another way, we focus on three different types of agents whose activities help provide answers to the paradox of global governance. The second section identifies key challenges facing the evolution of the global political economy. These challenges are: development and economic growth, equality and justice, and democracy and regulation.

What is global governance and how does it work?

The contemporary discourse on global governance is located within the debate on globalization. Because the debate on globalization is so wide-ranging, we begin by clarifying key terms in the chapter (globalization and global governance). The second section examines the role of regimes, legal and financial coercion, moral appeals and the existence of structural power in the construction and maintenance of structures of governance. The third section assesses the impact of various actors (states, corporations and civic associations) on the transformation of global rules. This chapter, therefore, is centrally concerned with a key issue in international relations, namely that of international cooperation. This may be put in the form of the following question – If people live in separate states, how is it possible that rules and codes of behaviour might influence activity across these borders?

In what follows we focus on the practical manifestation of global governance. This part of the chapter concludes by considering the implications of a recent attempt at reforming global governance, the Global Compact.

Definitions

The term 'globalization' is used very widely, but people often mean different things when they use the term. For example, some people use the term to imply internationalization (an increase in the volume of economic flows across borders), while others use it to indicate liberalization (the removal of restrictions to cross-border flows, such as the elimination of trade or investment barriers). Both internationalization and liberalization are often used in the context of economic activity. The term 'globalization' is also used in the context of the dissemination of knowledge or ideas rather than changes in economic indicators. For example, some analysts focus on universalization (particular ideas or principles being accepted by all people) while others emphasize westernization (the increasing prevalence of ideas and practices originating in Europe or the United States). These terms are most often used when discussing the spread of principles such as human rights or culture, such as the expansion of the US movie industry. The term 'deterritorialization' highlights the political impact of globalizing tendencies. While changes in economic activity and the spread of ideas capture some features of globalization from the perspective of global political economy it is political change that is paramount.

Thus, only deterritorialization adequately captures what is new about globalization. Following Scholte (2000a), we understand globalization to mean a process of relative deterritorialization. Territory is not disappearing, but it is becoming less important to human affairs. Deterritorialization involves the shrinking of time and space, as well as the creation of new sets of social relations and new centres of authority. We can see that time and space have become less significant obstacles to human interaction as technologies make it easier to travel across large distances or communicate with people around the world. The lowering of time and distance barriers allows people to become involved in the lives of other people in other parts of the planet much more easily. However, such an approach is also fully aware that this compression is extremely uneven. Some areas of the globe are left behind as advanced areas exploit technology and upgrade communication and transport infrastructure. That is, globalization is not occurring at the same rate and same pace in all countries or regions.

By 'global governance', we mean the overarching system which regulates human affairs on a worldwide basis. Another term would be the system of 'world order' (Cox, 1996a). The mechanisms and rules of global governance are created by the actions and agreements of key actors in the global system. The primary political actor is the state, but other actors such as corporations and civic associations can also influence and participate in global governance. A striking feature of global governance in the past 50 years has been the increasing role played by international (that is interstate) organization in facilitating governance. More recent developments have been the growing role of corporations and the mobilization of citizens through civic associations.

This chapter highlights one particular aspect of global governance – world or international organizations and their ability to address global problems (Hewson and Sinclair, 1999). These organizations are significant because they provide both the forum for negotiating globalization rules and the mechanisms for monitoring and enforcing rules.

Many different factors can regulate people's behaviour. Habit or custom may dictate how people behave. Religious beliefs may encourage particular forms of activity. Rules may be written down into laws which can be enforced by authority figures or policing agencies to ensure compliance. On a global scale, the rules that regulate activity and norms which condition behaviour are much looser than those that exist on a national or community level. Diversity in cultures makes agreement on modes of behaviour more difficult and the lack of a world government means that there is no global legislature passing binding rules nor any global police force to enforce them. States are reluctant to diminish their sovereignty by submitting themselves to higher authorities such as international organizations. Yet, despite the greater distance between global rules and local activity, there are a number of ways that global governance can function.

In the field of international relations, the governance arrangements put in place by states in particular issue areas are often referred to as regimes. Regimes are 'implicit or explicit principles, norms, rules and decision-making procedures around which actors' expectations converge in a given area of international relations' (Krasner, 1983, p. 2). Regimes are ideas and rules about how states should behave. A vast literature has been created in an attempt to explain the conditions under which regimes are created, maintained and destroyed. Most approaches see regimes as being created through state-to-state negotiations with states acting as self-interested, goal-seeking actors pursuing the maximization of individual utility (Hasenclever *et al.*, 1997). In other words, states create regimes because they believe that a regular pattern of cooperation will bring them benefits. In many cases, states will participate in regimes that are not ideal because the cost of conflict outside of the regime is greater than the bad deal they get inside the regime (Keohane, 1984). For example, developing states may object to many aspects of the trade regime, but they prefer to be a member than to operate outside the main trading institution.

We can identify a number of ways through which regimes influence behaviour. Some regimes have a strong legal framework which compel states to obey rules by the threat of economic sanctions. The WTO is an excellent example. It has a strong dispute settlement mechanism which adjudicates trade conflicts based upon the rules contained in the agreements that created the WTO. Countries in violation of the rules must change their policies or face economic sanctions from the states they have injured. Even powerful states obey these rules, because they have an interest in a predictable system of rules that fosters increased trade and economic activity. The WTO puts the value of free trade above other goals, leading to conflict with those people who feel that free trade undermines environmental standards. In this case liberal values and market mechanisms are privileged over other approaches. Environmental protection must take place in the context of free trade.

The distribution of money and provision of credit can also be used to foster compliance with particular rules. This is the approach used by the World Bank and the IMF. These organizations loan money to states that are in need of funds to weather an economic crisis or to assist in long-term development strategies. The loans are usually conditional upon the recipients undertaking certain policies. These policies have varied over time, but usually ask states to liberalize their economies so that they earn money to pay back the loans. Institutions which disperse money are influenced by their largest financial contributors. In the case of the World Bank and the IMF, voting rights are distributed in proportion to the financial contributions of member states. Because the US is the largest contributor to both institutions, it has the largest share of votes and influence. Thus, policies that the US advocates are the most likely to be spread through this channel of influence in the global governance process. For example, IMF loans to South Korea during the East Asian financial crisis stipulated that Korea open up its manufacturing and financial industries to foreign investors, many of whom were from the United States.

At other times, state behaviour can be influenced by appeals to morality. This is the approach used by the International Labour Organization (ILO). The ILO conducts research on labour issues and highlights the abuse of workers rights through reports and investigations. It facilitates negotiations between states to set minimum standards for countries to follow and publicizes failure to comply with the standards. The organization's work is based upon the belief that states may change their behaviour if they face international condemnation. Although the ILO has been operating for almost 100 years, its ability to influence state behaviour is limited by its lack of enforcement measures. Many states ignore its reports and advice.

Expertize can also be used to convince actors that it is in their best interest to behave in a particular way. For example, organizations such as the OECD and the IMF issue reports on the economic policy of particular states and suggest how they should adapt to globalization. Reports do not order states to change their policies, but they advise that a particular change will help foster economic growth. These institutions tend to offer liberal approaches to economic restructuring and until very recently were unlikely to advocate policies that might protect society by reducing the influence of unregulated markets.

A final element that influences behaviour is the structure of the global system itself. This is known as structural power. Drawing upon theories of the privileged power position of business in a national context, Gill and Law (1993) have argued that the internationalization of economic activity has increased the direct and indirect power of business in relationship to the state. The nature of the system makes particular types of behaviour more likely and punishes some forms of behaviour more harshly than others. For example, states must pay attention to the desires of international investors if they want to attract capital for investment or keep national wealth and businesses from fleeing to other locations. This encourages state leaders to move their economies in a more liberal direction.

It is important to note that in the system of global governance, the institutions that are tasked with liberalizing the global economy and increasing the role of the market are more influential than those seeking to protect society from economic failures. On the market liberalization side, the IMF and World Bank are able to use the provision of finance for influence and the WTO has its important dispute settlement mechanism. However, the ILO, which protects labour standards, is confined to an advocacy role. Other institutions with social mandates such as UNICEF which assists poor children or the World Health Organization, must work within the economic policies advocated by the liberal institutions. The structure of governance seems to favour the increasing power of the market at the expense of social values. Returning to Polanyi's (1957) view of the dislocating effects of the liberal market, this is likely to lead to social turbulence and conflict over the rules of global governance.

Agents for change

One of the most important questions facing students of, and practitioners within the global political economy concerns the management of change. That is, what determines changes in the rules under which a particular form of global governance operates? For example, how do actors with a commitment to environmentalism shift the system in a direction which puts a higher emphasis on environmental protection? The relatively brief history of world orders or global governance warns against expecting rapid change and highlights the link between crisis and changes in governance. Dramatic transformations in governing relations between states have tended to follow large-scale wars. For example, in the aftermath of the Napoleonic Wars at the beginning of the nineteenth century the European state system was managed by the Concert of Europe. The next large change in organizing the international system followed the terrible destruction of the First World War. The League of Nations and a number of other international organizations and treaties were created to try and improve governance and maintain peace. The Second World War marked the end of that system and ushered in a new world order in 1945. Many of today's international organizations such as the United Nations, the IMF, the World Bank and the NATO date back to this era. The end of the Cold War between the United States and the Soviet Union in 1989 resulted in the strengthening of existing Western institutions rather than the creation of a new form of international organization.

Large-scale changes in reforming or replacing existing global governance structures are unlikely unless there is a devastating crisis in the international system. With the relatively peaceful end to the Cold War, the chances are low that a new world war will erupt in the near future to cause major change in global governance. It is more likely that wholesale change would come about as a result of a severe financial crisis which plunged the world into economic depression. Financial collapse would force decision makers to change the existing system or replace it with a new set of rules. Since such a collapse would impoverish millions and probably lead to violent conflict within and between states, it is not a method of changing global governance that many people would choose. Such a scenario is only attractive to those who have nothing to gain from the existing system. Financial collapse may come about by mistake, but not as a strategy for reform. It is unlikely to improve global governance or relations.

In the absence of change on a grand and destructive scale, we must look to particular actors to foster innovations that might gradually guide the globalization process in a more positive direction. The three most important actors are states, corporations and civic associations. We'll examine each in turn.

States. The state retains a pivotal role in creating and maintaining governance in the global system because of the centrality of the connection between law and political authority. The state is the central legal actor and primary representative of individuals in the international system. Agreements binding the population of a country can only be made by a state. While its representative function is often imperfect, the state is the only institution that can make a legitimate claim to represent all of the people within its territory. Attempts to reform global governance must work through the state system.

Not all states are equally important for transforming global governance. The most developed and wealthy states are the most significant because they can veto changes or coerce other states to follow particular sets of policies. Thus, the United States is a central actor because of its wealth and power. Changes in US domestic politics can have a significant influence on the process of global governance. For example, the election of a Republican to the US presidency in 2000 made international agreement to slow climate change much more difficult. President George W. Bush has much closer ties to the oil industry than his Democratic predecessor. Many suggestions for slowing global warming threaten the profits of US oil companies and are not welcomed by the Republican president. Since the United States is the world's largest producer of the pollutants which contribute to global warming, a treaty without US participation will not be very effective. In a similar way, on different issues, the position of the European Union and its member states is crucial to securing or blocking changes in global regulation.

The George W. Bush presidency has posed a decisive question for global governance as to whether the US would continue to work through international organizations and treaties to build a negotiated system of rule (multilateralism) or whether it would increasingly exercise domination over other states by striking out on its own (unilateralism). Under Bush, the US has increasingly parted company with other states' policies and asserted its power to act unilaterally. Prominent examples include: the decision not to participate in a treaty banning the use of landmines; refusing to adhere to the Kyoto Protocol on climate change; withholding support for an International Criminal Court; taking military action to overthrow the Iraqi government without the authorization of the UN. If the US continues along such a path, the label 'Empire' may be more accurate than global governance to describe the system of rule in the global political economy.

Other states in the system are important for different reasons. China's views carry some weight because it represents a quarter of the world's population. In military terms it is a force to be considered because of its large army and nuclear weapons. In economic terms, the Chinese state controls access to what is potentially the largest market when it reaches a sufficient stage of development. Thus, corporations and states tread more lightly when they deal with China than with small, less powerful states. It is much easier to exert pressure on a small country such as Nicaragua to respect universal human rights than on China.

Another example of a developing state whose views can carry some weight is South Africa. The South African state has a great deal of legitimacy to speak on behalf of oppressed people in Africa and the developing world because of its struggle to overthrow apartheid. In addition, because South Africa is a democratic state, its views carry more weight in global discussions than the views of a similar-sized authoritarian state. An interesting example of the role that the South African state is playing in challenging the existing form of global governance is its campaign to challenge the patent protection afforded to multinational drug companies that produce anti-AIDS drugs. The South Africans are trying to make a moral argument for violating patent protection that is enshrined in the WTO.

Despite the importance of the state to global governance, some groups have moved away from concentrating all of their effort on influencing state power. The major explanation for this is that the ability of the state to offer protection from the harmful aspects of globalization seems to have been reduced. The populations of the weakest states in the developing world have been at the mercy of Western states and large corporations for many years. Recently, however, it appears that even advanced industrialized states seem less able to protect their citizens from increasing global competition. This has been described by one observer as the state shifting its role from providing welfare for its citizens to preparing the population for increased competition (Cerny, 2000). The state does not shrink or disappear, but changes its role. The process of globalization is seen to have made it more difficult to support the traditional welfare state which cushioned the effects of competition (Mishra, 1999).

The view that the state is losing power has been widely challenged. Some have suggested that globalization is exaggerated, by arguing that the degree of internationalization as measured by percentages of trade and investment flows has precedents in the early 1900s (Hirst and Thompson, 1996). Citing the persistent differences between North American, European and Asian models of capitalism, students of comparative politics dispute that there has been a movement to policy convergence (Garrett, 2000). These scholars deny that the state is weaker or is unable to protect its citizens. They suggest that if political forces advocating social protection gather the political will and organize themselves properly, the government can be pointed in the direction of social protection. From this perspective globalization has very little to do with increasing inequality or decreasing social protection.

Controversies about the relative importance of state–corporate power continue to rage, but some trends appear undeniable. First, most states around the world, in stark contrast to the 1970s, actively seek multinational investment. Secondly, in contrast to earlier decades states seem more intent upon furnishing those companies with an attractive environment than with regulating their activity. Some have referred to states engaging in 'beauty contests' in an effort to attract foreign investment (Palan and Abbott, 2000). Of course, the balance of power between any particular state and any particular firm will vary depending upon their position in the global economy.

Corporate actors. Although a global governance system which privileges the market as an allocator of resources brings benefits to particular states and people, it is often seen to be driven by corporate strategy. Transnational corporations are seen as an increasingly influential factor in formulating the polices that are instituted at a global level and as an actor influencing the decision of state elites.

In the early 1990s, some observers argued that the growing power of transnational corporations in relation to the state necessitated a revision of international relations and international business theory. Drawing upon a study of investment relations in Brazil, Malaysia and Kenya, Stopford and Strange (1991) argued that state–firm and even firm–firm bargaining was becoming more important to the international system. States are increasingly interested in attracting foreign investment and firms are increasingly capable of influencing governmental investment policy. Thus, a key feature of how rules are created and enforced in the global economy is the negotiation conducted between states and firms.

A good example of how corporations can influence global governance is provided by the insertion of intellectual property rights (IPRs) into the WTO. IPRs include things such as copyright protection for books and music, as well as patent protection for inventions and scientific discoveries. They do not really fall under the umbrella of free trade because their enforcement does not increase the flow of goods between states. However, in the 1980s many Western corporations in industries such as pharmaceuticals, computer software, movies and music became concerned that competitors were copying their products. An association of leading US transnational corporations such as Du Pont, General Electric, IBM, and Monsanto convinced the US government that IPRs should be protected in trade agreements. Eventually the corporations were able to have rules that they largely drafted inserted into the WTO (Sell, 1999). These are some of the rules that the government of South Africa is battling against in an attempt to provide affordable drugs to combat the large numbers of deaths from AIDS in southern Africa.

In addition to the trend of increasing corporate influence over state policy makers one can also point to the rise of private authority. Private authority exists where firms exercise decision-making power over a particular issue area and this activity is viewed as legitimate. Cutler *et al.*, (1999) have identified six mechanisms for the exercise of private authority: industry norms; coordination service firms (for example, bond rating); production alliances; cartels; business associations; and private regimes. They argue that private firms are increasingly exercising authority in particular issue areas in the global economy. Studies of the telecommunications industry, insurance business, accountancy and cartels support the notion of private authority (Strange, 1996).

It is important to note that recognizing the role and significance of corporate activity does not imply that state power is unimportant or that all corporations behave the same way. One can acknowledge the role of corporate activity in global governance while at the same time agreeing with authors (Doremus *et al.*, 1998) who argue that there are differences in behaviour between corporations from different states and that states often support the behaviour of corporations headquartered in their territory. Corporations have an interest in influencing the terms of global governance even if their particular interests are not identical.

In their pursuit of profits corporations will attempt to influence the structures of global governance. Not all corporations will have the same immediate goals, nor follow the same tactics. Indeed, business conflict theory (Skidmore-Hess, 1996) advises us to expect clashes of interest between corporations in international as well as domestic realms. Corporations from particular states or sectors may demonstrate distinctive characteristics. Firms that are internationally competitive will have different preferences from those that are not internationally competitive. Despite or because of these differences corporations will attempt to shape governance structures by influencing state, international organization, corporate and civil society behaviour. The role of the corporation in international relations has grown to such an extent that attempts to understand or influence global governance must take the role of corporations into account.

Civic Associations. In addition to key states and resource rich corporations, voluntary citizen organizations are playing an increasing role in influencing the principles of global governance. Indeed, in the 1980s and 1990s, prominent civic actors played the role of unofficial opposition to global governance agencies and interstate agreements. They stressed an agenda that puts citizen autonomy and security at the centre of governance questions. Peace groups have opposed particular weapons systems and military strategies. The campaign to ban the production and use of landmines is the most recent example. Development, women's, environmental and labour groups have opposed the dominance of liberal policies emanating from international economic institutions. Citizen action across state borders to overcome the anti-democratic actions of their own states has been described as 'democratic internationalism' (Gilbert, 1999).

The global civil society sphere is the space where civic actors meet to engage in debate and political activity in an effort to shape the direction of global and national society (Scholte, 2000b). It is primarily composed of voluntary, non-profit associations. To differentiate them from profit-seeking non-governmental organizations such as corporations this chapter uses the term 'civic associations.' The most visible organizations tend to be those working in high-profile areas such as Greenpeace and Friends of the Earth in the environmental field or Amnesty International in the human rights area. However, there are many other forms of organization. For example, international trade-union bodies such as the International Confederation of Free Trade Unions claim a representative (127 million members) as well as advocacy role. Religious organizations are also very active. In terms of numbers of formal organizations, the bulk of activity takes place in relatively uncontroversial forms such as industry associations and scientific knowledge organizations (medicine, sciences, communications) (Boli and Thomas, 1999, p. 41). Aggregating visible NGOs with less visible local activity, one can point to the emergence of fluid social movements around issues such as human rights, peace and women's issues.

The global civil society arena is occupied by several actors which do not share the characteristics of being non-profit voluntary equity-seeking civic associations. One prominent group is composed of business associations. These associations seek to create an environment where corporations can maximize profits. A prominent example is the International Chamber of Commerce. In addition to lobbying state and civil society actors, it attempts to foster an environment which encourages self regulation (Schneider, 2000).

Although it goes against the grain of our understanding of domestic civil society, there are civic associations that lack civility. Civility, or the agreement to manage interaction according to a common set of rules and without recourse to violence, is a hallmark of domestic notions of civil society. Those who choose not to be bound by such rules are considered to be outside the bounds of civil society. An example would be criminal organization such as the Mafia. In the global system there is less agreement about common rules and much less enforcement than in most national societies. As a result, there is a greater space for uncivil groups to operate alongside peaceful civic associations. Examples include organized crime, violent ethnic nationalists and terror organizations. They are shunned by the majority of civic associations, but they exist in a similar space.

While there are many different groups with specific agendas, most politically active groups would describe themselves as pursuing the objectives of equity or social justice. Equity and justice could be sought in respect to gender relations (women's groups), distribution of resources (development groups) quality of life (environmental groups), human security (human rights). There are, of course, differences between members of civil society, just as there are conflicts between states or corporations. Organized labour is challenged by NGOs claiming to speak on behalf of the informal sector.

Women's groups in the developing world have an ambivalent and some-times conflictual relationship with Northern feminist groups. Environ-mentalists seeking radical changes to the doctrine of economic growth are in conflict with more conservative conservationist groups. Various NGOs claim to speak on behalf of social movements or constituencies, but the plethora of groups and lack of transparency makes it difficult to determine the legitimacy of their claims.

Although the precise nature of global civil society is debatable, it is less contentious that transnational civic actors are having an influence on world politics and interstate relations. Scholarly attention has tended to focus upon human rights, environmental and women's groups attempts to influence norms and values in the global system (Keck and Sikkink, 1998). International NGOs seeking social transformation operate on a number of levels to influence global governance – they create and activate global net-works, participate in multilateral arenas, facilitate interstate cooperation, act within states to influence policy and enhance public participation (Alger, 1997). Even in areas often considered to be the sole domain of states such as international security, civil society groups can play a role in shaping the agenda and contributing to policy change (Price, 1998).

At the minimum we can say that civic actors increasingly serve a role as disseminators of information, mobilizers of public opinion, articulators of dissent and protest. Ignoring their role, as the architects of the Multilateral Agreement on Investment did (Mayne and Picciotto, 1999), is likely to lead to governance breakdown. Civic associations can be instrumental in undermining the legitimacy of international organizations, even as states continue to support them.

The Global Compact

If global governance is to push ahead, one would imagine some form of accommodation is required between the three different types of key actors (state, corporate and civic). For example, a trade regime would have to simultaneously be sensitive to the interests of developing states for increased equity, corporate interests for expansion and profit, and social interests for restricting human and environmental exploitation. This is an enormously complicated task. An example of such an approach is the Global Compact developed by the Secretary-General's office of the United Nations.

The Global Compact asks corporations to incorporate nine principles drawn from the Universal Declaration of Human Rights, the ILO's Fundamental Principles on Rights at Work and the Rio Principles on Environment and Development into their corporate practices. The Compact does not monitor corporate practice nor does it assess corporate performance. It is designed to identify and disseminate good practices. The Global Compact asks leaders of some of the world's most prominent corporations to publicly commit themselves to good labour and environmental practices.

The Global Compact simultaneously addresses the concerns of some corporate, state and civic associations. From a developing country point of view, the initiative is tolerable because it is aimed at influencing the policy of multinational corporations rather than restricting state policy or punishing developing states for poor labour conditions. This is preferable to the WTO enforcing of standards because it removes the threat of Northern protectionism. From the corporate viewpoint, it is tolerable because regulations are voluntary and allow continued expansion of the global economy and accumulation of profits. They can claim to be good corporate citizens without being bound by compulsory regulation. For some civic actors, it represents a limited advance in enshrining some principles of social protection. It is a small step that might lead to more binding forms of regulation.

To be sure, the social compact has severe shortcomings. Many of the companies participating in the venture are those which have been attacked as abusers of environmental and human rights or accused of engaging in super exploitation of workers. The list includes Shell, Nike, Disney and Rio Tinto. Each of these companies has been or is subject to boycotts or anti-corporate campaigns by civic associations. One can question the degree to which such companies will actually change their stripes. Domestically, reliance only upon voluntary regulation of corporate behaviour is unacceptable. Why would such activity at the global level prove any more satisfying? The ILO has hundreds of conventions but sees many abused because of a lack of enforcement powers. How would this initiative be any different? Another problem is that the selection of participating civic associations in the Compact was very narrow and not reflective of the wider community. The UN selected civic groups based on their judgement of who would be the most likely to cooperate. Reaction from many other groups has been very critical. The initiative has been condemned because it threatens the integrity of the UN, as corporations attempt to 'bluewash' their record by association with the UN (TRAC, 2000).

This example of the Global Compact is informative for our efforts to understand global governance reform for three reasons. Firstly, it illustrates that the concerns of civic actors about the damaging aspects of globalization are being taken seriously by other actors in the system. The United Nations is responding to public unease about the costs of globalization. This initiative follows public demonstrations against institutions such as the WTO and the IMF. The UN Secretary-General is trying to put a more humane face on globalization so that the process will continue, but in a less brutal manner. The goal is to restrain competition that is based upon the abuse of labour and environmental standards so that the public will not fight the liberal rules under which globalization is taking place. Corporations are also being forced to respond to civic pressure by setting up codes of conduct and projecting the image of moral behaviour.

Secondly, it highlights the failure of existing global governance arrangements. We already have an institution that is designed to bolster labour standards – the ILO. However, the ineffectiveness of the ILO has forced labour activists to turn to the enforcement mechanisms found in the WTO to support labour standards. Many developing states oppose dealing with labour standards because they fear that developed states might increase their protectionism through the device of labour standards. Those groups in civil society trying to improve labour standards find themselves blocked at the WTO and faced with a weak ILO. Existing global governance mechanisms seem unable to improve social standards. Thus, new initiatives such as the Global Compact are being devised in an urgent attempt to resolve difficult dilemmas.

Finally, the Global Compact illustrates just how difficult it is to create new governance arrangements. The cost of freer markets is creating more public resistance, but many states and corporations resist instruments that would require better labour, environmental or social standards. Agreements which secure widespread corporate and state support are unlikely to satisfy the social interests which are pressing for protection. At the moment social interests may have to accept incremental steps towards reforming institutions and polices on the global level.

The point here is not to argue the merits or demerits of the Global Compact. It is to illustrate a recent response to the difficult problem of regulating the economic aspects of globalization. The Compact may be an inadequate response, but it is a leading example of state – corporate – civic association action that may increasingly guide the global political economy.

21st century challenges

Inhabitants of the global political economy face numerous challenges in the twenty-first century. In this section we outline three pressing issues: economic development and growth, equality and justice, democracy and regulation.

Development and growth

World leaders have pledged to eradicate global poverty by 2015. The Millennium Declaration (UN, 2000) states that 'we will spare no effort to free our fellow men, women and children from the abject and dehumanising conditions of extreme poverty'. Such an achievement would be truly staggering but no one seriously believes that this objective will be fulfilled. Nevertheless, the fate of most of humanity remains desperate in a world of plenty. At the dawn of the twenty-first century modern economic growth has still not been dispersed to the majority of the world's six billion inhabitants. The challenge of economic development became an international issue in the years immediately following the Second World War and was driven by the leaders of newly independent states. In order to maintain their hold on power political elites were obliged to respond to what in the 1960s was frequently referred to as the revolution of rising expectations. Some 40 years after the UN proclaimed the First Development Decade prospects remain bleak. One of the major challenges for the early years of the twenty-first century is therefore to meet the development needs of peoples living in Third World countries. What exactly does this entail at the current historical conjuncture? And what conditions are currently considered necessary to bring this change about?

In Chapter 9 we examined the changing meaning of the concept of development, and showed how the focus has shifted from a concentration on economic growth to a consideration of social factors. In the absence of an agreed definition of development, we can nevertheless suggest certain key features of the concept as it is currently understood. An improvement in material capabilities remains central to most conceptions of development. At the heart of national and international development efforts is the objective of raising material living standards. In effective terms this translates into the provision of basic necessities such as adequate foodstuffs, clean water, electricity, shelter, improved transportation, and better sanitation. It will in time lead to the consumption of a wider range of products but in essence development consists in satisfying basic needs. Of course, clean water, electricity and so on is meaningless outside the context of human beings. Directly linked to the provision of these needs are another set of equally basic services without which people will be unable to fulfil their life chances. These include education and health care. But development has increasingly come to mean the attainment of non-material values. In this respect we need to think about the ability of people to make their own decisions and to have greater control over their own lives. Amartya Sen (1981), the Indian Nobel laureate developed his theory of entitlements to show that famine arose not because of the absence of food but in circumstances where those starving lacked the bundle of resources that enabled them to have access to food. Development clearly entails increased participation and the empowerment of marginalized groups.

Early efforts at promoting development were gender-blind but we are aware that one of the main challenges of development in the twenty-first century will be to ensure that women are fully integrated into national development strategies. For a number of reasons this remains a daunting task. The problems facing women in developing countries remain the subject of analysis and policy prescriptions (Datta and Kornberg, 2002). In the light of the experience of women in the advanced industrial countries the mainstreaming of gender will not in itself lead to equality. Although women in Western developed societies have achieved legal equality they continue to experience many forms of discrimination and structural exclusion. In terms of formal equality women in the West have made the most significant gains but the concept of the glass ceiling is well understood, and is an actuality for many women. The glass ceiling refers to the existence of an invisible barrier that limits women from attaining the highest positions in many sectors and firms. Thus the battle to produce development policies that will support women's livelihoods in the developing world remains a daunting task.

How are the mechanisms of global governance responding to the challenge of economic development? As will have been apparent from previous chapters, the answer to this question depends on the perspective of the observer. We have rehearsed many of these arguments already and so we will not repeat them here. There are a number of identifiable problems of governance which the various perspectives will have to address and it is to these that we now turn. The first problem we will discuss is that of coordination of various initiatives. There are a number of agencies – national, regional and international – attempting to promote development but no means of co-ordinating the various activities exists at present. Indeed, governmental, intergovernmental and non-governmental actors can pursue diverse and conflicting objectives within a single country or region. Moreover, no system of allocation exists to ensure that resources are delivered where they are most needed, and duplication of effort is avoided. A second problem also relates to the overall framework in which economic development is promoted. In Chapter 8 we discussed the global financial system and raised problems of regulation. We have seen a number of financial crises, most notably in Mexico, East Asia and Argentina that have reversed decades of progress. In the absence of reform of the international financial architecture hard won gains will most likely be lost within a matter of days. Governance has been identified as a crucial issue in the promotion of development and it is now widely accepted that in the absence of effective governance mechanisms there will be limited achievement of development goals. However, at the moment there is an absence of consensus concerning how good governance is to be pursued. Lectures from developed countries on good governance ring hollow when political motives still play such a large part in the foreign aid policies of leading donor nations.

Equality and justice

Current discussions may lead one to conclude that global inequality is unique to globalization which it is claimed is wreaking havoc on the development prospects of Third World countries, and creating an underclass in advanced industrial societies. As we have seen in this book the global economy and international economic exchange has always created winners and losers. To point to the historical existence of a phenomenon is not, however, to claim that it is unimportant. It makes us aware that these issues have been of concern to people for a very long time. At the beginning of the twenty-first century the search for equality and justice is as pressing as ever. The Human Development Report noted 'a breathtaking globalization of prosperity side by side with a depressing globalization of poverty' (UNDP, 1994, p. 1), and it is the existence of such glaring disparities that drives part of the agenda for greater social equity.

Governments around the world and international institutions will have to give greater attention to social justice issues in the coming decades. To some extent, the dominance of neo-liberal ideology masked issues of equity and justice in its naive faith in market solutions. At the end of the twentieth century these issues began to be taken more seriously and there was evidence of a move away from the Washington Consensus. The search for equality and justice is being driven by the impact of changes in the global economy and the reaction of various groups to these developments. The process of globalization is leading to increasing inequality within and between nations. In other words, the challenge of inequality is not to be seen simply in terms of differences between states but also in terms of internal inequality. Caroline Thomas reminds us that, 'two-thirds of the global population seem to have gained little or nothing from the economic growth that has occurred as a result of globalization to date' (2000, p. 11). Globalization is affecting income inequality within countries and it has the potential to adversely affect the standards of living of workers in developed countries (Kitching, 2001, p. 266).

If left unchecked this will give rise to greater tensions and instability within and between nations. One example of the response to increasing inequality within many advanced industrial societies has been the rise of ethno-nationalist parties blaming foreigners for loss of employment, and a range of social ills. As governments have cut back on public spending, reduced social safety nets, and increased privatization, the poor and disadvantaged in industrial countries have become even more marginalized. Centre-left and centre-right governments have increasingly lost the ability to appeal to large segments of those left behind by economic and technological change. The result has been an increase in support of right-wing, populist parties. Of course, while this phenomenon is occurring in a number of countries, there is nothing automatic about these developments and the success of these parties also depends on domestic circumstances. Moreover, the timing of increased support reflects developments in local politics.

The link between domestic politics, global processes and the search for international solutions is illustrated in the crisis over asylum seekers which has erupted in Western Europe and Australia in 2000–2002. One direct and visible effect of rising inequality between states is reflected in current debates on asylum seekers, and the debate is also a reflection of rising levels of inequality in affluent societies. Among the refugee flows are so-called economic migrants seeking a better life are responding to the lack of opportunity in their home countries. The existence of glaring disparities between rich and poor nations will continue to fuel a trade in people-smuggling and illegal migration. The uncharitable reception of asylum seekers also reflects the attitude of those who feel that they are currently losers in the process of globalization. They resent what they see as scarce resources being spent on foreigners. The solution to this problem does not lie in individual initiatives by single governments but requires international cooperation.

While it is important to remember that shifting patterns of equality are not to be seen in simple North–South terms, the impact of change in the global political economy is experienced differently within the South. While globalization has the potential to create significant benefits for developing countries, these countries will only gain if they institute effective management systems at the domestic level and attain support from international agencies. Unless states find ways to cope with the adjustment and social costs attendant on further integration into the global economy they will be unable to reap the benefits of globalization (Cook and Kirkpatrick, 1994, p. 64). We can see evidence of major variations among regions in the developing world: while Africa seems to be falling further behind, the countries of South-east Asia appear to have benefited from their incorporation in the global economy. This is obviously not a straightforward process as the Asian financial crisis demonstrated, but the economies in Asia hardest hit by the crisis are now returning to higher growth rates.

By influencing the location and distribution of wealth and productive power in the world economy, globalization defines and reshapes global patterns of hierarchy and inequality. The challenge for global governance in the twenty-first century is to devise structures so that persistent inequality and widening income disparities do not lead to a more unstable and unruly world. The extent to which national and global leaders currently have the understanding and political will to respond creatively to these challenges remains open to doubt. One set of actors within the global political economy has prioritized issues of equality and justice. Many national and transnational civic associations are actively involved in seeking to promote a social justice agenda. We will illustrate this movement by reference to one campaign.

As noted in Chapter 8 the debt crisis has had a profound impact on the developing world. Efforts to reduce Third World debt provide an example of the struggle currently being waged to address social justice in the context of the global economy. One of the key actors in this struggle is a civic organization known as Jubilee 2000. Members of the Jubilee 2000 coalition base their strategy on the belief that total debt remission is both economically feasible and ethically defensible. As two of their proponents ask, 'How many more deaths are needed before [debt] unsustainability is recognized and treated?' (Dent and Peters, 1998, p. 15). The aim of Jubilee 2000 is to inject justice into an economic system given over to profit and stability. The coalition has used a diverse range of tactics to grab the attention of world leaders. These range from normal lobbying tactics to mass actions designed to hit the international headlines. For example, Jubilee 2000 activists have engaged in street protests at G7 summits, including forming a human chain around the meeting site of the 1997 G7 Denver summit (Michael, 2001, p. 11). The campaign has not succeeded in its aim of total debt cancellation but the Heavily Indebted Poor Countries Initiative (HIPC) was one response by creditor governments to calls for debt cancellation. Subsequent G7 decisions on debt such as the decision at the Cologne summit in 1999 to cancel $27 billion reflect the influence of the coalition. Jubilee 2000 is part of a larger movement of citizens seeking the promotion of global security, democracy and justice.

Another component of this search for justice in the global economy is the Fair Trade movement. Advocates of fair trade argue that the current trading order is fundamentally biased against the developing world and seek to initiate a more just trading order. This position usually takes two forms. One central concern relates to the prices paid to producers in the developing world, and the campaign is for more equitable prices. In this scenario the market confines poor countries to export goods whose prices are vulnerable to fluctuations and also historically low. The other issue of concern relates to labour standards. In this view international trade is unfair because the internationalization of production leads to the exploitation of workers in the developing world (Sengenberger and Wilkinson, 1995, p. 112). Trade is an important part of this process since production is largely for export.

Democracy and regulation

The increasing globalization of the world economy has been accompanied by increasing global regulation. For example, since the early 1990s international institutions such as the IMF, World Bank and WTO have taken on a more prominent role in governing the global economy. Rules and norms are needed to guide state, corporate and citizen activity in this environment. However, new forms of regulation raise difficult issues about democratic control over the regulators and the process of creating rules and norms. The impression that existing regulatory structures serve the needs of the rich and powerful has led to considerable public unease about global governance.

A good example of this unease can be found in the area of financial regulation. Following the East Asian financial crises, a wide range of actors called for a new form of financial architecture that would safeguard the public interest. During financial crisis the regulations governing capital mobility and debt seemed to privilege the owners of capital and punish poor people in developing countries. During 2002 a series of financial scandals at a number of large US companies such as Enron raised serious questions about the degree to which accounting regulations and stock market practices hurt the public interest because they facilitated corporate theft and plunder. Public unease over the direction of the global economy was heightened by these regulation failures.

In April 2000 Joseph Stiglitz, a former chief economist and Senior Vice-President of the World Bank wrote, 'Next week's meeting of the International Monetary Fund will bring to Washington D.C., many of the same demonstrators who thrashed the World Trade Organization in Seattle last fall. They'll say the IMF is arrogant. They'll say the IMF doesn't really listen to the developing countries it is supposed to help. They'll say the IMF is secretive and insulated from democratic accountability. They'll say the IMF's economic 'remedies' often make things worse – turning slowdowns into recessions and recessions into depressions' (2000). Stiglitz concedes that the demonstrators do have a point – an opinion in sharp contrast with the views of most mainstream commentators. Stiglitz's comments go to the heart of a current challenge to institutions of global governance. A critical issue that we have touched on at various times in this book is the subject of the legitimacy of institutions of global governance, and this issue will remain important in the early part of the twenty-first century. There is currently official and popular dissatisfaction with many institutions of global governance and one of the challenges ahead will be to find ways to ensure that these institutions meet current tests of democratic control.

Few theorists or practitioners would disagree with the claim of a former UN Secretary-General that 'Respect for democratic principles at all levels of social existence is crucial in communities, within states, and within the international community'. (Boutros Ghali, 1995, p. 2) While consensus exists concerning the spread of democracy none is forthcoming concerning the reasons for the upsurge of interest in global democracy. The final two decades of the twentieth century witnessed a sharp increase in the number of democratic states giving rise to what has been termed the 'third wave' of democratization (Huntington, 1991). As a result of democratization processes in Asia, Africa, Latin America and Europe, democracy has become an unquestioned global norm. There has been a burgeoning literature on the causes of democratization, the theory and practice of democracy, and the global order and democracy. But democracy remains an aspiration for many of the world's peoples, a goal proclaimed by almost all politicians wherever they reside, and a crucial political value in the twenty-first century. It is difficult envisaging a serious political party or politician that did not claim attachment to the values embodied within democratic constitutions. The reality may well fall far short of the ideal and it may be that the date for a transition to democracy is postponed into the future but across the globe democracy has triumphed as the preferred form of government. Democracy thus stands as a crucial test of the legitimacy of political arrangements in the contemporary world. In other words, institutions lacking in democratic features are held to be illegitimate, and by extension unjust. The ramifications of the triumph of democracy are evident in subnational, national and international politics. There has been a diffusion of democratic norms – at the core of recent protests against the international economic institutions the central issue is one of democratic governance.

The changing global economic order poses fundamental questions for the exercise of global democratic governance. Three disjunctures in the global system challenge the image presented above. A key aspect of globalization has been the creation of new non-state centres of authority. One feature of this is what can be termed the privatization of regulation (Sinclair, 1994; Cutler, 1995). Policy decisions taken by, for example, financial institutions can have profound effects on the policies of governments and intergovernmental organizations. Secondly, there are limitations on state sovereignty in the sense that the authority and power of national authorities is undermined by the creation of regional and global organizations. In other words, international organizations are not to be conceived as solely the instruments of states. Another centre of authority is to be found in the increased influence of international organizations. Through the expanded mandate of organizations like the European Union, and the WTO their member governments and their citizens are increasingly subject to new forms of regulation over which there is little direct control. Finally, the development of international economic law is creating a system in which political authority is migrating to regional and global centres without a proper system of checks and balances.

One response to these developments is to claim that these international economic organizations (IEOs) remain firmly intergovernmental, and therefore are democratic because they are accountable to their member states. It can be argued that this claim fails to recognize shifting authority patterns and structures in a changing world order. For example, both through the impact on state preferences and directly on the bureaucracy of such organizations, non-state actors influence the agendas and functioning of global institutions. Any assessment of the role of international economic institutions must therefore begin from a recognition of the transformation in multilateralism (O'Brien *et al.*, 2000). No longer can multilateralism be conceived solely in state-centric terms, that is states are no longer the only salient actors in the construction of multilateral regimes. IEOs in this perspective are assessed not solely on their ability to fulfil the needs of states but rather on whether they meet the aspirations of social movement actors as well as states. It is within this context of change that the democratic credentials of IEOs have to be assessed. From this perspective representation can be conceived as concern for the interests of stakeholders. Institutions of global governance will fail to meet the test of democratic control in the absence of transparent procedures, access for non-governmental groups, and mechanisms through which policy can be explained and justified to the range of stakeholders.

Some political theorists (Held, 1995) have attempted to project national democratic institutions onto the international stage to remedy the problem of democratic deficits in a globalizing era. Attempts to have international parliaments seem premature given the decentralization of the international system. An alternative approach has been developed by Coleman and Porter (2000) who have suggested the application of six criteria to judging the degree of democracy surrounding a particular institution or regime. The criteria are: transparency, openness to direct participation, quality of discourse, representation, effectiveness and fairness. They argue that international governance arrangements can be modified to improve performance on these measures without rebuilding domestic institutions such as legislatures at the international level. For example, transparency can be increased by providing clear and timely information about an institution's operations. Participation in the policy process can be increased by greater consultation with a wide range of interests. The quality of discourse can be improved by launching education campaigns and fostering debate around key issues. Representation concerns can be mitigated by creating institutional linkages with concerned parties. Effectiveness may be increased by streamlining decision-making processes and developing institutional autonomy. Fairness would be bolstered by procedures deemed to be legitimate and policy outcomes that were sensitive to the distribution of costs and benefits.

Conclusion

This chapter focused attention on one of the themes running through the book, namely the issue of governance. In the first section of the book we examined governance structures (or the lack of them) in various historical periods. In the second part of the book, examining key frameworks in the contemporary global political economy, we noted the importance of governance institutions for the functioning of the global economy. In this chapter we outlined how governance is accomplished in the contemporary global political economy, and have discussed the actors involved in this process. The second section of this chapter provided a brief introduction to three key challenges to institutions of governance. We have not suggested solutions to these challenges but have raised some of the difficulties in addressing these issues.

As globalization intensifies, the fate of peoples around the world is increasingly interconnected. Despite rapid advances in technology and production the world faces daunting challenges of inequality, environmental degradation and democratic governance. Attention to, and action in, the global political economy is needed now more than ever.

References

Abernethy, D.B. (2000) *The Dynamics of Global Dominance: European Overseas Empires 1415–1980* (New Haven, CT: Yale University Press).

Abu-Lughod, J.L. (1989) *Before European Hegemony: The World System A.D. 1250–1350* (New York: Oxford University Press).

Alger, C.F. (1997) 'Transnational Social Movements, World Politics and Global Governance', in J. Smith, C. Chatfield and R. Pagnucco (eds), *Transnational Social Movements and Global Politics: Solidarity Beyond the State* (Syracuse: Syracuse University Press).

ALU (1995) 'Towards a UN Labour Rights Convention, Conclusions of the National Consultation concerning the social clause in World Trade agreements', *Asian Labour Update*, 20, pp. 11–12, 17.

Amin, S. (1976) *Unequal Development* (New York: Monthly Review Press).

Amin, S. (1997) *Capitalism in the Age of Globalization* (London: Zed Books).

Amsden, A.H. (1989) *Asia's Next Giant: South Korea and Late Industrialization* (New York: Oxford University Press).

Andrews, D.M. (1994) 'Capital Mobility and State Autonomy: Towards a Structural Theory of International Monetary Relations', *International Studies Quarterly*, 38, pp. 93–218.

Ashfar, H. and Berrientos, S. (1999) *Women, Globalization and Fragmentation in the Developing World* (Basingstoke: Palgrave).

Axelrod, R. and Keohane, R. (1986) 'Achieving Cooperation Under Anarchy: Strategies and Institutions', in K. Oye (ed.) *Cooperation Under Anarchy* (Princeton: Princeton University Press).

Bangura, Y. and Beckman, B. (1991) 'African Workers and Structural Adjustment: The Nigerian Case, in D. Ghai (ed.) *The IMF and the South: The Social Impact of Crisis and Adjustment* (London: Zed Books).

Bannock, G. (1971) *The Juggernauts* (London: Weidenfeld and Nicolson).

Banuri, T., M. Mahmood, Khan, S.R., Mehmood, M. and Rafi, K.H. (1997) *Just Development: Beyond Adjustment with a Human Face* (Karachi: Oxford University Press).

Barnett, R.J. and Müller, R.E. (1975) *Global Reach* (London: Jonathan Cape).

Barraclough, G. (1967) *An Introduction to Contemporary History* (New York: Penguin).

Barrett, S. (1993) 'International Cooperation for Environmental Protection, in R. Dorfman and N.S. Dorfman (eds), *Economics of the environment*, 3rd edn, (New York: W.W. Norton).

Bauer, P.T. (1971) *Dissent on Development* (London: Weidenfeld and Nicolson).

Bauer, P.T. (1981) *Equality, the Third World and Economic Delusion* (London: Weidenfeld and Nicholson).

Bauer, P.T. (1984) *Reality and Rhetoric* (London: Weidenfeld and Nicolson).

Beckerman, W. (1995) *Small is Stupid: Blowing the Whistle on the Greens* (London: Duckworth).

Beckford, G. (1972) *Persistent Poverty* (New York: Oxford University Press).

Bello, W. (2000) 'Why Reform of the WTO is NOT the Agenda', World Wide Web <http://http://www.zmarg.org/CrisesCurEvts/Globalism/notreformbello>.

Bennett, A.L. and Oliver, J.K. (2002) *International Organizations: Principles and Issues*, 7th edn, (New Jersey: Prentice Hall).

Bernard, M. (1994) 'Post-Fordism, Transnational Production and the Changing Global Political Economy', in R. Stubbs and G.R.D. Underhill (eds) *Political Economy and the Changing Global Order* (London: Macmillan).

Biersteker, T.J. (1992) 'The Triumph of Neoclassical Economics in the Developing World', in J.N. Rosenau and E.O. Czempiel (eds) *Governance without Government: Order and Change in World Politics* (Cambridge: Cambridge University Press).

Blackhurst, R. and Subramanian, A. (1992) 'Promoting Multilateral Cooperation on the Environment', in K. Anderson and R. Blackhurst (eds) *The Greening of World Trade Issues* (London: Harvester Wheatsheaf).

Block, F.L. (1977) *The Origins of International Economic Disorder* (Berkeley: University of California Press).

Blustein, P. (2001) *The Chastening: Inside the Crisis that Rocked the Global Fnancial System and Humbled the IMF* (New York: Public Affairs).

Boli, J. and Thomas, G.M. (1999) *Constructing World Culture: International Nongovernmental Organizations Since 1875* (Stanford: Stanford University Press).

Boserup, E. (1989) *Woman's Role in Economic Development* (London: Earthscan).

Bouchon, G. and Lombard, D. (1987) 'The Indian Ocean in the Fifteenth Century', in A. Das Gupta and M.N. Pearson (eds) *India and the Indian Ocean 1500–1800* (Calcutta: Oxford University Press).

Bourgignon, F. and Morrison, C. (1992) *Adjustment and Equity in Developing Countries: A New Approach* (Paris: OECD).

Boutros Ghali, B. (1995) *An Agenda For Peace* (New York: United Nations).

Brandt Commission (1983) *Common Crisis: North–South Cooperation for World Poverty* (London: Pan).

Braudel, F. (1979) *The Perspective of the World Civilization and Capitalism 15th–18th Century* vol. 3 (New York: Harper and Row).

Braudel, F. (1994) *A History of Civilizations* (New York: Allen Lane).

Braverman, H. (1974) *Labor and Monopoly Capital: The Degradation of Work in the Twentieth Century* (New York: Monthly Review Press).

Burnell, P. (1993) 'Good Government and Foreign Aid' (University of Warwick, Department of Politics and International Relations Working Paper 115).

Burtless, G., Lawrence, R.Z., Litan, R.E. and Shapiro, R.J. (1998) *Globaphobia: Confronting Fears about Open Trade* (Washington, DC: The Brookings Institution).

Caldwell, L. (1988) 'Beyond Environmental Diplomacy: The Changing Institutional Structure of International Cooperation', in J.E. Carroll (ed.) *International Environmental Diplomacy* (Cambridge: Cambridge University Press).

Carlson, L.J. (2000) 'Game Theory: International Trade, Conflict and

Cooperation', in R. Palan (ed.) *Global Political Economy: Contemporary Theories* (London: Routledge).

Carr, E.H. (1939) *The Twenty Years' Crisis 1919–1939: An Introduction to the Study of International Relations* (London: Macmillan).

Casson, M. (1991) 'Modelling the Multinational Enterprise: A Research Agenda', *Millennium*, 20(2), pp. 271–285.

Castells, M. (1996) *The Rise of the Network Society* (Oxford: Blackwell).

Caves, R.E. (1974) 'The Causes of Direct Investment: Foreign Firms' Share in Canadian and UK Manufacturing Industries', *Review of Economics and Statistics*, 56(3), pp. 279–93.

Cerny, P.G. (1993) 'The Deregulation and Re-regulation of Financial Markets in a More Open World', in P.G. Cerny (ed.) *Finance and World Politics: Markets, Regimes and States in the Post-Hegemonic Era* (Aldershot: Edward Elgar).

Cerny, P.G. (1995) 'Globalization and the Changing Logic of Collective Action', *International Organization*, 49(4), pp. 595–625.

Cerny, P.G. (2000) 'The Competition State', in R. Stubbs and G.R.D. Underhill (eds), *Political Economy and the Changing Global Order*, 2nd edn (Toronto: Oxford University Press).

Chamberlain. M.E. (1985) *Decolonization: The Fall of European Empires* (London: Basil Blackwell).

Chang, G. (2000) *Disposable Domestics: Immigrant Women Workers in the Global Economy* (Boston: South End Press).

Chenery, H.B. and Strout, A.M. (1966) 'Foreign Assistance and Economic Development', *American Economic Review*, 56, pp. 679–733.

Cheru, F. (2002) 'Debt, Adjustment and the Politics of Effective Response to HIV/AIDS in Africa', *Third World Quarterly*, 23(2), pp. 299–312.

CIA (2001) *World Factbook* (Washington: Brassey's).

Clapp, J. (1998) 'The Privatization of Global Governance: ISO 1400 and the Developing World', *Global Governance*, 4(3), pp. 295–316.

Cohen, E.A. (1996) 'A Revolution in Warfare', *Foreign Affairs*, 75(2), pp. 37–54.

Coleman, W. and Porter, T. (2000) 'International Institutions, Globalisation and Democracy: Assessing the Challenges', *Global Society*, 14(3) pp. 377–98.

Coleman, W. and Underhill, G. (eds.) (1998) *Regionalism and Global Economic Integration* (London: Routledge).

Conrad, J. (1902/1999) *The Heart of Darkness* (New York: Penguin).

Cook P. and Kirkpatrick, C. (1994) 'Globalisation, Regionalization and Third World Development', *Regional Studies*, 31(1) pp. 55–66.

Cooper, R.N. (1987) *The International Monetary System: Essays in World Economics* (Cambridge: MIT Press).

Coote, B. (1992) *The Trade Trap* (Oxford: Oxfam).

Cox, R.W. (1977) 'Labor and Hegemony', *International Organization*, 31, pp. 385–424.

Cox, R.W. (1979) 'Ideologies and the NIEO: Reflections on Some Recent Literature', *International Organisation*, (33) pp. 370–95.

Cox, R.W. (1983) 'Gramsci, Hegemony and International Relations: An Essay in Method', *Millennium*, 12(2), pp. 162–75.

Cox, R.W. (1986) 'Social Forces, States and World Order: Beyond International Relations Theory', in R. Keohane (ed.) *Neorealism and its Critics* (New York: Columbia University Press).

Cox, R.W. (1987) *Production, Power, and World Order: Social Forces in the Making of History* (New York: Columbia University Press).

Cox, R.W. (1996a) (with T. Sinclair) *Approaches to World Order* (Cambridge: Cambridge University Press).

Cox, R.W. (1996b) 'Civilisations in World Political Economy' *New Political Economy*, 1(2), pp. 141–56.

Cox, R.W. (2002) (with M. Schechter) *The Political Economy of a Plural World: Critical Reflections on Power, Morals and Civilization* (London: Routldege).

Cox, R.W. and Jacobson, H.K. (1974) *The Anatomy of Influence: Decision Making in International Organization* (New Haven: Yale University Press).

Craig, G.A. and George, A.L. (1983) *Force and Statecraft: Diplomatic Problems of Our Time* (New York: Oxford University Press).

Croce, B. (1941) *History as the Story of Liberty* (London: George Allen and Unwin Limited).

Crosby A.W. (1996) *Ecological Imperialism: The Biological Expansion of Europe, 900–1900* (Cambridge: Cambridge University Press).

Curtain, P.D. (2000) *The World and the West: The European Challenge and the Overseas Response in the Age of Empire* (Cambridge: Cambridge University Press).

Cutler, C. (1995) 'Global Capitalism and Liberal Myths: Dispute Settlement in Private International Trade Relations', *Millennium*, 24(3), pp. 377–97.

Cutler, C., Haufler V. and Porter, T. (eds) (1999) *Private Authority and International Affairs* (Albany: State University of New York Press).

Darwin, J. (1988) *Britain and Decolonisation: The Retreat from Empire in the Post-War World* (Basingstoke: Macmillan).

Datta, R. and Kornberg, J. (2002) *Women in Developing Countries: Assessing Strategies for Empowerment* (Boulder: Lynne Rienner).

David, N. (1996) *Worlds Apart: Women and the Global Economy* (Brussels: International Confederation of Free Trade Unions).

Davies, N. (1982) *The Ancient Kingdoms of Mexico* (London: Allen Lane).

Dean, J.W. and Globerman, S. (eds) (2001) *Dollarization in the Americas?* (Boulder: Westview).

Denemark, R. and O'Brien, R. (1997) 'Contesting the Canon: International Political Economy at UK and US Universities', *Review of International Political Economy*, 4(1), pp. 214–38.

Dent, M. and Peters, B. (1998) 'Poverty and Debt in the Third World: Confronting a Global Crisis', *Conflict Studies*, 310, 1–24.

Dicken, P. (1992) *Global Shift: The Internationalization of Economic Activity*, 2nd edn (London: Paul Chapman Publishing).

Dicken, P. (1998) *Global Shift: Transforming the World Economy* (New York: Guilford Press).

Dickenson T. and Schaeffer, R. (2001) *Fast Forward: Work, Gender and Protest in a Changing World* (Boston: Rowan and Littlefield).

Dickson, A.K. (1997) *Development and International Relations* (Cambridge: Polity).

Dobson, A. (1990) *Green Political Thought* (London: Routledge).

Doremus, P., Keller, W.W., Pauly, L.W. and Reich, S. (1998) *The Myth of the Global Corporation* (Princeton, NJ: Princeton University Press).

Dos Santos, T. (1970/1991) 'The Structure of Dependence', in G.T. Crane and A. Amawi (eds), *The Theoretical Evolution of International Political Economy: A Reader* (Oxford: Oxford University Press).

Dos Santos, T. (1970) 'The Structure of Dependency', *American Economic Review*, 60(21), pp. 231–6.

Doyle, M.W. (1996) *Empires* (Ithaca: Cornell University Press).

Dryzek, J. (1996) 'Foundations for Environmental Political Economy: The Search for *Homo Ecologicus*', *New Political Economy*, 1(1), pp. 27–40.

Dunford, M. (2000) 'Globalisation and Theories of Regulation', in R. Palan (ed.), *Of Global Political Economy: Contemporary Theories* (London: Routledge).

Dunning, J. (1973) 'The Determinants of International Production', *Oxford Economic Papers*, pp. 289–336.

Dunning, J. (1981) *International Production and the Multinational Enterprise* (London: Allen and Unwin).

Dunning, J. (1985) *Multinational Enterprises, Economic Structure and International Competitiveness* (Chichester: John Wiley and Sons).

Dunning, J. (1988) *Explaining International Production* (London: Unwin Hyman).

Dunning, J. (1991) 'Governments and Multinational Enterprises: From Confrontation to Cooperation, *Millennium*, 20(2), pp. 225–39.

Eckersley, R. (1992) *Environmentalism and Political Theory* (London: UCL Press).

Eichengreen, B. (1996) *Globalizing Capital: A History of the International Monetary System* (Princeton, NJ: Princeton University Press).

Ekins, P. (1989) 'Trade and Self-Reliance', *The Ecologist*, 19(5), pp. 186–90.

Ellwood, W. (1998) *The A to Z of World Development* (Oxford: New Internationalist).

Emmanuel, A. (1972) *Unequal Exchange* (London: NLB).

Escobar, A. (1995) *Encountering Development: The Making and Unmaking of the Third World* (Princeton, NJ: Princeton University Press).

Fanon, F. (1963) *The Wretched of the Earth* (New York: Grove Press).

Feldstein, M. (1992) 'The Case Against EMU', *The Economist*, June 13, pp. 19–22.

Finlayson, J.A. and Zacher, M.W. (1981) 'The GATT and the Regulation of Trade Barriers: Regime Dynamics and Functions', *International Organization*, pp. 561–602.

Finnemore, M. and Sikkink, K. (1998) 'International Norm Dynamics and Political Change', *International Organization*, 52(4), pp. 887–917.

Fontana, M., Joekes, S. and Masika, R. (1998) 'Global Trade Expansion and Liberalisation: Gender Issues and Impacts', *BRIDGE Report*, no. 42. (Brighton: Institute of Development Studies).

Frank, A.G. (1967) *Capitalism and Underdevelopment in Latin America* (New York: Monthly Review Press).

Frank, A.G. (1969) *Latin America: Underdevelopment or Revolution* (New York: Monthly Review Press).

Frank, A.G. (1998) *ReOrient: Global Economy in the Asian Age* (Berkeley: University of California Press).

Freedman, L. (1985) *The Evolution of Nuclear Strategy* (London: Macmillan).

Frieden, J. (1981) 'Third World Indebted Industrialization: International Finance and State Capitalism in Mexico, Brazil, Algeria and South Korea', *International Organization*, 35(1), pp. 407–31.

Frieden, J. (1987) *Banking on the World* (New York: Harper and Row).

Frobel, F., Heinrichs, J. and Kreye, O. (1980) *New International Division of Labour* (Cambridge: Cambridge University Press).

Fukuyama, F. (1992) *The End of History and the Last Man* (New York: Free Press).

G20 (2000) News release. Meeting of the G20 Finance Ministers and Central Bank Governors Montreal (October 25).

Galbraith, J.K. (1996) *Money: Whence it Came and Where it Went* (Boston: Houghton Mifflin).

Gamble, A. and Payne, A. (eds.) (1996) *Regionalism and World Order* (Basingstoke: Macmillan).

Garrett, G. (2000) 'Shrinking States? Globalization and National Autonomy', in N. Woods (ed.), *The Political Economy of Globalization* (London: Macmillan).

Germain, R. (1997) *The International Organization of Credit: States and Global Finance in the World-Economy* (Cambridge: Cambridge University Press).

Gerth, H. H. and C.W. Mills (eds.) (1958) *From Max Weber: Essays in Sociology* (New York: Oxford University Press).

Gertzl, C. (1995) 'The New World Order: Implications for Development', *Briefing Paper* No 35, Development Bulletin Canberra.

Gilbert, A. (1999) *Must Global Politics Constrain Democracy? Great Power Realism, Democratic Peace, and Democratic Internationalism* (Princeton: Princeton University Press).

Gill, S. (ed.) (1993) *Gramsci, Historical Materialism and International Relations* (Cambridge: Cambridge University Press).

Gill, S. (2003) 'Globalizing Elites in the Emerging World Order', *Power and Resistance in the New World Order* (New York: Palgrave).

Gill, S. and Law, D. (1988) *The Global Political Economy* (Baltimore: Johns Hopkins University Press).

Gill, S. and Law, D. (1993) 'Global Hegemony and the Structural Power of Capital', in S. Gill (ed.), *Gramsci, Historical Materialism and International Relations* (Cambridge: Cambridge University Press).

Gilpin, R. (1981) *Change and War in World Politics* (Cambridge: Cambridge University Press).

Gilpin, R. (1987) *The Political Economy of International Relations* (Princeton: Princeton University Press).

Goldin I., Knudsen, O. and van der Mensbrugghe, D. (1993) *Trade Liberalisation: Global Economic Implications* (Paris: OECD).

Goldstein, J., Kahler, M., Keohane, R.O. and Slaughter, A. (2000) 'Introduction: Legalization and World Politics', *International Organization*, 54(3), pp. 385–99.

Goodin, R.E. (1992) *Green Political Theory* (Cambridge: Polity Press).

Goodman, J. and Ranald, P. (eds.) (2000) *Stopping the Juggernaut: Public Interest Versus the Multilateral Agreement on Investment* (Annandale: Pluto Press).

Gordender, L. and Weiss, L. (1999) 'Pluralizing Global Governance: Analytical Approaches and Dimensions', in L. Weiss and L. Gordender (eds) *NGO, the UN and Global Governance* (Boulder, CO: Lynne Rienner).

Greenaway, D. and Hine, R.C. (1991) 'Introduction: Trends in World Trade and Protection', in D. Greenaway, R. Hine, A. O'Brien and R. Thornton (eds), *Global Protectionism* (London: Macmillan).

Griffin, K.B. (1970) 'Foreign Capital, Domestic Savings and Economic Development', *Bulletin of the Oxford Institute of Economics and Statistics*, 32(2), pp. 99–112.

Griffin, K.B. and Enos, J.L. (1970) 'Foreign Assistance: Objectives and Consequences', *Economic Development and Cultural Change*, 18(1), pp. 313–27.

Haas, P.M. (1990a) 'Obtaining International Environmental Protection Through Epistemic Consensus', *Millennium*, 19(3), pp. 347–63.

Haas, P.M. (1990b) *Saving the Mediterranean* (New York: Columbia University Press).

Halliday, F. (1983) *The Making of the Second Cold War* (London: Verso

Hamilton, A. (1791/1991) 'Report on manufactures', in G.T. Crane and A. Amawi (eds), *The Theoretical Evolution of International Political Economy: A Reader* (Oxford: Oxford University Press).

Harmes, A. (1998) 'Institutional Investors and the Reproduction of Neoliberalism', *Review of International Political Economy*, 5(1), pp. 92–121.

Harrod, J. and O'Brien, R. (eds.) (2002) *Global Unions? Theory and Strategy of Organised Labour in the Global Political Economy* (London: Routledge).

Hasenclever, A., Mayer, P. and Rittberger, V. (1997) *Theories of International Regimes* (Cambridge: Cambridge University Press).

Hayter, T. (1971) *Aid as Imperialism* (London: Penguin Books).

Heckscher, E. (1919) 'The Effect of Foreign Trade on the Distribution of Income', *Ekonomisk Tidskrift*, 21, pp. 497–512. Reprinted in H.S. Ellis and L.A. Metzler (eds), (1949) *Readings in the theory of international trade* (Homewood: Irwin).

Held, D. (1995) *Democracy and the Global Order: From the Modern State to Cosmopolitan Governance* (Cambridge: Polity Press).

Helleiner, E. (1996) 'International Political Economy and the Greens', *New Political Economy*, 1(1), pp. 59–77.

Henderson, J. (1991) *The Globalization of High Technology Production* (London: Routledge).

Herod, A. (1997) 'Labor as an Agent of Globalization and as a Global Agent', in K. Cox (ed.) *Spaces of Globalization* (New York: Guilford Press).

Hewson, M. and Sinclair, T.J. (eds.) (1999) 'The Emergence of Global Governance Theory', in *Approaches to Global Governance Theory* (New York: SUNY Press).

Higgott, R. (1998) 'The Asian Economic Crisis: A Study in the Politics of Resentment', *New Political Economy*, 4(1), pp. 333–56.

Hines, C. (2000) *Localization: A Global Manifesto* (London: Earthscan).

Hirst, P. and Thompson, G. (1996) *Globalization in Question* (Cambridge: Polity).

Hobsbawm, E.J. (1987) *Industry and Empire: From 1750 to the Present Day* (Harmondsworth: Penguin).

Hobson, J. (1902) *Imperialism: A Study* (London: George Allen and Unwin).

Hochschild, A. (1999) *King Leopold's Ghost: A Story of Greed, Terror and Heroism in Colonial Africa* (New York: First Mariner Books).

Hoogvelt, A. (1997) *Globalisation and the Postcolonial World* (London: Macmillan).

Huck-Ju, K. (2001) 'Globalization, Unemployment and Policy Responses in Korea: Repositioning the State?', *Global Social Policy*, 1(2), pp. 213–34.

Hughes, H. (ed.) (1988) *Achieving Industrialization in Asia* (Cambridge: Cambridge University Press).

Hughes, H. (1989) 'Catching Up: The Asian Newly Industrializing Economies in the 1990s', *Asian Development Review*, 7(2), pp. 128–44.

Hugill, P.J. (1993) *World Trade since 1431: Geography, Technology and Capitalism* (Baltimore: Johns Hopkins University Press).

Huntington, S.P. (1991) *The Third Wave of Democratization in the Late Twentieth Century* (Norman: University of Oklahoma Press).

Huntington, S.P. (1993) 'The Clash of Civilizations?', *Foreign Affairs*, 72(3), pp. 2–49.

Hurrell, A. (1995) 'Explaining the Resurgence of Regionalism in World Politics', *Review of International Studies*, 21(4), pp. 331–58.

Hurrell, A. and Kingsbury, B. (1992) 'The International Politics of the Environment: An Introduction', in A. Hurrell and B. Kingsbury (eds), *The International Politics of the Environment* (Oxford: Clarendon Press).

Hurrell, A. and Woods, N. (1995) 'Globalization and Inequality', *Millennium*, 24(3), pp. 447–70.

Hymer, S. (1976) *The International Operation of National Firms* (Cambridge, MA: MIT Press).

Hymer, S. (1979) *The Multinational Corporation: A Radical Approach* (Cambridge: Cambridge University Press).

ICFTU (1995a) *From the Ashes: A Toy Factory Fire in Thailand* (Brussels: International Confederation of Free Trade Unions).

ICFTU (1995b) 'Rethinking the Role of the IMF and World Bank: ICFTU Proposals to the Annual Meetings of the Board of Governors of the IMF and World Bank', Washington, October 10–12.

ICFTU. (1996a) *Behind the Wire: Anti-union Repression in the Export Processing Zones* (Brussels: International Confederation of Free Trade Unions).

ICFTU. (1996b) *No Time to Play: Child Workers in the Global Economy* (Brussels: International Confederation of Free Trade Unions).

IHT (1998) 'World Bank Targets the Next Asian Danger: Growing Social Unrest', *International Herald Tribune*, February 2, p. 4.

Iliffe, J. (1995) *Africans: The History of a Continent* (Cambridge: Cambridge University Press).

International Commission on Peace and Food (1994) *Uncommon Opportunities: An Agenda for Peace and Equitable Development: Report of the International Commission on Peace and Food* (London: Zed Books).

Jackson, J.H. (1969) *World Trade Law and the GATT: A Legal Analysis of the General Agreement on Tariffs and Trade* (Indianapolis: Bobbs-Merrill).

Julius, D. (1990) *Global Companies and Public Policy: The Growing Challenge of Foreign Direct Investment* (London: RIIA/Pinter).

Kahn, M.S. and Knight, M.D. (1986) 'Fund-Supported Adjustment Programs', *Occasional Paper* no. 42 (Washington, DC: International Monetary Fund).

Kaldor, M. (1997) 'Introduction', *Restructuring the Global Military Sector: New Wars* (London: Pinter).

Kant, I. (1795/1991) 'Perpetual Peace: A Philosophical Sketch', in H. Reis (ed.) *Kant: Political Writings* (Cambridge: Cambridge University Press).

Kaplinsky, R. (1991) 'TNCs in the Third World: Stability or Discontinuity', *Millennium*, 20(2), pp. 257–68.

Kearney N. (1999) 'Corporate Codes of Conduct: the Privatized Application of Labour Standards', in R. Mayne and S. Picciotto (eds), *Regulating International Business – Beyond Liberalization* (Basingstoke: Macmillan/Oxfam).

Keck, M. and Sikkink, K. (1998) *Activists Beyond Borders: Advocacy Networks in International Politics* (Ithaca, NY: Cornell University Press).

Kemp, T. (1983) *Industrialization in the Non-Western World* (London: Longman).

Kennedy, P. (1987) *The Rise and Fall of the Great Powers: Economic Change and Military Conflict from 1500 to 2000* (New York: Random House).

Keohane, R. and Nye, J. (1977) *Power and Interdependence: World Politics in Transition* (Boston: Little, Brown and Company).

Keohane, R.O. (1984) *After Hegemony* (Princeton, NJ: Princeton University Press).

Keohane, R.O. (1989a) 'A Personal Intellectual History', *International Institutions and State Power: Essays in International Relations Theory* (Boulder, CO: Westview Press).

Keohane, R.O. (1989b) *International Institutions and State Power: Essays in International Relations Theory* (Boulder, CO: Westview Press).

Keohane, R.O. (2002) 'Introduction: From Interdependence and Institutions to Globalization and Governance', *Power and Governance in a Partially Globalizing World* (London: Routledge).

Keynes, J.M. (1936) *The General Theory of Employment, Interest and Money* (London: Macmillan).

Khagram, S., Riker, J.V. and Sikkink, K. (eds) (2002) 'From Santiago to Seattle: Transnational Advocacy Groups Restructuring World Politics', in *Restructuring World Politics: Transnational Movements, Networks and Norms* (Minneapolis: University of Minnesota Press).

Kindleberger, C.P. (1969) *American Business Abroad* (New Haven: Yale University Press).

Kindleberger, C.P. (1986) *The World Depression 1929–1939* (Berkeley, CA: University of California Press).

Kindleberger, C.P. (1993) *A Financial History of Western Europe*, 2nd edn (Oxford: Oxford University Press).

Kitching, G. (2001) *Seeking Social Justice Through Globalization* (University Park, PA: Pennsylvania State University Press).

Klein, N. (2001) *No Logo: Taking Aim at the Brand Bullies* (New York: St Martin's Press).

Kock, K. (1969) *International Trade Policy and the GATT, 1947–1967.* (Stockholm: Almqvist and Wiksell).

Kovach, H., Neligan, C. and Burall, S. (2002/2003) *Power Without Accountability?* (London: One World Trust).

Krasner, S.D. (1976) 'State Power and the Structure of International Trade', *World Politics*, 28(3), pp. 317–48.

Krasner, S.D. (ed.) (1983) *International Regimes* (Ithaca, NY: Cornell University Press).

Krugman, P. (1987) 'Is Free Trade Passé?', *Journal of Economic Perspectives,* 1(2), pp. 131–144.

Krugman, P. and Venables, A.J. (1995) 'Globalization and the Inequality of Nations', *Quarterly Journal of Economics*, 110(4), pp. 857–80.

Kuznets, S. (1966) *Modern Economic Growth* (New Haven, CT: Yale University Press).

Laferrière, E. (1994) 'Environmentalism and the Global Divide', *Environmental Politics*, 3(1), pp, 91–113.

Lall, S. and Streeten, P. (1977) *Foreign Investment, Transnationals and Developing Countries* (London: Macmillan).

Lall, S. (1991) 'Multinational Enterprises and Developing Countries: Some Issues for Research in the 1990s', *Millennium*, 20(2), pp. 251–6.

Landes, D.S. (1998) *The Wealth and Poverty of Nations* (New York: Norton).

Lasch, C. (1995) *The Revolt of the Elites and the Betrayal of Democracy* (New York: Norton).

Lenin, V. (1917/1969) *Imperialism, the Highest Stage of Capitalism* (New York: International).

Letuchamanan, R. (2000) 'Testing the Pollution Haven Hypothesis', in P. Könz *et al.* (eds), *Trade, Environment and Sustainable Development: Views from Sub-Saharan Africa and Latin America* (Geneva: ICTSD, Tokyo: UNU/IAS).

Lever, H. and Huhne, C. (1986) 'The Demand for Credit and the Supply of Credit', *Debt and Danger* (Boston: Atlantic Monthly Press).

Levy, D. (1997) 'Environmental Management as Political Sustainability', *Organization and Environment*, 10(2), pp. 126–47.

List, F. (1885/1991) 'Political and Cosmopolitical Economy', in G.T. Crane and A. Amawi (eds), *The Theoretical Evolution of International Political Economy: A Reader* (Oxford: Oxford University Press).

Madeley, J. (1992) *Trade and the Poor* (London: Intermediate Technology Publications).

Maier, C.S. (1977) 'The Politics of Productivity: Foundations of American International Economic Policy after World War II', *International Organization*, 31, pp. 607–33.

Maizels, A. and Nisanke, M.K. (1984) 'Motivations for Aid to Developing Countries', *World Development*, 12(9), pp. 879–900.

Marchand, M. and Runyan, A. (2000) *Gender and Global Restructuring* (London: Routledge).

Marcus, R. (1993) 'Woman Chosen as Attorney General', *Washington Post*, Feburary 12, p. 2.

Marshall, R. (1993) *Storm from the East* (London: BBC Books).

Marx, K. and Engles, F. (1848/1977) 'The Communist Manifesto', in D. McLellan (ed.), *Karl Marx: Selected Writings* (Oxford: Oxford Unviersity Press).

Mayne, R. and Picciotto, S. (eds.) (1999) *Regulating International Business: Beyond Liberalization* (Basingstoke: Macmillan and Oxfam).

McLeod, R.H. and Garnaut, R. (1998) *East Asia in Crisis: From Being a Miracle to Needing One?* (London: Routledge).

McMichael, P. (1996) *Development and Social Change: A Global Perspective.* (Thousand Oaks, CA: Pine Forge Press).

McMichael, P. (1997) 'Rethinking Globalization: The Agrarian Question Revisited', *Review of International Political Economy*, 4(4), pp. 630–62.

McNeill, J., Winsemius, P. and Yakushiji, T. (1991) *Beyond Interdependence: The Meshing of the World's Economy and the Earth's Ecology* (New York: Oxford University Press).

McNeill, W. (1982) *The Pursuit of Power: Technology, Armed Force, and Society Since A.D. 1000* (Chicago: University of Chicago Press).

Meadows, D. and Meadows, D. (1972) *The Limits to Growth* (London: Earth Island Ltd).

Meadows, D., Meadows, D. and Randers, J. (1993) *Beyond the Limits: Global Collapse or a Sustainable Future* (London: Earthscan).

Michael, M. (2001) 'Jubilee 2000: Drop the Debt, Not the Campaign', *Dollars and Sense*, vol. 11, p. 11.

Mihevc, J. (1995) *The Market Tells Them So: The World Bank and Economic Fundamentalism in Africa* (London: Zed Books).

Mill, J.S. (1859/1980) *On Liberty* (Harmondsworth: Penguin).

Milner, H. (1997) *Interests, Institutions and Information: Domestic Politics and International Relations* (Princeton: Princeton University Press).

Mishra, R. (1999) *Globalization and the Welfare State* (Cheltenham: Edward Elgar).

Miskimin, H.A. (1975) *The Economy of Early Renaissance Europe 1300–1460* (Cambridge: Cambridge University Press).

Moody, K. (1997) *Workers in a Lean World: Unions in the International Economy* (London: Verso).

Morris, D. (1989) 'Free Trade: The Great Destroyer', *The Ecologist*, 19(5), pp. 190–5.

Mote, F.W. (1999) *Imperial China: 900–1800* (Cambridge: Harvard University Press).

Mudzafar, J. (2001) 'Transfer of Technology in Marketing', World Wide Web <http://www.sibelink.com.my/g15magazine/>.

Myrdal, G. (1968) *Asian Drama: An Enquiry into the Poverty of Nations* (London: Penguin).

Narayan, D., Patel, R., Schafft, K., Rademacher, A., and Koch-Schulte, S. (2000) *Can anyone Hear Us? Voices of the Poor*, Vol. 1 (New York: Oxford University Press).

Nikiforuk, A. (1996) *The Fourth Horseman: A Short History of Plagues, Scourges and Emerging Viruses* (Toronto: Penguin).

Nordstrom, H. and Vaughan, S. (1999) *Trade and Environment* (Geneva: WTO).

Norris, P (2001) *Digital Divide: Civic Engagement, Information Poverty, and the Internet Worldwide* (New York: Cambridge University Press).

Nye, J.S. and Donahue, J.D. (eds.) (2000) 'Introduction', in *Governance in a Globalizing World* (Washington, DC: Brookings).

O'Brien, R. (1995) 'North American Integration and International Relations Theory', *Canadian Journal of Political Science*, 28(4), pp. 693–724.

O'Brien, R. (1998) 'Shallow Foundations: Labour and the Selective Regulation of Free Trade,' in G. Cook (ed.) *The Economics and Politics of International Trade* (London: Routledge).

O'Brien, R. (2000) 'Labour and IPE: Rediscovering Human Agency', in R. Palan. (ed.) *Global Political Economy: Contemporary Theories* (New York: Routledge).

O'Brien, R. (2002) 'The Varied Paths to Minimum Global Labour Standards', in J. Harrod and R. O'Brien (eds), *Global Unions? Theory and Strategy of Organised Labour in the Global Political Economy* (London: Routledge).

O'Brien, R. (2003) 'Paths to Reforming Global Governance', in R. Sandbrook (ed.) *Civilizing Globalisation* (New York: SUNY Press).

O'Brien, R., Goetz, A.M., Scholte, J.A. and Williams, M. (2000) *Contesting Global Governance: Multilateral Economic Institutions and Global Social Movements* (Cambridge: Cambridge University Press).

O'Grady, R. (1994) *The Rape of the Innocent* (Bangkok: ECPAT).

Ohlin, B. (1933) *Interregional and International Trade* (Cambridge, MA: Harvard University Press).

Ohmae, K. (1990) *The Borderless World* (London: Fontana).

O'Riordan, T. (1976) *Environmentalism* (London: Pion Press).

Pakenham, T. (1991) *The Scramble for Africa 1876–1912* (London: Abacus).

Palan, R. (2000) 'The Constructivist Underpinnings of the New International Political Economy', in R. Palan (ed.) *Global Political Economy: Contemporary Theories* (London: Routledge).

Palan, R. (1998) 'Trying to Have Your Cake and Eating It: How and Why the State System has Created Offshore', *International Studies Quarterly*, 41, pp. 625–44.

Palan, R. (2002) 'Tax Havens and the Commercialization of State Sovereignty', *International Organization*, 56(1), pp. 151–76.

Palan, R. and Abbott, J. (with Phil Deans) (2000) *State Strategies in the Global Political Economy* (London: Pinter).

Parker, G. (1996) *The Military Revolution and the Rise of the West 1500–1800* (Cambridge: Cambridge University Press).

Pauly, L.W. (2000) 'Capital Mobility and the New Global Order', in R. Stubbs and G.R.D. Underhill (eds), *Political Economy and the Changing Global Order*, 2nd edn, (London: Macmillan).

Pauly, L.W. and Reich, S. (1997) 'National Structures and Multinational Corporate Behaviour: Enduring Differences in the Age of Globalization', *International Organization*, 51(1), pp. 1–30.

Pearce, D. (1990) 'Economics and the Global Environmental Challenge', *Millennium*, 19(3), pp. 365–87.

Pearce, D., Markandya, A. and Barbier, E. (1989) *Blueprint for a Green Economy* (London: Earthscan).

Pearson, L.B. (1969) *Partners in Development* (New York: Praeger).

Pearson, R. and Seyfang, G. (2001) 'New Hope or False Dawn? Voluntary Codes of Conduct, Labour Regulation and Social Policy in a Globalizng World', *Global Social Policy*, 1(1), pp. 49–78.

Penrose, E.T. (1968) *The Large International Firm in Developing Countries: The International Petroleum Industry* (Cambridge, MA: MIT Press).

Pepper, D. (1996) *Modern Environmentalism: An Introduction* (London: Routledge).

Persaud, R.B. (2001) 'Racial Assumptions in Global Labor Recruitment and Supply', *Alternatives*, 26(4), pp. 377–99.

Peterson, S.V. and Runyan, A.S. (1993) *Global Gender Issues* (Boulder, CO: Westview).

PGA. (1997) 'First Conference of the Peoples' Global Action against "Free" Trade and the World Trade Organisation' (Philippines: PGA Secretariat).

Pio, A. (1994) 'The Social Impact of Adjustment in Africa', in G.A. Cornia and G.K. Helleiner (eds), *From Adjustment to Development in Africa: Conflict, Controversy, Convergence, Consensus?* (New York: St Martin's Press).

Polanyi, K. (1957) *The Great Transformation* (Boston: Beacon Hill Press).

Pomeranz, K. and Topik, S. (1999) *The World that Trade Created: Society, Culture and the World Economy, 1400 – the Present* (London: M.E. Sharpe).

Price, R. (1998) 'Reversing the Gun Sights: Transnational Civil Society Targets Land Mines', *International Organization*, 52(3), pp. 613–44.

Prugl, E. (1999) *The Global Construction of Gender: Home Based Work in the Political Economy of the 20th Century* (New York: Columbia University Press).

Pye, L.W. (1988) 'The New Asian Capitalism: A Political Portrait', in P.L. Berger and H.M. Hsia (eds), *Search of an East Asian Development Model* (Oxford: Transaction Books).

Radice, H. (ed.) (1975) *International Firms and Modern Imperialism* (London: Penguin Books).

Radosh, R. (1969) *American Labour and United States Foreign Policy* (New York: Random House).

Redclift, M. (1987) *Sustainable Development* (London: Routledge).

Reding, A. (1994) 'Chiapas is Mexico', *World Policy Journal*, 11(1), pp. 11–25.

Reich, R. (1992) *The Work of Nations* (New York: Vintage Books).

Ricardo, D. (1817/1992) *The Principles of Political Economy and Taxation* (London: Everyman's Library).

Rich, B. (1994) *Mortgaging the Earth: The World Bank, Environmental Impoverishment and the Crisis of Development* (London; Earthscan).

Risso, P. (1995) *Merchants and Faith: Muslim Commerce and Culture in the Indian Ocean* (Boulder: Westview Press).

Robinson, R. (1972) 'Non-European Foundations of European Imperialism: Sketch for a Theory of Collaboration', in R. Owen and B. Sutcliffe (eds), *Studies in the Theory of Imperialism* (Bristol: Longman).

Rodman, K. A. (1998) 'Think Globally, Punish Locally: Nonstate Actors, Multinational Corporations and Human Rights Sanctions', *Ethics and International Affairs*, 12 pp. 19–41.

Rostow, W.W. (1960) *The Stages of Economic Growth* (Cambridge: Cambridge University Press).

Ruggie, J.G. (1982) 'International Regimes, Transactions and Change: Embedded Liberalism in the Postwar Economic Order', *International Organization*, 36(2), pp. 379–415.

Rupert, M. (1995a) *Producing Hegemony: The Politics of Mass Production and American Global Power* (Cambridge: Cambridge University Press).

Rupert, M. (1995b) '(Re)Politicizing the Global Economy: Liberal Common Sense and Ideological Struggle in the US NAFTA Debate', *Review of International Political Economy*, 2, pp. 658–92.

Sahn, D.E. (1994) 'The Impact of Macroeconomic Adjustment on Incomes, Health and Nutrition: Sub-Saharan Africa in the 1980s', in G.A. Cornia and G.K. Helleiner (eds), *From Adjustment to Development in Africa: Conflict, Controversy, Convergence, Consensus?* (New York: St Martin's Press).

Saurin, J. (1996) 'International Relations, Social Ecology, and the Globalisation of Environmental Change', in J. Vogler and M.F. Imber (eds), *The Environment and International Relations* (London: Routledge).

Schechter, M.G. (2002) 'Critiques of Coxian Theory: Background to a Conversation', in R.W. Cox (with Michael G. Schechter) *The Political Economy of a Plural World: Reflection on Power, Morals and Civilization* (London: Routledge).

Schmidheiny, S. (1992) *Changing Course: A Global Business Perspective on Development and the Environment* (Cambridge, MA: MIT Press).

Schneider, V. (2000) 'Global Economic Governance by Private Actors: The International Chamber of Commerce', in J. Greenwood and H. Jacek (ed.) *Organized Business and the New Global Order* (New York: St Martin's Press).

Scholte, J.A. (2000a) *Globalization: A Critical Introduction* (New York: St Martin's Press).

Scholte, J.A. (2000b) 'Global Civil Society', in N. Woods (ed.), *The Political Economy of Globalization* (London: Macmillan).

Seers, D. (1969) 'The Meaning of Development', *International Development Review*, 11(4), pp. 2–6.

Sell, S. (1999) 'Multinational Corporations as Agents of Change: The Globalization of Intellectual Property Rights', in C. Cutler, V. Haufler and T. Porter (eds), *Private Authority and International Affairs* (Albany: State University of New York Press).

Sell, S. (2000) 'Structures, Agents and Institutions: Private Corporate Power and the Globalisation of Intellectual Property Rights', in R.A. Higgott, G.R.D. Underhill and A. Bieler (eds), *Non-state Actors and Authority in the Global System* (London: Routledge).

Sen, A. (1981) *Poverty and Famines: An Essay on Entitlement and Deprivation* (Oxford: Clarendon Press).

Sen, G. (1983) *The Military Origins of Industrialization and International Trade Rivalry* (New York: St Martin's Press).

Sengenberger, W. and Wilkinson, F. (1995) 'Globalisation and Labor Standards', in J. Michie and J.G. Smith (eds), *Managing the Global Economy* (Oxford: Oxford University Press).

Servan Schreiber, J.J. (1968) *The American Challenge,* trans. by Ronald Steel (New York: Athenaeum).

Shillington, K. (1995) *History of Africa* (New York: St Martin's Press).

Shrybman, S. (1990) 'International Trade and the Environment: An Environmental Assessment of the General Agreement on Tariffs and Trade', *The Ecologist,* 20(1), pp. 30–4.

Sikkink, K. (2002) 'Restructuring World Politics: The Limits and Asymmetries of Soft Power', in S. Khagram, J.V. Riker and K. Sikkink (eds), *Restructuring World Politics: Transnational Movements, Networks and Norms* (Minneapolis: University of Minnesota Press).

Sinclair, T. (1994) 'Passing Judgement: Credit Rating Processes as Regulating Mechanisms of Governance', *Review of International Political Economy,* 1(1), pp. 133–60.

Sisson C.A. (1986) 'Fund-supported Programs and Income Distribution in LDC', *Finance and Development,* 231, pp. 33–8.

Skidmore, D. (1997) *Contested Social Orders and International Politics* (Nashville: Vanderbilt University Press).

Skidmore-Hess, D. (1996) 'Business Conflict and Theories of the State', in R.W. Cox (ed.) *Business and the State in International Relations* (Boulder, CO: Westview).

Sklair, L. (2001) *The Transnational Capitalist Class* (Blackwell: Oxford).

Sklias, P. (1999) *Non-Governmental Organisations and the International Political Economy, with Special Reference to the European Union's Development Policy* (Athens: Nubis).

Smith, A. (1776/1983) *The Wealth of Nations* (New York: Penguin).

Smythe, E. (2000) 'State Authority and Investment Security: Non-state Actors and the Negotiation of the Multilateral Agreement on Investment at the OECD', in R.A. Higgott, G.R.D. Underhill and A. Bieler (eds), *Non-state Actors and Authority in the Global System* (London: Routledge).

Spero, J. (1981) *Politics of International Economic Relations* (London: Unwin Hyman).

Spruyt, H. (1994) *The Sovereign State and its Competitors* (Princeton: Princeton University Press).

Spruyt, H. (2000) 'New Institutionalism and International Relations', in R. Palan (ed.) *Global Political Economy: Contemporary Theories* (London: Routledge).

Stalker, P. (2001) *The No-Nonsense Guide to International Migration* (Oxford: New Internationalist).

Stearns, P.N. (1993) *The Industrial Revolution in World History* (Boulder, CO: Westview Press).

Stewart, F. (1995) *Adjustment and Poverty: Options and Choices* (London: Routledge).

Stewart, F. and Berry, A. (1999) 'Globalization, Liberalization and Inequality: Expectations and Experience', in A. Hurrell and N. Woods (eds), *Inequality, Globalization and World Politics* (Oxford: Oxford University Press).

Stiglitz, J. (2000) 'The Insider: What I learned at the World Economic Crisis', *The New Republic*. (April 17) <http://www.tnr.com/041700/stiglitz041700.html>.

Stiglitz, J. (2002) *Globalization and its Discontents* (London: Penguin).

Stopford, J.M. and Strange, S. (1991) *Rival States, Rival Firms: Competition for World Market Shares* (Cambridge: Cambridge University Press).

Strange, S. (1982) 'Cave Hic Dragones: A Critique of Regime Analysis' *International Organization*, 36(2) pp. 337–54.

Strange, S. (1985) 'Protectionism and World Politics', *International Organization*, 39(2), pp. 233–59.

Strange, S. (1986) *Casino Capitalism* (Oxford: Blackwell).

Strange, S. (1987) 'The Persistent Myth of Lost Hegemony', *International Organisation*, 41 pp. 551–74.

Strange, S. (1988) *States and Markets* (London: Pinter).

Strange, S. (1991) 'Big Business and the State', *Millennium*, 20(2), pp. 245–50.

Strange, S. (1994a) 'Rethinking Structural Change in the International Political Economy: States, Firms and Diplomacy', in R. Stubbs and G.R.D. Underhill (eds), *Political Economy and the Changing Global Order*, 2nd edn (London: Macmillan).

Strange, S. (1994b) 'Wake Up, Krasner! The World has Changed', *Review of International Political Economy*, 1(2), pp. 209–20.

Strange, S. (1996) *The Retreat of the State: The Diffusion of Power in the World Economy* (Cambridge: Cambridge University Press).

Strange, S. (1998) *Mad Money: When Markets Outgrow Governments* (Manchester: Manchester University Press).

Strange, S. (2002) 'I Never Meant to be an Academic', in R. Tooze and C. May (eds), *Authority and Markets: Susan Strange's Writings on International Political Economy* (New York: Palgrave).

Stubbs, R. (1999) 'War and Economic Development: Export-Oriented Industrialization in East and Southeast Asia', *Comparative Politics*, 31(3), pp. 337–55.

Stubbs, R. and Underhill, G.R.D. (eds), (2000) *Political Economy and the Changing Global Order*, 2nd edn (Toronto: Oxford University Press).

Sundrum, R.M. (1983) *Development Economics: A Framework of Analysis and Policy* (Chichester: John Wiley and Sons).

Sutcliffe, B. (2001) *100 Ways of Seeing an Unequal World* (London: Zed Books).

Swann, D. (1992) *The Economics of the Common Market*, 7th edn (London: Penguin).

Swartz, H.M. (1994) *States Versus Markets* (New York: St Martin's Press).

Thomas, C. (2000) *Global Governance, Development and Human Security* (London: Pluto).

Thomas, C. and Reader, M. (1997) 'Development and Inequality', in B. White, R (Little and M. Smith (eds), *Issues in World Politics* (London: Macmillan).

Thomas, C.Y. (1974) *Dependence and Transformation* (New York: Monthly Review Press).

Thompson, W.R. (2000) *The Emergence of the Global Political Economy* (New York: Routledge).

Thorne, C. (1978) *Allies of a Kind: The United States, Britain, and the War Against Japan, 1941–1945* (London: H. Hamilton).

Tilly, C. (1999) *Coercion, Capital, and European States AD 990–1992* (Oxford: Blackwell).

Toffler, A. (1980) *The Third Wave* (New York: Morrow).

Tooze, R. and May, C. (2002) 'Authority and Markets: Interpreting the Work of Susan Strange', in R. Tooze and C. May (eds), *Authority and Markets: Susan Strange's Writings on International Political Economy* (New York: Palgrave).

Transnational Resource and Action Center. (2000) *Tangled up in Blue: Corporate Partnerships at the United Nations*. World Wide Web: <http://www.corpwatch.org>.

UN (2000) *The Millennium Declaration* UN General Assembly Resolution 55/2; adopted 18/9/00.

UNCTAD (1999) *World Investment Report 1999: Foreign Direct Investment and the Challenge of Development* (New York: United Nations).

UNCTAD (2000) *World Investment Report* (New York: United Nations).

UNDP (1990) *Human Development Report* (Geneva: UNDP).

UNDP (1994) *Human Development Report* (Geneva: UNDP).

UNDP (2000) *Human Development Report* (Geneva: UNDP).

UNDP (2002) *Human Development Report* (Geneva: UNDP).

UNICEF (1999) *The Progress of Nations 1999* New York: UNICEF, United Nations Publication. Retrieved May 5, 2003, from the World Wide Web <http://www.unicef.org/pon99/pon99_5.pdf>

Vaitsos, C. (1975) 'Power, Knowledge and Development Policy: Relations Between Transnational Enterprises and Developing Countries', in G.K. Helleiner (ed.), *A World Divided: The Less Developed Countries in the International Economy* (Cambridge: Cambridge University Press).

Vernon, R. (1966) 'International Investment and International Trade in the Product Cycle', *Quarterly Journal of Economics*, 80(2), pp. 190–207.

Vernon, R. (1971) *Sovereignty at Bay* (London: Penguin Books).

Vernon, R. (1977) *Storm Over the Multinationals: The Real Issues* (London: Macmillan).

Wade, R. (1990) *Governing the Market: Economic Theory and the Role of Government in East Asian Industrialization* (Princeton, NJ: Princeton University Press).

Wade, R. and Veneroso, F. (1998) 'The Asian Crisis: The High Debt Model vs. the Wall Street–Treasury–IMF Complex', *New Left Review*, 228, pp. 3–22.

Waley-Cohen, J. (1999) *The Sextants of Beijing: Global Currents in Chinese History* (New York: Norton).

Walton, S. (2002) 'The Danger of Global Finance: A Reassessment of the Asian Crisis', *Journal of Asia-Pacific Affairs*, 4(1), pp. 107–21.

Waterman, P. (1998) *Globalization, Social Movements and the New Internationalisms* (London: Mansell).

Weiss, L. (1999) 'State Power and the Asian Crisis', *New Political Economy*, 4(3), pp. 317–42.

Weiss, T.G., Forsyth, D.P. and Coates R.A. (2001) *The United Nations and Changing World Politics* (Boulder, CO: Westview).

Wendt, A. (1987) 'The Agent-Structure Problem in International Relations Theory', *International Organization*, (41) pp. 335–70.

White, G. (Ed.) (1988) *Developmental States in East Asia* (London: Macmillan).

Wilkins, M. (1970) *The Emergence of the Multinational Enterprise* (Cambridge, MA: Harvard University Press).

Williams, E. (1944) *Capitalism and Slavery* (Chapel Hill: University of North Carolina Press).

Williams, M. (1993) 'International Trade and the Environment: Issues, Perspectives and Challenges', *Environmental Politics*, 2(4), pp. 80–97.

Williams, M. (1994) *International Economic Organisations and the Third World* (London: Harvester Wheatsheaf).

Williams, M. (1999) 'The World Trade Organisation, Social Movements and "democracy"', in A. Taylor and C. Thomas (eds), *Global Trade and Global Social Issues* (London: Routledge).

Williams, M. (2001) 'Trade and Environment in the World Trading System: A Decade of Stalemate?' *Global Environmental Politics*, 1(4), pp. 1–9.

Wilson, W. (1918/1986) 'The Fourteen Points', in J.A. Vasquez (ed.) *Classics of International Relations* (London: Prentice-Hall).

Winham, G.R. (1986) *International Trade and the Tokyo Round Negotiations*. (Princeton, NJ: Princeton University Press).

Wolf, E.R. (1982) *Europe and the People Without History* (Berkeley: University of California Press).

Wollstonecraft, M. (1792/1992) *A Vindication of the Rights of Woman* (London: Penguin).

World Bank (1980) *World Development Report* (New York: Oxford University Press).

World Bank (1987) *World Development Report* (New York: Oxford University Press).

World Bank (1989) *World Development Report* (New York: Oxford University Press).

World Bank (1990) *World Development Report* (New York: Oxford University Press).

World Bank (1991) *Pacific Island Economies: Towards Higher Growth in the 1990s* (Washington, DC: World Bank).

World Bank (1993) *The East Asian Miracle: Economic Growth and Public Policy* (Oxford: Oxford University Press; Washington, DC: World Bank).

World Bank (1994) *World Development Report* (New York: Oxford University Press).

World Bank (1995) *Mainstreaming the Environment* (Washington, DC: World Bank).

World Bank (1996) *World Development Report* (New York: Oxford University Press).

World Bank (1998) *Partnerships for Development: A New World Bank Approach* (Washington, DC: World Bank).

World Bank (2000) *World Development Indicators* (Washington, DC: World Bank).

World Bank (2001) *Global Development Finance 2001* (Washington, DC: World Bank). Retrieved May 5, 2003, from the World Wide Web: <http://www.worldbank.org/prospects/gdf2001/vol1-pdf/pdf>

World Bank (2002) *The World Bank Annual Report 2002* (Washington, DC: World Bank).

World Bank (2003) *Global Development Finance 2003* (Washington, DC: The World Bank). Retrieved May 5, 2003, from the World Wide Web: <http://www.worldbank.org/prospects/gdf2003/GDF_vol_1_web.pdf>

World Commission (1987) World Commission on Environment and Development (The Brundtland Report) *Our Common Future* (Oxford: Oxford University Press).

World Guide 2001/2002 (2001) (Oxford: New Internationalist).

WTO (1998) *International Trade Statistics 1998* (Geneva: WTO).

WTO (2000) *International Trade Statistics 2000* (Geneva: WTO).

WTO (2001) *International Trade Statistics 2001* (Geneva: WTO).

WTO (2002) *International Trade Statistics 2002* (Geneva: WTO).

WTO (2002) *Annual Report* (Geneva: WTO).

Young, O. (1989) 'The Politics of Regime Formation: Managing Global Resources and the Environment', *International Organization*, 43(3), pp. 349–377.

Young, O. (1994) *International Governance: Protecting the Environment in a Stateless Society* (Ithaca and London: Cornell University Press).

Zakaria, F. (1994) 'Culture is Destiny: A Conversation with Lee Kuan Yew', *Foreign Affairs*, 73(2), pp. 109–26.

Index